Palgrave Studies in Financial Services Technology

Series Editor
Bernardo Nicoletti
Rome Campus
Temple University
Rome, Italy

The Palgrave Studies in Financial Services Technology series features original research from leading and emerging scholars on contemporary issues and developments in financial services technology. Falling into 4 broad categories: channels, payments, credit, and governance; topics covered include payments, mobile payments, trading and foreign transactions, big data, risk, compliance, and business intelligence to support consumer and commercial financial services. Covering all topics within the life cycle of financial services, from channels to risk management, from security to advanced applications, from information systems to automation, the series also covers the full range of sectors: retail banking, private banking, corporate banking, custody and brokerage, wholesale banking, and insurance companies. Titles within the series will be of value to both academics and those working in the management of financial services.

More information about this series at
http://www.palgrave.com/gp/series/14627

Bernardo Nicoletti

Procurement Finance

The Digital Revolution in Commercial Banking

palgrave
macmillan

Bernardo Nicoletti
Rome campus
Temple University
Roma, Roma, Italy

Palgrave Studies in Financial Services Technology
ISBN 978-3-030-02139-9 ISBN 978-3-030-02140-5 (eBook)
https://doi.org/10.1007/978-3-030-02140-5

Library of Congress Control Number: 2018960486

This Palgrave Macmillan imprint is published by the registered company Springer Nature Switzerland AG
The registered company address is: Gewerbestrasse 11, 6330 Cham, Switzerland

To my Parents for all the tacit lessons

Contents

Abbreviations

4PL and 3PL	Fourth- and third-party logistics providers
AI	Artificial intelligence
AMA	Advanced measurement approach—one of the three possible operational risk methods under Basel
AML	Anti-Money Laundering (regulation/controls/activity)
AMLD	Anti-Money Laundering Directive
AnaCredit	European Analytical Credit Dataset
API	Application programming interface
AR	Acquisition request or accounts receivable
ASF	Available stable funding
ATO	Assemble-to-order
B2B	Business-to-business
BaaS	Blockchain as a Service
BAU	Business as Usual
BCT	Blockchain technology
BI	Business intelligence or business indicator method for risk measurement
BL	Business line (type classification for risk)
BOL or B/L	Bill of lading
BPO	Bank payment obligation or business process outsourcing
BRRD	Bank Recovery and Resolution Directive
BTO	Build-to-order
C2C	Cash-to-cash cycle
C2M	Consumer-to-machine
CCC	Cash-to-cash cycle or cash-to-cash cycle of organizations
CCCTB	Common consolidated corporate tax base
CCF	Credit conversion factor (Basel risk weighting)

CCR	Central credit register
CEBS	The EBA's Committee of European Banking Supervisors
CEO	Chief executive officer
CET	Core equity tier
CFO	Chief financial officer
CI	Credit institution
CIF	Cost, insurance, and freight
CMU	Capital Markets Union
CODP	Customer order decoupling point
COGS	Cost of goods sold
CPFR	Collaborative planning, forecasting, and replenishment
CRR 2, CRD 5	Proposals to update the Capital Requirements Regulation (1) and Directive (4) Reviews
CRR, CRD 4	The third iteration of the Capital Requirements Regulation and Directive Reviews, effective January 2014
CS	Consignment stock
CSP	Customer security program
CVC	Corporate venture capital
Dapp	Decentralized application
DCF	Discounted cash flow
DGS	Deposit guarantee scheme
DL	Deep learning
DLT	Distributed ledger technology
DP	Data protection
DPO	Days payable outstanding
DSO	Days sales outstanding
DTC	Digital trade chain
E2E	End-to-end (total supply chain, including all steps)
EAD	Exposure at default (of a loan)
EBT	Earnings before taxes
ECA	Export credit agency
EDI	Electronic data interchange
EMEA	Europe, Middle East, and Africa
EMS	Environmental management system
EMU	European Monetary Union
e-SCM	e-Supply chain management
EUF	Federation for the factoring and commercial finance industry in the EU
FATCA	Foreign Account Tax Compliance Act
FCF	Factoring and commercial finance
FEC	Financial and economic crime
FI	Financial institution

FSP	Financial service provider
FTT	Financial transaction tax
FX	Foreign exchange
GDP	Gross domestic product
GPI	Global payment initiative
ICO	Initial coin offering
ICT	Information and communication technology
ID	Identity
IFRS	International financial reporting standards
IoT	Internet of Things
IRB	Internal ratings-based system approach to capital requirements for credit risk under Basel III
ITD	International Trade Department
ITP	International Trade Portal
JIT	Just-in-time
KPI	Key performance or process indicator
KRI	Key risk indicator
KYC	Know your customer
LC	Legal Committee of the EUF or letter of credit
LCR	Liquidity coverage ratio
LGD	Loss given default (of an exposure)
LMA	Loan Market Association: standard lending documentation
LOC	Line of credit
LSL	Lower stock limit
LSP	Logistics service provider
M2M	Machine-to-machine
MBO/MBI	Management buy-out/in
MCTFL	Multi-product capacitated facility location
MiFID II	Directive on markets in financial instruments
ML	Machine learning
MMR	EUF monthly monitoring report
MNE	Multinational enterprise
MTO	Make-to-order
MTS	Make-to-stock
NLP	Natural language processing
NLU	Natural language understanding
NOD	National options and discretions
NOI	Net operating income
NPL	Non-performing loan
NSFR	Net stable funding ratio
NWC	Net working capital
O2O	Online-to-offline

O2P	Order to pay
OCR	Optical character recognition
OM	Operations management
OR	Operational risk
OWC	Operating working capital
P2P	Peer-to-peer or purchase-to-pay
PD	Probability of default (of an exposure)
PF	Procurement finance
PO	Purchase order
PoW	Proof-of-Work
PRC	Prudential Regulation Committee of the EUF
PSC	Physical supply chain
Pub-PL	Public and permission-less (blockchain)
QMS	Quality management system
RF	Reverse factoring
RSF	Required stable funding
RTS	Regulatory technical standards
RWA	Risk-weighted assets
S&OP	Sales and operations planning
SA	Standardized approach—one of three possible operational risk methods under Basel
SC	Supply chain
SCC	Supply chain council
SCF	Supply chain finance or supply chain flexibility
SCI	Supply chain integration
SCM	Supply chain management
SCTFL	Single-product capacitated facility location
SG&A	Selling, general, and administrative (expenses)
SKU	Stock keeping unit
SMA	Standardized measurement approach (to risk)
SME SF	Small and medium-sized enterprise supporting factor which allows for a reduction in capital requirements for banks which lend to SMEs under the CRR
SME	Small and medium-sized enterprise
SMS	Safety management system or short message service
SO	Sales order
SREP	Supervisory report and evaluation process
SSCM	Sustainable supply chain management
STP	Straight-through processing
TSU	Trade services utility
TA	Total assets
TLTRO	Targeted longer-term refinancing operations

TMA	Transaction matching application
TTIP	Transatlantic trade and investment partnership
USL	Upper stock limit
VAS	Value-added services
VMI	Vendor-managed inventory
WACC	Weighted average cost of capital
WC	Working capital
WCM	Working capital management
WIP	Work in progress
XML	eXtensible Markup Language

Institutions and Associations[1]

ABFA	The Asset-Based Finance Association UK and Ireland. www.abfa.org.uk
AEF	Asociacion Española de Factoring Spain. www.factoringasociacion.com
AILOG	Associazione Italiana Logistica. www.ailog.it
APBF-BBF	Association Professionnelle Belge des Sociétés de Factoring. www.febelfin.be/fr/node/3012
ASF	Association Française des Sociétés financières France. www.asf-france.com
ASSIFACT	Associazione Italiana per il Factoring in Italy. www.assifact.it
BCBS	Basel Committee on Banking Supervision. www.bis.org/bcbs
BIS	Bank for International Settlements. www.bis.org
BOE	Bank of England. http://www.bankofengland.co.uk/Pages/home.aspx
CFA	Commercial Finance Association (USA). www.cfa.com
CIPS	Chartered Institute of Procurement and Supply. www.cips.org
CLFA	Czech Leasing and Finance Association Czech Republic. www.clfa.cz/
DFV	Deutscher Factoring-Verband Germany. www.factoring.de/
DG FISMA	Directorate-General for Financial Stability, Financial Services and Capital Markets Union. ec.europa.eu/info/departments/financial-stability-financial-services-and-capital-markets-union_en
EBA	Euro Banking Association (the less likely use of this abbreviation). www.abe-eba.eu
EBA	European Banking Authority (the more likely use of this abbreviation). www.eba.europa.eu
EBF	European Banking Federation. www.ebf-fbe.eu

EBRD	European Bank for Reconstruction and Development. www.ebrd.com.
ECB	European Central Bank. www.ecb.europa.eu
EFRAG	European Financial Reporting Advisory Group. www.efrag.org
EPA	Emerging Payments Association. http://emergingpayments.org/
EPC	European Payments Council. http://www.europeanpayments-council.eu/
ESC	Economics and Statistics Committee of the EUF. https://euf.eu.com/what-is-euf/organisation/economics-and-statistics-committee.html
ESMA	European Securities and Markets Authority. www.esma.europa.eu/
ESRB	European Systemic Risk Board. www.esrb.europa.eu
EUF	European Union Federation for the Factoring and Commercial Finance Industry. www.euf.eu.com
ExCom	Executive Committee of the EUF. https://euf.eu.com/what-is-euf/organisation/economics-and-statistics-committee.html
FAAN	Factoring & Asset-Based Financing Association Netherlands. www.factoringnederland.nl/over-faan
FATF	Financial Action Task Force (on Money Laundering). www.fatf-gafi.org
FCA	Financial Conduct Authority. www.fca.org.uk/
FCI	Factors Chain International. www.fci.nl
FiREapps	The Leader in Global Fx Management Technology. Available at www.Fireapps.com
FLA	Associação Portuguesa de Leasing, Factoring e Renting Portugal. www.alf.pt
FoL	Finans og Leasing Denmark. www.finansogleasing.dk
FSB	Financial Stability Board. www.fsb.org
HFA	The Hellenic Factors Association Greece. www.hellenicfactors.gr
ICC	International Chamber of Commerce. iccwbo.org
ITFA	International Trade and Forfaiting Association. itfa.org
LiquidX	The largest marketplace for liquidity. Available at liquidx.com/marketplace-in-action
NACHA	National Automated Clearing House Association. www.nacha.org/
OECD	Organisation for Economic Co-operation and Development. www.oecd.org/about
OFV	Österreichischer Factoring Verband Austria. www.factoring.at
PSR	Payment Systems Regulator. www.psr.org.uk/
PUK	Payments UK. http://www.paymentsuk.org.uk/
PZF	Polski Związek Faktorów Poland. www.faktoring.pl
SBA	Swedish Bankers Association Sweden. www.swedishbankers.se

Swift	The global provider of secure financial messaging services. www.swift.com
UCA	UK Cards Association. http://www.theukcardsassociation.org.uk/welcome/
UEAPME	European Association of Craft, Small and Medium-Sized Enterprises. www.ueapme.com
UNCITRAL	The United Nations Commission on International Trade Law which may be Foundation F-IRB or Advanced A-IRB. www.uncitral.org/

Note

1. All sites accessed 10 February 2018.

List of Figures

List of Tables

CHAPTER 1

Introduction to Procurement Finance

Concept of Procurement Finance

The financial crisis of 2008 brought strong competitive pressures on the organizations. Large organizations are challenged by small ones that are more specialized. On the other side, the small and medium-sized enterprises (SMEs) have difficulties in accessing to the credit.

The aim of this book is to demonstrate how it is possible and useful to exploit the digital transformation to support and innovate the procurement organizations and the financial institutions. The aim is to demonstrate that all the actors involved in the procurement ecosystem can benefit from the digital transformation.

To reach this objective, it is important to consider an integrated approach, including[1]:

- trade finance;
- supply chain finance;
- payments management.

This integrated vision is called procurement finance. It is represented by the dashed lines in Fig. 1.1. Procurement finance goes beyond the trade finance, supply chain finance, and payments management. It encompasses the entire extended procurement processes. To clarify this statement, it is useful to consider what has been defined as the ultimate supply chain.[2]

B. Nicoletti, *Procurement Finance*,
Palgrave Studies in Financial Services Technology,
https://doi.org/10.1007/978-3-030-02140-5_1

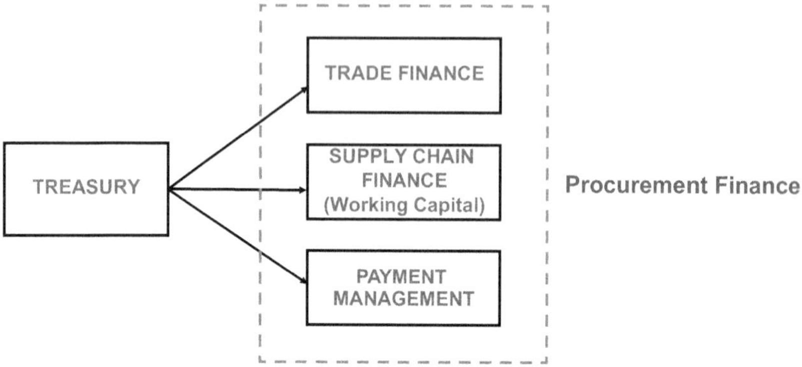

Fig. 1.1 Procurement finance

More and more of the operations of an organization are network shaped rather than single flow shaped. Besides, the real objective of the process is to add value to the organization: the supply should involve co-design, co-development, cooperations, and co-marketing and sales. For all these reasons, this book considers procurement finance as an optimization of the value network processes rather than only of the supply chain.[3]

There are several pillars to consider in procurement finance (Table 1.1).[4]

All three components of procurement finance are challenging. In approaching procurement finance, it is necessary to consider the current global scenario. Globalization creates a complex combination among outsourcing, global supply, and distribution networks. This leads to an increase in the number of actors and of their relationships. Globalization of processes and relationships is commonly referred to as one of the underlying factors of the ever-increasing vulnerability of procurement for the organizations.[5] In this new situation, multinational organizations, followed more and more by SMEs, need to take new approaches to better support the increasing global trade and at the same time to act on the new challenges and remediate to the risks.

Organizations are adapting to the new competitive scenarios by managing complexity, disintermediation, innovation, networking, and flexibility. This is the base to rethink, restructure, and innovate all processes and relationships along the value network, starting with the procurement. It is important to take into account that an innovative solution brings benefits but can bring also several risks and uncertainty regarding the desired results with the actual ones. This aspect is one of the main barriers to inno-

Table 1.1 Pillars in procurement finance

Financing	*Risk management*	*Payment*	*Information*
Available to all parties (buyer/vendor/logistical operator)	Risk sharing	Secure	Shipment and storing status
Available at several steps in the transaction	Country, financial institutions, and transaction risks	Timely and prompt	Quality of products shipped and services delivered
	Logistics risks	Global	Total cost of products shipped and services delivered
	Export credit	Taking into account currency fluctuations	
	Insurance		

Adapted by the author based on Malaket, A. (2014). *Financing Trade and International Supply Chain.* Gower Publish, Farnham, UK

vate. It is essential to manage it. This book considers the ways to cope with these risks, by managing them and understanding the main key factors within procurement finance.

The creation of value by an organization is determined by its ability to generate long-term cash flows through operational management.[6] Cash flows are an indicator of an organization's sustainable development capacity and the ability to remunerate and repay debt and capital. This is an objective measure of the organization performance.

The digital transformation is introducing deep changes also in treasury tools, systems, and processes.[7] Treasury needs to be prepared for these changes not only to capture all the potential benefits but also to manage possible challenges and risks.

Treasury is the underlying asset of the correct cash inflows and cash outflows management. It is required to help maintain an efficient structure of working capital, given the increasing competitive environment. To maintain the proper day-to-day management, treasury needs to lean and digitize as much as possible its own processing. It must have secure systems and processes to minimize operational risks by maximizing efficiency in managing working capital and optimize liquidity.

Technological evolution in payment systems is perhaps one of the most obvious aspects for procurement finance since scope, cost, and quality performance are perceptible in day-to-day business management. The main efforts are focused on shrinking payment execution times, visibility, and traceability of transactions.[8] In addition, the digital transformation is deeply changing the architectural landscape of payment systems.[9] It could turn towards distributed solutions that can potentially provide faster and traceable transfers between counterparts. New solutions bring improvements and benefits. They also bring operational risks and potential frauds that must be known, monitored, and mitigated.

Being in an increasingly globalized ecosystem, the international trade transactions are increasing. With the slowdown in the world economic growth, the trade finance industry has also suffered a certain impact. It is still maintaining a relatively optimistic growth. There are several estimations not completely consistent for this potential growth. All of them confirm the growth of the market. Trade finance market size is expected to maintain the average annual growth rate of 10.58 percent from $25,290 million in 2014 to $34,200 million in 2017.[10] BisReport analysts believe that in the next few years, trade finance market size will expand. They expect that by 2022 the market size of the trade finance will reach $54,890 million.[11] With increased focus on global trade, the trade finance market is likely to witness a strong growth in the coming years. The global trade finance market is expected to reach USD 71,000 million by the end of 2023, growing at a compound annual growth rate (CAGR) of 3.0 percent between 2017 and 2023.[12]

For this reason, it is necessary to consider an advanced payments management taking into account especially the different currencies in the international transactions. New solutions are important in facilitating the cross-border transactions. In this international ecosystem, the actors require innovative solutions of procurement finance oriented to increasing value added. Innovative procurement finance solutions allow especially SMEs in financing their operations in an effective, efficient, and economical way.

To deal with the changes in the current trade, it is necessary to consider not only the physical flow of procurement but also the financial and information flows with an integrated vision. It is necessary to bridge the gap between the business and financial worlds. An integrated approach is necessary while being useful for taking into account simplification and digitization at the same time.

The development of smart approaches and collaboration in procurement can accelerate the modernization and transformation of the entire organization. The task of the procurement is to be a model of use of new solutions, encouraging its use intelligently to support collaboration.[13]

Structure of This Book

In the light of the analysis of the previous section, this book intends to focus on the management of the financial flows along the full procurement cycle. It shows how innovative solutions are able to play a relevant role in an integrated context supporting the procurement transactions, also international, in terms of agility, rapidity, visibility, flexibility, and compliance.

The objective of this book is to emphasize some innovative areas useful in transforming procurement finance thanks to process optimization and digital transformation especially for SMEs.

This book considers the entire procurement ecosystem, including organizations, financial institutions, and public central and local organizations. In this vision, the role of the financial institutions is more relevant. They should recognize their role as platforms.[14]

This book is structured through eight chapters. At their basis, there is the presentation, in a coordinated way, of new solutions.

The first chapter defines procurement finance. This function is increasingly positioned as a strategic function within an organization. Considering the importance of this function and taking into account the dynamic, volatile, and global scenario in which the organizations need to operate, this chapter proposes the necessity of an increased agility in the organizations, especially in the procurement finance sector.[15] The agility can be improved through new solutions. They allow adapting to a changing environment in a flexible and rapid way. New concepts are emerging, such as the ones connected with the fintech approach: the fusion between technology and finance.[16] The fintech organizations often compete with the traditional financial institutions to provide innovative financial services in rapid, easy, direct, and transparent ways. They are able to satisfy the needs of a large number of customers and not only of a specific privileged range of customers of the financial institution. The digital transformation allows easier access to any organization which needs financial services. Some financial institutions have started to collaborate with the fintech ecosystem to create an environment able to satisfy all customer needs.

The second chapter examines in depth the procurement processes. It describes and underlines the three important phases of the function: information/digital flow, physical flow, and financial flow. This distinction is important especially for the following chapters. It underlines the importance of the collaboration within and among organizations along the entire extended value network not only in regard to physical and information flows but also considering the financial flows.

The third chapter describes the useful linkage between procurement, finance, and information and communication technology (ICT). It shows the possibility to get a shared objective and thus obtaining trusted relations among all the actors in the ecosystem. The physical and the financial flows in procurement need an alignment. Such an alignment helps to overcome the gap between the industrial vision and the financial vision under an integrated vision increasingly necessary in this current global scenario. This chapter describes the roadmap from trade finance to supply chain finance (SCF), and to procurement finance. It defines the transition from one to another. It stresses the importance of procurement finance in a market that is evolving globally. This chapter underlines the need for streamlining the processes supporting the information/digital flows and facilitating the access to financial support—trying to mitigate challenges and risks related to procurement, especially if global. Procurement finance is represented as a holistic vision of the procurement and finance considering it an ecosystem of relationships and not only a bilateral transaction. The payment times increase in all the chains, and the optimization of working capital is needed in the organizations. Considering these needs, procurement finance is presented as an innovative approach able to optimize the working capital and the cash flows along the value network through the collaboration among partners. Procurement finance is a new integration concept that includes trade finance, supply chain finance, and payments management. It supports the organizations with an integrated vision related to the linkage between finance and procurement. The final part of the chapter deals with the key performance indicators (KPIs) to monitor and support the implementation and management of the new solutions.

The fourth chapter describes the vision of this book of an agile procurement finance. Agility is essential in the current volatile environments, to be able to adapt and catch all the opportunities which might arise. Agile procurement finance is based on an integrated lean and digitized approach to take into account at the same time the improvements in the processes and their simplification and digitization.[17]

The fifth chapter describes in depth the new solutions supporting procurement finance. It reports several examples of concrete applications. The examples are classified based on the following sections: portals, marketplaces, risk management, advance payments, and document management. It shows how the digital transformation can support each of these aspects. It highlights the opportunities offered by the new solutions to optimize payment times, dematerialize documents, improve transactions' traceability, and mitigate risks. The vision is of an increasing digital future.

The sixth chapter has a longer-term perspective. It provides examples, which should find in the near future many practical applications. These applications move towards an integrated ecosystem which sees a role of platforms for the financial institutions. This chapter focuses on the organizational and technological procurement finance solutions. Fintech organizations are the paradigm of organizational innovations, while some of the relevant innovative solutions are connected with blockchain, cloud computing, and artificial intelligence. The combination of these solutions leads to a procurement finance 4.0 fully embedded and supportive of the Industry 4.0 initiatives. This chapter clarifies how all these innovative solutions can be increasingly exploited to obtain benefits especially in the financial aspects but also from an organization point of view.

The seventh chapter focuses on the role of SMEs in the economy, and the difficulty for them to access to the credit from the financial institutions. This chapter reports an empirical study on the application of procurement finance in large European organizations. This study supports a new vision which is important also for the SMEs. It is a vision of the procurement finance as a collaborative platform which allows the SMEs to get substantial benefits. It is useful to reach an integrated credit rating that considers a procurement perspective and not only partial financial perspectives.

The eighth chapter draws the conclusions of the book. The final part of the book contains an extensive glossary, reference, and website lists.

The book is full of business cases relative to the concrete applications of the concepts described.

Conclusions

Looking at a single organization may not be enough to provide credit to the organizations for supporting them in times of difficulty while at the same time growing procurement finance as part of the digital transformation. By considering the ecosystem allows organizations to find new and rewarding opportunities. It is only necessary to reap and manage them in the proper way.

Notes

1. Nicoletti, B. (2016), Innovazione e Tecnologia nel Procurement dei Servizi Finanziari, *The Procurement*, 2(2), Apr./Mag., 26:27.
2. Mentzer, J. T., DeWitt, W., Keebler, J. S., Min, S., Nix, N. W., Smith, C. D., & Zacharia, Z. G. (2001). Defining supply chain management. *Journal of Business Logistics*, *22*(2), 1–25.
3. Nicoletti, B. (2017), *Agile Procurement. Volume I: Adding Value with Lean Processes*, Springer International Publishing, London, UK. ISBN 978-3-319-61082-5.
4. Adapted by the Author based on Malaket, A. (2014). *Financing Trade and International Supply Chain*, Gower Publish, Farnham, UK.
5. Rao, S., & Goldsby, T. J. (2009). Supply chain risks: a review and typology. *The International Journal of Logistics Management*, *20*(1), 97–123.
6. Morden, T. (2017). *Principles of management*. Routledge, London, UK.
7. Coleman, S., & Thomas, B. (2017). *Organizational Change Explained: Case Studies on Transformational Change in Organizations*. Kogan Page Publishers, London, UK.
8. Nicoletti, B. (2014). Using operational analytics to achieve a digitized, visible supply chain. *Inbound Logistics, 1*.
9. de Reuver, M., Sørensen, C., & Basole, R. C. (2017). The digital platform: a research agenda. *Journal of Information Technology*, 1–12.
10. newshawktime.com/trade-finance-market-with-manufacturers-application-regions-and-swot-analysis-2022/. Accessed 20 June 2018.
11. www.bis.org/publ/arpdf/ar2018e.htm. Accessed 25 June 2018.
12. industrytoday.co.uk/finance/trade-finance-2018-global-market-to-reach-us%2D%2D71000-million-and-growing-at-cagr-of-3-0%2D%2Dby-2023. Accessed 02 August 2018.
13. Laudon, K. C., & Laudon, J. P. (2016). *Management information system*. Pearson Education India, Noida, India.
14. Nicoletti, B. (2017), *The Future of Fintech*, Springer International Publishing, London, UK. ISBN 978-3-319-51414-7.
15. Nicoletti, B. (2017), *Agile Procurement. Volume II: Designing and Implementing a Digital Transformation*, Springer International Publishing, London, UK, ISBN 978-3-319-61085-6.

    Nicoletti, B. (2017), *Agile Procurement. Volume I: Adding Value with Lean Processes*, Springer International Publishing, London, UK. ISBN 978-3-319-61082-5.
16. Nicoletti, B. (2017), *The Future of Fintech*, Springer International Publishing, London, UK. ISBN 978-3-319-51414-7.
17. Nicoletti, B., (2012), *Lean and Digitize: An Integrated Approach to Process Improvement*. Gower Publishing, Farnham, UK. ISBN-10: 1409441946.

CHAPTER 2

Procurement Processes and Finance

Introduction

This chapter defines the procurement cycle and describes its various processes. It analyzes the details of the relevant procurement processes. Procurement is considered to include the entire cycle from the moment of an acquisition request up to the payment to a vendor.

The procurement processes are both strategic and operational. In the procurement processes, there are essentially three levels[1] (Fig. 2.1):

- a physical flow of the products and services;
- a financial flow;
- an information/digital flow.

The physical flow encompasses services or products that move between the suppliers and buyers within the supply chain. The financial flow consists of invoices, credit notes, investments, cash, and payments. It flows typically in the opposite direction of the flow of goods and services. The information flow comprises information associated with products and services as well as payment flows through the value network. It includes purchase orders (POs), inventory documents, confirmations, and invoices, among others. The information flow initiates the other two flows. Information handling is more and more done via information and communication technologies. This flow is also indicated as the digital flow.

B. Nicoletti, *Procurement Finance*,
Palgrave Studies in Financial Services Technology,
https://doi.org/10.1007/978-3-030-02140-5_2

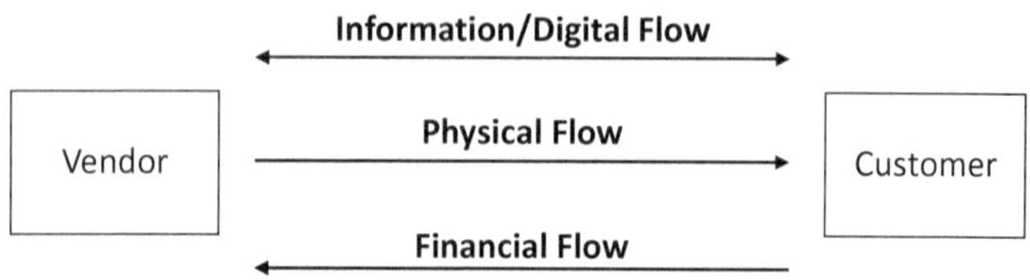

Fig. 2.1 The three flows in procurement

Table 2.1 Flows within procurement finance

	Products
Material flow	Services
======>	
	Plans/budget/forecasts
	Demand/orders information
Information/digital flow	Procurement documentation
<======>	Alerts
	Quality
	Knowledge
	Costs
Financial flow	Funds
<======	Financial resources
	Human resources

Adapted from the author from Pfohl, H. C., & Gomm, M. (2009). Supply chain finance: optimizing financial flows in supply chains. *Logistics research*, *1*(3–4), 149–161

These flows can be further analyzed (Table 2.1).[2]

This chapter considers the first two processes. Later chapters examine the financial flow. These three flows are interconnected. Finance providers offer their services in the context of the financial requirements triggered by purchase orders or contracts, invoices, receivables, claims, and related pre-shipment and post-shipment processes along the entire and extended value network. Consequently, the financial flow is largely "event-driven".[3] Each intervention (finance, risk mitigation, or payment) in the financial flow is driven by an event or a trigger in the physical and informational flows.[4] The development of advanced technologies and procedures to track and control events in the physical/digital flow creates opportunities to digitize the initiation of the financial flow interventions in the value network.

At the beginning of this chapter, the procurement processes are described starting with procurement marketing, acquisition request, and sourcing up to the payment to a vendor. This chapter analyzes also the physical distribution, considering transportation, warehousing, and delivery. Finally, the chapter examines the important vendor rating process.

Procurement

Procurement includes all processes able to ensure that the products and services are available for the customer according to the agreed schedule.[5] It can create a win-win situation for both the buyers and the vendors since it impacts on the overall procurement performance.

According to CIPS, the Chartered Institute of Procurement and Supply, procurement is:

> The business management function that ensures the identification, sourcing, access, and management of the external resources that an organization needs or may need to fulfill its strategic objectives.[6]

Procurement includes all activities related to the acquiring and managing the material and services required by the organization.

Procurement is present in the public and the private organizations. In both cases, it is important that the procurement operators be effective, efficient, economical, and ethical. The procurement function analyzes the potential opportunities that the supply market offers. It then applies the agreed strategies to obtain the best possible outcome from the market to satisfy the organization and all its stakeholders and customers.[7] The term procurement does not refer to a single action, but it covers all the processes connected with external resources used by the organization: from the identification of the organization needs up to the disposal or cessation of the necessary products and services that satisfy such needs.

The current economic environment influences the evolution of the concept of procurement also in the literature. This evolution has moved procurement from a transactional and administrative role towards a strategic role.[8] This last aspect includes strategic partnerships and value network management. Procurement objectives are no longer considered only primarily cost reduction. Procurement is strategic for the creation of value for the organization; as such, it is considered a core competency in many types of organizations.[9]

The procurement is not just the procedure of buying materials and services. It is not considered any more a passive function in the organization. Its new strategic role inside the organization implies that it has the capability to recognize the pressures on the organization and the best ways in which it is possible to react and possibly exploit these pressures in favor of the organization. Being a strategic function, the procurement has to be active in the identification of the products and services that are critical for a sustainable organization.

Already in the past, organizations have attributed a relevant importance to the procurement because they recognize the value added that this function is able to provide to the organizations, which is responsible up to the 75 percent (and even more in some cases) of the average manufacturing sales.[10] The organizations realize that the correct management of the procurement adds a relevant value to the organization. For this reason, they started to invest more in this strategic area. The procurement function has to focus more on core processes as supply coordination, market research, cost analysis, and strategic planning to be able to face the challenges of the current dynamic environment and to maintain the competitiveness of the organization.[11] Thanks to the introduction of new solutions as e-procurement, it is possible for the procurement area to have more time to expand its core processes.[12]

Procurement should become one of the main competencies to improve the profitability of the organization. This strategic role of the procurement can generate a strong procurement integration internally or externally to the organization. To this end, the procurement cannot work in isolation. It is important that all the functional areas in the procurement are linked to the business objective of the organization.

The CIPS has identified some relevant potential benefits for the management of this area[13]:

- securing the supply;
- lowering costs;
- adding greater value;
- reducing risks;
- improving quality;
- increasing efficiency;
- innovating.

It is clear that the optimization of the procurement area is important. When procurement is given the right importance in an organization, the organization achieves a greater efficiency and the best match for the delivery of products and services. Procurement adds value to the organizations as a whole.

The last few years have seen changes that influence all sectors of the organizations, including procurement. These changes bring some key challenges:

- The key customers, vendors, and buyers often suffer from a poor end-to-end customer journey experience.[14] Often the processing of a transaction follows overly complicated and manual processes, long waiting times with low visibility, and a relatively high residual settlement uncertainty.
- The parties involved in procurement face risks, such as fraudulent shipments and delays in the delivery.[15]
- The procurement of products and services can be associated with high costs for both the buyer and the vendor. Since transactions may be highly complex, global, and expensive, the organizations are in dire need of adding value to the organization also through procurement, by both significant reductions in cost, as well as innovative sources of funds to provide a broader, more stable procurement for the business.[16]
- The scarcity and cost of capital in the wake of the credit crunch creates an incentive to explore procurement finance programs as the spread between investment-grade and non-investment-grade rates widens. One of the main benefits of procurement finance programs is in enabling non-investment-grade vendors to benefit from investment-grade financing rates.[17]
- Increased regulations: management of global risks, such as sanctions and trade barriers, along with fraud prevention, KYC (know your customer), and AML (anti-money laundering) requirements, is becoming an important part of the procurement, further increasing operational overheads.[18]
- The globalization is a relevant factor of the actual dynamic economic environment. The spread of globalization and the relevance of international trade have led the organizations to be more competitive.[19] To cope with this challenge, it is necessary for the organizations to be agile, that is, responsive and flexible. The market increasingly

international attributes an important role to the procurement. It leads the management of this sector to become more complex because the markets have now vendors, logistical operators, warehouses, distributors, and customers distributed globally. To be competitive, it is necessary to guarantee globally faster, more profitable, and more efficient operations. In a global market, the competitiveness is no longer focused on increasing the sales volume. It is oriented towards the customer satisfaction taking into account that customers are diverse. This orientation in turns brings sales volume. To win the competition, the organizations have to guarantee the satisfaction of the customer requirements regarding products characteristics, the terms of sales, but also efficient methods of payments. The competition is becoming more rapid and aggressive also due to the diffusion of technologies. The difference between vendors is no longer measured on product quality or price levels rather on effective procurement procedures, quick deliveries, and an effective customer journey.[20]

- Procurement can gain strategic benefits if it succeeds in finding new approaches in delivering the service to the customers through the digital transformation.[21] The maturing of new solutions, coupled with network effects, contributes to the take-up of procurement. The simplification and digitization of the full procure-to-pay (or accounts payable) and order-to-cash (or accounts receivable) processes enable event-triggered financing services. For instance, a pre-shipment financing negotiation can be triggered by an order confirmation. The availability of procure-to-pay digitization on independent third-party platforms allows the buyers and the vendors to use several financial services. It allows easy access to multiple liquidity providers, including small financial institutions and fintech organizations. Big financial institutions still claim 68 percent of the small business market (versus only 41 percent of retail consumers).[22] Even though small organizations are more likely to bank with a large financial institution, that does not mean they want to. Many would prefer to have a relationship with a smaller institution: one which knows the local market and takes the time to understand their business. The concern of small and medium-sized enterprises (SMEs) is that community banks and credit unions are less likely to have the technology conveniences they crave.

- At the same time, there is an increasing interest in outsourcing.[23] This mode of procurement has several benefits, but it must be managed carefully.
- Due to the increasing and rapid changes in the environment, it is difficult to forecast and hence plan.[24]

These challenges have influenced, especially, the procurement sector. To analyze in depth where the procurement function is positioned in the organization and why it is considered in such an important way, it is possible to refer to the Porter's value chain, represented in Fig. 2.2.[25]

The value chain, modeled by Porter, represents the overall value network composed by value-adding activities and margins.[26] The value-adding activities are the activities performed by every organization. Instead, the margins represent the difference between all the value activities and all the costs necessary to perform these activities. The value chain allows the splitting of the strategic activities in an organization in a way that makes possible to understand how the costs behave and how it is possible the optimization.[27]

The main distinction, within the value activities, is between primary and support activities. The first category is connected to the physical transformation of the products or the provision of the services. The primary activities stand out among themselves on the basis of the industry's types and the industry's strategies. The support activities are those activities that

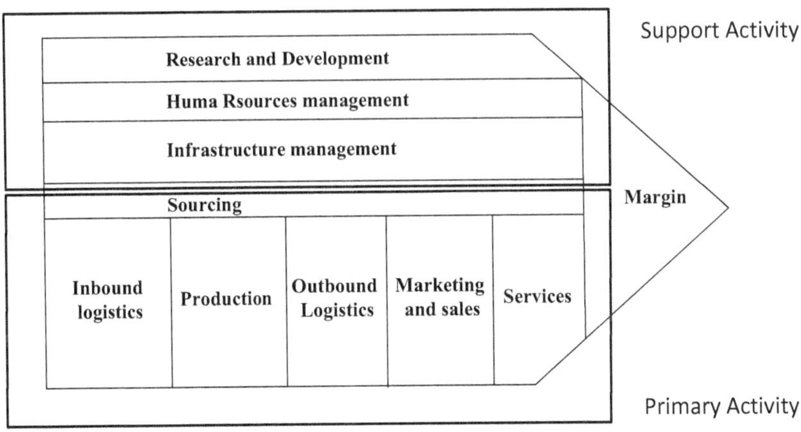

Fig. 2.2 Porter's value chain

support the primary ones. Among all activities which represent the support activities, the procurement activity is the only one that is a large impact activity because it is able to support both the primary activities and the support activities.[28] Procurement is a channel with participants who are associated to make easier the transactions among them.[29] The transactions are relative to the buying and selling of products and services viewed as inputs for the participants of the value chain.[30] Procurement supports the primary activities so that the requirements of products and services from the operations, inbound and outbound logistics, are satisfied correctly. It supports the activities in a way that services and products necessary also to all the other support activities are available at the right time, the right location, and the right quality.

Procurement for direct products and services should be considered a primary function. Procurement is a large and increasing part of the costs of an organization. Procurement can impact substantially on the margins. Indirect procurement for all other supplies is instead a support function.

Procurement is the process that covers a whole cycle that starts from the identification of the needs of organizations to the termination of an order or a contract including the evaluation of proposals and the "make or buy" decision. The function qualifies new vendors, provides different kinds of inputs, and evaluates the performance of the vendors. For this reason, it is a significant link among the members of the value chain. Obtaining the best value for money means selecting the vendors or choosing the bids that are not based on the lowest possible price but the ones that combine costs and benefits to best meet the requirements of the customers.

Procurement should perform activities before and after the ordering or contracting with a vendor[31]:

- pre-contract: planning, marketing, identification of the needs, analysis, and sourcing;
- post-contract: management of contracts, value network management vendor rating, and disposal;
- general activities: corporate governance, vendor management relationship, and regulatory compliance.

This large capacity of procurement in influencing the overall costs and differentiation of the organization as a whole gives procurement a significant role within the organizations.

Procurement Cycle

The procurement cycle is the process of the key steps to procure products or services. The activities in the procurement cycle start from the selection and management of the vendors' offers until the bill's accounting and payment. They pass through the orders management and the documentation of transport of the entry products or the provision of services.

The main processes of the procurement cycle are called "P2P" (purchase to pay) and "O2P" (order to pay). The purchase-to-pay cycle regards the sourcing by an organization.[32] During the cycle of producing products and delivering services, the organization proceeds in the selection, the reception, and the payment of all the necessary materials and the other inputs. The days payable outstanding (DPO) formula measures how many days on average are necessary for the organization to pay creditors within a defined period.[33] From the working capital point of view, it would be appropriate that the DPO is as high as possible allowing the organization to keep cash for more time. The vendors are interested in the opposite. Procurement finance can help to satisfy both requirements.

The order-to-pay cycle provides two simple and distinct phases: the former concerns with the beginning of the cycle, in which the preparation of a quote for a customer is the main object; the latter regards the end of the cycle, characterized by the reception of the payment and its reconciliation with the appropriate invoice.[34]

The phases of the procurement cycle can be clustered into two parts: primary and support processes:

- primary processes:
  - determination of needs (or acquisition request)
  - sourcing
  - logistics:
    - transportation
    - warehousing
    - delivery
  - supply chain

- support processes
  - procurement marketing
  - vendor qualification
  - vendor management
  - vendor rating

All these activities allow the organization to commit to the vendors, provide the products and/or services, and manage the expenses incurred.

From an organization point of view, any inefficiency means added costs. Simplification and digitization allow the support of the communication processes and of the documents processing. They bring benefits in terms of reduction of billing times, shortening of payment times, elimination of transmission errors, and easier and timely information access.[35]

Primary Processes

The primary processes in procurement are connected with the primary activities in the Porter's value chain.[36]

Acquisition Request

A procurement process supports the acquisition of products and/or services from the market. The acquisition request (AR) is the document through which any business structure can provide inputs to the procurement department to begin the procurement activities of a product or service.

The AR must contain all the information necessary to identify the product or service to purchase:

- name;
- description;
- quantity;
- technical and/or functional specifications;
- any technical and/or construction/installation drawing or requirement;
- location(s) of delivery;
- required supply times and locations;
- available budget for that purchase;
- authorization to spend within the limits of the budget;
- any suitable or previously used eligible vendors.

The acquisition requests allow the operators of various departments to communicate to the procurement their material or service needs. The buyer verifies that the acquisition request defines well all those requirements. It is important that a schedule of deliveries is specified based on when the organization needs the products or services. Procurement analyzes all the acquisition requests, deciding whether to reject them (motivating the rejection with a note and suggesting modifications), put them on hold, or create an order/contract for the required item. The better the acquisition request describes the features of the product or services to be acquired, the faster and more precise it is the buyer's job in completing the procurement in accordance with the desired characteristic and respecting the organization's budget and compliance.

Sourcing

Sourcing is the determination of the acquisition method, requests for bids, selection of the preferred vendor(s), and the negotiation.

Determination of the Acquisition Method

An important aspect in sourcing is the choice between an order and a contract. The former is mainly for one-time procurement, while the latter is for a more continuous purchase. The trend is now mainly in the direction of contracts in such a way to create stable relationships with the vendors. There are essentially three types of contracts: the cost-reimbursement contract, the fixed price contract, and the incentive contract.[37]

The cost-reimbursement (or cost-plus) contract occurs when the buyer reimburses all documented production costs to the vendor and pays a supervision or overhead fee. In this case, the vendor is assured against possible discrepancies between the actual production costs and the estimated ones. With this type of contract, the vendor is not incentivized to cut costs. This type of contract is suitable in situation in which the quality is non-verifiable, namely, non-contractible quality, because the vendor has no incentive to cut the quality. Therefore, it is suitable when the supply cannot be properly specified. Cost-reimbursement contract is used when uncertainties involved in the contract do not allow estimating costs in a proper way. For this type of contract, the negotiation with the vendor is preferred rather than the competitive tendering.

In the fixed price/fixed time contract, the contractor is paid a fixed price in a fixed time to perform the contract. The vendor is not insured by possible cost overruns. In this situation, the vendor is incentivized to reduce its costs. Unlike the cost-reimbursement contract, in this case, competitive tendering is preferred. The fixed price contract is preferred by most of the buyers since the commodity price is set at the beginning and is not subject to change unless changes are made to the specifications of the purchase. For any increase in costs due to unfavorable services, the vendor is responsible, since it is obliged to complete the commitment. This type of contract is mainly preferred for simple projects or commodity products and services and in situations in which the uncertainty is low. In drafting this contract, particular care should be devoted to the change management of the specifications on respect to the initial ones.

The incentive (or *bonus/malus*) contract is in the middle between the previous two types of contract. In this situation, the total price of the contract is connected with the performance of the contractor. The latter is not fully responsible for the fluctuations of the costs of implementation. This type of contract allows high incentives for the contractor to perform cost reduction activities and, at the same time, it creates incentives for better quality.

Tenders or Requests for Bid

There are long list and short list for the vendors in a tender. The first one occurs when several vendors meet the pre-qualification criteria and they are requested to submit the first proposal. The short list occurs when only some vendors meet the pre-qualification criteria. They are requested to submit a detailed bid.[38]

The important first steps in a bid are:

- Preparation of:
  - The Request for Information (RFI) invites vendors to submit general information regarding past experiences of qualifications. The Request for Information is normally followed by a Request for Quotation and/or a Request for Proposal.
  - The Request for Quotation (RFQ) invites vendors to submit detailed bids to meet the organization's requirements. It is relative only to the price quote and presupposes a pre-qualification of the vendors and standard or pre-approved requirements.

- The Request for Proposal (RFP) is used to receive the offers and to compare them to each other. This request invites vendors to submit their offers according to the terms and conditions stated in the request itself. This request does not involve only the provision of a price but also the demonstration of functional and technical capabilities consistent with the acquisition request.

Selection

Following the receipt of the bids, the procurement starts the evaluation process based on the criteria defined before sending the requests and normally described in the bidding document (evaluation grid). On the basis of the bids received, the organization selects the better vendor(s) and starts the negotiation with it/them.

The criteria on which the selection is based are[39]:

- technical capability;
- experience;
- seriousness;
- financial and economic capacity;
- more favorable conditions.

The vendors must have the capabilities to perform the requested supply, in the necessary quantities and times and at competitive prices. The objective is to reach the compliance of supplies with operational requirements, namely, quality, timeliness, and service levels, and possibly improve on them.

The buyer is required to know the market to guarantee alternative sources, to foster competitiveness, and to use successfully the vendor rotation or consolidation opportunities. It is important to evaluate the knowledge of the potentiality of a vendor including its technical capabilities, the production volumes, and the market positioning. Furthermore, the buying organization has to control each bid evaluating the vendor performance according to the organization requirements as the basis for the continuous improvement of the procurement services.

Negotiation

Following the selection of the vendor(s), there is the negotiation for agreeing the pricing, terms, and conditions. The negotiation starts in this phase and covers the total cost of the supply, logistics services, and accessory services. It is particularly important to include a precise management of the potential changes in the course of the supply (change requests or change management).

Logistics

According to the Italian Association of Logistics (AILOG), the definition of logistics is[40]:

> The process of planning, organizing, and controlling all handling and storage activities of products and information from the acquisition points of raw materials, through the production process of the organization, to the delivery of finished products to the end-customers.

Logistics is relative to materials management and physical distribution (transportation). Logistics has two objectives: minimization of costs and maximization of the quality of the services. It needs to ensure the lowest possible cost, but it has to ensure timeliness, reliability, and flexibility.[41]

The logistics processes are transportation, warehousing, distribution, and connected services.

The traditional approach defines logistics as the set of transportation and storage activities for the distribution of the products to the customers. Logistics has evolved mainly due to the globalization that has increased the distribution networks and the availability of new solutions. Integrated logistics is an extension of transportation activities considering as the main objective the optimization and integration of warehouse processes and the distribution of products and, in some cases, of the services.[42]

Transportation

Transportation activities can be divided into three interrelated phases relative to the inbound logistics, the transformation, and the outbound logistics. The first one allows the organization to acquire raw materials, parts, and components from the vendors, to have the supply in the locations, ways, and times required by the organization processes available at the lowest total costs.

During the process of transformation, the logistics follow the flow of work in process, ensuring its timely and economical utilization in the various production phases, until the finished products are placed in their warehouse(s) or delivered to the intermediaries or to the end customers.

Warehousing

Warehousing is relative to the design and management of logistics infrastructure and facilities used for the collection, storage, and handling of products.[43] It has the objective to make them available in the required times and quantities to the organization. It is one of the main functions of the logistics. The warehouse is a typical logistic network, which is able to receive, store, and prepare materials for sorting, shipping, and delivery. In the face of a constantly evolving market, warehousing is an important asset that the organizations can use to improve their competitiveness. On the other side, inventory is a cost to the organization. The smaller and emptier the warehouse, the less "waste" for the organization.[44]

The competitive benefits of the warehouse are not only found in the potential uncoupling of the production from the demand but also in the improvement of the service levels. The end price of a product depends on the production and distribution costs that are influenced by the storage costs, while the service level is determined by the effectiveness of the warehousing activity.

Warehousing acts as a junction between the sourcing of the organization and the process of transformation, and between the process of transformation and the sales processes. It ensures the continuity of the production process and the timeliness in the satisfaction of the customer needs.

Warehousing management includes inventory management. It falls within the scope of the physical flow control within a logistics/production process. Its objective is to minimize the costs of maintaining the products in stocks while ensuring a proper supply of production and sales flows. Warehouse management needs to ensure the availability of materials and to cut the order-delivery cycle time.

New information and communication technologies (ICTs) and automation solutions allow the improvement of most of the warehouse operations. The warehouse operators can receive orders in a more rapid way, pick them in an efficient manner, and can track the inventories related to these orders.[45]

This chapter does not consider the case where inventories are used for financial reasons (for instance, for speculating on prices). Plenty of literature is available on this subject.[46]

Delivery

The organizations adopt a delivery strategy depending on the characteristic of the products, the customers, and the context in which it operates.[47] The objective is to obtain a sufficient control of the final demand by improving the services offered and reducing costs.

The organization can have two types of distribution strategies[48]:

- Direct delivery: The products are shipped directly from the vendor to the end customer without passing through intermediaries.
- Indirect delivery: It consists of intermediaries between the vendor and the end customer. The indirect delivery can occur through deposit (warehousing) in which the vendor transfers the product to a deposit that performs the activities of storage and sorting out products for the customer. The delivery of the product when it is indirect can occur through transit points called cross-docking in which the sorting out of the products is prevalent.[49] They are called transit point to underline that the products should pass quickly through them.

Supply Chain

The supply chain is the connected series of activities involving the planning, coordination, and control of physical the flow, components, and finished products from the vendor to the customer.[50] Another definition for supply chain is a system where several parties transform the raw materials in finished products for the end customers.[51] The supply chain is a dynamic system where supply meets demand and where the raw materials become products that are sold to intermediaries and/or to end customers.[52] LaLonde and Masters use the term supply chain to refer to a group of organizations moving materials forward.[53] This definition entails a concept where there is a one-way movement, from the first raw material vendor to the end customer. According to these authors, delivery to the end customer is part of the supply chain. It is possible to consider the supply chain as the system made by all the organizations that consequently bring a product or a service to the market.[54] To sum up, inside a supply chain there must be at least two organizations and an end customer. The organizations involved have to operate both for the supply and distribution of products.

A supply chain can be more or less complex, hence short or long, and as the number of players increases, so do the number of relationships and links, bringing its complexity to arise (Fig. 2.3). Any organization involved in a supply chain can also be part of another one (that is, inside one there can be a vendor while inside another the customer). Let alone the length and complexity degree of a supply chain, this includes[55]:

- upstream vendors, who are responsible for the delivering of the inputs;
- internal functions of an organization, that is, all the processes needed to transform inputs into outputs;
- downstream intermediaries, who are responsible for bringing the products to the end customer.

There are several degrees of complexity that characterize a supply chain[56]:

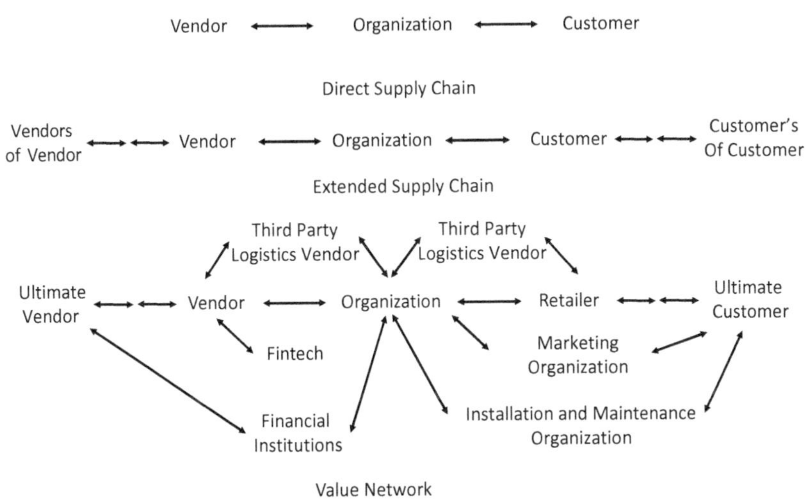

Fig. 2.3 Types of supply chains

- direct supply chain;
- extended supply chain;
- ultimate supply chain.

A direct supply chain consists of an organization, a vendor, and a customer involved in the upstream and/or downstream flows of products, services, finances, and/or information. An extended supply chain includes vendors of the immediate vendor and customers of the immediate customer, all involved in the upstream and/or downstream flows of products, services, finances, and/or information. An ultimate supply chain includes all the organizations involved in all the upstream and downstream flows of products, services, finances, and information from the ultimate vendor to the ultimate customer.

This is the traditional supply chain definition. Other authors pointed out to a broader concept that goes beyond the traditional supply chain and that includes also other players involved in the packaging, recycling, or re-use of finished products (reverse logistics).[57]

To run a supply chain, some practices are needed. This is where the concepts of supply chain management (SCM) emerge. The definition of SCM is "the management of upstream and downstream relationships with vendors and customers to deliver superior customer value at less cost to the supply chain as a whole".[58] It is also possible to define SCM as the management of the organizations and activities they have to perform to create a sustainable competitive advantage.[59]

Support Processes

There are essentially four support processes in the procurement cycle: procurement marketing, vendor qualification, vendor management, and vendor rating.

Procurement Marketing

Procurement marketing is an important base for the other procurement processes. It is an effective and necessary tool to discover and know the markets, and to maximize the effectiveness, efficiency, and economics on the choice of the vendors.[60] The objective of procurement marketing is to optimize procurement activities by identifying where and how to purchase the best items and adding value to the customers.[61] In this way, it is possible to minimize all the risk components of the procurement processes while at the same time establishing a profitable relationship with the vendors.

Procurement marketing helps to answer questions such as:

- What is the most appropriate sourcing market for the needs of the organization?
- Which are the vendors in that market and categories which best meet the needs of the organization?

Procurement marketing involves the systematic study of the procurement environment: markets, products, and vendors.[62] That analysis aims to get, from its own acquisition system, benefits able to improve the business competitiveness and add value to the organization. It analyzes the procurement markets, their risks, and opportunities. Procurement marketing helps also in the definition of the acquisition strategy for each specific procurement and of the mix of product-money-source-relationship policies.

Procurement marketing looks at the primary characteristics of the organization's needs and places them at the base of the relevance and structure of the procurement market to underline criticalities and opportunities for improvement. This phase is the cornerstone of the procurement process. Its absence may bring a loss of value for the organization.

It is useful to define, among the organization needs to procure, which have more strategic characters and which have less ones. The Kraljic matrix allows to understand this distinction in depth.[63] This model divides the sourcing into four categories according to the complexity of the supply market and the strategic importance of procurement. This matrix distinguishes four categories of items (leverage, strategic, non-critical, and bottleneck) with the needs of different procurement approaches (exploitation of contractual power, partnership, delegation of management, and long-term collaboration) (Fig. 2.4).[64]

An important aspect of the procurement marketing is the study of the innovation in the products/procurement markets to purchase and the procurement actions of the competition (market intelligence).[65]

Vendor Qualification

According to the American Society for Quality, vendor qualification is "the process of demonstrating whether an entity is capable of fulfilling the specified requirements".[66]

Vendor qualification means assuring that the vendor can get the job done to the standards the organization expects. Its objective is to learn of the vendor qualifications and what they mean for the procurement process.

Supply Risk

Importance	LOW	HIGH
HIGH	**Leverage Purchases** Emphasis on profitability (negotiation, bargaining power, volume, fluid flows) Exploit purchasing power and minimize costs	**Strategic Purchases** Emphasis on long-term availability (guarantee supply, alliances, demand forecasting) Form partnerships
LOW	**Non-critical Purchases** Emphasis on efficiency (irrilevant purchases) Simplify and Digitize	**Bottleneck Purchases** Emphasis on the stability of supplies (guarantee of supply, long-term contracts, safety stocks) Ensure supply

Fig. 2.4 The supply matrix (Kraljic)

There are several methods for the vendor qualification. A six-step process offers a comprehensive way to evaluate vendors[67]:

- Step 1: Certification. When a vendor has a certification (such as the ISO certification), it means their products and services meet the standard quality expectations of the customers. Checking the vendor's certifications can ensure they are in compliance.
- Step 2: Examination of the vendor's quality manual. In this step, the organization asks the potential vendor to provide its quality manuals and inspects them. This inspection includes the analysis of the vendor's procedures and documentation.
- Step 3: Vendor questionnaires. The questionnaire should cover all the aspects of information the organization needs to know of the vendor.
- Step 4: SPC (Statistical Process Control). The organization uses the information provided by the vendor in the manuals and the questionnaire to determine the SPC capabilities. Here too, certifications and standards can help. The potential vendors are categorized and inspected further on their ability to perform.

- Step 5: Process validation. The organization validates the vendor's processes against the standards provided in the manuals and the questionnaire.
- Step 6: Vendor auditing. The buyer organization can audit the vendor to ensure that the standards are still over time as documented. If necessary, adjustments could take place during the vendor auditing.

Picking the right vendor can simplify the way the organization receives the best supplies. It is necessary to decide which method of screening is the right one for the specific organization. For example, the pharmaceutical or biopharmaceutical organizations use the QUEST approach when they want to screen their vendors[68]:

- Question: In this step, the organization decides which products it needs the vendor to supply. The vendor needs to meet Food and Drug Administration (FDA) (or similar in the other countries) standards or other qualifications. This stage defines also a potential purchasing budget.
- Understand: The next step is to decide how the vendor is going to meet the requirements. It might be useful to request all the potential vendors for a sample of their products or of their services.
- Evaluate: All the potential vendors are evaluated to decide which candidate is going to meet the requirements established, based on the information acquired.
- Audit: All the potential critical vendors need to go through a site audit. Their facilities are inspected, and depending on the type of audit, off-site evaluations may also be required.
- Track: When a vendor is selected, the last step is to continuously monitor their progress and work performance.

Vendor Management

The term vendor management describes the activities in managing the definition of the contracts with the vendors, managing the relationships, assigning jobs, evaluating performance, and ensuring that correct payments are made.[69] A more complete definition is that vendor management is a set of processes, activities, systems, and information management tools (data and document repositories, and so on) that allows an organization to manage and have maximum visibility into all activities associated with a vendor. This visibility should encompass the definition of the vendor profiles based on the needs of the organization, the selection (RFx), the onboarding, the tracking, the scoring, and all the transactional activities and systems in the procure-to-pay process.[70] Key to all these activities is providing an organizational/management structure to manage and take ownership of all vendor-related activities.

The activities connected with the vendor management processes are:

- support the procurement and legal personnel in the definition of the commercial relationships and the terms and conditions of the contract with the vendors;
- define a service-level agreement with the vendors;
- manage a certain number of vendors supporting the organization either in the product or in the service delivery;
- work together with the management in charge of the projects, services, and initiatives supported by the vendors to optimize the relationships with the vendors;
- help in the transition of the service from the incumbent vendor or the organization to the new vendor;
- work in defining and improving the dashboards and cockpits to monitor the activities of the vendors;
- monitor the respect of the contractual relationships and follow the level of service actually delivered by the vendors;
- define and monitor the actions of the vendors and the organizations in case there are substantial deviations in respect to the level of service offered or there are emergency situations or there are major incidents;
- manage the change control process;
- organize and attend periodic meetings with the vendor's management;
- monitor the respect of the security requirements of the vendors;
- organize the lessons learned session at the end of the delivery (or periodically) of the relationships with the vendors.

Vendor Rating

Vendor rating represents the process of assessment, evaluation, and monitoring the performance of the vendor(s).[71] It is important to the procurement processes since it allows:

- a better selection of vendors;
- the correction, also during the supply, of any defects or inadequate performance;

- an involvement of the entire organization in the procurement processes.

The vendor rating should be done at different times:

- before the order is issued or at the time of the vendor selection;
- during the provision of services or the supply of products purchased;
- at the end of the service or supply.

The vendor rating is a driver for the improvement, in qualitative terms, of the current and future procurement relationships with the vendors. It allows to store the expected and past behaviors of the vendors and to influence the results of a new negotiation. It consists in the overall rating of a vendor's performance to see if the results are able to satisfy the customer requirements/needs. It is based exclusively on objective and complete data that must synthesize the effective performance of the vendor.

Due to the complexity and diversification of the modern procurement base, the handling of the vendors and the obtainment of the performances of quality and efficiency from the management on a vendor have become difficult. The non compliance of the supply can have results in the short term (delivery delays, higher costs, or unsatisfactory quality) and in the long term, such as negative consequences on the strategic objectives in the market.

In this context, vendor rating is important. It allows evaluating the vendors by using a reputable index based on relevant economics and qualitative and quantitative dimensions of perceived performances. From an objective point of view, if a vendor is evaluated, normally it performs better.

An accurate system of vendor rating allows reaching significant benefits:

- high level of value for money;
- achievement of long-term strategic objectives;
- qualitative improvement of the vendors' portfolio;
- sharing of the organization priorities with the vendors;
- spending rationalization.

Everybody in the organizations agrees with the previous observations. In reality, very rarely the process of vendor rating is followed throughout the life of a supply. For example, once the supply has been completed, it is quite difficult to obtain from the internal users of the services and products provided by a vendor:

- a proper evaluation;
- in a written and comprehensive format.

The problem is that people in the organizations are often over-committed and do not have time to provide a fair assessment of the vendors.

It is worthwhile to see how the five most significant technological solutions in a digital transformation can help also in the vendor rating:

- Internet of Things (IoT). The IoT can help organizations to automatically collect a variety of data. The information extracted by these data can support from a management and operational point of view but also in the evaluation of the vendors when the vendors are involved in providing the service or products using IoT. Thanks to IoT, it is possible, for instance, to record the time of start, the timing of the service, the items which do not pass the quality controls, and so on.
- Big Data. The IoT can collect a lot of data. There are also other digital tools used to collect data on procurement. An example is provided by the service desk. Several organizations are now using applications that enable the creation of the support tickets for incidents, problems, service and change requests, and knowledge management processes. Many of these tools have the ability to report on the compliance with the levels of service (SLA). In this way, the organizations can automatically register data on vendor performance, compliance with contractual clauses, and trends. In this way, the organizations can evaluate the vendors and, if necessary, take action before the situation goes out of control. All this data can be stored using the Big Data technologies. It is then relatively easy to access or produce statistical reports and dashboards on the vendor performance.
- Artificial intelligence. The Big Data allows the organizations to use advanced tools of artificial intelligence. These applications can provide an operational- and a management-level support. They can also be used to evaluate vendors and support them for better delivery.

- Mobile. Where there is the need for the manual evaluation of the vendors, it is possible to develop simple apps that allow recording the procurement performance by using cell phones or tablets. Simple apps can remind and alert the operators to perform vendor evaluation with a few clicks.
- Cloud computing. Cloud computing extends the use of the tools mentioned above in all the business organizations involved in the extended value network.

In the future, with the spread and the use of e-procurement functionality, organizations can connect the applications mentioned in this section with management tools to support the procurement processes. It is possible the automatic buildup of a black list and a gold list of vendors. Moreover, the information gathered can be shared in real time directly with the vendors in the entire procurement ecosystem.

Conclusions

In recent years, there has been an in-depth refinement of the procurement processes. It is recognized as a strategic function, able to strength collaboration and the use of new solutions. The analysis of procurement processes makes possible to define and support the relevant role of the procurement inside the organization.

Procurement costs are an increasing share of sales volume. Organizations need vendors which are able to satisfy their requirements in terms of procurement and sales. Qualified personnel need to properly select the vendors that meet the organization needs and have a collaborative mode with them. It is increasingly necessary that the procurement processes create more value for the customers. The collaboration and proximity to the vendors through new solutions can support efficiently the procurement processes shortening the time of information exchange and integrating fully the vendors in the organization's value network. Procurement is not only "saving" but it is the generation of value for the organization. For this reason, the procurement department can contribute considerably to the organization success because it can intercept the upstream needs and to guide, in a strategic way, the procurement processes.

The vendors can represent also a source of risks for the procurement. It is necessary to manage, in an integrated way, the process of qualification and evaluation of the vendors. The word "integrated" is important.

It is necessary an efficient integration of the vendors, producers, warehousing, deposits, and intermediaries in order that the products and services are produced and deployed at the right quantity, at the right place, at the right time, and at the right economics. This allows minimizing the costs, reducing wastes, increasing the service levels, and adding value to the customers and the organization.

Notes

1. Pfohl, H. C., & Gomm, M. (2009). Supply chain finance: optimizing financial flows in supply chains. *Logistics research*, *1*(3–4), 149–161.
2. Pfohl, H. C., & Gomm, M. (2009). Supply chain finance: optimizing financial flows in supply chains. *Logistics research*, *1*(3–4), 149–161.

   Mentzer, J. T., DeWitt, W., Keebler, J. S., Min, S., Nix, N. W., Smith, C. D., & Zacharia, Z. G. (2001) Defining supply chain management. *Journal of Business Logistics* 22(2): 1–25.

   Croom, S, Romano P., & Giannakis, M (2000) Supply chain management: an analytical framework for critical literature review. *European Journal of Purchasing and Supply Management.* 6(1): 67–83.

   Cooper, M. C., Lambert, D. M., & Pagh, J. D. (1997). Supply chain management: more than a new name for logistics. *The International Journal of Logistics Management*, *8*(1), 1–14.
3. cdn.iccwbo.org/content/uploads/sites/3/2017/01/ICC-Standard-Definitions-for-Techniques-of-Supply-Chain-Finance-Global-SCF-Forum-2016.pdf, Accessed 24 February 2018.
4. Chakuu, S., Masi, D., & Godsell, J. (2017). A Systematic Literature Review on Supply Chain Finance Actors, Instruments and Processes. *DEStech Transactions on Engineering and Technology Research*, (icpr).
5. Van Weele, A. J. (2009). *Purchasing and supply chain management: Analysis, strategy, planning and practice.* Cengage Learning EMEA, Andover, UK.
6. CIPS (2013). *The definition of Procurement.* www.cips.org/Documents/CIPSAWhitePapers/2006/Definition_of_Procurement.pdf
7. CIPS (2013). *The definition of Procurement.* www.cips.org/Documents/CIPSAWhitePapers/2006/Definition_of_Procurement.pdf
8. Tunisini, A., & Sebastiani, R. (2015). Innovative and networked business functions: customer-driven procurement. *Journal of Business & Industrial Marketing*, *30*(3/4), 302–311.
9. Tassabehji, R., & Moorhouse, A. (2008). The changing role of procurement: Developing professional effectiveness. *Journal of Purchasing and Supply Management*, *14*(1).

10. Cousins, P. D., & Spekman, R. (2003). Strategic supply and the management of inter-and intra-organisational relationships. *Journal of Purchasing and supply Management*, *9*(1), 19–29.
11. Tassabehji, R, & Moorhouse, A (2008), *The changing role of the procurement: Developing professional effectiveness,* Journal of Purchasing and Supply Chain Management 14, 55–68.
12. Kurbel, K. E. (2016). *Enterprise resource planning and supply chain management.* Springer-Verlag Berlin, Germany.
13. CIPS (2013). *The definition of Procurement.* www.cips.org/Documents/CIPSAWhitePapers/2006/Definition_of_Procurement.pdf, Accessed 12 February 2018.
14. www.mckinsey.de/files/customer-experience-compendium-2016.pdf, Accessed 31 March 2018.
15. ijbssnet.com/journals/Vol_4_No_9_August_2013/20.pdf. Accessed 31 March 2018.
16. Mena, C., Christopher, M., & Van Hoek, R. (2014). *Leading procurement strategy: driving value through the supply chain.* Kogan Page Publishers, London, UK.
17. Helper, S., Nicholson, J., Noonan, R., & Callen, J. (2015). The economic benefits of reducing supplier working capital costs. www.sba.gov/sites/default/files/aboutsbaarticle/The_Economic_Benefits_of_Reducing_Supplier_Working_Capital_Costs.pdf. Accessed 18 July 2018.
18. Wandhöfer, R. (2014). Post-Crisis Regulatory Change. In *Transaction Banking and the Impact of Regulatory Change* (pp. 5–57). Palgrave Macmillan, Houndmills, UK.
19. Steger, M. B. (2010). *Globalization.* John Wiley & Sons, Ltd., Hoboken, NJ.
20. Hobson, H. (1978). *Indirect journey.* London: Weidenfeld and Nicolson, London, UK.
21. Maedche, A., vom Brocke, J., & Hevner, A. (Eds.). (2017). *Designing the Digital Transformation: 12th International Conference, DESRIST 2017, Karlsruhe, Germany, May 30–June 1, 2017, Proceedings* (Vol. 10243). Springer, Berlin, Germany.
22. thefinancialbrand.com/72541/community-bank-credit-union-small-business-banking-lending-trends/, Accessed 31 May 2018.
23. Ketler, K., & Walstrom, J. (1993). The outsourcing decision. *International journal of information management*, *13*(6), 449–459.
24. Christopher, M. (2016). *Logistics & supply chain management.* Pearson, London, UK.
25. Porter, M. E. (2008). *Competitive advantage: Creating and sustaining superior performance.* Simon and Schuster, New York City, NY.

26. Porter, M. E. (2008). *Competitive advantage: Creating and sustaining superior performance.* Simon and Schuster, New York City, NY.
27. Barnes, D. (2001), *Understanding Business: Processes,* Routledge, London, UK. 52–53.
28. Porter, M. E. (2008). *Competitive advantage: Creating and sustaining superior performance.* Simon and Schuster, New York City, NY.
29. Porter, M. E. (1998). Clusters and the new economics of competition. *Harvard Business Review.* 76(6), 77–90.
30. Novak, R. A., & Simco, S. W. (1991), The industrial procurement process: A supply chain perspective, *Journal of Business Logistics,* 12, 145–167.
31. CIPS (2013). *The definition of Procurement.* www.cips.org/Documents/CIPSAWhitePapers/2006/Definition_of_Procurement.pdf, Accessed 12 February 2018.
32. Kristofik, P., Kok, J., de Vries, S., & van Sten-van't Hoff, J. (2012). Financial Supply Chain Management–Challenges and Obstacles. *Proceedings in Finance and Risk Perspectives '12.*
33. Kristofik, P., Kok, J., de Vries, S., & van Sten-van't Hoff, J. (2012). Financial Supply Chain Management–Challenges and Obstacles. *Proceedings in Finance and Risk Perspectives '12.*
34. Kristofik, P., Kok, J., de Vries, S., & van Sten-van't Hoff, J. (2012). Financial Supply Chain Management–Challenges and Obstacles. *Proceedings in Finance and Risk Perspectives '12.*
35. Ketterer, J. A. (2017). *Digital Finance: New Times, New Challenges, New Opportunities.* Inter-American Development Bank, Washington, DC.
36. Porter, M. E. (2008). *Competitive advantage: Creating and sustaining superior performance.* Simon and Schuster, New York City, NY.
37. Dimitri, N., Piga, G. Spagnolo, G. (2006). *Handbook of Procurement,* Cambridge University, Cambridge, UK, 87–90.
38. Van Weele, A. J. (2009). *Purchasing and supply chain management: Analysis, strategy, planning and practice.* Cengage Learning, Boston, MA, 29–33.
39. Weber, C. A., Current, J. R., & Benton, W. C. (1991). Vendor selection criteria and methods. *European journal of operational research, 50*(1), 2–18.
40. www.ailog.it, Accessed 12 February 2018. Nicoletti, B., (2013), *Lean Procurement,* FrancoAngeli, Milano, Italy.
41. Rushton, A., Croucher, P., & Baker, P. (2014). *The handbook of logistics and distribution management: Understanding the supply chain.* Kogan Page Publishers, London, UK.
42. Christopher, M. (2016). *Logistics & supply chain management.* Pearson U.
43. Richards, G. (2017). *Warehouse management: a complete guide to improving efficiency and minimizing costs in the modern warehouse.* Kogan Page Publishers, London, UK.

44. Keyte, B., & Locher, D. A. (2016). *The complete lean enterprise: Value stream mapping for administrative and office processes*. Productivity Press.
45. Mason, S. J., Ribera, P. M., Farris, J. A., & Kirk, R. G. (2003). Integrating the warehousing and transportation functions of the supply chain. *Transportation Research Part E: Logistics and Transportation Review*, *39*(2), 141–159.
46. Kilian, L., & Murphy, D. P. (2014). The role of inventories and speculative trading in the global market for crude oil. *Journal of Applied Econometrics*, *29*(3), 454–478.
    Casson, M. (1982). *The entrepreneur: An economic theory*. Rowman & Littlefield, Lanham, MD.
47. Chenhall, R. H. (2003). Management control systems design within its organizational context: findings from contingency-based research and directions for the future. *Accounting, organizations and society*, *28*(2–3), 127–168.
48. Mentzer, J. T., DeWitt, W., Keebler, J. S., Min, S., Nix, N. W., Smith, C. D., & Zacharia, Z. G. (2001). Defining supply chain management. *Journal of Business Logistics*, *22*(2), 1–25.
49. Hofmann, E., Maucher, D., Piesker, S., & Richter, P. (2011). *Ways out of the working capital trap: Empowering self-financing growth through modern supply management* (Vol. 1). Springer Science & Business Media, Berlin, Germany.
50. Stevens, G. C. (1989) Integrating the Supply Chain, *International Journal of Physical Distribution & Materials Management*, 19(8), pp. 3–8.
51. Kozlenkova, I. V., et al. (2015). The role of marketing channels in supply chain management. *Journal of Retailing*, 91.4: 586–609.
52. Sell, S. P. D. (1999). Introduction to supply chain management. www.academia.edu/download/32179904/Introduction_to_SCM.docx, Accessed 31 March 2018.
53. LaLonde, B. J., Masters, J. M. (1995). *Bibliography on Logistics Management*, Council of Logistics Management.
54. Lambert, D. M., Stock, J. R., & Ellram, L. M. (1998). *Fundamentals of logistics management*, McGraw-Hill, Irwin, NJ.
55. Handfield, R. B., & Nichols, E. L. (2002). *Supply chain redesign: Transforming supply chains into integrated value systems*. FT Press, London, UK.
56. Mentzer, J. T., DeWitt, W., Keebler, J. S., Min, S., Nix, N. W., Smith, C. D., & Zacharia, Z. G. (2001). Defining supply chain management. *Journal of Business Logistics*, *22*(2), 1–25.
57. Beamon, B. M. (1999). Designing the green supply chain. *Logistics information management*, *12*(4), 332–342.

58. Christopher, M. (2016). *Logistics & Supply Chain Management*, Pearson, London, UK.
59. Handfield, R. B., & Nichols, E. L. (2002). *Supply chain redesign: Transforming supply chains into integrated value systems.* FT Press, London, UK.
60. Aaker, D. A., & McLoughlin, D. (2010). *Strategic market management: global perspectives.* John Wiley & Sons, Hoboken, NJ.
Van Weele, A. J. (2010). *Purchasing & supply chain management: analysis, strategy, planning and practice.* Cengage Learning EMEA, Andover, UK.
61. Hugos, M. H. (2018). *Essentials of supply chain management.* John Wiley & Sons, Hoboken, NJ.
62. Koppelmann, U. (1998). *Procurement Marketing: A strategic concept.* Springer Science & Business Media, Dordrecht, The Netherlands.
63. Kraljic, P. (1983). Purchasing must become supply management. *Harvard business review*, *61*(5), 109–117.
64. www.nigp.org/docs/default-source/new-site/education/webinars/sourcing-business-modelsnigp582a86d6be6365359624ff000097fdb4.pdf?sfvrsn=1349e357_0. Accessed 31 March 2018.
65. Edler, J., Ruhland, S., Hafner, S., Rigby, J., Georghiou, L., Hommen, L. & Papadakou, M. (2005). Innovation and public procurement. Review of issues at stake. *ISI Fraunhofer Institute Systems and Innovation Research*, Karlsruhe, Germany.
66. www.asq.org. Accessed 12 June 2018.
67. www.gordonhorner.com/single-post/2017/11/10/What-Does-Vendor-Qualification-Mean. Accessed 6 May 2018.
68. www.pharmtech.com/how-develop-practical-and-compliant-vendor-qualification-program-0?id=&sk=&date=&%0A%09%09%09&pageID=2. Accessed 4 May 2018.
69. Palaniswami, S., & Lingaraj, B. P. (1994). Procurement and vendor management in the global environment. *International Journal of Production Economics*, *35*(1–3), 171–176.
70. www.icgconsulting.com/vendor-management-what-is-it. Accessed 5 May 2018.
71. Castellani, L., & Spagnolo, G. (2017). Introduction–Vendor rating, performance and entry in public procurement. In *Law and Economics of Public Procurement Reforms* (pp. 17–28). Routledge, London, UK.

CHAPTER 3

From Trade Finance to Supply Chain Finance to Procurement Finance

Introduction

After the economic and financial crisis of 2008, payment times in all the organizations have increased. This has led to larger financial needs to support working capital management and liquidity. This phenomenon, due to the simultaneous restriction of the credit grant criteria and the increase in financing costs, has jeopardized the financial stability of many organizations. In this scenario, procurement finance emerges as a possible solution to ease the credit situation of the organizations.

This chapter focuses on the financial flows in the procurement processes. It starts with the relationships between finance and procurement. It continues with the definitions of trade finance, supply chain finance, and procurement finance, clarifying the transition from one to another.

The final part of this chapter introduces the new concept of procurement finance. It identifies a set of solutions and services aimed at optimizing working capital and liquidity within the value network of the organization through an increased integration and coordination among all its components.

B. Nicoletti, *Procurement Finance*,
Palgrave Studies in Financial Services Technology,
https://doi.org/10.1007/978-3-030-02140-5_3

Relationships Between Procurement and Finance

Procurement and Finance[1]

Procurement has always been connected with the finance sector. In a certain number of organizations, the procurement sector is even within the finance department. Procurement can make a huge contribution to add value to the organization. These two functions (procurement and finance) share many things both at a strategic and tactical level. Examples of these relationships are vendor management, the integration of the corporate and procurement strategy, the implementation of procurement systems, and so on. To better describe the common points between finance and procurement, it is necessary to clearly understand the procurement priorities. They can be summarized in a triangle (Fig. 3.1).[2]

One of the main tasks of the procurement is to "meet an organization demand for the product and services required to achieve the objectives of that organization".[3] To make sure that the procurement negotiates and agrees on appropriate orders and contracts, it is necessary to understand the demand of the organization and know the vendors' markets. "Supply" is the name to summarize this aspect.

To comply with the process and authorized contracts, an organization must ensure that all employees use these guidelines. This aspect is called "Control".

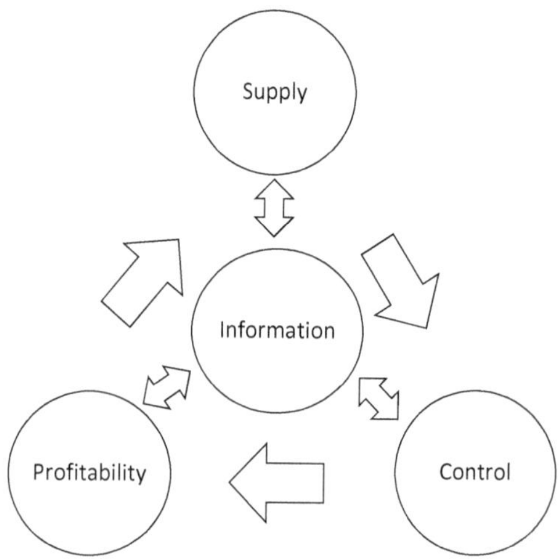

Fig. 3.1 The four pillars of procurement finance

The organization should value its customers the most. It is necessary to take into account also the satisfaction of the shareholders and of the employees of the organization. This underlines the importance of the "profitability". Profitability in procurement consists in understanding the needs of the organization, the progress of purchases, the characteristics and trends of the vendors' markets, the extent to which the available procurement processes and the accompanying systems are used. Profitability is also the best way to assure the survival and indeed the growth of the organization.

Information is the glue among all the previous aspects. Managing the information is a way to assure profitability and control of the organization's supply. All the information should be made available to all the stakeholders. It is important that the information be correct and quickly available. These two characteristics are sometimes in conflict. The best organizations combine the two aspects in an optimal way.

These aspects are the key touch points between procurement and finance. Since each category has its own characteristics that determine the requirements that products, services, and vendors must reflect, it is important to define a precise strategy for each of these aspects. The organization's strategic objectives should always be at the forefront. For example, considering an organization that targets innovation or product leadership, it is necessary to look for vendors who are able to fulfill those expectations. If the organization wants to implement a cost leadership or operational excellence strategy, it is necessary to look for less innovative vendors that are able to offer quality products at favorable cost conditions. If the organization has a strategy of customer intimacy, it is important to select vendors with expertise and experiences of the customer's business, possibly in the proximity of the customer. The vendors should be able to support the strategy of building the customer loyalty.

Supply

A critical aspect for a successful cooperation between procurement and finance is to have clear and strategic supply objectives. The organization strategy defines these objectives. Due to its role in the organization, the chief financial officer (CFO) has the responsibility to translate into financial actions the organization's overall strategy and to coordinate them with the strategies of the other departments. Based on the organization strategy, the supply of products and services can be prioritized and the procurement plan of action settled.

Another important point is the fact that finance translates the supply objectives into clear and measurable performance indicators. These indicators should support the organization in evaluating in a concise manner how procurement's performance is measured. Thus, the latter does not simply serve for the control of the costs. Some indicators can be the basis of the measurement of the competency and delivery factors of the vendors. They are important for creating added value for the organization. They should guarantee better quality management and greater reliability of supply.

Control

Supply is mainly relative to the organization's tactical procurement aspects. Control deals with the adaptation of the supply at an operational level. At this point, the issuing of the order of a product or services takes place. It is followed by the receipt of the products or the delivery of the services and the financial management of the payments. To control this phase, it is important that there are defined and achievable procurement processes, properly supported by the systems. Adequate methods and tools should support all employees in such a way to respect and monitor the compliance processes.

This aspect underlines an important connection between procurement and finance. The interest of procurement is that traded contracts are made available in time to the employees authorized to order products and services. Operators should have a more direct form of ordering items. This is possible thanks to automation and, whenever possible, to a self-service by the operators themselves. The information is uniformly registered in the systems, making it a source of knowledge for new procurement activities. In this way, finance can monitor costs and get information on ongoing financial commitments. To obtain a deeper collaboration between the procurement and other departments' activities, the design of the ordering process and the following administrative operation should be a joint operation.

Besides the compliance with processes, control refers with the respect of the contracts. It is essential that operators follow the correct ordering process. It is also necessary that purchases be based on procurement contracts avoiding maverick orders. This has financial convenience, simplifying risk control. Risk monitoring is complicated when the supply processes are not methodically followed.

Well-defined performance indicators are also needed for the control in both disciplines (procurement and finance) as from the "Supply" point of view.

Profitability

Profitability of the supply is also the result of the proper interactions between the procurement and the finance sectors. Through the profitability, the processes of procurement can be highlighted at a tactical and strategic level. The contribution that they provide in achieving corporate objectives is made visible. Thanks to the fact that the obligations are recorded for the compliance process, profitability allows a better management of the financial function as it shows the availability of liquid assets and the impact on the capital. Once reached full control of the operational procurement processes, more complex payment conditions can be negotiated with the vendors that include payment times, terms, and discounts.

The continuous traceability of all purchases helps procurement in its supply activities. It allows monitoring of the procurement behavior of the entire organization and to agree on the contract's terms with the vendors. It allows gathering information from the sales and the operations planning. Finally, all these processes allow real-time control of sales margins, helping the organization to take the right decisions and measures to achieve the desired objectives.

Procurement Performance

One of the main problems in many organizations is that they have not set any performance measures for evaluating procurement efficiency, effectiveness, and economics. Based on the strategic planning objectives and the pursuit of the quality, procurement should set some measures through which establish the results of its actions. This allows procurement to verify that its objectives are satisfied. Procurement performance is one of the main drivers to improve the performance of the organization. A poor performance can create obstacles to the changes in the organization and can bring to the failure of the procurement function.

Performance measurement is important for increasing the performance of the organizations. Procurement performance is considered the result of two elements: procurement effectiveness and procurement efficiency.[4] It is essential to consider also procurement economics. Measuring performance allows the analysis of the organization's progress and how much is needed to achieve its objectives. Therefore, it helps in finding strengths and weaknesses and helps in deciding future initiatives.

One of the principal needs is the implementation of pre-organized procedures, systems, and strategies that, on a continuous base, connect and align the procurement actions to the organization's objectives.

The organizations that apply these approaches, in a reliable and integrated way, gain in cost savings, management of the expenditures, compliance, vendor integration, and bigger contribution to the organization value.

Trade Finance

Trade finance refers to commercial credit and all connected services, such as loans to finance purchases, advance payments by buyers, and deferred payments.[5]

Trade finance has enabled the exchange of goods for millennia. Babylonian cuneiform tablets, dating back to 3000 BC, mention the kind of promissory notes and letters of credit that still underpin international trade.[6] The expansion of trade is growing globally. To maintain the competitiveness in this dynamic environment, facilitating trade is important. It occurs through streamlining processes, supporting information flows related to international trade, and facilitating access to financial support.

World trade volumes have seen a startling increase in open-account transaction over the recent years, and more are expected in the future (Table 3.1).[7] Already today more than 80 percent of the total world trade

Table 3.1 Growth in supply chain finance

	Europe	*Americas*	*Asia*
Estimated volume (billions of USD)	135	235	70.8
Estimated market size by funds in use (billions of USD)	55	98	11.8
Estimated annual volume growth (percent)	35	38	29
Key sectors using supply chain finance	Food, retail, telecoms	Retail, electronics, textiles, consumer goods	Food, retail, commodities

Adapted from the authors from https://bcrpub.com/news/global-supply-chain-finance-jumps-36-percent

volume (export) is settled by clean payments. This impressive ratio is expected to grow even further in the future. The following statistics are interesting on these aspects[8]:

- Short-term export credit insurance (new business volume 2013), USD 1.640 billion. The exposure at year end 2013 was USD 1.092 billion.
- Cross-border factoring volume 2013 amounts to USD 440 billion (domestic factoring volumes 2013: USD 2.667 billion).

A requirement from corporate customers is that the financial institutions they use should offer products that support fully automated processing as well as cost savings combined with payment assurance and financing options. The dynamic and volatile context requires agility and timeliness. The international transactions have limits and risks.[9] Buyers and vendors can be under different legislation or there can be a different currency for payments. For many organizations, the ability to start trading with foreign customers and vendors is an important milestone in their business plans because it impacts profitability. For many industries, the interesting markets are located abroad. Vendor activities can be an expensive and with uncertain paths. To limit these risks, the formalization of a commercial contract has to be guaranteed by a trusted third party: the financial system.

In international trade, there is an organization that sells products abroad and another that buys them. The exchange of products is governed by a negotiation that defines the terms and conditions. Often payments are deferred. Most transactions are conducted with terms of payments within a few months from the delivery. When complex transactions are connected with inventory normally, the payment terms are long. Organizations need to manage in the best way the financial relationships and the risks related to payments when they trade especially with foreign countries. The vendors have to ensure that they are paid, while the buyers have to receive the products for which they have paid.

The concept of trade finance comes in. Trade finance is a set of solutions that manage cash, credit, and investments and make them useful for trade.[10] Trade finance is able to facilitate the information asymmetry among actors of the transactions.[11] The lack of financing support is a great limit to the development of the business. Especially the small and medium-sized enterprises (SMEs) experience big difficulty in achieving credit, because of the lack of guarantees. By contrast, the development and growth of the SME segment, which represents over half GDP globally, has to be supported and developed.[12]

Before explaining in depth the relevant methods of financing trade, it is useful to underline the importance of the assessment of the financial needs of an organization.

Assessment of the Financial Needs

One of the main financing needs of the organizations is connected with the working capital and the need for managing liquidity.[13] It is an indicator for verifying the financial equilibrium of the organization in the short term. It is interesting to quote the *leitmotiv* of the FCA General Assembly of June 1, 2018: "Net cash, how sweet it is."[14]

The net working capital represents the difference between current assets and current liabilities.[15] The first one corresponds to the assets that have to be converted into cash within a year. The current liabilities represent short-term debts that have to be paid within that year.

To ensure the continuity of operations, the organization needs to manage the net working capital in an efficient way. It must satisfy the daily needs of cash flow, payment of the vendors, of salaries, and other expenses. The objective of the management of the working capital is to optimize the net working capital. This implies reaching a liquidity level able to meet the organization's obligations without having too much cash on hand.[16] The ordinary management of the working capital is to receive cash as soon as possible and, at the same time, delay as late as possible the payments. A survey of 337 US and Europe, Middle East, and Africa (EMEA) companies found that median payable days increased 14 days in 2014. That is the highest level since 2017. The total value of payables increased by $327 billion.[17]

There are other financial ways to help in the management of the net working capital. This is the subject of this chapter.

Methods for Financing Trade

It is important to distinguish between domestic and international transactions. The international transactions imply risks that are not present in the domestic transactions. Being at a global level, the international transactions can be in different currencies (with related exchange risks) for payments, different legislation and regulations. There are also difficulties related to logistics, transport costs, communication related to distance even if new technologies have mitigated some of these difficulties.

The methods of financing trade can mitigate the risks related to the international transactions. There are several traditional instruments for financing trade, such as letters of credit, documentary collections, international guarantees, factoring, pre-shipment loans, and commercial loans. These products are able to facilitate payments supporting both vendors and buyers.

The letter of credit is the most used and secure payment method in trade finance[11]. This product is more common in international transactions and it is a trade finance solution if there is a decoupling in the payment to the vendor and the collection from the buyer.[18] With a letter of credit, the financial institution of the buyer (the issuing financial institution) undertakes to pay a certain amount at the submission of documents conforming to terms and conditions stipulated in the letter of credit. The issuing financial institution issues the letter of credit at the request of the buyer and becomes liable to the financial institution of the vendor for the transfer of the indicated sum.[19] In a situation in which it is difficult to reach reliable information of credit relative to the buyer, the letter of credit represents a secure tool for the vendors. At the same time, it can be a secure method also for the buyers. There is no obligation of payment until the products or the services are delivered. It is a useful method when the buyer and vendor do not know (or trust) each other and there is uncertainty regarding the solvency of the buyer.

The letter of credit is normally provided by the financial institution as an intermediary.[20] The financial institutions intervene as the third party of the transaction. It assumes an independent obligation to those assumed by the vendor and the buyer. In addition, the financial institution acts as a guarantor of payment in the event of the delivery of the merchandize by the vendor attested by the delivery of requested documents and verified by the financial institution itself. An important step of the enforcement is the preparation of the required documents. The financial institutions only work on documents and make payments in the agreed terms if the submitted documents are in accordance with the parties' agreement. Non-conformity of the documents determines for the vendor the inability to receive payments from the financial institution and, consequently, the loss of the guarantee.

In the current volatile and dynamic context, where the timeliness is one of the primary requests, the instrument able to respond to the need for certainty and rapidity in the international operations is the first-time guarantee.[21] It is a faster and more effective protection form. With it, the financial institutions make available to their customer organizations a series of guarantees to support the operations with foreign customers/vendors. The financial institution guarantee is a tool through which a financial institution, the guarantor, ensures to the beneficiary the payment of a certain amount of money at a simple request of the beneficiary in the event that the principal obligor does not fulfill its commitments.

A documentary collection is a transaction where the vendor consigns the payments collection to the vendor financial institution, called remitting financial institution. It is this institution that sends the document to the buyer financial institution, called the collecting financial institution.[22] The buyer receives the funds and then these funds are sent to the vendor through the financial institutions in exchange for documents.[23] The documentary collection is an instrument cheaper than the letter of credit. With it, the vendor entrusts the collection of the payments to its financial institution. This financial institution sends the documents to the buyer financial institution. The payments of a certain amount are guaranteed after the delivery of the documents with the chin of financial institutions. Financial institutions only acquire the function of a trustee. They do not assume any commitment. This financial instrument is useful when the buyer and the vendor know each other well and there are no doubts on the solvency of the buyer or on its intention to pay. Payments are issued at the collection of the products as documented.

The cash in advance (or advance payment) allows the vendor the mitigation of the risk of credit because the payments are done before the products are delivered. This method is the least attractive to the buyer.

The open account is a commercial agreement for which the products are shipped from the vendor to a foreign buyer, without any written document attesting that the buyer will pay. It is an international sale to a trusted buyer, as usual for a domestic sale. The vendor bears the potential risk related to the failure to pay by the buyer after the product delivery. The vendor proceeds to the delivery of the products covered by the contract (and any document representative of such products). The buyer, through its financial institution, pays the price by credit to the vendor's financial institution account. This instrument, which has benefits in terms of transaction costs and the rapidity of the procedures, exposes the parties to a significant risk of failure to pay the sale price or failure to the delivery of products or delivery, not in compliance with contractual provisions.

Intense competition for buyers has forced vendors to offer more favorable transaction terms, often by forgoing lengthy and expensive letters of credit in favor of the open-account transactions.

- In open-account transactions, products are sold and shipped before payment is due, which is normally within 30, 60, or 90 days.
- With unassisted open-account transactions, the financial institutions' role is limited to processing payments. There is no guarantee for the vendor that the buyer will make the payment.

In addition, the low level of involvement of financial institutions in open-account operations makes it more difficult to provide funding to the vendors and the buyers because the financial institution itself is generally unlikely to run the risk of financing (pre-shipping financing or post-shipping financing) not having information on the content and performance of the underlying business.

Thanks to the payment of the sales price by letter of credit, the above-mentioned risks are considerably cut (as well as the non-payment and the failure to deliver the products). The reduction of the risks associated with the use of the letter of credit as a means of payment allows the lenders to provide more awareness and ease of funding to the vendors and to the buyers, even in the forms of pre-financing of transport or post-shipment financing.

The letter of credit involves high costs related to the issuance procedures and emission procedures of the document itself. The rapidity of the transaction can be strongly hindered by the complexity of obligations that the financial institutions have to carry out to complete the payments.

The guarantees (or bank guarantees) are tools with which the financial institution, or the guarantor, ensures the beneficiary the payment of a certain amount of money in the case when the buyer does not fulfill its commitments. The beneficiary of a guarantee may be the buyer, to protect itself from the risk of failure to carry out the supply or construction of the work, or the vendor, as a protection against the risk of insolvency. In the international transactions, guarantees are increasingly important as the buyer of a commodity, the customer of a service, and the vendor of a commodity ensure the fulfillment of a contractual obligation assumed by the counterparty.

There are two forms of guarantees: financial institution guarantee and first-on-demand financial institution guarantee.[24] The second one is preferred in the international trade for its rapidity and efficiency.

The financial institution guarantee represents accessory commitment made by the financial institutions that depend on the contract they originate, following their fate, as they cannot exist. They are characterized by the accessory to the principal obligation, by the link between the beneficiary of the guarantee and the ordering party.

The first-on-demand financial institution guarantee is an autonomous guarantee containing the guarantor's obligation to pay at the request of the beneficiary. It is a stand-alone, irrevocable commitment undertaken by a financial institution to perform a financial service if a third party fails to fulfill an obligation. The commitment does not allow the beneficiary to object with any objections by the principal. Therefore, it is not necessary to prove the legality of the request for its enforcement.

The standby letter of credit is a tool that, similar to the letter of credit, provides for an assessment of documents for its use, but in which the guarantee function is preeminent. The standby letter of credit is the issuing financial institution's commitment to the vendor to honor its claim for reimbursement, within the limits of the obligation assumed, if the buyer does not meet its obligations. Therefore, the standby letter of credit differs from a normal documentary credit, since it is not a payment instrument but a guarantee instrument. It is intended to protect the vendor against the risk of default of the counterparty. For this reason, the fulfillment of the beneficiary is not intended to ensure the shipment of the products but the failure of the buyer to pay. Following the opening of the standby letter of credit, relations continue to take place directly between the buyer and the vendor, with the use of traditional payment instruments. If the debtor does not fulfill its obligation upon expiry, the vendor will activate the standby letter of credit.

A traditional possibility for credit is inventory financing.[25] This is a type of asset-based lending. It is a short-term working capital loan secured by the inventory purchased. As the inventory is converted into sales, the loan is gradually paid off. When it is fully used, new inventory is bought with a new loan. The cycle starts all over again. Inventory financing interest rates are normally higher than for accounts-receivable financing because in the latter case products have already been sold. Inventory financing is not for any organization. Those who qualify can benefit from better product acquisition deals and more disposable cash for non-inventory-related investments.[26] There are limitations to this instrument, including added inventory accountability and potentially higher interest rates. If an organization is growing and moving products quickly, inventory financing may be a good move. A typical inventory financing arrangement occurs when a financing institution purchases inventory from a manufacturer on behalf of the buyer.[27] The financing organization holds the inventory until there is a committed buyer for the products. Then the funds are put into the lender's account and paid towards the inventory loan. These loans are often short term. Inventory financing requires some track record of sales where inventory is consistently turned into cash. It does not always work with startups.[28] Organizations seeking inventory financing are normally eligible if they have plenty of inventory, high demand, and high inventory turnover. Interesting to the financial institutions are a steady sales history, a mature product, and low debts. Organizations with aging inventory, poor sales performance, and high debts, or those looking for long-term loans, are not good candidates for inventory financing.

Financial institutions are often very stringent about inventory control and product movement. Organizations must provide lenders with timely accounts receivable, shipping, and especially returns information on products on inventories. This means using a detailed and appraised inventory system. This is often not available in SMEs. In some cases, financial institutions want to see the merchandize. It is important to safeguard items from damage. Financing also often requires proof of sales orders. There is the need for a current business plan that shows that organization growth is expected. This is a way to reassure the financial institutions of the repayment. Inventory financing allows an organization to use liquidity that is otherwise invested in inventory on other items. It can often lead to discounted purchases.[29] With more money to buy inventory, bulk sales are often sold at more affordable prices. Acquiring the added financing may also assure organizations of more favorable payment options with the vendors, resulting in more time to pay and fewer late fees. There are some drawbacks to inventory financing. Financial institutions often want to make sure the loan's collaterals are used properly. So they might require some additional measures for security. If the organization runs in trouble, losses may occur, because inventory must be sold quickly. Additionally, high interest rates and other fees may slow down the organizations' operations abilities. Inventory financing is not available at every financial institution. It may take extra work to find a deal suitable to all parties.

From Trade Finance to Supply Chain Finance

Supply chain finance (SCF) can be defined as the use of financing and risk management methods and tools to optimize the management of working capital and liquidity and support the financial supply chain.[30] The term covers a wide range of financing and risk mitigation practices, from payables finance to pre-shipment finance.[31]

There are two dimensions in the financing of procurement, especially international, transactions[32]:

- The providers of trade finance tend to focus on solutions that meet the preferences, related to trade, of the actors of the transactions. These preferences are oriented to open-account methods moving away from the traditional methods as the letters of credit.
- The diffusion of technology regarding the traditional transactions eliminates the paperwork procedures.

The technology solutions, used to make easier trade finance and supply chain finance, start to be seen as an alternative to traditional tools.

There are different points of view regarding the relations between the concept of trade finance and SCF. Some providers think that trade finance is a part of SCF. Others think the opposite: SCF is a part of trade finance. This area is increasingly evolving, and the organizations, to remain competitive at a global level, operate increasingly on improving their business processes. For this reason, it is necessary to handle financial resources along the entire supply chain.[33]

Supply chain finance considers trade in a holistic way, involving all the relationships throughout the supply chain. Trade finance involves only a bilateral transaction of financing. SCF is considered as a financing program (Fig. 3.2).

Based on a PricewaterhouseCoopers survey, the principal reasons for implementing a supply chain finance program are shown in Table 3.2.[34]

Supply Chain Finance Definition

As trade finance supports directly most of the international transactions, it is equally important to underline that the most efficient value network operators are starting to take into account the liquidity as an important support of the business. Supply chain finance is the inter-organization

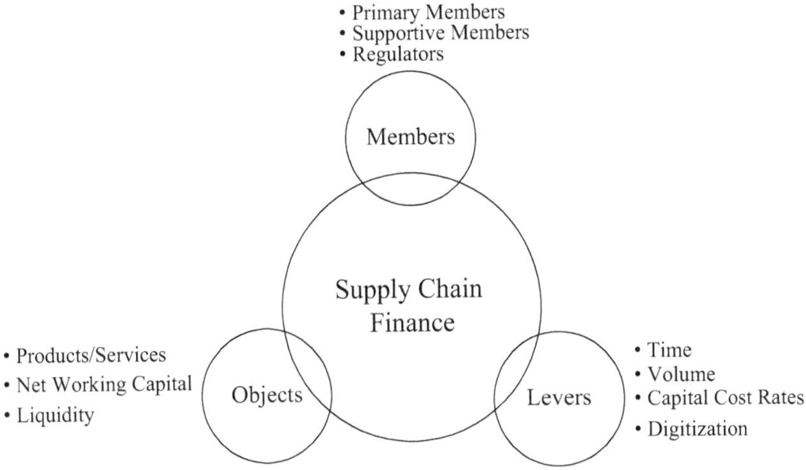

Fig. 3.2 Dimensions of supply chain finance

Table 3.2 Objectives for procurement finance

Primary reason	*Percentage (%)*
Working capital optimization	42
Vendor liquidity needs	18
Vendor relationships improvement	18
Supply chain stability improvement	12
Others:	10
Additional revenues, cost reduction	
Utilize cash surplus	
Optimize corporate finance (including asset financing)	

Elaboration of the author on the PwC survey www.pwc.com.au/publications/pdf/supply-chain-finance-jul17.pdf

financing within the supply chain. It consists of programs of financing throughout the supply chain and not relative to the single organization.

There are several definitions of this concept because the SCF market is still evolving. Pfohl and Gomm define supply chain finance as[35]:

> Inter-organization optimization of financing as well as the integration of financing processes with customers, vendors, and service providers to increase the value of all participating organizations.

According to Hofmann, SCF is[36]:

> An approach for two or more organizations in a supply chain, including external service providers, to jointly create value through the means of planning, steering, and controlling the flow of financial resources on an inter-organizational level.

According to Aberdeen, SCF is[37]:

> A combination of trade financing provided by a financial institution, a third party vendor or a corporation itself, and a technology platform that unites trading partners and financial institutions digitally and provides the financing triggers based on the occurrence of one or several supply chain events.

From a practical point of view, supply chain finance can be defined as an approach that seeks to increase the value of two or more organizations, which are part of a supply chain, through the implementation of financial solutions. These solutions, exploiting the strength of the supply chain links, provide alternative means of financing. These solutions do not always require the presence of a financial institution but help in decreasing the working capital and optimizing the liquidity as measured by the weighted average cost of capital (WACC).[38]

The use of the term supply chain finance was introduced at the beginning of 2000.[39] Initially, the literature focused on the management and optimization of the so-called logistically induced financial flows.[40] Over time, the concept of supply chain finance has evolved arriving at embracing the optimization of financial needs from the whole supply chain perspective, or for each size of organization,[41] including the SMEs.[42]

SCF focus is on creating liquidity in the supply chain through various buyer- or vendor-led solutions with or without the support of technology. The role of SCF is to optimize both the availability and cost of capital within a given buyer-vendor supply chain.[43]

The basic idea of the SCF is to provide more liquidity to all the actors of the value network and to handle in the best way the financial flows throughout the value network. Its aim is to reach a high level of supply chain financial efficiency and to optimize the working capital and the liquidity of the organization. Over time, SCF has transformed to new models zeroing in on garnering efficiency, collaboration, reduced operating expenses, and ensuring better security.

Historically, players in the supply chain have always sought the maximization of their own profit, being customers or vendors but also financial institutions.[44] The cash-to-cash cycle of organizations can be defined as:

$$\text{CCC}\left(\text{cash} - \text{to} - \text{cash cycle}\right) = \text{days of receivables} + \text{days of inventory} \\ - \text{days of payables.}$$

CCC is a truly comparative advantage. It is clearly related with the cash flow of the organization and indirectly it is related to its size and the weighted average cost of capital (WACC).[45] The literature focused on the exploitation of these differences from the whole supply chain point of view, increasing the value for each supply chain partner involved.[46]

This broad concept is the base on which SCF emerges. SCF represents an opportunity for collaboration in the credit chain to overcome the main difficulties that organizations face, from credit reduction to the duration of payment and hence to the needs for sustainable values of working capital and liquidity.

SCF attributes more importance to solutions and relationships rather than products and transactions.[47] SCF has a holistic vision related to trade. It considers trade as an ecosystem of relationships and not only a bilateral transaction between actors. Some studies show that it may cut the working capital of the focal company by 40 percent, as well as the costs of capital (because of the better credit rating of the focal company). For the purpose of this work, an organization value is defined as V = P∞t = 0 (1 + WACC).[48]

SCF helps on liquidity management.[49] After the financial crisis of 2008, the basics of liquidity management have changed. The management of the working capital has reached a large importance along the supply chain. There has been a severe restriction of access to the credit and a reduction in the financial institution system. The financial rating of the organizations has worsened, and the payment times have increased. Organizations are pressured on improving cash flow. This has led to an increased pressure on vendors. Buyers request vendors to extend their receivables or raising their working capital at their disposal.

A collaboration among partners of the entire supply chain is necessary because a financial difficulty of one actor can become obstacles for others throughout the supply chain. The need for working capital and for the stability of supply chains is clear. For this reason, organizations realized even more that reliable financing alternatives are becoming necessary to manage the cash flow and the financial flows within the supply chain.

SCF allows the optimization of the cash flows and the allocation of the capital throughout the supply chain thanks to the integration and collaboration of all parties along the supply chain. SCF allows leveraging specific supply chain relationships to control and optimize working capital and liquidity. It is an approach aimed at increasing the effectiveness of inter-organization financial exchanges. Its objectives are the reduction of the imbalance between capital demand and supply demand, through the implementation of solutions that exploit the deep knowledge of supply chain relationships. SCF is a tactical improvement for both sides of the supply chain generating a win-win situation. The buyer can extend the terms of payments and the vendors can cash earlier.

To measure how many days on average are necessary for an organization to collect the payment from completed sale in a defined period, it is possible to use the days sales outstanding (DSO) formula. The lower DSO, the better for the stakeholders, so that the payments are collected in a faster way and the cash is used quicker for other purposes. SCF works on them. SCF optimizes the cash flow extending the term of payments to vendors and, at the same time, allows vendors to be paid earlier. SCF extends days payable outstanding (DPO) of the buyer and it allows vendors to accelerate DSO.

The expressions financial supply chain and supply chain finance are similar. They represent different concepts. The first one regards the transactions among the actors of trade. SCF is relative to the provision of liquidity to the vendors through financing, most of the time with the support of technological solutions. SCF facilitates the access to credit, improving financing conditions, and allowing its extension to the weaker members of the chain.[50]

Dimensions of Supply Chain Finance

To analyze the concept of supply chain finance, the dimensions, shown in the Fig. 3.3, are interesting to consider.[51]

Supply chain finance allows financing of both fixed investments and working capital, and at the same time improves liquidity, essential for the operations of an organization. The cash-to-cash cycle is the indicator used to estimate the amount of net working capital (NWC) needed to operate an organization's operating activities. It represents the amount of time necessary to convert the cash outflows, due to the payment of the vendors,

	Source	**Make**	**Deliver**	**Pay**
SCM	Marketing Plan Contracting Order Deliver	Design Material Acquisition Manufacture Assembly Test	Pack Scan Transportation Install Track & Trace	Warehouse Merchandise Collect
	PO or Contract	**Credit & Financing**	**Documentation Management**	**Control & Payment**
FSCM	Budget Negotiate Amend Track	Credit Protection Vendor/Inventory/ Distributor Financing Liquidity Management Import/Export Financing	Invoicing Packing Lists PL Proof of Delivery Inspections	Fund Movement Documentary Defect Management Advance Payments Reports
	Information/Digital Flow			
	Cross-organization Workflow Management			
	Rules of Engagement and Legal Setting			

Fig. 3.3 Relationships between Supply Chain Management and Financial Supply Chain Management

in receivables from customers. The longer cash-to-cash cycle is, the more the organization will need to borrow funds to finance the bigger requirements of working capital. The longer the cash-to-cash cycle is, the more the working capital is liquid. The cash-to-cash cycle can be considered as a reference point to reach since it represents a key factor to estimate the requirements of financing.

In supply chain finance, there are two types of actors: the primary members and the support members. The first group is the reference organization (industrial or commercial), vendors, and customers. The second group refers to logistics service providers and financial intermediaries. They are support members because they are just as service providers to one or more members of the supply chain.

The levers for SCF have essentially three dimensions of financing: the volume (the number of assets to be financed), the duration, and the rate of the capital cost (interest rate).[52] The latter depends on investor expectations on profitability and investment risk, external creditor claims, and the organization's financial structure. Supply chain finance considers the interest rate as the lever to cut the cost of financing. For this reason, to cut the capital costs, it is useful to act on these three levers at the same time.

Supply Chain Finance and Digitization

To optimize the processes and realize savings, it is possible to implement several digital solutions to support SCF, for instance, e-invoicing.[53] This solution eliminates (or at least reduces) manual and paper-based processes. The simplification and digitization need to integrate with the systems and processes within the organizations.[54] It must comply with the storage, retrieval, and removal regulations in each jurisdiction.

The information and communication technologies (ICTs) allow improving the efficiency, effectiveness, and economics of the new solutions of SCF. Digital technologies help in managing customers, documents, and information more quickly, initiate financing solutions, and improve riskiness sensitivity. Digital relationships allow analyzing and monitoring more accurately the role of each actor in the supply chain end to end: from the vendor to the customer.

The factors necessary to implement correctly the solutions of SCF are the simplification, the digitization, and the dematerialization. They are important prerequisites for accelerating financial and information flows. Therefore, the introduction of the e-invoice within the financial supply chain is a prerequisite for the proper implementation of SCF projects. SCF allows an organization to cash in sooner its credits and to be able to extend the payment times to its vendors in a sustainable way. The e-invoice makes all this possible, becoming an essential requirement for the SCF.

The traditional process of invoices exchange makes the reception time long. It requires longer evaluation times and approvals of incoming invoices. A digital exchange provides the vendor with immediate visibility that the invoice has been approved by the customer. In this way, it reduces the time period in which the vendor can decide how best to finance its own working capital and liquidity. In addition, there is also a benefit for the debtor because the SCF links to advance financing: the possibility of repaying a debt in longer times compared to the contractual expiration date.

Benefits of a Supply Chain Finance Program

The benefits of an SCF program vary with the program itself. One of the main benefits is the improvement of the components of the cash-to-cash cycle (CCC). It can be achieved through different SCF solutions, which also help to improve the ability to forecast cash flows.[55] Another source of benefits that can be important for organizations with capital needs comes from the adoption of solutions that optimize the WACC exploiting the links in the supply chain to obtain cheaper debt. A financial institution involved has the burden of collecting payments and optimizing the costs of such a process. It has benefits too: its revenues increase, as well as the certainty of payments. In the case of SMEs, it can implement a one-by-one risk assessment.[56] From a wider point of view, SCF programs provide better visibility on the supply chain, strengthening the links among partners, and offering new means of collaboration.

A possible classification of the benefits of SCF is the following[57]:

- Strategic benefits:
  - Support to the supply chain partners by re-balancing the economic and financial availability of the supply chain to reduce the risk of bankruptcy of financially weak actors, which might be strategic for the market;
  - Development of new business opportunities, such as the possibility to provide financing by reducing and controlling with greater awareness the risks associated with these credits.
- Financial and economic benefits:
  - The organization leader of the supply chain collaborates with the financial system to launch innovative solutions to facilitate the access to credit to larger and weaker members of the supply chain. SCF is one of the fields through which some fintech organizations help the SMEs to access to credit, representing platforms through which vendors can apply for loans, or advance payments, on active invoices;
  - Reduction in the net working capital, thanks to the reduction in inventories and trade receivables and the increase in trade payables, and improvements of the liquidity;
  - Margin improvement, thanks to lower financial charges and discounts on purchase costs for products and services.

- Process benefits:
  - It allows financial institutions, vendors, and buyers obtaining benefits from cost reduction and mitigation of risks.[58] In addition, it provides benefits such as higher visibility in the negotiating process that provides trust for the financial institutions. For the latter, it is easier to know the number of flows of money within the supply chain;
  - Efficiency either throughout the supply chain or in the relationships with financial actors thanks to the high digitization needed for the application of most solutions of SCF.

From Supply Chain Finance to Procurement Finance

Procurement can benefit from the simplification and digitization of the value network and of the optimization of the working capital and the liquidity. These are an important aspect of the relationships between finance and procurement. It is also very important to consider the current evolution of relationships with the vendors. There is the need to improve and to streamline relations with the whole organization but also with the vendors, increasingly considered partners. The priority becomes to examine in a holistic way the relationships between finance and procurement. This relationship needs to be optimized from the point of view of the four Ps: people, processes, platforms, and partners.

- people: how talent, training, and tenure contribute to procurement finance;
- processes: the combination of activities and procedures end to end to support operations and management;
- platforms: the systems and applications supporting in a strategical, tactical, and operational way the organization;
- partners: the vendors, the financial institutions, the retailers, and even the customers which provide services.

This is what this book calls procurement finance.

The procurement function has become a strategic function within the organization. The competitive scenario in which organizations develop their own business is dominated by phenomena that make the competitiveness increasingly important on the economic profitability and financial sustainability of the organizations. The increased dynamicity and complexity of the markets lead to important changes in the procurement processes to ensure overall supply efficiency objectives. Every organization, to be able to complete successfully its own activities, needs to purchase continuously products and services, optimize its value network, and improve the accounts payable.

The development of intelligent and collaborative approaches in the procurement fields represents an accelerator able to modernize and to change the entire organization. Procurement should be a model of use of innovative solutions. In this respect, new solutions have an important role to help the procurement sector to deal with the new financial challenges caused by a constantly changing scenario. The rapid technological evolution of the procurement market underlines the need to identify innovative solutions able to support the digital transformation of the entire organization (and possibly its vendors). The best response to a volatile context is a greater agility to make the services provided more flexible and responsive.

Regarding the innovation of services in the financial field, procurement is, for instance, developing internal marketplaces that allow the organization to increase its productivity and provide a better and quicker service. This innovation is often on a technological basis but also on processes. The benefits for the buyers from the marketplace are linked also to the simplification and digitization of the sourcing processes, reducing processing times and transaction costs, and improving client satisfaction. Those three ingredients allow increasing margins. There is a higher visibility of information thanks to the use of consolidated online catalogs. In addition, the marketplace allows tracking purchases and then controls spending. It helps in the elimination of maverick purchases, getting a better compliance.

In procurement finance, there are two important aspects to consider:

- The relationships between finance and procurement are more a triangle: finance, procurement, and ICT.
- Risks must be properly managed.

Procurement is characterized by three flows (Fig. 3.4 and Table 3.3[59]), which needs to be considered holistically:

- the physical flows of material and products;
- the information flows of documents, more and more digital;
- the financial flows from procure to pay.

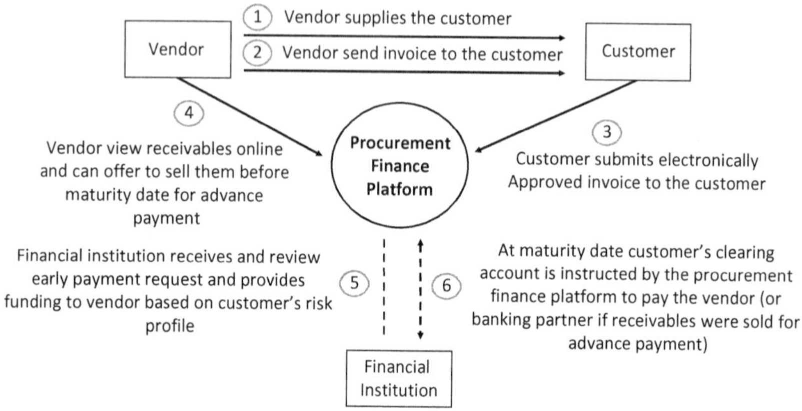

Fig. 3.4 Procurement finance process

Table 3.3 Supply chain flows

Flow	*Description*
Physical	The actual transportation and movements between and within organizations It includes the activities of transportation, service mobilization, delivery movement, storage inventories, and logistics
Information/ digital	Flows of cash between organizations and consumers, incurrence of expenses, accounts receivable and accounts payable processes and systems, DPO and DSO managements
Financial	Processes and electronic systems, data movement triggers, access to key information and knowledge, capture and use of data, enabling processes, and market intelligence

Adapted by the author from Mathis, J. F., & Cavinato, J. (2010). Financing the global supply chain: growing need for management action. *Thunderbird International Business Review*, 52(6), 467–474

Procurement finance aims at aligning these three flows and optimizing them at an inter-organizational level[60] by leveraging a stronger coordination and cooperation between extended value network players, financial institutions, and technology providers.[61] The procurement finance approach often results in an increase of trust, commitment, and, thus, profitability throughout the value network.[62]

The information/digital flows synchronize the physical flows with the financial flows. The organizations must be able to communicate with vendors, distributors, and customers. In parallel, they must also manage the relationships with the financial institutions and the entire procurement ecosystem. The diversity of financial communications, within an organization, its vendors, and the various financial institutions possibly in different countries, gives rise to a wide range of transactions and services. They range from cash management services of reconciliation, delivery of financial institution statements, routing, and execution of orders and connected flow of funds.

The result is the need to integrate different areas of the procurement, operational and financial, connected to each other, both inside and outside the organization, through an environment of multi-organization collaboration in the ecosystem.

The challenge of combining the financial and physical procurement is a complex project.

The financial excellence requires efficient financial transactions. In the absence of effective financial management processes, optimized and designed to cut costs and limit the demand for resources, it is difficult to achieve the increasing and challenging organization's objective. Manual processes on financial procurement cannot help the organizations' productivity. It is not only a problem of efficiency of the processes. The processes and systems must optimize and improve the accuracy of the financial processes.[63] They should help, for instance, the reporting cycles and the management of the accounts receivable, the monitoring and managing of the expenditures at the organization level, and the achievement of economies of scale, for instance by enabling shared services.

It is necessary to respect the four Es:

- effectiveness: optimize the closing of the financial cycles by improving the digitization and collaboration to cut the time of closing of the fiscal or legal periods;
- efficiency: increase the productivity of the financial management, allowing organizations to conduct also international operations with fewer resources, simplifying the processes, while maintaining the control of the costs;
- economics: automate the processes of accounts receivable, billing, computation of cash flows, reconciliation of cash, and the improvement of the cycle times for completing the order;
- ethics: be compliant with the several regulations in the jurisdictions where procurement finance is applied.[64]

There is also another important E often not considered: the environment. Procurement must be as much as possible sustainable or green.[65]

The financial management solutions must provide the basis for the simplification and digitization of critical processes in financial management, including sales, sourcing, and vendor and financial institutions management. They must provide the flexibility to configure processes according to the best practices.

Some surveys show that roughly 75 percent of the working capital is tied up in the procurement.[66] It is not common in traditional value networks, such as apparel or durables, to have cash-to-cash cycles of six months or more. Working capital inefficiencies combine with cross-border risks related to exchange and interest rate movements. They tend to increase the costs of the products and cut the service levels.

The following two sections examine these two aspects.

Characteristics of Procurement Finance

Procurement finance in this book refers to the use of short-term credit to balance and finance working capital across vendor-buyer-customer organizations systems. In this way, it aims to minimize the aggregate value network cost, that is, the base value of the network costs plus the cost of financing, and make it more effective and efficient. Procurement finance works in such a way that buyers can keep their long payment terms and simultaneously ensures that vendors are paid quickly and with certainty (through letters of credit and guarantees or other innovative instruments).[67]

Procurement finance is supported by to risk management practices and transactions that facilitate the purchase of, and payment for, products and services, especially internationally. Examples of this type are the exchanging of purchase orders and invoices, the management of liquidity, the financing of the working capital finance, and making payments if necessary taking into account several currencies (Fig. 3.5).[68]

Business processes increasingly run across and outside organizational and geographical boundaries. This increases risks and requires greater collaboration:

- internally, among sales, marketing, procurement, operations, treasury, and receivables and payables management;
- externally, among buyers, vendors, customers, financial institutions, and solution providers.

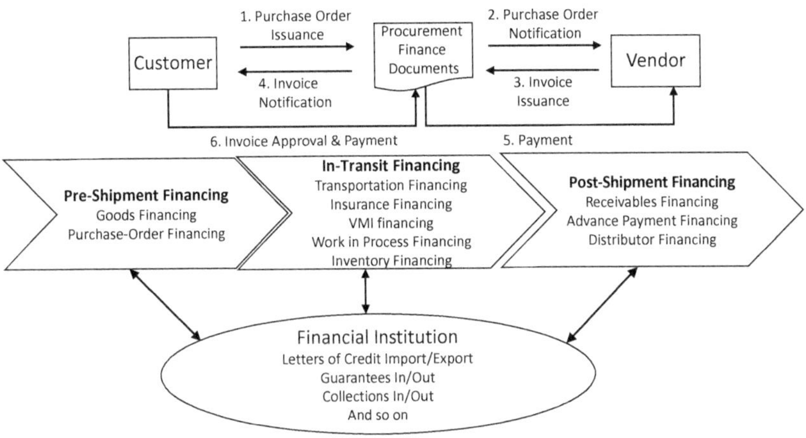

Fig. 3.5 Procurement finance model

The ecosystem of the providers of procurement finance resources, information, and components are internal corporate functions, vendors, and external partners, such as[69]:

- collaborating trading partners;
- corporate treasuries;
- financial institutions, fintech organizations, logistics, and insurance providers;
- business process outsourcers or services;
- B2B integration networks;
- e-invoicing and e-business service providers;
- market analysts and advisers;
- governments, regulatory bodies, global, customs, or regional institutions.

Procurement finance is becoming more important, due to[70]:

- increased globalization and complexity in the value network management;
- acceleration of the growth in open-account trading and cutting the use of classical trade finance instruments;

- digitization as technology is leveraged to improve physical, informational/digital, and financial value network flows;
- focus on working capital management, liquidity, and the need to manage costs at all levels and add value to the customers;
- increasingly globalized and interrelated value networks.

Procurement is also becoming more complex due to the trend towards servitization: the joint provision of products and related services.[71]

The key risk indicators (KRIs) of procurement finance are[72]:

- credit risks
  - trading partners' financial stability
  - buyers' default
  - vendors' default
  - payment assurance
  - payment execution and performance
- liquidity risks
  - cash flow and liquidity
  - availability of finance, credit, or guarantees
- market risks
  - financial impact of demand volatility
  - exchange and interest rate risks
- operational risks
  - fraud and errors
  - systems and network availability

Procurement finance works on interest rate arbitrage between a creditworthy buyer and a less well-established vendor. The finance institution purchases the vendor's accounts receivable at a discount, securing cash against the buyer's credit. The discount assessed on the vendor's invoice amount, minus the risk premium, constitutes the financial institution's margin. Typical procurement finance spreads range from around 20 to 500 basis points.[73]

Compared to the traditional letters of credit or guarantees, procurement finance encompasses new trade finance and supply chain instruments. It is a field still under development and improvement. Procurement finance includes, for instance, advance payments, reverse financing, payables financing, factoring, and dynamic discounting.[74] The money may flow from the buyer's treasury, a financial institution with an active transaction financial institutions practice, or a trade finance fintech startup.[75]

The increasing collaboration and integration create demand for:

- standards and standardization as a platform for improving competition;
- visibility, which is driving buyers, vendors, and financial institutions to achieve simplification and digitization and better tracking of physical and financial flows for the management and compliance reasons.

The inter-relationship between the physical and financial value networks can be clarified referencing process maps which show:

- the components of the physical value network;
- the components of the combined physical and financial value network;
- the events in the physical and financial value networks that represent opportunities for financial institutions and solution providers to introduce financial value network products, services, and solutions.

The challenge for providers of procurement finance solutions is to recognize the key components of procurement finance to be included into and to support the complete value network.

To understand better the role of the financial institutions in procurement finance, the opportunities and the solutions can be classified as follows:

- value network simplification and digitization;
- working capital management;
- trade and procurement finance;
- risk mitigation;
- business intelligence and Big Data analytics.

These categories overlap. As is the case, for example, with trade and value network finance with risk mitigation.

In the past, procurement finance has focused on a single value network (between a buyer and a vendor) to show the components and interrelationships in physical and financial value networks. In reality, the actual transaction flow between buyers, vendors, and customers in the ecosystem likely consists of multiple parties meshed together in a value network.

Physical and financial value networks are very much linked. They are becoming evermore integrated, digitized, and characterized by collaboration among all stakeholders involved. Several points along the value network create opportunities for financial institutions to offer procurement finance solutions.

Buyers, vendors, and providers of procurement finance solutions should move beyond a silo view of the traditional value network. They should take a holistic approach to fully understand and act upon the overall opportunities.[76]

In the implementation of procurement finance, it is important to consider the costs supported for their development and operational usage. Starting from the analysis of the implementation process of a generic procurement finance solution with a total cost of ownership perspective, it is important to consider all the procurement finance's costs and benefits.[77]

Stakeholders in the Procurement Finance

The categories of stakeholders in the procurement finance framework do not coincide with the ones of the typical supply chain context.[78] It is useful to list them:

- The industrial and commercial organizations that are the backbone of the value network. The simplest interaction in the value network is between a vendor and its customer, where both can be an industrial, a service, a public administration, or a commercial organization.[79]
- The logistics service providers (LSPs) are another important typology of players. They are providers of logistics services that perform the logistics functions on behalf of their customers.[80] LSPs are not always considered members of the traditional supply chain framework.[81] They assume a more relevant role with the introduction of procurement finance: from general logistics service providers to administrative, SMEs guarantee, and even financial service providers themselves.[82]

- Other players in the procurement finance context include every stakeholder that provides financial services, including both financial institutions and private/public investors.[83] The need for external financial services in procurement finance is widely recognized in the literature, whether it is the need for a generic lender or for a financial institution.[84]
- Internal institutional actors, that is, departments traditionally left out from the framework of the value network. All departments dealing with financial activities should be included in a procurement finance framework.

Procurement, Finance, and Digitization

As procurement of products and services represents a large and increasing percentage of an organization's entire spending, there is the need of innovation for managing such spending. Such innovation requires alignment among procurement, finance, and ICT.[85] A successful alignment can occur when procurement, finance, and ICT are oriented commonly on pursuing the strategic objectives of the organization and have an effective collaboration. In this way, there are common objectives that foster new solutions generating more trust among partners and, as a consequence, a higher capability to reach customer satisfaction and profitability of the organization.

Digital solutions provide to these three important fields a possibility to communicate and to collaborate on platforms that create benefits for all of them. Through the digitization, the visibility of spend is high. There is higher productivity and improvement of the relationships among all the actors in the procurement ecosystem.

An ideal context that allows reaching a best solution of procurement finance is structured in a way through which procurement and finance study solutions, complementarily, so as satisfying the requirements relative to business processes. At the same time, ICT regards the provision of user-friendly integrated solutions, implementing technology and satisfying the organization's requirements.

The ICT function supports the collaboration between procurement and finance. Thanks to the collaboration among ICT, finance, and procurement, the organizations can select the best solutions able to achieve great objectives as[86]:

- streamlining the source-to-pay cycle to reach lower costs;
- developing higher collaboration with vendors, partners, and the rest of the organization;
- facilitating the ICT applications to achieve more agility;
- supporting the requirements of compliance of the organization.

Before doing any development or restructuring, it is important to take into account the architecture for the e-procurement digitization (Fig. 3.6).[87]

An important component of the collaboration among these three sectors is provided by the digital spend analysis in support of spend management.[88] The spend management aims to optimize the use of economic resources and acquire from the market the resources necessary for the operation of the organization. It must allow a cost structure manageable over time and consistent with the organization strategic objectives. Managing spending is more than reducing costs, it is a strategic decision-

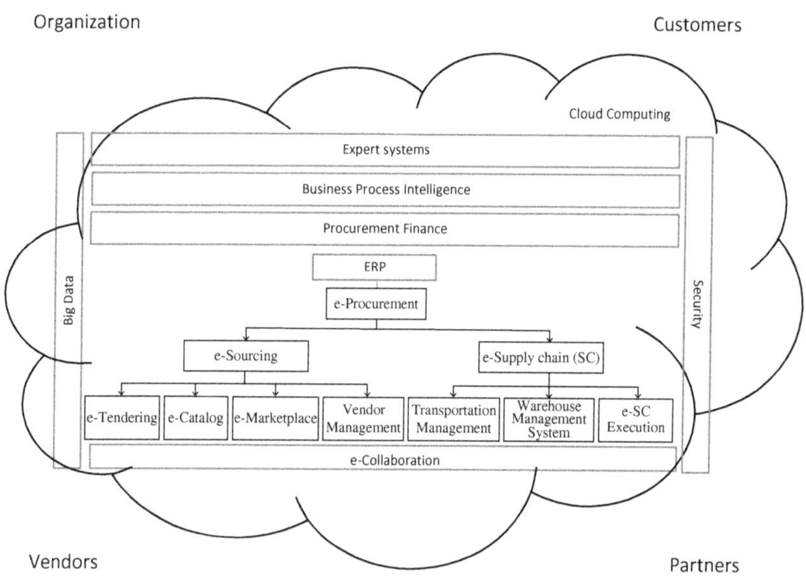

Fig. 3.6 E-procurement architecture. (From Nicoletti, B. (2014), Lean and Digitize e-procurement, paper presented at the *e-Public procurement in Europe: public management, technologies and processes of change*, Lisbon, Portugal, 27th May)

making about where and how to spend, in terms of strategic organization development and value creation, optimizing and making the use of resources more flexible. It is necessary to make spending visible and to involve internal users in collaborative demand management processes and systems.

New solutions assume a relevant role in this dynamic context. They improve visibility and control of spending, contracts, and global vendors.[89]

Motorola Inc.[90]

Motorola Inc. was an American multinational company founded in 1928, based in Schaumburg, Illinois. The company was split into two independent public companies, Motorola Mobility and Motorola Solutions, on January 4, 2011. Motorola Solutions is generally considered to be the direct successor to Motorola, as the reorganization was structured with Motorola Mobility being spun off.[91]

The supply chain finance is an integral component of Motorola's overall supply chain management strategy. Physical products, information systems, and financial flows are closely aligned with each other throughout the value network incorporating Motorola, its customers, vendors, and banks. The overall trend is towards the development of an integrated global procurement finance in which cash flows mirror product flows. Motorola shares financial data with its vendors as part of a cooperative strategy that generates cost savings for Motorola and its vendors in areas such as foreign exchange and cash balances. The cooperative strategy also improves the quality of the payments process measured by Six Sigma tools.[92] A strategy of this type is only possible by taking a global perspective of the procurement finance.

Taxonomy of Procurement Finance Solutions

Procurement finance solutions can be segmented through several dimensions: geographical aspects, payment methods, different types of platforms, players involved, and characteristics.[93]

One possible distinction is between finance-oriented, buyer-driven, supply chain-oriented, and vendor-driven (Table 3.4)[94]:

Table 3.4 SCF perspective

Perspective	*Focus*	*Procurement definition*
Finance-oriented	Organization's financial position and its ability to finance the operative business; the financial institution plays a key role	Set of innovative short-term financial solutions commonly provided by financial institutions, which have proven with a positive effect on the financial performance of procurement players
Buyer-driven	Organization's cash-to-cash (CCC) cycle optimization by working on DSO and DPO	Modified form of reverse factoring by enabling a broader portfolio of customers which can access capital at a lower rate, enhanced transparency, flexibility improvements, and a higher involvement of new players as third-part logistics providers
Supply chain-oriented	Supply chain CCC cycle optimization by working on all its three components	Set of solutions that include supply chain processes, inventories, fixed asset financing (that is, through a pay per production solution), for instance, in vendor-managed inventory (VMI) solutions; financial institutions may not be involved
Vendor-driven	Vendor-driven programs such as: factoring invoice discounting inventory financing	This is where a financial institution purchases the vendor's accounts receivable, with or without recourse, and assumes the responsibility for the buyer's financial ability to pay. In the case of invoice discounting, the sales accounting functions are retained by the business; the buyers are unaware of the involvement of a financial institution

- Finance-oriented is a set of innovative short-term financial solutions commonly provided by financial institutions, which have proven to have a positive effect on the financial performance of supply chain players.
- Vendor-based finance or trade finance is a common financing scheme that has existed for a long time. Under this financing scheme, a vendor allows the buyer to postpone payment to a date after the invoice date. The benefits are essentially transaction costs, enforcing repayments, no dependence on central control of credit, and similar. The issues are coping with risks such as demand uncertainty, retail prices, product assortments, production technologies, return processes, and the associated strategic interactions between vendors and buyers.[95]

In the sales finance, a vendor with a trusted portfolio of customers enables them to have extended payment terms, in exchange of becoming their preferential buyer (normally carried out with the support of a financial institution that acquires the discounted invoices from the vendors and collects the inflated invoices from the customers).[96]

- Supply chain-oriented is a set of solutions that include supply chain processes, inventories, fixed asset financing (that is, through a pay per production solution). For instance, in vendor-managed inventory (VMI) solutions, financial institutions may not be involved.
- Buyers-based finance was born out of the globalization of the value network. The emergence of e-commerce platforms has provided opportunities for entrepreneurs to reach end customers. Vendors, especially small- and medium-sized vendors in developed countries, have challenges in accessing capital markets. Innovative financing schemes have emerged to address those challenges. Examples of such instruments include reverse factoring and purchase order financing.

This chapter considers the classification of procurement finance instruments in details. It is based on four categories:

- traditional solutions;
- innovative solutions;
- collaborative solutions;
- emerging solutions.

The first two categories include various financing methods that involve collaboration between the value network partners. The third group combines collaborative solutions between members of the value network that, through the optimization of working capital, cuts mainly the need to resort to external financing. The fourth group includes various alternative finance techniques being offered to organizations.[97] In the practice, the same organizations use several of these solutions, with an optimization of their selection.[98]

Traditional Solutions

Traditional solutions are consolidated financing instruments designed to provide the single organization with instruments for accessing short-term capital.

Some relevant traditional solutions have been analyzed in a previous section. Some additional examples are:

- Invoice discounting is an operation through which an organization obtains financing by a financial institution, in the face of a commercial credit against its own customer, surrendering an invoice as a pledge.[99] Through this instrument, organizations can get cash in advance of their customer payment times. Vendors contract short-term debt in the face of increased liquidity that funds net working capital. The simplification and digitization and in particular e-invoicing can provide more control over the capital by a better handling of the invoices and can optimize the relationships with the vendors.
- Factoring is an instrument through which an organization can obtain short-term capital. Unlike the invoice discounting, it is a continuous relationship. Factoring is a contract whereby an organization grants part (or all) of its commercial credits portfolio to a financial intermediary called factor. This instrument is also called a key accounts receivable sales program.[100] A group of vendor sells invoices issued to and approved by a trustworthy key customer (also called anchor buyer) to a financial institution. In exchange for a percentage of its value, the financial institution will recuperate the entire invoice amount from the key customer after a pre-established amount of time. It is possible to split this type of program into pre-shipment (vendor payment by the financial institution triggered by the key customer order) and the more common post-shipment program (vendor payment triggered by invoice acceptance).[101] This contract involves three categories of subjects in the transaction. These subjects are: the creditor-surrender, that is the holding organization of receivables which are the subject of the cession, the buyers, that are the surrendered debtors, and the factor that intervenes in the financial regulation of the relationship between the two previous parties. Factoring is not only aimed at funding. Collecting credits in advance cuts the amount of working capital by reducing the amount of cash-to-cash cycle. A critical issue can be the need of investments in technologies, digitization, and communication by one or more of the three parties.
- Reverse factoring is a particular form of factoring aimed at medium-large-sized organizations called big debtors. By the nature of their business, these organizations operate with a large number of ven-

dors. In the reverse factoring, the flow of money and products proceeds exactly as in the key accounts receivable sales program. It is the financial institution that promotes the initiative proposing to the vendors of the key customers the acquisition of the accounts receivable for a discounted percentage that reflects the vendors' creditworthiness.[102] The benefits of the application of reverse factoring are the cost savings by simplifying payment procedures to vendors, the relationships improvement with the vendors, and the optimization of the payment flows. From the vendor perspective, reverse factoring allows the reduction of the net working capital and an increase in the liquidity. It provides access to the credit at lower cost. From the customer perspective, it allows the delay of payments and the simplification of trade payables. It allows the customer organization to use factoring as a trading tool to obtain more favorable payment terms and cut purchase prices. The financial institutions are also expanding the use of this instrument because of their regulatory treatment due to the potential impact of the Basel III requirements on other trade finance instruments.[103]
- Forfeiting is a form of receivables purchase, consisting in the purchase of future payment obligations represented by financial instruments or payment obligations (normally in negotiable or transferable form), at a discount or at face value in return for a financing charge.

Innovative Solutions

The innovative solutions are financing models born as procurement finance solutions. Following the expansion of the world of fintech organizations, these innovative solutions have grown in relevance.

All these innovative solutions use digital documents and technological platforms. These platforms are able to connect digitally the procurement finance parties digitizing the processes related to the procurement finance. These platforms in these innovative solutions are used for increasing the efficiency and the control of the processes.

Digital solutions are a powerful enabling factor. They allow managing operationally a great massive structure of information which would not be otherwise possible to correctly manage the processes in real time. The simplification and digitization of the organizations' processes, inside the organization and in support of the relationships, allow the organization to get bigger efficiency with respect to the traditional models of financing.

Some relevant innovative solutions are:

- Dynamic discounting is an agreement between buyers and vendors that the payment of the product or service can be made in advance of the date indicated on the invoice in return for a discount.[104] The discount applied is dynamic since it depends on the date of actual payment. Major discounts are applied for payments made more in advance. Trade credit is a well-known managerial practice when a vendor allows a customer to extend payment terms.[105] It gained popularity as a procurement finance solution,[106] in which two parties involved in a transaction may agree on payment terms. These terms are normally composed by three parts: a discount percentage (for instance, 5 percent), the period within which the customer should pay to gain the discount (for instance, 30 days), and the final day, on which the credit is completely due (for instance, 60 days). In this way, the customer may decrease its costs of products sold, and the vendor may decrease its CCC through a smaller receivable collection period.
- Advance reverse factoring is an innovative version of the traditional reverse factoring. In it, credit delivery occurs in the presence of more operational information. In this way, potentially the risks are lower and this instrument allows a reduction in the cost of financing. A digital solution is necessary in order to use this instrument.[107] A possible critical aspect is the need to move to the simplification and full digitization of documents. This might generate problems with international trade, as in many countries legal and accounting standards do not recognize these documents as legally binding invoices.
- Cleaning house is an evolution and extension of reverse factoring. In it, a third party, normally a financial institution, exploits the visibility of one or more branches of a chain to gather information about business transactions in a set of organizations to allow the financing of flows of which it is a guarantor.
- SMEs do not necessarily need to finance themselves through financial institutions such as banks.[108] This phenomenon was particularly clear during the financial crisis. Alternative financing is a procurement finance solution without recourse to financial institutions. The capital comes from another player in the supply chain[109] or organizations can get money through trade credits.[110] This approach allows non-bankers with capital availability buying invoices against an interest by operating through an online marketplace that is considered as a guarantor. Invoices are

uploaded to a cloud platform, a marketplace of commercial invoices, where an auction mechanism is triggered among different potential lenders.

- Fintech organization represents a variation of alternative financing. These organizations are making inroads by keeping the cost of payments low. Saxo Payments Banking Circle did a survey on SMEs.[111] The study revealed that low interest rates would encourage 58 percent of organizations to select a non-bank for a loan and 44 percent said low arrangement fees or flexible loans would persuade them to look outside banks.[112]

Collaborative Solutions

The traditional and innovative solutions are financial instruments of financing of working capital and liquidity, while the collaborative solutions are practices of operational collaboration in the value network. They are made up of collaborative value network management models. The aim of these collaborative solutions is to decrease the inventory and receivables value through greater collaboration and visibility among partners of the value network.

These models, applied according to the procurement finance approach, can be used for ensuring the financial sustainability of the value network.

The most representative models of collaborative solutions are[113]:

- Distributor finance includes forms of direct financing represented by loans or advance payment directed to the distributors of large manufacturers/exporters. Financing is normally used to fund inventory and receivables on a short-term basis. They fill a liquidity gap generated from the postponed receipt of payments of resales from intermediaries or end customers. It is a buyer-led instrument as the distributor can benefit from lower cost of capital through the endorsement of the large manufacturer (anchor enterprise), with which various types of risk-sharing arrangements are settled.
- Vendor-managed inventory. The vendor is authorized to handle the inventories of certain products at the customer's premises. Thanks to the sharing of information, this instrument allows both the vendor and the customer to cut inventories and consequently operational working capital.
- Consignment stock. The vendor makes available products to the customer at the premises of the latter, keeping the property until the

products are picked up. This cuts the customer's inventory and consequently the requirement of working capital. To ensure the correct operation of the instrument, information on consumption have to be shared with a high frequency.

- Collaborative planning, forecasting, and replenishment (CPFR). It is a commercial practice involving collaboration among several network value members to develop jointly production and purchase plans, demand forecasts, and inventory management policies. The model necessarily requires the use of technology platforms capable of managing, analyzing, and synthesizing high volumes of data from different sources. Cloud computing solutions are the ideal for this type of instrument.[114]
- The uniform credit is a procurement finance solution in which an organization receives money from a logistical supply provider (LSP), as a loan, pledging its inventories, and uses cash from selling those inventories to repay the loan. This is one of the cases in which LSPs extend their roles from the mere transportation and warehousing also to the procurement of financial services.[115]

Emerging Solutions

There are several new types of procurement finance solutions, such as[116]:

- Merchant cash advance was originally structured as a lump-sum payment to an organization in exchange for an agreed-upon parentage of future credit card and/or debit card sales.
- In e-Factoring, single invoice or group of invoices activate traditional factoring by applying new underwriting instruments via one of the three invoice sources: accounting software, e-invoicing platforms, and uploads by the customers.
- In purchase-to-pay and other networks, third-party finance can fund the invoice with third-party capital, using an approved invoice from a network (e-procurement, original equipment manufacturer (OEM), dealers, e-invoicing).
- Marketplace lenders provide a marketplace, using either their balance sheet or others to make small business loans.
- Single-use virtual cards or p-cards to replace a real card account with a unique virtual card account (VCA) for purchases and payment settlement.

- Working capital platforms where vendors name their price of funds. Vendors provide a rate at which they are willing to discount their invoices for early payment. This is a significant point of distinction. Vendors have the ability to set their own price for early payments.
- Supply chain finance is a solution that enables a buyer to lengthen their payment terms to their vendors while providing the option to their larger vendors to access funding or receivables to the buyer based on the buyer's credit rating.
- Auction-based invoice financing is the online platform where finance providers bid to advance money to small- and medium-sized organizations based on trade receivables' invoices issued. The finance providers that make these advances are largely made up of institutional investors, such as hedge funds and asset managers, and wealthy individuals. Since August 2013, the UK government has also provided finance for this new market.[117]

Structured Financing

The variations of procurement finance products considered until this point can be classified in:

- pre-shipment finance, such as financing based on inventories with warehouse certificates as collateral, based on a purchase order or on assumption of liability for payment by another institution based on the purchase order;
- shipment finance, such as discounting of export letters of credit;
- post-shipment finance, such as financing based on receivables towards the buyers—purchase of receivables, the discount of draft bills, factoring, and reverse factoring.

There is a more sophisticated instrument which is structured financing. This instrument implies financing the customers from foreign sources (cross-border finance) based on the transaction structure resulting in the isolation of the cash flow and its direction towards the repayment of the concerned exposure.[118]

Structured financing is targeted mainly at emerging markets and focused on the transaction liquidating. It is repaying itself based on the movements of the financed products, that is, the underlying cash. The transaction is based on securing and isolating the cash flow, or, in other words, on the structure of the transaction, instead of on the customer's rating, that is, its creditworthiness. In the majority of cases, the transaction is implemented through a newly established company (the so-called special purpose vehicle).

Some products within structured trade finance are the following[119]:

- Finance based on warehouse certificates is similar to pre-shipment finance. The difference is that the finance is backed by a cross-border credit line of the parent's financial institution, while the local financial institution controls the process of registering collaterals and endorsing warehouse certificates in its favor.[120]
- Finance based on the ratio of working assets' value and granted loan's value (borrowing base financing). The local financial institution, together with the monitoring agency, controls the reports submitted by the customer on a weekly basis. They are relative to the working assets pledged by the financial institution, and concerning new assets, new inflows, new products, inventories, new buyers' export agreements, and so on.
- Financing the production of a customer without any production capacities (tolling or throughput contract).[121] Financing the fees for production, packaging costs, shipment, and so on of a customer who submits raw materials to another organization so that it could manufacture the final product. The customer organization does so because it does not have (enough) production capacities of its own. In this way, it is possible to finance the procurement of raw materials to be supplied to the manufacturer so that it could manufacture the final product. For this service, the organization pays a fee to the manufacturer. In most of the cases, the value of the inventories is many times higher than the value of the production, that is, the fee paid for that production, which is another factor mitigating the transaction risk.
- Financing the purchase (import) by means of advance payment (pre-export (prepayment) finance))—financing the purchase of products from a foreign vendor storing its products in a certified warehouse, with warehouse certificates serving as proof of ownership. The products are purchased by means of advance payment. The buyer gets a loan and effects an advance payment to the exporter.
- Finance based on future receivables and inventories (export receivables-backed finance)—financing of the purchase of products from domestic and/or foreign vendors, with the establishment of a

pledge over the working assets (products and receivables occurring as a result of the finance), with the purpose of selling to domestic and/or foreign buyers, after they commit to settling the debt by paying the local bank's account.[122]

Choice Among the Instruments for Procurement Finance

The choice among the procurement finance instruments depends on different factors: the financial strategy of the organizations, the type of products, the markets, the distribution channels, and so on. It might be interesting to examine the results of a survey by the Osservatorio Supply Chain Finance del Politecnico di Milano.[123]

With an average collection time of 98-day trade receivables and 124-day payables to vendors (data for 2016), the potential supply chain finance market in Italy is equal to €637 billion (of which 74 percent of loans to customers and 26 percent to subsidiaries). It is the most important in Europe, bigger than the German (€582 billion), France (€529 billion), the UK (€411 billion), Spain (€341 billion), and the Netherlands (€170 billion) markets. The market served goes up to 23 percent of the total (29 percent if one considers only the receivables from the customers), amounting to over €146 billion. The market is still based on the traditional solutions, such as the advance invoice, that is, the financing of invoices that have not yet been collected, which went from €87 billion in 2015 to €75 billion in 2016 (−13.8 percent), and factoring, the sale of trade receivables claimed by an organization to debtors rising by +6, 6 percent to €58 billion. In 2016, the reverse factoring has grown, allowing vendors to exploit the creditworthiness of a customer organization to obtain lower prices (€3 billion, +7 percent). Innovative solutions have also taken hold, such as invoice auction, purchase order finance, dynamic discounting, and equipment finance. The market is expected to have grown strongly in 2017 thanks to the fintech organizations' boom and the use of innovative technologies such as blockchain, Big Data, and the Internet of Things.

Procurement Finance and Risk Management

Every business operates in a certain economic, political, and social context. In this context, it is inevitably exposed to certain risks. To deal with them adequately, each organization should use tools for risk management. They aim to safeguard the organization (and its assets) and ensure the continuity and the value-added to the business processes.

The application of risk management to the procurement processes is becoming increasingly critical and important for the need of integration among partners throughout the value network and for the more rapid process speed requested by the market. An organization should be aware that the financial risk management, due to the volatile context, requires that the procurement strategies remain linked to the overall organization's objectives and its financial objective. The two objectives need to be aligned and in sync with the rest of the organization. Finance and procurement must collaborate on risk management.

An inclination on managing the risk is within the procurement finance propensities.[124] The most important aspects are:

- handling the volatility of both demand and supply side;
- assuring economic-financial stability;
- collaborating within the risk management field through the use of financial resources to support the procurement function;
- working more closely with the finance function to achieve means able to identify and to measure the impact of savings on the total cost;
- integrating the ICT applications to achieve mechanisms of analysis and compliance able to support the initiatives of the organization.

Conclusions

Procurement and finance departments, through individual work, can provide immediate results regarding the economics of procurement. When these two sectors collaborate, there could be other opportunities related also to effectiveness, efficiency, and ethics of the organization's processes. This collaboration is becoming a reference point for many organizations. Collaboration between procurement and finance does not only refer to a better communication and collaboration towards converging objectives. It is also relative to a clearer visibility and data sharing, attainable only through shared and digitized solutions.

The CFO's role is expanding in the procurement sector in three areas: capital allocation, performance management, and risk management.[125] This expansion of the CFO's role is important for the procurement finance. It leads to a strong collaboration between the procurement and finance sectors allowing them to evolve in coordinated ways[126]:

- the procurement sector borrows financial tools from finance and gets the support on the management on the financial risks;
- the finance sector supports the procurement processes addressing them financially;
- the two sectors focus on how the value network financing instruments can bring better returns and more flexibility, managing together the complex financial aspects of procurement.

The physical and financial procurement flows need to be synchronized. They need to communicate with vendors, customers, and distributors. At the same time, they need to handle the relationships with financial institutions. In this situation, new solutions assume a relevant role through digitization, for instance through e-invoicing. The two main objectives of implementing this form of dematerialization solutions are the reduction of the administrative costs associated with invoicing and the improvement of their traceability along the procure-to-pay processes.

The finance sector has the accountability for dematerialization projects. For being successful, the collaboration with the procurement and the ICT functions is necessary. This collaboration is based on reaching shared objectives: the management of working capital, the increase in the cash flow, the reduction of the expenses, and the management of the risks.

The collaboration between finance, ICT, and procurement brings great benefits:

- faster decision-making and higher efficiency of processes;
- improvement of relationships with the vendors;
- high bottom-line savings.

Finance, ICT, and procurement when working closely can optimize the procure-to-pay cycle guaranteeing benefits for the entire organization that becomes a driver of higher, effectiveness and efficiency, and ensures compliance.

The collaboration and transfer of information throughout the value network is a key to doing business in a different way. A holistic vision regarding the handling of the working capital and of the liquidity can increase effectiveness, efficiency and economics in the procurement processes due to the use of innovative solutions, for instance, the use of e-procurement including e-invoicing and advanced payment solutions. The digital transformation of the procurement plays a key role in generating value and driving the competitiveness of the organizations.

The financial area has to be more innovative in the management of the liquidity especially in this current context characterized by dynamicity and competitiveness. In the face of the current financial crisis, organizations have to do as much as possible to free up working capital. The globalization of the economy and the increasing financial inclusion necessarily require the full simplification and digitization of the financial services, especially in connection with procurement.

Notes

1. www.capgemini.com/consulting/2013/09/a-dream-team-procurement-and-finance/#, Accessed 28 January 2018.
2. Elaboration of the Author on www.capgemini.com/consulting/2013/09/a-dream-team-procurement-and-finance/#, Accessed 28 January 2018.
3. www.capgemini.com/consulting/2013/09/a-dream-team-procurement-and-finance/#, Accessed 28 January 2018.
4. Van Weele, A. J. (2009). *Purchasing and supply chain management: Analysis, strategy, planning and practice*. Cengage Learning EMEA, Andover, UK.
5. Ahn, M. J. (2011). *A theory of domestic and international trade finance* (No. 11–262). International Monetary Fund, Washington, DC.
6. usblogs.pwc.com/emerging-technology/blockchain-to-disrupt-trade-finance/. Accessed 12 June 2018.
7. Adapted from bcrpub.com/news/global-supply-chain-finance-jumps-36-percent. Accessed 19 July 2018.
8. bebeez.it/wp-content/blogs.dir/5825/files/2015/02/BPO.pdf, Accessed 27 December 2017.
9. Rajan, R. G. (2006). Has finance made the world riskier?. *European Financial Management*, *12*(4), 499–533.
10. Burkart, M., & Ellingsen, T. (2004). In-kind finance: A theory of trade credit. *American Economic Review*, *94*(3), 569–590.
11. ITC (2009). *How to Access Trade Finance: A Guide for Exporting SME*. ITC, Geneva, CH.
12. Dunning, J. H., & Lundan, S. M. (2008). *Multinational enterprises and the global economy*. Edward Elgar Publishing, Cheltenham, UK.
13. Christopher, M. (2016). *Logistics & supply chain management*. Pearson, London, UK.
14. Bertoldi, B. (2018), Focus. Fiat e Chrysler, Destini Incrociati, *Il Sole 24 Ore*, 3 June 2018.
15. ITC (2009). *How to Access Trade Finance: A Guide for Exporting SME*. ITC, Geneva, CH.

16. Kristofik, P., Kok, J., de Vries, S., & van Sten-van't Hoff, J. (2012). Financial Supply Chain Management–Challenges and Obstacles. *Proceedings in Finance and Risk Perspectives '12.*
17. www.pymnts.com/news/b2b-payments/2018/fitch-ratings-supply-chain-financing-corporate-debt/. Accessed 07 August 2018.
18. Camerinelli, E. (2009). Supply chain finance. *Journal of Payments Strategy & Systems*, 3 (2), 114–128.
19. Guide, T. F. (2008). *A Quick Reference for US Exporters*, US Department of Commerce. International Trade Administration, Washington, DC.
20. International Trade Administration, 2012. *Trade Finance Guide.* Office of Public Affairs, U.S Department of Commerce, Washington, DC.
21. www.oecd.org/finance/financial-markets/44260489.pdf. Accessed 28 July 2018.
22. www.linkedin.com/pulse/international-trade-glossary-terms-zahira-oubaiche/. Accessed 28 July 2018.
23. International Trade Administration, 2012. *Trade Finance Guide.* Office of Public Affairs, U.S Department of Commerce, Washington, DC.
24. Bloch, C. (2015). Double trouble-the giving of guarantees with others. *Brief*, *42*(9), 30.
25. www.businessdictionary.com/definition/inventory-financing.html, Accessed 31 March 2018.
26. smallbusiness.chron.com/definition-inventory-financing-3192.html, Accessed 31 March 2018.
27. www.Entrepreneur.com. Accessed 31 March 2018.
28. www.Startupjunkies.com Accessed 31 March 2018.
29. www.Entrepreneur.com. Accessed 31 March 2018.
30. cdn.iccwbo.org/content/uploads/sites/3/2017/01/ICC-Standard-Definitions-for-Techniques-of-Supply-Chain-Finance-Global-SCF-Forum-2016.pdf, Accessed 24 February 2018.
31. Murphy, S. (2014). Trade Finance Applications Technology Analysis Abstract, *CEB Tower Group White Paper*, August.
32. Malaket, M. A. (2014). *Financing trade and international supply chains: commerce across borders, finance across frontiers.* Ashgate Publishing, Abingdon, UK.
33. Malaket, M. A. (2014). *Financing trade and international supply chains: commerce across borders, finance across frontiers.* Ashgate Publishing, Abingdon, UK.
34. www.pwc.com.au/publications/pdf/supply-chain-finance-jul17.pdf. Accessed 9 July 2018.
35. Pfohl, H. C., & Gomm, M. (2009). Supply chain finance: optimizing financial flows in supply chains. *Logistics research*, *1*(3–4), 149–161.

36. Hofmann, E. (2005). Supply chain finance: some conceptual insights. *Beiträge Zu Beschaffung Und Logistik*, 203–214.
37. Steeman, M. (2014). The Power of Supply Chain Finance. *Windesheimreeks Kennis en Onderzoek*, (50).
38. Weighted average cost of capital: WACC = kE · E/(D + E) + kD · D/(D + E), where kD is the cost of debt, kE the cost of equity, D and E the book values of debt and equity.
39. Hartley-Urquhart, W. R. (2000). *U.S. Patent No. 6,167,385.* Washington, DC: U.S. Patent and Trademark Office.
40. Stemmler, L. & Seuring, S. (2003). Finanzwirtschaftliche Elemente in der Lieferkettensteuerung–Erste Überlegungen zu einem Konzept des Supply Chain Finance. *Logistik Management*, *5*(4), 27–37.
41. Chen, X. & Hu, C. (2011), The value of supply chain finance, in Habib, M. (Ed.), *Supply Chain Management - Applications and Simulations*, InTech, Rijeka, Croatia, 111–132.
42. Xu, Y., & Zhong, H. (2011). Analyzing innovative model of the Small and Medium Enterprises financing: Supply chain financing. *2011 International Conference on Management Science and Industrial Engineering* (MSIE), 1033–1036.
43. Kouvelis, P. et al. (2017), Supply Chain Finance, special issue of *Foundations and Trends in Technology, Information and Operations Management.* 10(3–4).
44. Meca, A., & Timmer, J. B. (2007). *Supply chain collaboration.* (Trabajos I+D; No. 1/CIO-2007-31). CIO (Centro de Investigación Operativa), Universidad Miguel Hernández de Elche, Elche, Spain.
45. Randall, W. S., & Farris, T. M. (2009). Supply chain financing: using cash-to-cash variables to strengthen the supply chain. *International Journal of Physical Distribution & Logistics Management*, *39*(8), 669–689.
46. Randall, W. S., & Farris, T. M. (2009). Supply chain financing: using cash-to-cash variables to strengthen the supply chain. *International Journal of Physical Distribution & Logistics Management*, *39*(8), 669–689.
47. Malaket, M. A. (2014). *Financing trade and international supply chains: commerce across borders, finance across frontiers.* Ashgate Publishing, Abingdon, UK.
48. Hofmann, E. (2010). A supply chain-oriented approach of working capital management. *Journal of Business Logistics*, 305–330.
49. Song, H., Yu, K., & Lu, Q. (2018). Financial service providers and banks' role in helping SMEs to access finance. *International Journal of Physical Distribution & Logistics Management*, *48*(1), 69–92.

50. Pezza, S. (2011). Supply Chain Finance: Gaining control in the face of uncertainty. *Aberdeen Group*, Waltham, MA.
51. Adapted by the Author based on Pfohl, H. C., & Gomm, M. (2009). Supply chain finance: optimizing financial flows in supply chains. *Logistics research*, 1(3–4), 149–161.
52. Higgins, R. C. (2012). *Analysis for financial management*. McGraw-Hill/Irwin, New York City, NY.
53. Korkman, O., Storbacka, K., & Harald, B. (2010). Practices as markets: Value co-creation in e-invoicing. *Australasian Marketing Journal (AMJ)*, *18*(4), 236–247.
54. Srai, J. S., & Lorentz, H. (2018). Developing design principles for the digitalisation of purchasing and supply management. *Journal of Purchasing and Supply Management*.
55. Lamoureux, J. F., & Evans, T. (2011). Supply chain finance: A new means to support the competitiveness and resilience of global value chains. papers.ssrn.com/sol3/papers.cfm?abstract_id=2179944, Accessed 17 March 2018.
56. Xu, Y. & Zhong, H. (2011). Analyzing innovative model of the Small and Medium Enterprises financing: Supply chain financing. *2011 International Conference on Management Science and Industrial Engineering* (MSIE), 1033–1036.

    Hofmann, E. (2005). Supply chain finance: some conceptual insights. *Beiträge Zu Beschaffung Und Logistik*, 203–214.
57. Caniato, F., Gelsomino, L., Maestrini, V., Moretto, A., Perego, A., & Ronchi, S. (2016). The benefits of supply chain finance: a value assessment model. In *23rd EurOMA Conference* (pp. 1–10).
58. Kristofik, P., Kok, J., de Vries, S., & van Sten-van't Hoff, J. (2012). Financial Supply Chain Management–Challenges and Obstacles. *Proceedings in Finance and Risk Perspectives '12*.
59. Mathis, F. J., & Cavinato, J. (2010). Financing the global supply chain: growing need for management action. *Thunderbird International Business Review*, *52*(6), 467–474.
60. Hofmann, E., & Belin, O. (2011). *Supply chain finance solutions* (pp. 644–645). Springer-Verlag Berlin, Germany.
61. Wuttke, D. A., Blome, C., Foerstl, K., & Henke, M. (2013). Managing the innovation adoption of supply chain finance—Empirical evidence from six European case studies. *Journal of Business Logistics*, *34*(2), 148–166.
62. Randall, W. S., & Farris, M. T. (2009). Supply chain financing: using cash-to-cash variables to strengthen the supply chain. *International Journal of Physical Distribution & Logistics Management*, *39*(8), 669–689.

63. Navatte, P., & Bironneau, L. (2017). La mise en place d'un marché interne du capital au sein de la chaîne logistique: un nouveau défi. *Logistique & Management*: 1–11.
64. Directive 2001/115/Ec. eur-lex.europa.eu/LexUriServ/LexUriServ.do?uri=OJ:L:2002:015:0024:0028:EN:PDF, Accessed 24 April 2017.
65. Meehan, J., & Bryde, D. (2011). Sustainable procurement practice. *Business Strategy and the Environment*, *20*(2), 94–106.
66. www.sdcexec.com/article/12247812/supply-chain-finance-on-the-blockchain-enables-network-collaboration, Accessed 3 March 2017.
67. Templar, S., Findlay, C., & Hofmann, E. (2016). *Financing the End-to-end Supply Chain: A Reference Guide to Supply Chain Finance.* Kogan Page Publishers, London, UK.
68. Adapted by the Author from More, D., & Basu. P. (2013), Challenges of Supply Chain Finance, *Business Process Management Journal*, 19(4): 624–647.
69. Ross, D. F. (2013). *Competing through supply chain management: creating market-winning strategies through supply chain partnerships.* Springer Science & Business Media, Berlin, Germany.
70. Christopher, M. (2005). *Logistics and supply chain management: creating value-adding networks.* Pearson Education, London, UK.

    Lysons, K., & Farrington, B. (2006). *Purchasing and supply chain management.* Pearson Education, London, UK.
71. Lodefalk, M. (2017). Servitization of organizations and trade policy implications. *World Trade Review*, *16*(01): 59–83.

    Kowalkowski, C., Gebauer, H., Kamp, B., & Parry, G. (2017). Servitization and deservitization: Overview, concepts, and definitions. *Industrial Marketing Management.*
72. Recor, J., & Xu, H. (2017). GRC Technology Fundamentals. In *Commercial Banking Risk Management* (333–392). Palgrave Macmillan US, New York City, NY.
73. issuu.com/supplydemandchainfoodlogistics/docs/sdc0916, Accessed 20 April 2017.
74. When the buyer's cash is used to finance vendors, the practice is called dynamic discounting. Functionally it is the same as procurement finance.
75. www.sdcexec.com/article/12247812/supply-chain-finance-on-the-blockchain-enables-network-collaboration, Accessed 20 April 2017.
76. Bryant, C. & Camerinelli, E. (2014), *Supply Chain Finance: EBA European market guide*, European Banking Association, Paris, France.
77. Piccolo, S. & Di Meco, F. (2016), *Development of a cost and benefit model for supply chain finance solutions.* Thesis at the Politecnico di Milano, Milano, Italy.

78. Hofmann, E. (2005). Supply chain finance: some conceptual insights. *Beiträge Zu Beschaffung Und Logistik*, 203–214.
79. Boon-itt, S., Wong, C. Y., & Wong, C. W. (2017). Service supply chain management process capabilities: Measurement development. *International Journal of Production Economics, 193*, 1–11.
80. Coyle, J. J., Bardi, E. J. & Langley, C. J. (1996) *The Management of Business Logistics* 6th edn, *West Publishing*, St Paul, MN.
81. Hofmann, E. (2005). Supply chain finance: some conceptual insights. *Beiträge Zu Beschaffung Und Logistik*, 203–214.
82. Xu, Y. & Zhong, H. (2011). Analyzing innovative model of the Small and Medium Enterprises financing: Supply chain financing. *2011 International Conference on Management Science and Industrial Engineering* (MSIE), 1033–1036.
    Chen, X. & Hu, C. (2011), The value of supply chain finance, in Habib, M. (Ed.), *Supply Chain Management - Applications and Simulations*, InTech, Rijeka, Croatia: 111–132.
    Zhang, L., & Yan, G. (2009, February). The complex economic system of supply chain financing. In *International Conference on Complex Sciences* (pp. 763–772). Springer, Berlin, Germany.
83. Hofmann, E. (2005). Supply chain finance: some conceptual insights. *Beiträge Zu Beschaffung Und Logistik*, 203–214.
84. Xu, Y. & Zhong, H. (2011). Analyzing innovative model of the Small and Medium Enterprises financing: Supply chain financing. *2011 International Conference on Management Science and Industrial Engineering* (MSIE), 1033–1036.
    Zhang, L., & Yan, G. (2009). The complex economic system of supply chain financing. In *International Conference on Complex Sciences,* 763–772. Springer, Berlin, Germany.
    Raghavan, N. S. & Mishra, V. (2011).Short-term financing in a cash-constrained supply chain. *International Journal of Production Economics*, 134(2), 407–412.
85. Thompson, J. (2016). *IT+Procurement+Finance: a powerful triade.* www.digitalistmag.com/cio-knowledge/2016/07/11/it-procurement-finance-powerful-triad-04299256, Accessed 12 February 2018.
86. sapinsider.wispubs.com/Assets/Articles/2016/August/SPI-The-Power-of-Collaboration, Accessed 12 February 2018.
87. Nicoletti, B. (2014), Lean and Digitize e-procurement, paper presented at the *e-Public procurement in Europe: public management, technologies and processes of change,* Lisbon, Portugal, 27th May.
88. Pandit, K., & Marmanis, H. (2008). *Spend analysis: The window into strategic sourcing.* J. Ross Publishing, Plantation, FL.

89. Bienhaus, F., & Haddud, A. (2018) Procurement 4.0: factors influencing the digitisation of procurement and supply chains, *Business Process Management Journal*, doi.org/10.1108/BPMJ-06-2017-0139.
90. Blackman, I. D., Holland, C. P., & Westcott, T. (2013). Motorola's global financial supply chain strategy. *Supply Chain Management: An International Journal*, *18*(2), 132–147.
91. Ante, S. E. (2011). "Motorola Is Split Into Two". *The Wall Street Journal*. Accessed 21 July 2018.
92. Akpolat, H. (2017). *Six sigma in transactional and service environments*. Routledge, London, UK.
93. Hofmann, E., & Belin, O. (2011). *Supply chain finance solutions* (pp. 644–645). Springer-Verlag Berlin, Germany.
94. Invernizzi, M. G. (2018). Supply chain finance as a sustainability enabler. *Tesi, Politecnico di Milano*, Milano, Italy.
   Kouvelis, P. et al. (2017), Supply Chain Finance, special issue of *Foundations and Trends in Technology, Information and Operations Management*. 10(3–4).
95. Hofmann, E., Strewe, U. M., & Bosia, N. (2017). *Supply Chain Finance and Blockchain Technology: The Case of Reverse Securitisation*. Springer, Berlin, Germany.
96. Dyckman, B. (2011). Supply chain finance: Risk mitigation and revenue growth. *Journal of corporate treasury management*, *4*(2).
97. Politecnico di Milano (2014), *Supply Chain Finance: nuove opportunità di collaborazione nella filiera*, Politecnico di Milano, Milano, Italy.
98. Gelsomino, L. M., de Boer, R., Steeman, M., & Perego, A. (2018). An optimisation strategy for concurrent Supply Chain Finance schemes. *Journal of Purchasing and Supply Management*.
99. Lea, T., & Trollope, W. (1996). *A guide to factoring and invoice discounting: The new bankers*. Chapman & Hall.
100. Camerinelli, E. (2009). Supply chain finance. *Journal of Payments Strategy & Systems*, 3 (2), 114–128.
101. Lamoureux, J.-F. & Evans, T. A. (2011), Value network finance: a new means to support the competitiveness and resilience of global value chains, Working Paper 2179944, *Social Science Research Network*, Rochester, NY.
102. Camerinelli, E. (2010). Trends in cash, liquidity and working capital management digitization: The role of technology. *Journal of Corporate Treasury Management*, *3*(2).
103. Elliot V., & Lindblom T. (2018) The Impact of Recent Regulatory Reform on the Use of Supply Chain Finance: The Case of Reverse Factoring. In: García-Olalla M., Clifton J. (eds) *Contemporary Issues in Banking*. Palgrave Macmillan Studies in Banking and Financial Institutions. Palgrave Macmillan, Cham, Switzerland.

104. Hofmann, E., Strewe, U. M., & Bosia, N. (2018). Background I—What Is Buyer-Led Supply Chain Finance?. In *Supply Chain Finance and Blockchain Technology* (pp. 7–23). Springer, Cham, Switzerland.
105. Petersen, M. A. & Rajan, R. G. (1997), Trade credit: theory & evidence, *The Review of Financial Studies*, 10(3), 661–691.
Biais, B., & Gollier, C. (1997). Trade credit and credit rationing. *The Review of Financial Studies*, *10*(4), 903–937.
106. Lee, C. H. H. & Rhee, B. D. B.-D. (2011), Trade credit for value network coordination, *European Journal of Operational Research*, 214(1), 136–146.
107. Ascari, M. (2015). An analysis of supply chain finance in Europe: unexploited potential and future improvements. Thesis at Politecnico di Milano, Milan, Italy.
108. Luo, S., Zhang, Y., & Zhou, G. (2018). Financial Structure and Financing Constraints: Evidence on Small- and Medium-Sized Enterprises in China. *Sustainability*, *10*(6), 1774.
109. Pfohl, H. C., & Gomm, M. (2009). Value network Finance: optimizing financial flows in value networks. *Logistics research*, 1(3–4), 149–161. Springer, Berlin, Germany.
110. Carbo-Valverde, S.; Rodriguez-Fernandez, F.; & Udell, G. F. Trade Credit. The Financial Crisis, and SME Access to Finance. *J. Money Credit Banking* **2016**, *1*, 113–143.
111. www.bankingcircle.com/whitepapers. Accessed 7 July 2018.
112. La Cour, M. (2018). Saxo Payments' Virtuous Circle. *Fintech Finance*, issue 9, 16–19.
113. Whipple, J. M., & Russell, D. (2007). Building supply chain collaboration: a typology of collaborative approaches. *The International Journal of Logistics Management*, *18*(2), 174–196.
114. Panahifar, F., Heavey, C., Byrne, P. J., & Fazlollahtabar, H. (2015). A framework for collaborative planning, forecasting and replenishment (CPFR) state of the art. *Journal of Enterprise Information Management*, *28*(6), 838–871.
Davenport, T. H., & Brooks, J. D. (2004). Enterprise systems and the supply chain. *Journal of Enterprise Information Management*, *17*(1), 8–19.
115. Gelsomino, L. (2012). A model for the supply chain representation and financial assessment. *Thesis at the Master of Science in Management, Economics, and Industrial Engineering*, Politecnico di Milano, Milano, Italy.
116. spendmatters.com/research/alternative-finance-market-update-treasury-considerations/. Accessed 14 June 2018.
117. www.accaglobal.com/gb/en/student/exam-support-resources/fundamentals-exams-study-resources/f9/technical-articles/going%2D%2Dgoi

ng%2D%2Dgone%2D%2D%2D%2Dauction-based-invoice-financing.html. Accessed 14 June 2018.

118. Kerfoot, M. K., Alicandri, J. R., & Perkins, R. G. (2017). The ABCs of fund finance: credit facilities for secondaries funds and funds of funds. *Journal of Investment Compliance, 18*(4), 8–12.
    Schwarcz, S. L. (1993). Structured finance. *New York.*
119. Kasavica, P. (2014). Finansiranje Lanca Snabdevanja. *Bankarstvo Magazine*, (3).
120. Youssef, F., finance and energy unit, UNCTAD, Commodity finance and risk management, 2010, p. 6.
121. www.risk.net/definition/tolling-agreement. Accessed 29 July 2018.
122. Youssef, F., finance and energy unit, UNCTAD, Commodity finance and risk management, 2010, p. 8.
123. www.thepaypers.com/expert-opinion/access-to-payment-accounts-under-psd2-which-accounts-are-in-scope-/763682. Accessed 8 July 2018.
124. Busch, J. (2013). *Risk Management: 3Ps—Predictive, Proactive, Prescriptive.* spendmatters.com/2013/08/12/supply-chain-and-risk-management-3ps-predictive-proactive-prescriptive/, Accessed 12 February 2018.
125. www.ey.com/Publication/vwLUAssets/EY-infinite-possibilities-procurement-in-2025/$FILE/EY-infinite-possibilities-procurement-in-2025, Accessed 12 February 2018.
126. Lind, M., & Barner, K. (2017). *Finance Unleashed: Leveraging the CFO for Innovation.* Springer, Berlin, Germany.

CHAPTER 4

Agile Procurement Finance and Its KPI

Introduction

In the current volatile, dynamic, global, and competitive context, the procurement sector is fully immersed in this evolutionary process. It is becoming a strategic function inside the organization. This chapter defines the characteristic of the procurement finance concept considering the challenges in the current context. The constant economic and social evolution forces to review and update the business models.

The previous chapters clarify the role and the importance of procurement through the analysis of the Porter's value chain.[1] This chapter underlines the linkage between the current dynamic context and the consequent changes in procurement and in financial services due to the digital transformation, globalization, and difficulties in obtaining the credit especially for small and medium-sized enterprises (SMEs).

The right approach in the presence of this volatile context is to become agile. This chapter develops the concept of agility. It clarifies how this term should be applied to procurement finance increasing the value of this sector for the organization and the customers, internal and external to the organization.

Procurement finance must necessarily become more flexible and rapid to respond quickly to the volatile customer demand. For monitoring the progress in this direction, it is important to analyze in depth which key performance indicators (KPIs) are relevant for procurement finance.

B. Nicoletti, *Procurement Finance*,
Palgrave Studies in Financial Services Technology,
https://doi.org/10.1007/978-3-030-02140-5_4

Agile Organizations

Definition of Agility

Organizations are facing changes in the market competition, innovation, and customer demand. This dynamic and unpredictable environment pushes to focus on how the organizations need to cope with these constant and rapid, internal and external changes.[2]

The current situation is characterized by these relevant factors[3]:

- scarce resources against the constant pressures of a dynamic environment;
- fast development of new solutions;
- globalization;
- volatile global market;
- volatility of information and the increase of their availability;
- difficulty in getting credit for many organizations, especially the SMEs.

There are different objectives for the organizations to improve their processes and their systems. This chapter concentrates on agility.

One of the best ways for the organization to cope with these challenges is to become agile.[4] To move in this direction, it is important to clarify what the agility concept means and implies. This term underlines the importance, as the primary characteristics, of the speed and the flexibility of an organization and the fast response that it should have to face the pressures of the dynamic environment.[5] The main characteristics of agility is to find the proper ways to face the unpredictable changes and actually to benefit from these changes. An unstable and dynamic environment leads the organizations to prefer less formalization and more flexibility to be able to respond to these changes any time and in any possible way.

Agility and Flexibility

Flexibility is relative to the volume of products, the organizations, the model of products, and people competencies. It is the capability to achieve different objectives with different processes without relevant difficulties. The flexibility, along with responsiveness, competency, and quickness, needs agility with these relevant attributes[6]:

- responsiveness: anticipating changes and reacting faster to them;
- competency: the ability of users of the technologies, an high rate of new product introduction, efficiency, and effectiveness of operations, quality of products and services, cooperation (internal and external), and integration;
- quickness: rapid reaction times to changes in the market, rapid operations, and rapid delivery of products and services. It requires shorter processing times, including in procurement.

Flexibility is a particularly important aspect in the agility. It is also a relevant requirement in today's world. The majority of research from the last decades focused on building conceptual models to describe the relationships among constructs of supply chain flexibility.[7] These conceptual models studied the relationship among multiple constructs and how they are related, the direction, and the size of the effects. In the case of procurement finance, flexibility is the robustness of the buyer-vendor-financial institution relationship under changes in the organization and procurement conditions.[8]

There are no mathematical models for something called "procurement finance flexibility". It is possible to describe 22 flexibility dimensions.[9] The majority of these flexibility dimensions are difficult to translate in quantitative terms, like coordination flexibility, information flexibility, response to market flexibility, and sourcing flexibility. However, quantitative terms can be defined for delivery flexibility, new product flexibility, mix flexibility, and volume flexibility.[10] It is possible to describe how to measure these dimensions in terms of range and response.[11]

Some definitions of these aspects of the flexibility are:

- Delivery flexibility is the ability to change planned delivery dates according to the customer needs.[12]
- Mix (product) flexibility is the ability to manufacture multiple products in the same capacity, and the ability to reallocate procurement and capacity between products in response to realized demand.[13] Changing the mix of products might also be caused by changes in the customer demand distribution. Mix flexibility is essentially the amount of products that could be produced taking into account the changeover times.[14]
- Volume flexibility is the change in one product group, while changing the output level of multiple product groups is a combination of

volume flexibility and mix flexibility. Varying the output level of a production process to cope with seasonality occurs in almost every industry.[15] When evaluating volume flexibility and mix flexibility in a build-to-order (BTO) environment, procurement should prioritize one dimension over the other, since it is impossible to focus on all the dimensions.[16] Due to the correlation between these dimensions, the other dimension is already affected if it is not prioritized. It has been proposed to measure volume and mix flexibility of an organization by measuring the produced products and observing the customer demand in every time period.[17] It is possible to define four measurements for volume flexibility of an organization.[18] Their measurements are based on the standard deviation of sales, inventory, costs of products sold, and of the return on investment (ROI).[19]

Drivers of Agility

The main drivers of the agility in an organization are the changes in the environment, the market, and the technology. Today, the change is very fast. It is important for the organization to have the capabilities to avoid the great risks caused by the rapid changes.[20] In this context, the agility is the relevant role to allow the organization to face the changes of the market, the demand of customers, and the strong competitiveness that characterized this new economic context. The context requires a strong flexibility and capability to react with the greatest readiness. This is true especially for the SMEs that need to cope with the competition of larger organizations. Often agility is their competitive advantage.[21]

To understand what an agile organization is, it is interesting to refer to Fig. 4.1. It represents a conceptual model of an agile enterprise.[22]

The main objective of an agile organization is the fast satisfaction of the customer requirements even when the demand of the customers is very unpredictable. These situations stimulate the organizations for agility to achieve the satisfaction of the customer requirements and the achievement of the organization's objective. An agile organization needs also agile vendors. The agile vendors are characterized by a strategy based on collaborative relationships, an infrastructure based on information integration, operative mechanisms oriented to the responsiveness to the customer requirements, and, as the cardinal point, the process integration.

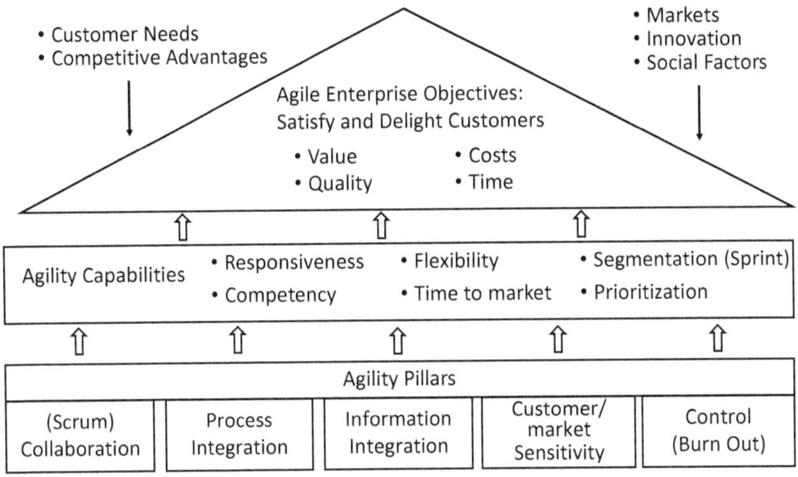

Fig. 4.1 Conceptual model of an agile enterprise. (Adapted by the author from Tseng, Y. H., & Lin, C. T. (2011). Enhancing organization agility by deploying agile drivers, capabilities, and providers, *Information Science,* 181)

In conclusion, it is important the linkage and coordination among the agility drivers and capabilities in a way that the vendors guarantee the agile organization to reach its objectives.

Agile Procurement Finance

In a globalized procurement finance, an agile organization requires some characteristics of services and products also from the financial institutions with which it works.

Starting from the customer perspective and from the characteristics the customers' desires, some key indicators have a relevant importance in a global, competitive, and dynamic procurement finance as shown in Fig. 4.2.

Procurement finance refers to financing procurement solutions in the face of these problems encountered by the organizations: the risk of credit, the export finance, and the funding of the organization's working capital.[23] Trade is the main driver of development, but to be effective it is necessary to have an acceptable and fair financing.[24] The international trade is growing over time, and the financial institutions are assuming a

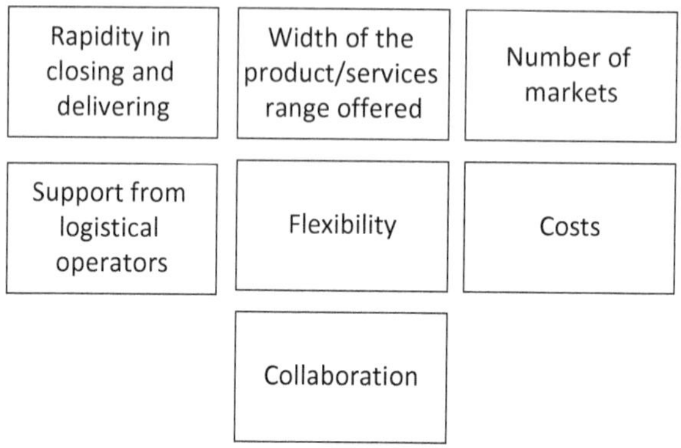

Fig. 4.2 Relevant KPI

relevant role regarding the trade services for supporting the organizations in their global trade.

The global market involves the transportation of products and the movement of services all over the world. In this context, the procurement sector assumes a greater importance. One of the biggest problems that operators of international trade have is to assure secure ways to receive the payments of their supplies. The consequence is the importance of procurement finance.

The reason of the importance of the procurement function lies in the fact that globalization has stimulated the externalization of parts of the activities outside of the organizations with the outsourcing of relevant processes and sub-processes. Globalization, besides stimulating the competitiveness, has also given great importance on the timeliness of the deliveries that represents an important competitive factor. The time factor matters in global trade. It has an important role to be supported above all by the procurement sector. This sector has to guarantee the timeliness and flexibility in response to the continuous market changes due to the volatility of customer demand. In this volatile context, forecasting is difficult. The customers expect the availability of products and services in a very short time. These expectations can create difficulties for the procurement sector. In order to be flexible and rapid in the delivery, procurement might be pushed to purchase more than needed. To avoid such a waste, the procurement function has to manage the information flow, procedures, systems, and services along the value network as a whole in an efficient, effective, economical, and ethical way.

The Procurement Finance Agile Management Framework

To analyze on which aspects to act for reaching an agile procurement finance management, it is useful to refer to a framework used as the basis for developing a research framework for financial supply chains.[25] The authors of this framework identify three interdependent procurement dimensions on which to act to get agility: business processes, management components, and network structure. Given that procurement finance operates in parallel with the product value network, it is interesting to adapt this framework and use it as the basis for the definition of an agile procurement finance.

Financial business process management refers to the activities relevant to the coordination and management of financial transactions between trading partners in a value network context. The business processes construct maps directly onto procurement finance. Management components are concerned with the integration and coordination of business processes. Processes must be managed using an agile approach.

In procurement finance, financial business management is done with the support of ICT systems and the sharing of information within and between organizations. To reflect this critical role of the ICT solutions combined with management systems, the term "financial and banking information systems" can be used in place of management components.[26] Financial and banking information flow refers to the extent of information sharing and visibility among the value network participants.[27] It is essential to support the agile management components of procurement finance;

Financial network structure identifies the composition and the typology of the relationships among all the actors involved in the financial and physical networks as well as the communication (collaborative infrastructure settled to integrate physical, information/digital, and financial flows). Network structure has been identified as a key feature in the procurement literature. This concept applies equally to the network structure of organizations and financial institutions involved in procurement finance.

Key Performance Indicators

The key performance indicators (KPIs) are factors through which the development, performance, or the position of the business of the organizations on respect to the competition can be measured effectively.[28] These indicators must be closely connected to the organization's objectives and strategy. Once the objectives of the organizations are identified, the KPIs need to be defined in such a way to allow the organization to be able to evaluate the performance of a specific activity or process.

The KPIs must be quantifiable and measurable, and they should be chosen from a long-term perspective. In a very dynamic and competitive economic environment as the current one, the measurement system of performance involves a wide and variable range of performances of business processes. For this reason, the KPIs are focused mainly on processes. The objective is to measure the entire range of performance that as a whole has to quantify the value of the outputs to the customer. In the selection of the KPIs, the primary aspect to consider is "which are the features that satisfy the customers need?".

KPIs for the Agile Procurement Finance

One of the most important KPI in procurement is time. Time to get to Yes refers also to the time for providing or getting financing. The time can be a benefit to the customers because it represents the rapidity from the moment of request to the delivery of the products or services. Customers request flexibility, quality, security, and speed. The virtual proximity to the customer is the primary aspect of performance growth.

Without the support of the financial system, an organization will never be competitive in the global market. For this reason, it is necessary to deepen the offer and to choose also financial services more in line with the objectives and characteristics of each business.

Another KPI is the width of the product ranges offered and the number of countries able to support for imports and exports. It is possible to evaluate the financial institution performances on the basis of their ability to offer a wide range of products to support the international financial operations. The financial institutions should provide a strong support to the global procurement through a range of products able to help customers with their payments and mitigate risks.[29]

The shipment of products requests time and involves risks. The partners of the procurement need to use different payment instruments to allocate risks and to finance costs between partners. These agreements could be divided into vendor finance (open account), buyer finance (cash in advance), and financial institution finance (letter of credit).[30] In a global procurement, there are different methods of payments for international operations. It is necessary to understand which methods are more useful and secure for the financial institution itself and for its customers.

A Model for the KPIs for Procurement Finance

The key performance indicators to assess the procurement finance from the point of view of its agility can be described by a model,[31] which takes into account the set of the relationships between procurement and finance presented in Chap. 3. It is based on the importance of the strategy of the supply, the control, the profitability, and the glue represented by the information management. Taking into account these four aspects, it is possible to arrive at a similar set of KPIs. They should evaluate the service, the costs, and the finance. Since information is the glue, the KPIs should take into account also the ways and the performance that the organization achieves in managing the data.

Procurement finance is a continuous trade-off between the customer service level, the total costs, the financial aspects, and the management of the related information. A graphical representation of the set of KPIs is shown in Fig. 4.3. These four dimensions are related to each other. It is important to look at these performance measurements. The KPIs should be balanced because it is almost impossible to have a higher service level, lower costs, lower financing needs, and an excellent management of the data connected with procurement finance. Finding the balance between these constructs is always a trade-off between the KPIs.

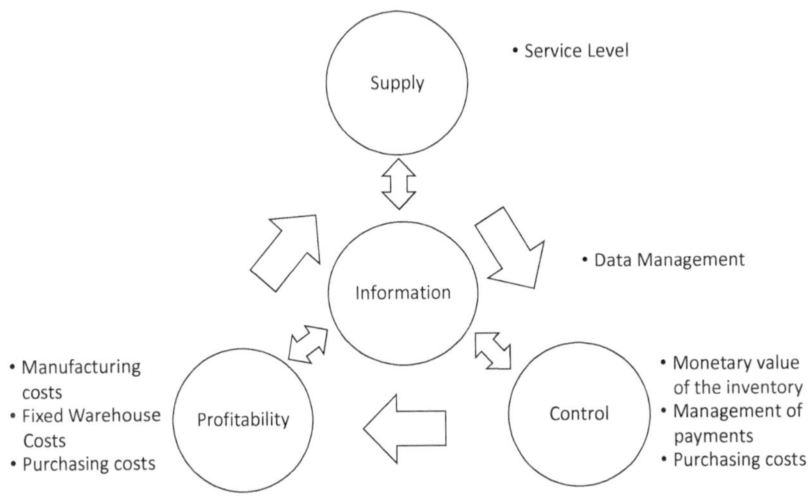

Fig. 4.3 The four pillars and their KPI

Going into the details of the KPI to measure the benefits of an agile procurement finance, it is necessary to take into account the following considerations.[32]

The service level can be measured by subtracting the expected number of backorders per time period from the expected period demand. Some of the main improvements that agile can bring to procurement finance are the ability to manage changing priorities, project visibility, and business/ICT alignment.

The performance measure for finance is the inventory and the management of the payments. The inventory and the finance are related to the costs. The finance angle can represent the number of products in the inventory of one product. It can also be calculated as the total monetary value of the products in the inventory. Both methods are used in practice. The main benefits that agility can bring are delivery speed/time to market, team morale, work predictability, risk reduction, engineering discipline, and improved management of distributed teams.

The costs related to this model are on the last triangle. The manufacturing costs, fixed warehousing costs, and purchasing costs should be taken into account. The total costs consist of transportation costs (logistics) and holding costs at preassemble sites and at the main production center. The main benefits that agility can bring are increased team productivity and cost reduction of the procurement actions and initiatives.

The management of the information is really the challenge. New and improved solutions make this task more achievable also in smaller organizations.[33]

Conclusions

Procurement finance is increasingly a strategic function within the organizations. Considering its relevance and the current economic scenario, organizations require more agility. This chapter underlines that agility can be more easily reached through the exploitation of new solutions. Business process management allows dealing with the volatility of information. It can be applied in the procurement sector in a way through which the handling of procurement processes is possible in a rapid and transparent way. In this current volatile and dynamic environment, the KPIs presented show that there is a need of a high flexibility. An agile perspective needs to deal with the challenges of an increasingly international trade.

Revenues from procurement finance now total several hundred of USD billion a year. Signs suggest that the good times may be ending, not because the growth of trade might be slowing but also because new entrants could capture attractive parts of the value network.

The ease of international communication and a new abundance of information on counterparties mean that buyers and vendors might be more confident about trading without necessarily the financial reassurance that a financial institution could provide. Competition for slices of a shrinking pie is pushing down prices. Simultaneously, regulation is making procurement finance costlier to supply.[34]

Adapting to shifts in demand is not straightforward. The global economy is precariously positioned, with causes for concern in China, the EU, and commodity-based economies. If trust falls, demand for credit guarantees may take off again. Financial institutions must be prepared to respond to rapid changes in the quantity and location of demand. The most lucrative transactions are those in which a financial institution serves both sides. But no cost-efficient financial institution can have a leading presence in every market.

To succeed in this challenging and uncertain environment, financial institutions' procurement finance offerings must be agile, low cost, and valued by customers despite the growing availability and security of alternatives to documentary finance.

Part of the answer lies in the digital transformation unfolding in procurement finance. Digital innovations in the customer interface can create "stickier", more valuable relationships. By automating many laborious paper-based processes and exploiting the wealth of data available to the financial institutions, new solutions can cut costs and expand a financial institution's operational footprint. They do not require more people on the ground. The next generation of trade technologies—electronic bills of lading (eBOLs) and bank payment obligations (BPOs)—may push procurement finance towards the paperless business long envisaged.

If financial institutions do not embrace these digital advances, their challenges will only grow. They are likely to find that tech-savvy upstarts have shunted them out of the lucrative role they have enjoyed for centuries, costing them not only the revenue from procurement finance but the customers that came with it.

Notes

1. Porter, M. E. (2008). *Competitive advantage: Creating and sustaining superior performance*. Simon and Schuster, New York City, NY.
2. Bohdana Sherehiy, B., Karwowski, W., & Layer, J. K. (2007). *A review of organization agility: Concepts, frameworks, and attributes*. International Journal of Industrial Ergonomics 37, 445–460.
3. Bag, S., Anand, N., & Pandey, K. K. (2017). Green Supply Chain Management Model for Sustainable Manufacturing Practices. In *Green Supply Chain Management for Sustainable Business Practice* (pp. 153–189). IGI Global.
4. Sherehiy, B., Karwowski, W., & Layer, J. K. (2007). A review of organization agility: Concepts, frameworks, and attributes. *International Journal of Industrial Ergonomics* 37, 445–460.

   Nicoletti, B. (2017), *Agile Procurement. Volume II: Designing and Implementing a Digital Transformation*, Springer International Publishing, London, UK, ISBN 978-3-319-61085-6.

   Nicoletti, B. (2017), *Agile Procurement. Volume I: Adding Value with Lean Processes*, Springer International Publishing, London, UK. ISBN 978-3-319-61082-5.
5. Williams, T. A., Gruber, D. A., Sutcliffe, K. M., Shepherd, D. A., & Zhao, E. Y. (2017). Organizational response to adversity: fusing crisis management and resilience research streams. *Academy of Management Annals, 11*(2), 733–769.
6. Sherehiy, B., Karwowski, W., Layer, J. K. 2007. A review of organization agility: Concepts, frameworks, and attributes. *International Journal of Industrial Ergonomics*, 37, 445–460.
7. van Someren, M. J. (2016). Influence of supply chain flexibility on slow moving capital products at Philips Healthcare. *Thesis at Eindhoven University of Technology*, Eindhoven, The Netherlands.
8. Duclos, L., Vokurka, R., & Lummus, R. (2003). A conceptual model of supply chain flexibility. *Industrial Management & Data Systems, 103*(6), 446–456.

   Sánchez, A., & Pérez, M. (2005). Supply chain flexibility and firm performance: a conceptual model and empirical study in the automotive industry. *International Journal of Operations & Production Management, 25*(7), 681–700.

   Kumar, V., Fantazy, K., Kumar, U., & Boyle, T. (2006). Implementation and management framework for supply chain flexibility. *Journal of Enterprise Information Management, 19*(3), 303–319.

   Charles, A., Lauras, M., & Van Wassenhove, L. (2010). A model to define and assess the agility of supply chains: building on humanitarian experience. *International Journal of Physical Distribution & Logistics Management, 40*(8/9), 722–741.

Singh, R., & Acharya, P. (2013). Supply chain flexibility: a frame work of research dimensions. *Global Journal of Flexible Systems Management, 14*(3), 157–166.

Das, S., & Abdel-Malek, L. (2003). Modeling the flexibility of order quantities and lead-times in supply chains. *International Journal of Production Economics, 85*(2), 171–181.

9. Singh, R., & Acharya, P. (2013). Supply chain flexibility: a frame work of research dimensions. *Global Journal of Flexible Systems Management, 14*(3), 157–166.
10. Slack, N. (1987). The flexibility of manufacturing systems. *International Journal of Operations & Production Management, 7*(4), 35–45.
11. Beamon, B. (1999). Measuring supply chain performance. *International Journal of Operations & Production Management, 19*(3), 275–292.
12. Beamon, B. (1999). Measuring supply chain performance. *International Journal of Operations & Production Management, 19*(3), 275–292.
13. Goyal, M., & Netessine, S. (2011). Volume flexibility, product flexibility, or both: The role of demand correlation and product substitution. *Manufacturing & service operations management, 13*(2), 180–193.
14. Beamon, B. (1999). Measuring supply chain performance. *International Journal of Operations & Production Management, 19*(3), 275–292.
15. Beamon, B. (1999). Measuring supply chain performance. *International Journal of Operations & Production Management, 19*(3), 275–292.
16. Salvador, F., Rungtusanatham, M., Forza, C., & Trentin, A. (2007). Mix flexibility and volume flexibility in a build-to-order environment: synergies and trade-offs. *International Journal of Operations & Production Management, 27*(11), 1173–1191.
17. Metternich, J., Böllhoff, J., Seifermann, S., & Beck, S. (2013). Volume and mix flexibility evaluation of lean production systems. *Procedia CIRP, 9*, pp. 79–84.
18. Jack, E., & Raturi, A. (2003). Measuring and comparing volume flexibility in the capital products industry. *Production and Operations Management, 12*(4), 480–501.
19. Schütz, P., & Tomasgard, A. (2011). The impact of flexibility on operational supply chain planning. *International Journal of Production Economics, 134*(2), 300–311.
20. Tseng, Y. H., & Lin, C. T. (2011). Enhancing organization agility by deploying agile drivers, capabilities and providers, *Information Science*, 181, 3693–3708.

21. Liao, J., Welsch, H., & Stoica, M. (2003). Organizational absorptive capacity and responsiveness: an empirical investigation of growth-oriented SMEs. *Entrepreneurship Theory and practice*, *28*(1), 63–85.
22. Tseng, Y. H., & Lin, C. T. (2011). Enhancing organization agility by deploying agile drivers, capabilities and providers, *Information Science*, 181, 3693–3708.
23. Garioni, G. (2004), Trade Finance: un caso pratico, *Commercio internazionale*.
24. World Trade Organization (2016). *Trade finance and SMEs. Bridging the gaps i provision.*
25. Lambert, D. M., Stock, J. R., & Ellram, L. M. (1998). *Fundamentals of logistics management.* McGraw-Hill, Irwin, NJ.
26. Blackman, I. D., Holland, C. P. & Westcott, T. (2013), Motorola's global financial Supply Chain strategy, *Supply Chain Management: An International Journal*, 18(2), 132–147.
27. Lambert, D. M., & Cooper, M. C. (2000). Issues in supply chain management. *Industrial marketing management*, *29*(1), 65–83.
28. Report Leadership, 2007. *Guide to Key Performance Indicators.* Communicating *the measures that matter*, PricewaterhouseCoopers.
29. Committee on the Global Financial System (2014). *Trade finance: developments and issues*, Banks for international settlement, Washington, DC.
30. Schmidt-Eisenlohr, T. (2013). *Towards a theory of Trade Finance,* Journal of International Economics 91, 96–112.
31. Desmet, B. (2016). Balancing Cash, Cost, and Service: The supply chain triangle blog.arkieva.com/balancing-cash-cost-service-supply-chain-triangle Accessed 21 March 2018.

    Desmet, B. (2016). The Impact of Strategy on Supply Chain and Forecasting. *Foresight: The International Journal of Applied Forecasting*, (43).

    van Someren, M. J. (2016). *Influence of supply chain flexibility on slow moving capital products at Philips Healthcare.* Thesis at Eindhoven University of Technology, Eindhoven, the Netherlands.
32. VersionOne. (2018). 12th Annual State of Agile Development Survey. Retrieved from explore. versionone.com/state-of-agile/versionone-12th-annual-state-of-agile-report. Accessed 2 June 2018.
33. Nguyen, T., Li, Z. H. O. U., Spiegler, V., Ieromonachou, P., & Lin, Y. (2017). Big data analytics in supply chain management: A state-of-the-art literature review. *Computers & Operations Research.*
34. Hugos, M. H. (2018). *Essentials of supply chain management.* John Wiley & Sons, Hoboken, NJ.

CHAPTER 5

New Solutions for Procurement Finance

Introduction

This chapter presents some new solutions for procurement finance. The applications are presented along the procure-to-pay process, dividing them in:

- Ordering and tendering
  - Portals
  - Marketplace
- Credit and financing
  - Risk management
- Advance payments
- Document preparation and collection
  - Document management

Each section includes relevant examples of these new solutions applied by financial institutions and organizations through the increasingly innovative use of technology. This shows how the future will increasingly be digital.

The final section introduces the concept of integrated platforms where different solutions are integrated into a comprehensive architecture.

B. Nicoletti, *Procurement Finance*,
Palgrave Studies in Financial Services Technology,
https://doi.org/10.1007/978-3-030-02140-5_5

Portals

Procurement finance customers have similar expectations from financial institutions of any other corporate customer: process visibility, risk reduction, credit when needed, and the rapid, low-cost facilitation of transactions.

Financial institutions use digital technology to be user-friendly and cheaper for customers to get their services. An example is provided by the German financial institution's Autobahn platform.[1] It offers customers a large variety of mobile apps for cash flow management, value network management, procurement finance, and more. For procurement finance, best-in-class innovation has come mainly from fintech organizations, active in the value network and receivables financing.[2] They offer customer interfaces that simplify interactions and cut time-to-cash. There are normally larger gaps between fintech organizations and traditional financial institutions.

To keep up with the online era, the necessary and initial steps for the organizations and financial institutions are to have an excellent entry point, labeled as the portal.

Financial institutions should give importance to high-quality digital front ends. These interfaces do more than improving the customer use of the financial services. By acting as gateways for supplying complementary services over and above simple transactions, they can strengthen relationships. This could be a competitive advantage with respect to fintech organizations. Getting the front end right allows financial institutions to be seen as service partners rather than document processors. This helps in justifying their fees in an increasing competitive digital world.

The most forward-looking organizations invest in creating their own corporate website. This step is important both in terms of communication and in terms of innovation and services provided to their customers. Organizations quickly realized that to attract new customers, it was not enough to have a website, but it is also necessary to promote it. The position of their website on the major search engines is the faster and cheap way to be recognized.

As the number of existing websites grew, organizations developed generalist portals. These sites in addition to a search engine offer an aggregate broad-spectrum content and services aimed at their customer community and to their prospects. The web is an unstructured information space. It is not an easy task to exploit such an open environment. Even when a resource meets the initial disclosure requirement, it is very difficult to evaluate its validity and exhaustiveness. The objective should be to develop an online portal that could attract as many users as possible for the longest possible time.

To this end, some of the pioneer financial institutions integrated into a unique site diverse features such as search tools, information and content website, virtual community, and access to advanced services.

The success and wide acceptance of the portal model have led to both enrichment and diversification of the original model. Over time, a distinction has become important between horizontal and vertical portals. A horizontal portal represents the web gateway for users. They are generalist sites, containing pages and links from a variety of topics. They include a search engine. In short, they aim to offer 360° services.

Vertical portals are thematic spaces that represent for the users the front door to a specific function or topic. If compared to horizontal portals, they have the benefit of helping in the search of highly specific and sectoral subjects.

Portals (and now more and more apps on mobiles) are one of the key nodes in the transformation that has characterized the Web over the last few years and has facilitated its diffusion. One of the most important functions of the portals is to support the onboarding process with new customers or with repeating business. The current status of this function in the financial services is not good. Many organizations agree that to create an optimal customer journey is important. Several financial institutions are behind in making it a reality. A survey report shows some facts on the state of the digital customer journey[3]:

- Most financial institutions still do not provide a totally digital account opening process.
- Most institutions do not have an application process that includes an omnichannel function which reports the same data in multiple digital channels.[4]
- Forty-five percent of functional services institutions do not have a structured onboarding process.

Commercial banks lag beyond retail banks, even if it is important to create a better experience for small and medium-sized enterprise (SME) banking (especially micro organizations) due to their importance to the financial institutions' well-being. This is important since most financial institutions do not offer to this valuable segment any value-added services despite a proven record that these customers are willing to pay for value.

Some recommendations for the portal design and implementation are important[5]:

- take the customers' viewpoint
  - pre-fill in advance as many as possible fields
  - enable a save and resume functionality from data entered through other channels (omnichannel approach)[6]
  - offer a personal touch and especially a satisfactory customer journey
- streamline the processes to increase effectiveness, efficiency, and cut errors
  - integrate without disruption
  - reap the benefits of straight-through processing (STP)[7]
- build in third-party integration capabilities and take into account the ecosystems around the financial institutions and its corporate customers[8]
- make the experience consistent for the customer wherever and on whichever device they do business
- continuously improve the customer experience and journey

Lloyds Bank[9]

Lloyds Bank is a British bank with presence in several countries. The international markets are growing, and, as a consequence, the opportunities of supporting organizations' procurement are growing.

The access to new international markets is not easy for any company, but especially for SMEs. It is important to know to deal with the difficulties and risks of these foreign markets:

- Difficulties:
  - understanding of the new international environment;
  - understanding the new market;
  - analyzing the factors that influence the new area's needs;
- Risks
  - economic and political risks;
  - currency risks in selling and procuring within an international trade;
  - risks in ensuring that the products are the ones expected, in the right quantity, and quality.

(*continued*)

(continued)

Lloyds Bank has introduced new solutions able to overcome these difficulties and mitigate these risks. They provide to its corporate customers' ease of access to new markets and hence new opportunities of trading and growth. Lloyds Bank's International Trade Portals (ITP) provides access to these functionalities. It is an online platform, which allows accessing information on foreign markets and opportunities of business, useful to expand into new international markets. The ITP is able to provide comprehensive information about a determined country and how to start penetrating and dealing in it. It lists also potential trading partners.

This online platform also provides information on the regulations of a determined country, tariffs, cost of shipment, and customs supporting the trading. It is able to change the global market in favor of the Lloyd Bank customers since it allows them detecting some of the most international profitable opportunities.

The offers of ITP for an organization are:

- complete information about foreign countries supporting the choice of the correct market;
- information about customs, regulations, cost of shipment to a determined country, and what is necessary to be fully compliant with local regulations;
- support in the search for the more profitable opportunities of trading in the international trade;
- access to trade events related to the bank customers' specific sector;
- access to international trading tenders in real time;
- availability of calculators for computing the cost of import, the currency conversion, and the export modes to optimize the shipment costs;
- support in establishing relationships with partners, thanks to the presence in the databases of thousands of buyers and vendors contacts.

Vietnam Ministry of Finance and the World Bank[10]
Some emerging countries have started to use trade portals as a means to facilitate access to trade intelligence on global markets. Vietnam has launched VTIP (Vietnam Trade Information Portal). Through VTIP, SMEs have the possibility to obtain information about imports, exports and market, and trends through one portal. This portal contributes to the improvement of the visibility and forecasting for trade transactions and to a fast access to Vietnam trade rules comprising all national regulations.

VTIP is characterized by several elements:

- an overview of national economies;
- information about exports and imports;
- information about particular economic areas;
- information about international or regional trade agreements which affect the country;
- information on cross-border trade transactions.

This portal is a tool able to provide sufficient and necessary trade information through a better and rapid accessibility to stimulate exports and imports transactions.

PrimeRevenue[11]
PrimeRevenue delivers a multi-funder value network financing platform as part of an integrated source-to-pay process. With this solution, by combining relationship, transactions, and financial data, the organizations can integrate procurement and finance. This solution provides the insights and visibility buyers and vendors need to optimize their relationships and cash flows. In an internal survey, PrimeRevenue found that 90 percent of vendors associated with a PrimeRevenue program have accepted term extensions in the last 12 months, up from 78 percent during the 3 years prior.[12]

In connecting the Ariba Network to PrimeRevenue, SAP Ariba can provide a single, easy-to-use interface through which buyers and

(*continued*)

(continued)

vendors can collaborate, in a seamless way, on several aspects from purchase orders and invoices to discounts and value network financing.

The connection of this cloud-based solution to SAP Ariba's business network can revolutionize financial value network management by providing an innovative way for organizations around the world to optimize working capital, to manage liquidity, and strengthen the organization's' procurement finance.

Using the platform, buyers can use payables from balance sheet liabilities as strategic organization assets. Vendors can cut their financing costs and improve their working capital and liquidity management.

Health iQ[13]

Health iQ was founded in 2011. This British company provides healthcare analytics to the pharmaceutical industry.

Health iQ has a large blue-chip customer base, which means they deal with payment terms of up to 100 days after the invoice. The customers can use MarketInvoice to bring cash forward for the research and development of new products. This online platform provides quick and easy access to funding, and the integration with the other application Xero makes managing invoices simple. Health iQ customers can spend less time on financial administration and more time coming up with new ideas to revolutionize the pharmaceutical industry.

The UK's MarketInvoice operates in the peer-to-peer lending space by enabling organizations to raise money from institutional investors and high net worth individuals by selling outstanding invoices.

DFCC Bank PLCC[14]

DFCC Bank is a commercial bank in Sri Lanka.[15] Its solution DFCC iConnect includes a fully integrated financial supply chain management (FSCM) system, virtual accounts (VA), and a state-of-the-art mobile application with fingerprint recognition capabilities for payment authorizations. The FSCM solution provides customers with a procurement finance platform where their dealers and vendors receive an end-to-end financing solution along with a straight-through processing (STP) solution for invoice settlement. The key benefits are the enablement of channel financing while shortening the time to market. Customers can identify their payers automatically without issuing a reference code through virtual accounts. In this way, they have full visibility of their current transactions.

Marketplace

Regarding the volatile and constant changes related to financial services, procurement has an increasing relevant role in developing innovative solutions. These solutions refer to an organization model and to processes to provide services. From the latter perspective, procurement finance has developed also external and internal online marketplaces able to increase strongly the productivity of these services.[16]

The marketplace is the place where the exchanges are made. Through the increasing use of the Internet technology, it has developed its own virtual dimension, called e-marketplace.[17] The latter refers to an intermediated place that favors the meeting between supply and demand of products and services. This is possible thanks to an infrastructure developed on the web that allows market actors interact with information and data exchanges.[18]

The e-marketplace makes available virtual spaces. They are able to increase the market liquidity and to cut the costs of the transactions aggregating in the same virtual space both buyers and vendors. It allows an easy search of vendors and buyers. In this way, it guarantees a visibility on prices and the integrity of the transactions.

E-marketplaces are very popular in Customer to Business (C2B) and Customer to Customer (C2C) context. They are expanding also in Business to Business (B2B). Amazon Business has expanded in Europe, Japan, and India. Many regions of the world have been served by large industrial marketplace in the last decades; some examples are Alibaba, Global Sources, TradeIndia, IndiaMART, DHGate, and HAIZOL, among others.[19] According to the market data and research portal Statista, B2B e-commerce revenue in 2017 was 6.5 trillion euros, triple that of B2C e-commerce revenue. In a survey of 400 B2B decision-makers in Europe and the USA, Salesforce CloudCraze found that 89 percent expect e-commerce to be a key growth driver in B2B. The survey found that for the first time, nearly half (48 percent) of B2B businesses are selling their full line of products online. All these refer to the B2B e-commerce.[20] They are the ideal platform to develop also procurement finance supports.

E-marketplaces provide vendors the opportunity to showcase their products and services and to distribute their offers to market operators. Buyers can use advanced search engines to find specific vendors, to select products, and to view the offers of participating actors in the marketplace. They can spread their requests quickly to a wide range of potential vendors.

From the point of view of the vendors, participating in a e-marketplace extends the ability to find new customers and partners, to capitalize on investments already made on the web through their own site. From the operational point of view, e-marketplaces allow limiting travels and the need of physical encounters with vendors and customers, and reducing acquisition costs.

Fintech organizations are active in setting up e-marketplaces. The fintech segment is characterized by strong vivacity and agility, able to act in several directions creating new markets and business. It is able to overcome the inefficiency and lacks from the financial system. It becomes instrumental to the economy growth through the development of new and often global marketplaces, capable of supporting the matching of demand and supply of capital, investments, and financing in a more effective, efficient, and economical way.

Regarding the fintech evolution, the marketplace lending represents an alternative financing channel compared to the one represented by the traditional financial institutions. In the marketplace, organizations can be funded also directly by a multitude of investors. The encounter between finance demand and supply is on an online platform. Although it is unlikely that marketplace lending be a major threat to the operations and profitability of the financial institution's system, it has the potential for stimulating traditional intermediaries to review their business models and to set up alternative financing sources for the organizations.

E-marketplace lending increases the degree of competition in the financial sector, contributing to cut the costs of brokerage, with positive effects on the economic growth.

LiquidX Inc[21]

LiquidX Inc manages an international marketplace for the liquidity. The assets of procurement finance have been developing but the market does not yet have a global platform. LiquidX Inc can provide a solution. It is a platform of digital exchange, through which the different buyers, that is, single actors, financial institutions, and other non-financial institutions, can exchange assets of procurement finance. These assets include letters of credit, receivables, and payables.[22]

The platform is based on an auction method. This leads to higher visibility in the marketplace regarding the financial activities and make possible increasingly competitive pricing. The platform allows gathering liquidity from different providers, and the participants can exchange risks and they can invest in financial activities. LiquidX Inc acts as an additional source of financing with respect to the traditional financial institutions. These different providers from the traditional financial institutions have a huge amount of capital that they can invest.

Both buyers and vendors can obtain benefits from this platform. The buyers consider the marketplace as the most efficient way to achieve the activities of procurement finance. The vendors see the marketplace as a strategic choice for sourcing the liquidity and for managing risks.

The membership in LiquidX Inc is free. This marketplace can present itself as the cheapest provider of capital.

The benefits of this global marketplace for liquidity are:

- high visibility that improves the execution of orders and creates trust on price, improving the savings;
- opportunity for corporate treasurers to access different financial institutions, through a unique portal;
- diversified presence of buyers, making the financing more flexible;
- contacts with a large number of providers of liquidity on a valid online platform;
- lowering the counterparty risks not being tied to a single financial institution;
- lower time of implementation and fast transaction execution;

(*continued*)

(continued)

- competitive pricing;
- improved ease of use for trading actors;
- higher efficiency through the standardization;
- lower legal costs thanks to a single agreement on financial assets.

The innovative concept of this online platform is based on the possibility to enter, through one account, in the international network of trading. It provides the opportunity to choose the entire solution or only a specific component, relevant to the customer's objectives.

Risk Management

Risk management is the identification, assessment, and prioritization of risks (defined in ISO 31000 as "the effect of uncertainty on objectives, whether positive or negative") followed by coordinated and economical application of resources to minimize, monitor, and control the probability and/or impact of unfortunate events or to maximize the realization of opportunities.[23] Risk management can also be defined as the continuous process of identifying, analyzing, evaluating, and managing exposures to loss and controlling risk and financial resources to minimize the negative effects of a loss.[24]

The concepts of risk and risk management are becoming more important. To compete, grow, and gain competitive advantages, organizations need to take risks. The market and credit risks existed since the trade was born. Now, the risks are more complex due to the globalization, the economic crisis, the development of new solutions, and supply markets in high turbulence and volatility.

On the other side, the organization's protection from the risks in the procurement is still very low. There is a lack of structured capacity to manage procurement risks. Most organizations either do not have a risk management function or it is within their finance organizations. That is not enough.

The new business models are all based on the "risk-based thinking". The ISO itself guides the organizations to structure according to "risk-based thinking", that is, to adopt all the criteria that allow proper risk management appropriate to the context.[25]

Every risk leads to a positive and/or negative effect. For this reason, risks management's objective is to identify the related opportunities by defining a strategy and understanding in advance how to respond to these events or at least to remediate to them.

In the procurement processes, it is convenient to determine the amount of time and resources to implement and to use in each of the processes. If the process is less complex and it involves only a few stakeholders, risk management can help in reaching a successful implementation, reducing costs and delays. If the project is complex and involves many different shareholders, risk management is crucial to avoid losses and possible gain benefits from it.

Risk Management in Procurement Finance

The procurement finance risks are several[26]:

- buyer or vendor default;
- demand volatility;
- exchange and interest rates;
- availability of finance and the connected problems of cash flow and liquidity;
- payment assurance;
- payment execution and performance;
- fraud and errors.

These risks matter, since they can affect[27]:

- the competitiveness, financial health, and survival of the trading parties;
- the overall stability of the local, regional, and global value network;
- the support for the value networks especially in emerging markets.

Due to the development and growth of the financial trade, the needs of better control on the procurement transactions are necessary. In trading, it is important to know how to manage the risks of losses since, in this actual volatile and dynamic context, it is possible that not always the expectations are met.

The finance sector has made massive investments in ICT resources and technologies. Risk management solutions are among the most important areas of investment. The management of the risks is critical in coping with the uncertainties of the reference market.[28]

In the current digital transformation, also finance is using more Big Data analytics for collecting, organizing, and analyzing large datasets. The objective is to find out the patterns, trends, data correlations, and other useful information for supporting risk management, to comply with regulatory standards, and to increase the internal efficiency and economics. The continuous monitoring of transaction data and the actions for detecting suspicious anomalies in payment transactions can support the compliance processes of the financial institutions. It supports anti-money laundering and the detection of other unlawful acts. The new solutions support efficiently and economically real-time internal communication flow analysis. In this way, they also help to prevent fraudulent behavior from inside the organization. They can cut the risks and costs of insolvency and litigations.

Using Big Data with the transaction data, it is possible to change the risk management approach. Traditionally, risk management is based on collecting input data, like financial data of the potential lenders and quantitative data, like inventories or sales. Collecting the transaction data in Big Data repositories, it is possible to perform creditworthiness analysis using performance data and predictive risk management. This is particularly useful for evaluating creditworthiness of SMEs.[29]

Especially in the forex market, risk management is a very useful methodology since, in this market, it is necessary to take into account the volatility of the environment while at the same time to maximize margins by trying to cut the risk of losses.

Despite the unpredictable and unplanned accidental losses, there are methods involved in risk management that can detect the likelihood of risk events. More predictable is an event, the lower the risk since it can be removed, insured, or mitigated. Regarding the predictability, the use of technology can improve and make the control on the anomalies of the transactions more effective and efficient.

Financial institutions have historically gained access to their customers' data and have pursued a tradition of analytical innovation in areas such as fraud prevention and risk management. Innovative digital organizations have adopted a non-traditional approach to data analysis by redefining the number of sources available to create new market trends. In this sense, the challenge for financial institutions consists of a change of mentality that from the possession of proprietary data can come to a more open approach to a broader analysis of the customers.

In the current economic climate, organizations are required to operate based on their strategic choices on quality and real-time information. This approach can keep their current and prospective exposure under control from different types of risks. In all areas, efficient measurement and management of risks are elements that differentiate the organizations which aim to excel or at least to survive in an increasingly competitive environment. This applies in particular to the finance sector. Here, the financial crisis has shown the need to adopt a more advanced approach in assessing key risk indicators such as liquidity risks, market risks, and counterparty risks, and the possible presence of anomalies in the transactions and potential frauds.

Having a fraud prevention system in such a competitive market should not be considered a cost but an investment for the profitability of the organization. Reducing administrative costs for manual revision of orders and the ability to cut reload procedures can provide to the own market a competitive boost in operational timing and in saving time.[30] This allows organizations to concentrate on the business of looking for new vendors or selling/acquiring new customers.

In risk management, it is necessary to take into account the reconciliation of security, privacy requirements with the opening to customers, and flow rates.

DBS Bank Ltd.[31]

Due to the development and growth of the financial trade, there is the need for a better control on the trade transactions. Some solutions are able to improve and to make more efficient the control of the anomalies of the transactions. The traditional control on the trade transactions is done in a manual way. This requires a long time and a low efficiency due to the possible human errors or fraud. The use of new data management solutions (Big Data and analytics) allows the Singapore DBS Bank to improve its risk management processes through an innovative program called Trade Alerts. It is a solid platform to discover anomalies in the transactions. The innovative feature of this program is its focus not on the single transaction with the customers but on the trends of trade transactions. Big Data allows managing the general transactional trends. It ensures DBS Bank to handle them, to cut anomalies, and to manage the risks in a highly efficient way.

SIA and INFORM[32]
Financial institutions around the world are reporting an increase in the number of fraud in payments where cash is not used. The current systems for fraud prevention are often unable to react quickly to new mechanisms of fraud. Furthermore, the criterion used by the systems is rarely able to classify one transaction as too risky, rejecting it.

The collaboration between SIA, an Italian company active in digital payments, and INFORM, a German company which deals with risk management and fraud prevention, has led to an innovative solution called RiskShield. This is a software solution for fraud prevention and risk assessment for financial institutions, payment systems, and insurance organizations.

It uses a fuzzy logic (the best mathematical model for the representation of human experience). It offers to the experts the ability to power the system by entering rules of fraud prevention in natural language in a way through which these rules of fraud prevention can be easily defined and included in the system.

The real-time authorization system of payment service providers receives the transaction request and can submit it to the RiskShield server for one risk assessment. RiskShield responds to these requests in a few milliseconds. This solution offers the possibility to react in a fast way to fraud cases providing alerts in real time with some important information.

RiskShield provides to the operators, subject to fraud in their transactions, sophisticated tools of forecasting analysis able to provide detailed and useful information about financial transactions, possible fraud situations, and specific trends. This is possible through intuitive interfaces that allow observing and analyzing visually all the data.

Swift[33]
Swift is the acronym for "Society for Worldwide Interbank Financial Telecommunication". It is an international organization dealing with financial messaging services.

Swift has launched a real-time payment monitoring service designed to integrate and strengthen anti-fraud controls already

(*continued*)

(continued)
used by its customers. The new computer fraud and cybercrime service enables Swift customers to analyze payment messages according to their own parameters. It supports the timely identification of errors before their transmission. Customers can integrate the service directly into their Swift messaging streams. This enables a significant improvement in messaging monitoring activity. It allows fast detection of abnormal payment schemes. This solution improves the overall ability to prevent fraudulent transfer requests. Customers have the ability to define messages and analyze parameters based on their risk and compliance policies, as well as deciding whether to allow centralized message control or specific access verifications.

Thomson Reuters[34]
Thomson Reuters Corporation is a Canadian multinational mass media and information organization. The company was founded in Toronto, Ontario, where it is headquartered.[35] Thomson Reuters announced the introduction of a solution called TRAC to fight money laundering and fraud in trading. It was initially launched in Singapore and Hong Kong. The solution aims to tackle these threats to ensure an efficient and transparent procurement finance.

Through the promotion of an open network which conforms to the procurement finance, TRAC is able to ensure more visibility and a better business behavior. Being an end-to-end solution, it counteracts risks at all trade stages, from pre-trade to post-trade.

Risk Management Approach and Tools

There are different types of risks requiring an improved risk management.

- Market risk:
  - Risk of losses in positions arising from movements in the market prices or the economy in general. These risks can be identified and cut through a process of dialogue with selected groups in the economy, or in the value network, and in potential vendors of new solutions.

- Risk of turbulence due to unforeseen circumstances: for instance, another innovative product is introduced in the market, impacting on the success of its planned product. The risks of turbulence can be identified using conversational methods and brainstorming.

- Credit risk is the risk of default on a debt that may arise from a lender failing to make required payments.
- Liquidity risks are related to the budget or liquidity. They can be prevented through a prior analysis and calculation of internal costs, revision, and evaluation mechanisms to identify the availability of capital, cost, volatility, and potential surplus.
- Operational risks:
  - Financial risks.
  - Organizational and corporate risks involve a failure at an organizational level. They can be identified, reduced, and mitigated with a comprehensive support and consideration of all stakeholders.
  - Technological risk occurs when technical standards blocked the innovative idea because it is not feasible. Technological risks can be identified through careful selection of the vendors who must comply with high standards, must have a high reputation, and also must be supported by appropriate insurance schemes.[36]

Focusing too much on reducing the risks or their negative consequences leads to missing some other opportunities. This is a key factor for the procurement improvement.

The ISO 31000 general framework classifies the main phases of risk management, including communication and consultation placed opposite monitoring and assessment.[37] This is the basis for recognizing and responding to risks. The objective of this process is to find and select these threats and opportunities that have an impact and a likeliness to occur.

Figure 5.1 shows how to identify risks and apply risk management also in procurement finance.[38] The identification of risks must be repeated continuously during the end-to-end cycle of the procurement. This is true especially when transitioning to new solutions and vendors in a new phase of the organization when the risks occur or when the time progresses. The risk management tool allows organizations to identify risks and administer ownership, mitigation plans, and risk management strategies.

It is also important to include a description of the risk management procedures and of the responsibilities and mitigation plans for certain types of risks in a contract with the vendors or an insurance.

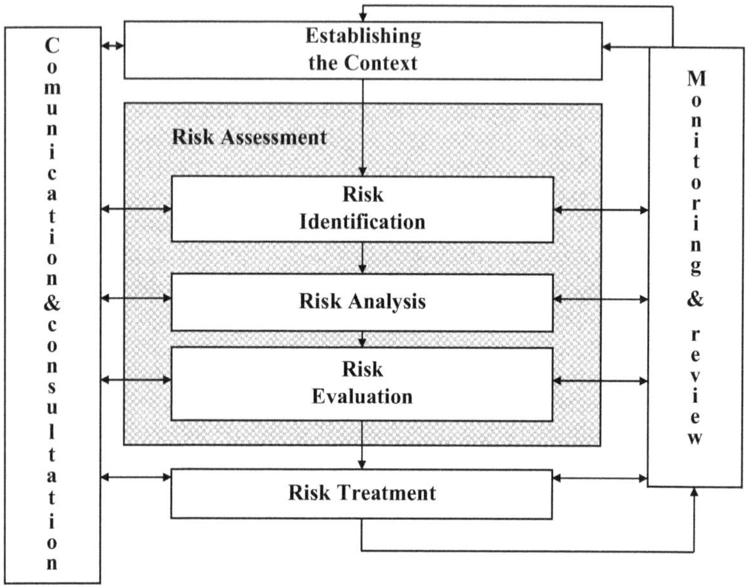

Fig. 5.1 Risk management processes

Risk management is a systematic process that consists of five well-defined phases.[39] To manage the risks, it is important to manage a crucial and important process for all the procurement stages. To conduct it optimally, it is requested to take many decisions directed towards success.[40]

- Risk identification: the buyer in charge to develop a procurement strategy should identify risks and issues for each market segment for a longer period rather than by initiatives in terms of potential impact on the objectives. Sources of risks can be divided into four categories: strategic/corporate, program, project, and operations. Once risks are identified, they must be registered in a detailed document identifying and evaluating the level of the risks in the key phases of the strategic procurement process. In this way, it is possible to have a general picture of the risks for the organization and their connection with the vendors most critical and connected with the organization.
- Risk assessment: the main objective is to identify the probability of occurring of the risks and assessing their potential impact and its frequency. The risk is evaluated also in terms of impacts and costs. This requires setting up an organization process to identify critical supply

categories and segmenting classified vendors based on their criticality for the business continuity. It is necessary to understand if the value network is sufficiently dynamic, if the organization has developed flexible operations, and if it has selected a diversified vendor portfolio with wide visibility. It is important to understand who the partners are from an operational risk and financial risk point of view and finally what are their third-party vendors and counterparts. If the organization depends only on a critical product (for instance, raw materials) from a single vendor, it may result in a competitive disadvantage. Finally, it is needed to understand how to identify, evaluate, and measure risks.

- Risk monitoring: it should be a continuous process passing through the following steps—risk identification number, risk owner, description of the risk, results of assessment and date of assessment, mitigating actions (what is the organization doing to reduce the impact or probability of the risks), and dates when the risks will be reviewed. This also leads to clarifying the roles and the responsibilities in the risk management. It is necessary to develop innovative ways to monitor risks and implement procedures and tools to cut the risk; to monitor the various categories of vendors and the different geographic and cultural aspects; to use external data sources for continuous monitoring of supply markets, the financial situation of vendors, and so on; to collaborate with selected critical vendors, agreeing and creating "alarm systems" for the prevention of risks; and to implement and monitor actions on the planning process to determine which monitoring activities are put in place to ensure that the risks are managed and that they follow appropriate actions as a risk assessment. Risk management processes must be consistent with the entire organization and must be linked with all other important business processes.
- Control is the next step. It includes the understanding on how to control the risks. It is important to find ways to mitigate the risks. This implies to develop a process to measure the impact of accidents, continually improve risk management procedures, and involve the entire organization in case of accidents with mitigation plans (determining who makes and who decides). It is useful to develop mitigation plans, especially for critical vendors. The degree of the control depends on the type of the risk. More in detail a risk can be tolerated if it is very low and the cost of taking an action maybe be higher than its potential benefits, so it will be just monitored. Otherwise, the risks can be treated to reduce their potential damages and probability of occurrences. The last solution under the risk's control is the option to trans-

fer it to a third party (for instance, an insurance company). Instead, if the level of risk is very high, it is necessary to review the entire approach. Sometimes, it is also necessary to stop the initiative when there is no chance to mitigate the risk to an acceptable level. When controlling risks at the management stage, cooperation and dialogue between the buyer and the vendor are important. There is the need to integrate risk management practices in all business functions to ensure their understanding, commitment, and alignment. It is necessary to define the roles and responsibilities to manage the risk internally or externally and to have the resources to verify the emerging trends, the progress, and the results obtained. This data collection and reports on sufficient data to identify effective supply risk management strategies needed to outline potential future scenarios. In addition, appropriate analytical tools must be provided to identify, measure, and monitor operational risks and to get improved risk management solutions. It is important to improve the resilience of the organization.[41]

- Risk occurrence. When risks do occur, it is important to manage them:
  - pay attention to the vendors' risk and price volatility when managing the relevant procurement strategies for the different product categories;
  - integrate risk management initiatives with the strategic procurement process (e.g., vendors' rating);
  - collaborate with the vendors to quickly detect risks and neutralize risk-related problems before they turn into "accidents".

The risks should not be measured case by case. There is a need for a structured risk management capacity within the procurement organization. Procurement professionals have to put in place decisions and actions in order not only for the organization to compete but specially to survive. It is necessary to develop also in the procurement area a structured management of the formal and substantial risks. This means creating a sufficient visibility on the problems of the performance of the vendors and the risks of procurement. This is the basis of a wider collaboration with vendors.

This topic is important, wide, and delicate. The following paragraphs present some of the potential actions to deal in a more structured and rational way the risk related to the procurement. The best practices for the management of the procurement risks are to follow international and well-proven standards.[42] The indications that come from the new ISO standards are certainly of extreme importance. Management systems have passed over time from the concept of corrective actions to preventive actions. The concept of preventive actions also becomes obsolete. Risk management allows a complete and structured analysis of all the risks of an organization, and the procurement sectors will certainly have to make its contribution.

Thus, it is important to manage the risk in the procurement, become aware of it, and begin to consider it an important part in the procurement management and of the whole value network, to be managed in an increasingly rational and structured way.

Advance Payment Solutions

The payment systems represent an integral and important part of the procurement finance. In the digital era, the payments are made mainly through ICT systems. They can assure the effectiveness and also the efficiency of international payments.

The payment currency, used in the international transactions, can generate an exchange rate risk, due to the need to use a currency other than that used in its own country. This situation brings the risk of collecting a cash amount in the domestic currency lower than expected or having to pay a sum higher than initially expected. To mitigate this risk, there are innovative solutions in the so-called foreign exchange (FX or forex) market. The markets are more and more global. They are in a substantial change mode. This brings the expansion of the forex market online and the diffusion of the online currency trade.

The development of the technology brings new solutions: the interconnection, the cashless activity, the real-time transactions, and the virtual portfolios. It is not only possible to purchase online. There is the opportunity to use global virtual currencies with virtual and real-time transactions all over the world. The continual growth in digital payments globally offers financial institutions the opportunity to provide better and advanced services to their customers, while organizations benefit from a more efficient procurement finance.

The money transfer services allow organizations to send and receive money at any time and in almost real time to/from anywhere. It is changing in line with the technology evolution, the mobile diffusion, and the constant research of innovative solutions and interfaces increasingly user-friendly, immediate, and with real-time efficiency. These solutions support the immediate transferability of money without the manual intervention of intermediate actors, as in the case of cryptocurrencies.

The concept of mobile transactions has developed over time. The transformation and evolution of payments have been a long-term strategy for many financial institutions. The priorities are now the integration of new channels (mobile, voices, and so on) on both payment transaction applications, the reduction of the complexity, the elimination of redundancies, the improvement of efficiency, and especially the reduction of the transaction costs. There are new factors of change such as new digital technologies, new business models, and new non-traditional operators. They force both financial institutions and technology providers to introduce new solutions, such as mobile networks, cloud, and peer-to-peer networks. This supports solutions that can cut costs and save time. Some of the challenges are security and scalability.

The transformation of payment systems by financial technology providers and financial institutions means new opportunities, platform opening, and concerted efforts to make payments simpler for developers and customers. The interface with the vendors, the customers, and the financial institutions is assured by data feed done via open application programming interfaces (APIs).[43] APIs are becoming a key element in the new solutions because they bring an integration and information exchange component that makes faster access while ensuring scalability, security, and flexibility of the application platforms.

EBS BrokerTec[44]

EBS BrokerTec provides services related to procurement finance. It is improving the rapidity of foreign exchange (FX) data management through its solution EBS Live Ultra. The key feature of this solution is its capability to provide to customer data within the forex market in real time. EBS Live Ultra provides feed of the data within a very short interval of five milliseconds. This rapidity is increasingly necessary for the volatile forex market.[45]

This solution allows markets to become more transparent, thus improving the efficiency in the trade transactions of customers and their liquidity. It is important that the actors of procurement participate in this new platform to improve data, creating constant benefits for the global market. To stimulate the participation, the intervals of publication are very short, represented by 20 milliseconds. In this way, it is possible to encourage actors to give their contributions to improve the overall market.[46]

Bank Payment Obligation (BPO)

The growth of international trade relations leads to a corresponding increase in international payments. In this context, the market requires faster, more efficient, and secure solutions. One of the solutions is the BPO (bank payment obligation). It is able to mix the benefits of the letter of credit and those of the open-account method.

The bank payment obligation constitutes an irrevocable undertaking of a financial institution (normally the financial institution of the buyer) in favor of the financial institution of the vendor to pay for the supply at sight or to pay at maturity. The payment is subject to the digital comparison of trade data between the financial institutions via a so-called transaction matching applications (TMA), such as Swift TSU.

On the TSU, the conditions (in the form of data transmitted via Swift's inter-financial institution messaging system) are specified, and the issuing financial institution will pay to the beneficiary financial institution.[47] The BPO provides the same benefits of a letter of credit in a digital way operating exclusively by exchanging of data via TSU platform. In this way, it allows substantial cost saving and the optimization of working capital.

The vendor will provide the required data for the payment of the BPO to its financial institution. The latter will through the TSU do the matching between the required data and those provided. When the requested data and the data provided by the beneficiary financial institution are equal, the financial institution may proceed with the collection of the BPO. Therefore, the bank payment obligation allows a near-complete dematerialization of the inter-financial institution information flows. In this way, it allows savings in terms of cost and time. The use of the BPO allows the direct delivery of the representative documents of the products from the vendor to the buyer, without intermediate passes, simply following the notice that the recipient financial institution sends to the vendor to inform him/her of the matching and subsequent collection of the BPO.

The instrument allows faster and more cost-effective payments, related to international trade transactions. It allows making easier and more secure the provision of export or import financing. It enables lenders to provide faster financing for business flows, in a simplified way. It allows significantly reducing of risks associated to the financing of open-account transactions.

With the BPO, the financial institutions are in a position to offer an enriched payment instrument that meets the demands of their customers in the open-account space. The BPO uses digital data matching to facilitate payments between the buyer's financial institution and the vendor's financial institution. It is quicker and normally cheaper for organizations than the letters of credit (partly because of a shorter credit utilization period). It also avoids the settlement risk of open-account trading.

The BPO is seen in the market as an alternative tool for price regulation, risk mitigation, and financing requirements for traders and financial institutions involved in international procurement operations.

The BPO supports and improves procurement finance tools, through the transition from paper presentations of the documents, with the need to analyze them, to their digital presentations with automatic data control. The BPO management process is essentially paperless. The result is a less complex. It involves cheaper payment systems, which cuts the payout cycle time.

The BPO does not intend to replace the existing settlement systems. It supports the current offers, allowing financial institutions to be more involved in the open-account methods.

The BPO provides several benefits[48]:

- improving the financing opportunities of financial institutions;
- reducing the inefficiencies of documentary trade products and open-account mixing the benefits of both;
- optimizing the working capital and the liquidity of the customer organizations:
- setting up procurement finance programs much faster and strengthening core relationships;
- improving the settlement processes, being traditionally expensive and slow;
- working on data and not on documents, thus allowing the reduction of discrepancies;
- allowing possible risk sharing among multiple financial institutions because more BPOs can be issued for the same operations;
- achieving lower operating costs with respect to a letter of credit thanks to the simplification and digitization of the end-to-end processes;
- meeting the market requirement for financial institutions to collaborate more on risk and customer onboarding;
- getting steady source of commissions and fees income;
- implementing a prudent use of the capital.

The bank payment obligation (BPO) has not been invented only as a useful instrument for procurement finance. It allows the collaboration among financial institutions developing new standards able to increase the procurement finance market size and to provide a complete range of services to corporate customers. It allows the optimization of working capital, reduction of operational risks, and the provision of liquidity.[49]

There are obstacles to a wider adoption of the BPOs. The parties on either side of the transaction must be BPO enabled. The installation and management of this capability are expensive. It requires an overhaul of well-integrated and long-standing processes and systems. The trade-off between cost and security presented by BPO does not suit all trading partners. Some prefer the greater security of the letters of credits. Others favor the lower cost of open-account trading.

With BPO, financial institutions face the adoption costs of developing new governance, marketing, systems, risk management, and operational expertise. BPO could cut financial institutions' transactional complexity and costs. There is also the fear that BPOs could cannibalize their fee-rich letter of credit business. As with the new Swift message MT798, these obstacles limit the possibility of a network effect. As long as the uptake is low, organizations and financial institutions have little incentive in adopting the BPO. This creates a vicious cycle.

Despite these obstacles, BPO has some strong advocates. BPO-secured transactions open doors to vendor receivables financing and foreign exchange transactions. Both of them are impossible with open-account trading. By taking the leap and adopting BPOs, financial institutions make worthwhile for other market participants to follow suit. If financial institutions can devise effective cross-selling and pricing strategies, BPO could significantly increase revenue instead of reducing them. To reach a significant role in the market, the financial institutions need to educate their customers about BPO and its applications and benefits.

BNP Paribas[50]

The French BNP Paribas was the first European bank to book a live BPO transaction in April 2014. This operation was a starting point for more recurring streams of BPO transactions. BNP Paribas has been closely involved in the BPO exercise and supported the initiative from the beginning. With the BPO, BNP Paribas offers flexible risk mitigation and financing services to all its corporate customers across their value network. Speed and flexibility are important challenges for every organization in every sector. BNP Paribas was also the first European bank to implement SwiftNet Trade connectivity for Corporates (MT798) in February 2010.

Cash Flow

Forex (FX) is the market where all currencies of the world are exchanged in every moment at a price determined by the market, called over-the-counter.[51] In a global trade, the FX exposure is referred to risks related to the changes in exchange rates that cause negative effects on the financial operations.

The future cash flow of an organization is influenced by these exchange rates changes. It is necessary for the organizations having the trust on data in a unique system, carrying them in a unique format, to foresee precisely the cash flow exposures and to soften their risks. Through using innovative technology, the exchanges in the FX markets can occur in a fully digital way.

Rim Tec[52]

The American fintech organization Rim Tec has launched a cloud-based product called FireApp for cash flow management. This cloud computing solution can transform the financial institutions because currently they spend a substantial amount of money to be compliant with the global regulations. In this sector, fintech organizations have been able to reduce the problems of compliance, to cut costs, and to increase competition.[53]

FireApps for cash flow allow the organization to handle the financial institution's forecasting of cash flows in an efficient way guaranteeing rapidity and better visibility. It calculates the actions of hedging, creating more trust in them. In this way, it allows better management of the foreign exchange (FX) exposure.

The innovative feature that allows these new financial products to differentiate from the traditional foreseeing instruments is that they are not based on certain steps in the forecasting of cash flow. They focus on the complete end-to-end process.[54] In this way, these new instruments can benefit the management of the cash flow risks at lower costs, higher efficiency, and higher precise predictability.

CitiBank: CitiFX Gateway[55]

When organizations have business relations across many countries, they have to exchange foreign currencies with their local currency when it comes to debts and credits. Foreign currencies present the risk that the exchange rate can change unfavorably before the currency exchange has taken place. Forex hedging is able to protect organizations from this risk.

CitiBank is a large operator with multinational organizations. Its digital solutions for the foreign exchange (FX) market are several. CitiFX Pulse is one of the most important. This digital platform allows customers to take into account what is happening in the market. CitiFX Pulse, along with an innovative solution called CitiFX Gateway relative to FX exposures, allows its customers to completely digitize the handling of FX risks.

CitiFX Gateway uses an API technology. This solution is an interface for data feeding of other applications and also of other financial institutions with the complete compatibility, to manage risks flexibly and economically.[56] In this way, the platform facilitates an online sharing of a range of information, such as the execution of trade transactions and the confirmation of orders.

Due to CitiBank global franchising, this new solution provides worldwide coverage to any of its customers. API technology elaborates every hedging requests sent to CitiBank, by automatically executing and sending them to CitiBank's local branches.

This solution allows keeping the hedging process both granulated in all the countries where customers are localized and, at the same time, integrated.

TD Securities[57]

The American fintech TD Securities aims to satisfying the requirements of customers through the provision of an overall vision of the market on the basis of fixed income and FX trading. To do it, it has developed an application called Valuation Services. This solution is a cross-asset platform able to act in FX market providing market analysis in real time. It is managed by multiple vendor systems, in a way through

(*continued*)

(continued)

which customers can obtain a full vision of the market thanks to the aggregation of different information. Being an overall vision, this platform allows customers to handle their risks in a more efficient way.

This solution focuses on the collaboration of teams and, at the same time, competition among them reaching a constant development of innovative ideas and a faster time to market.

Swift GPI[58]

Most of the international transactions are made through Swift channel, as transfers of money, confirmation of operations of exchange, and payments collection. This channel does not manage accounts of customers or it does not hold financing because it is only a communication network. The transfers of information are very fast in every part of the world compared to other channels of transmission. At present, financial institutions cannot monitor the position of their accounts in real time, since they do not have access to the infra-day reporting.

Swift launched Swift GPI (global payment innovation) to support cross-border payments. This solution starts from the need of financial institutions to have information on their real-time liquidity to manage in a better way funds during the operating day.

This solution aims to increase the speed, visibility, and end-to-end traceability of cross-border payments. The traceability service is in the cloud. It is based on a global database hosted by Swift. The initial phase aimed to help financial institutions address the challenges in monitoring and managing the international accounts. They are important to cross-border payment.

Tracker GPI[59]

Swift has a tracker service that allows traceability of cross-border payments in real time. Tracker is a key element of Swift's GPI initiative, which is revolutionizing cross-border payments by combining real-time payments monitoring with the speed and certainty of the availability of financing in international payments.

(continued)

(continued)

Swift GPI enables active international trading organizations to receive payment for services or delivery of products in a timely manner. It allows to speed up the entire value network. The GPI Tracker service allows business treasurers to have end-to-end and real-time visibility of their payments and to receive a confirmation when they are credited to the beneficiary's account. The service provides a more accurate reconciliation of payments and invoices. It optimizes liquidity management by improving cash forecasts. It cuts exposure to FX risk with the guarantee of funds accreditation on the same day, following the time zone of the beneficiary area. The Tracker is available through an open API. In this way, it can be used to interface any financial institution system. It helps to ensure the maximum spread of GPI benefits with a higher adoption speed. For this reason, this Swift solution has gained wide acceptance by the financial institutions' sector globally.

In addition, Swift is working on a distributed ledger technology (DLT), included in the GPI initiative. It can be used by financial institutions to improve the reconciliation of their real-time correspondence abroad accounts with the aim of optimizing liquidity management, lowering costs, and reducing operational risks.

Cambridge Global Payments[60]

The American Cambridge Global Payments launched a solution called Cambridge Link Mobile App. It allows customers managing their procurement necessities and FX payments through their own mobile phone directly.

This application has been designed for those Cambridge customers that sustain FX operations and have the necessity to have rapid access on mobile platforms. The customers have the possibility to:

- access to information on market trends in real time;
- facilitate trade and payments needs (for instance, notification of the requirements of payments on the basis of specific jurisdiction) through simple interface on mobile phones, simplifying the processing of the transactions;
- focus on their business growth while the platform deals with the payments.

Global Corporate Payments: The Corporate Procurement Cards

Working capital is an important tool for every type of organizations since positive results are necessary to ensure the correct and constant running of the organization's operations. Some credit card companies have solutions to allow the customer organizations, whether they are vendors or buyers, to obtain a substantial improvement in the flow of working capital over the entire value network, and consequently improve their profitability.[61]

This close collaboration between the financial institutions and their customers allows them to fully understand their credit and debt situation and to devise customized and effective solutions that add value to the organization.

A procurement or purchasing card (P-Card) is a type of commercial card that allows organizations to benefit from the existing credit card infrastructure to make electronic payments for a variety of organization expenses (for instance, products and services). Normally, a P-Card is a charge card, similar to a consumer credit card. However, the card-using organization must pay the card issuer in full each month, at a minimum. Some card companies offer P-Cards which can work as a full credit card. In some countries, the benefit of these cards is that the credit amount is not considered by central banks to evaluate the creditworthiness of the organizations using them. P-Cards are not necessarily plastic cards. They can also take the form of non-plastic virtual account numbers.

Variations of P-Cards are the following, where each one is intended to address different types of purchases and/or spend categories[62]:

- Ghost Card/Ghost Account: a card account that an end-user organization issues to a specific vendor or vendor type and the vendor processes all of the organization's purchases to the account, functions like a P-Card.
- Corporate Card: commonly used by organizations for employee travel and living (T&L) expenses, also referred to as a Travel Card.
- One Card: a single charge card that combines procurement with T&L and, in some cases, fleet charges.
- Fleet Card: a card product used by organizations to pay for fuel, maintenance, repair, and related expenses on company vehicles.
- Prepaid Card: debit-based card, allowing the user to pay now versus later, as the card transaction amounts are deducted from a funded account, for example, a Payroll Card "loaded" with an employee's earned wages.

- Declining Balance Card: a card that typically does not require a pre-funded account; a spending limit and/or expiration date is established up front, giving it a specific "shelf life" to accommodate a specific project budget or spend allowance, for example, a Project Card.
- Business Card: a credit card targeted for smaller organizations, commonly used for a variety of expense types (for instance, products services, travel, and so on). The customer organization may be allowed to carry a balance.
- Electronic Payables: a type of electronic payment, generally involving a vendor invoice (may be electronic or paper) and end-user approval process. It is followed by a "behind-the-scenes" payment to the vendor through the card network. These solutions are also known as electronic accounts payable, automated payables, e-payables, push payments, straight-through payments, buyer-initiated payments, single-use accounts, and electronic invoice presentment and payment.
- Convenience Checks: a payment instrument with characteristics resembling those of a common checking account, but they settle against a P-Card account.

V-Payments[63]

V-Payment is a digital platform that generates virtual card accounts for each payment order, without issuing a physical card. This virtual card account is equivalent to a credit card and can be used as a payment method in all American Express-approved shops. Implementing the solution simplifies the payment process by increasing the levels of efficiency, visibility, and control in managing the organization's expenses, related to business travel, but also of business costs, such as telephony, purchase of office supplies, and similar expenses.

V-Payment can provide detailed data related to the transaction itself with additional fields (e.g., reference numbers to cost centers).

V-Payment is available in two versions: On Demand and Integrated.

In the On Demand version, access to the V-Payment tool for generating virtual card accounts is via an American Express webpage

(*continued*)

(continued)
where authorized users must authenticate by entering user ID and password. This mode allows immediate operation on the payment platform. It does not require any special technical prerequisite.

In the integrated mode, the virtual V-Payment account can be generated directly in the organization operating process, making it the standard payment method. The integration is based on the most common data exchange formats (XML, Excel, csv, and so on) and allows the automatism of the payment method and the related reconciliation.

The benefits are:

- control: flexibility in defining the maximum amount and validity date of each transaction, both in single and recurring mode;
- security: virtual card accounts generated by the platform secure all transactions, especially in online transactions thanks to the default settings;
- reconciliation: availability of some additional fields that allow enriching the data related to the transaction to facilitate punctual and automated reconciliation;
- working capital: cash flow optimization through a maximum extension of up to 28 days and definition of the payment cycle according to specific needs.

V-Payment supports the elimination of manual processes to obtain different types of information.

It supports in resolving discrepancies within an order and online reporting. It takes care of ensuring compliance with the organization's policies. V-Payments allow comparison of the actual purchase data with contracted prices as per the framework agreement, based on the various levels of disclosure. It is therefore important to produce reports on the impact of the organization in terms of emissions harmful to the environment, to support the preparation of the social report.

To assure an easier compliance with regulations, a tax reporting has been introduced that uses updated and constantly available data. To improve the internal audit and control processes, American Express places considerable emphasis on monitoring the movements of working capital, as well as cost items at the cost centers of the organization.

Thanks to the accuracy and the expense details of V-Payments, it is possible to improve the bargaining power with vendors.

Document Management

Dematerialization of Documents

In procurement, the financial processes are almost all paperwork requiring high costs and low flexibility. The introduction of new solutions for managing paper documents and making them digital brings flexibility, agility, and lower costs. In this way, it is possible to provide solutions to two important challenges. On the one hand, it is possible to streamline and transform processes that regulate business transactions and dynamics between the organizations and third parties, be them vendors or customers. On the other hand, the inclusion, possibly fluid and automatic, of document content in the Big Data repositories is useful.

Document management systems were born to respond to the proliferation of documents and to improve in the efficiency of processes using paper documents. The objective is to simplify the automatic handling of large volumes of documents and the digitization of large quantities of paper that are still produced. The underlying idea is to convert to digital to manage in a better way document-heavy processes.

The specific objectives are[64]:

- digitizing paper documents;
- acquiring and classifying a large number of documents;
- searching and correlating data in different documents.

Document digitization does not transform documents, but processes. First, it is necessary to evaluate solutions taking into account the need of the customers which are now at the center of the digital transformation. Second, it is necessary to re-engineer the processes, in the light of the new needs and technologies.

The content and its processes are managed with an architecture capable of centralizing all kinds of information and providing visibility and accessibility to the operators, both inside and outside the organization, and to all other systems that produce or deliver content as portals, mobile apps, and outsourcing services, without creating closed silos.

Digitizing documents requires scanning the paper and archiving it. It consists also on the creation of a true digital culture in information management. The process requires storing and structuring the information in databases. It is necessary to manage information no longer through static document support, but with structured data streams.

The components of the document management processes are[65]:

- monitor the location of sensitive documents and their status;
- simplify and digitize the accesses, from workstations and mobile devices, to all archived documents to optimize their search and avoid the loss of important data;
- deliver real-time data and graphics on the document, printer, device usage, and user behavior that interact with them. In addition, the system, through algorithms, advocates how to improve machine efficiency and cut time and cost of the process management;
- provide access to sensitive data only to the authorized users and monitor their use, preventing loss or un-authorized access of relevant data.

Past attempts at moving to paperless in procurement have gained little traction. The main obstacle is the variety of participants in the process. Financial institutions and large organizations have the scale to benefit from investing in digital technology. Small traders and some logistics organizations, especially those in emerging markets, do not have the scale to invest in complex document management systems. Government agencies have the required scale. They often lack the incentives to improve efficiency or simply get the funds to do them.

End-to-end paperless procurement is thus unlikely to happen anytime soon. Nevertheless, all the actors involved in procurement finance can gain most of the benefit by going paperless internally, creating a digital ring fence around their operations. In this way, organizations incur the effort and costs of handling paper only at points of entry and exit.

Procurement finance is subject to several regulations, such as know-your-customer and anti-money-laundering policies, and trade embargoes. Such regulations are becoming more comprehensive and changing dynamically over time. They are also more strictly policed, exposing financial institutions to the risk of reputational damage and fines. From 2007 to 2014, fines imposed on the US and European financial organizations grew from USD 30 million to USD 58 billion.[66] A Boston Consulting Group (BCG) survey suggests that compliance accounts for up to 25 percent of servicing capacity. This percentage would increase without digital automation.[67] Effective compliance is thus a key driver of performance together with the reduction of the operational burden of managing paper documents.

The filtering technology that most financial institutions rely on today produces a high rate of false positives, increasing the need for manual checking and overrides. Basic solutions, which scan documents for blacklisted keywords, often fail to account for context. Artificial intelligence and Big Data can make filtering more effective. For example, Thomson Reuters World-Check uses both technologies to build profiles and identify high-risk entities before they are officially blacklisted. As a result, false positives have decreased by as much as 50 percent.[68]

The inflexibility of the traditional ICT architectures prevents financial institutions from realizing the full value of such tools. Significant effort and expense are required when adapting solutions to minor policy adjustments, let alone adopting the modern business intelligence technology. To keep up with policy and technological change, financial institutions must invest in scalable platforms. They must set up teams dedicated to maintaining and fine-tuning the Big Data that feeds those platforms. They must take actions on emerging technologies that promise profound transformations of procurement finance processes.

Using advanced document management systems, financial institutions can increase their revenues from procurement finance by ten percent and more. At the same time, they can cut operational and compliance costs by 15–25 percent if they embrace digital technology in procurement finance.[69]

Procurement is a sector of financial services that strongly requires advanced solution. The reason is based on the errors caused by paper-based procedures.

Optical Character Recognition (OCR)

It is important to consider the use of optical character recognition and machine learning in document management. Standard optical character Recognition (OCR) recognizes text in documents. It allows users to input data copying and pasting content into back-end fields. Although valuable, this provides no drastic change in efficiency.

Intelligent OCR solutions learn to recognize document templates and automatically transfer paper-based text and handwritten content into back-end fields. Some financial institutions are already using this technology, but it needs fine-tuning. CitiBank evaluated this intelligent OCR technology. They found that it could increase productivity in operationally intensive tasks by as much as 50 percent.[70] It also cuts the operational and compliance risks that arise from tracking activities on paper.

New Solutions

Under the pressure of the changes and thanks to the availability of new technologies, there are other solutions to support document management in procurement finance.[71] An example in this direction is provided by some new implementations in Swift messaging.

MT798, the so-called trade envelope, is a standardized Swift messaging protocol for direct-to-financial institution origination from within a customer's enterprise resource planning system.[72] MT798 for letters of credit and demand guarantees are supported on Swift's FIN and FileAct.[73] These solutions reduce process complexity and allow organizations to use the services from multiple financial institutions with ease.

MT798 cuts financial institutions' costs and increases their access to new customers. By eliminating the need for local financial institutions, it allows big players to sweep market share with limited investments. Some financial institutions fear that MT798 could undermine the stickiness of procurement finance business. MT798 works on multiple platforms. It reduces dependence on financial institution channels and might thereby reduce customers' willingness to pay for them. Rather than promoting MT798, some financial institutions are waiting to assess corporate demand. As long as many financial institutions do not offer MT798, however, organizations will have little use for it. This is a vicious circle which must be broken to accelerate its current rate of adoption. To be fair, more standardization in MT798 and less free formats would help in spreading its use thanks to the increased benefits in handling the messages.

CitiBank[74]

CitiBank sees real potential in the Swift message MT798.[75] It enables easier, faster, and more cost-effective adoption of digital-based solutions for procurement financing. The MT798 allows corporations to efficiently and affordably access the global Swift network. It presents a useful step ahead in the evolution of procurement finance. The wider context of international commerce, including customs clearance and logistics, is still heavily paper-driven. The demand from the corporate side for advanced technology-enabled models has not yet reached a tipping point. This is partly due to legacy practices and partly because the market does not have full visibility on the economics of such a transition.

The idea of the electronic bills of lading (eBOLs) has been around since the 1980s.[76] Now good functional solutions are available. These digital document platforms aim to lead the journey towards paperless trade by transferring shipping documents instantly between parties. The solution can be extended to the many other documents supporting procurement transactions.

By accelerating the transfer and presentation of documents, eBOLs shorten the payment cycle and thereby improve the working capital position of the vendors. Digitized documentation is cheaper to process, more traceable, and more secure. Financial institutions also benefit from the integration of eBOLs with Swift and proprietary financial institution platforms.[77]

The adoption of eBOLs is still limited by some obstacles. Many participants in the procurement ecosystem are, for reasons of size or lack of sophistication, unlikely to invest in the technology. As long as the adoption is limited to universal, financial institutions have little to gain by investing in it.

Wave BL[78]

Wave BL, backed by Barclays Accelerator, focuses on enabling the exchange of bills of lading across a decentralized ledger to decrease costs and risks. Wave BL focuses on integrating its product in one part of the value network process, seeking to take the place of traditional bills of lading (BOLs). Carriers issue these documents. They include details about a shipment, generally the type of product, quantity, and destination, and give the title of the property to a certain party.

Wave BL primarily deals with organizations that have finished products that need to be transported internationally, and they in turn hand over BOLs to vendors.

The vendors, once they receive the bill of lading, add the invoice, the certificates that go along the value network, put it all in an envelope and bring it to the local financial institution. The financial institution checks it, approves it, and sends it to the recipient. They check all the documents and trigger the receipt. When the recipient's financial institution receives the BOL, payments are triggered to the vendor and products are released.

Standard Chartered[79]

Paperless trade documents bring more flexibility and reduction of time and costs. The financial institutions can obtain significant benefits in reaching a complete internal digitization of their transactions as a digital scope that delimits them. In this way, financial institutions handle the paper issues only regarding the entry and the exit of the operations without dealing with these issues inside the processes, saving in terms of costs and efforts.

To reach this objective, Standard Chartered introduced the concept of standard OCR (optical character recognition). OCR is used by several international financial institutions. Through OCR, they can recognize the content of the procurement documents allowing conversion of a printed text into a format that can be easily edited and stored in a computer. This is a useful step. It is not sufficient to reach a substantial improvement in terms of efficiency.

Standard Chartered improved this approach through a new solution: intelligent OCR. This solution is able to recognize the models of the documents and to extrapolate precisely the important data. It then transfers the paper content, in an automatic way, in a back-end area.[80] In this way, the level of precision and visibility in the trade documents is increasingly enhanced.

Skuchain[81]

Skuchain is active in the digitization of procurement finance. It did the first procurement finance transaction on the blockchain. It involved Wells Fargo, Commonwealth Bank of Australia, and Brighann Cotton. That transaction supported the shipment of a bale of cotton from Texas, USA, to China.

Skuchain continued to work with financial institutions. They found that when it comes to procurement, financial institutions are only service providers. The party that really drives the transaction is the anchor buyer. Buyers' major pain point is the tracking and tracing of products as they move through the value network. While they seek that extra visibility, vendors consider this digitization as an additional cost without benefits.

(*continued*)

(continued)

Skuchain offers a solution for procurement finance and, in particular, inventory financing. Vendors taking on financing through the receivable can have substantial costs. They can purchase the inventory outright and get it financed from the buyer's cost of capital. The vendor gets an immediate working capital relief. The buyer gets a lower cost of products. Skuchain owns a subsidiary called IMT, which stands for Inventory Management and Trading Services. It is a special purpose vehicle (SPV).[82] The fund enables the procurement finance transactions of the type described. IMT directly purchases inventory from the vendor and holds that inventory for as long as the buyer needs it. When the vendor is ready to actually use that inventory, IMT sells it back to it.

The vendor gets paid immediately and the buyer is able to hold the inventory off their books for as long as possible. Most importantly, the vendor avoids paying the high-interest rates of receivable financing (8–15 percent depending on the cases, 30+ percent in emerging countries), so the products come out cheaper.

A blockchain solution supports these transactions. While third-party financiers would be hesitant to underwrite offline transactions, with this solution, they can see the clear chain of title attested to on the blockchain, from vendor to Skuchain to the buyer. They can see the payment guarantee from the buyer. Those two elements combined are sufficient for third-party financiers to consider this transaction virtually de-risked. In this way, they are willing to provide financing of the buyer's cost of capital. What the vendor was paying before in receivable financing becomes a financial gain. Skuchain takes a platform fee, dynamically priced based on the specific terms of each individual transaction.

Traydstream[83]

Artificial intelligence (AI) can play a pivotal role in procurement finance right from the first interaction when determining what coverage is best to ongoing customer service. Customers have started expecting personalized solutions from insurers. AI makes that pos-

(continued)

(continued)
sible by automatically understanding a customer profile and providing recommendations for only insurance products that are relevant for that customer and that would be the best for them based on set criteria. Chatbots that work with messaging apps are being used in the industry to resolve claims and answer simple questions.

Traydstream launched a software solution, with its same name, able to facilitate global transactions in an intelligent way and to make them more secure at a global level. It is a cloud computing platform. It converts the procurement paper documents into digital documents. It is able to extrapolate data in an efficient and intelligent way. It allows making documents valid with respect to several different trade regulations and compliance. It does that by automating the screening through AI solutions. The experts of financial institutions checking documents using this solution and process can cut this checking work from hours to minutes.

The innovative feature of this solution is that it deals with documents. It controls them in a detailed way against the several international regulations. In most financial institutions, this work is done manually. It takes a long time. The solution allows controlling in a fast way all procurement data about several different problems. It is a tool which not only reduces time but also improves accuracy. To convert procurement paper documents into digital documents, the solution uses intelligent OCR able to realize information from paper formats.

Integrated Platforms

This chapter analyzes several potential solutions in support of procurement finance. It is important prior to their implementation to have a clear view of the business architecture that the organization intends to adopt. This requires to analyze in depth how to consolidate and integrate the different applications and processes and how to evolve them into an integrated standardized platform supported by simplified processes. At the same time, it is also necessary to take into account the selection and education of the people involved, including the partner vendors or buyers.[84] In synthetic terms, it is necessary to act in a consistent way on the four Ps: platform, processes, people, and partners.

In terms of development over time of the solutions presented, CEB Tower Group defines three levels of platform convergence for a financial institution[85]:

- First level: the integration of front- and back-end procurement finance applications. The first level is the traditional procurement finance system. It has the following characteristics:
  - integrated corporate front-end and financial institution user back-end
  - support letters of credits, collections, standbys, and guarantees
  - enable workflow and simple document management
  - integrated credit and financing, including syndications
- Second level: the integration of trade and value network finance on a single system.
  - a single system with capabilities to support traditional trade and value network finance transactions
  - delivers factoring and forfeiting, shipment financing, BPO, and open-account financing
- Third level: the integration of trade and value network finance with treasury management.
  - integrated cash forecasting
  - liquidity and working capital management
  - seamless payments
  - ERP integration

What is distinctive of the new solutions is that they can integrate better methods for collaboration into the organization's processes. They can prevent an organization from regressing to its previous, less effective methods. Developing a balanced plan for supply and demand, for instance, requires input from multiple business functions. Without digital technology, those business functions would likely have submitted information to the sales and operations planning (S&OP) teams and left them to resolve any conflict. The latest digital S&OP platforms come with a standard planning process. It compels every business function to contribute to the planning exercise in a coordinated manner. As organizations prepare to transform their procurement finance with digital technologies, they need to envision the business and technical capabilities they want and plan to develop those capabilities at the same time.

Conclusions

In today's increasingly complex global economy, where financial institutions are risk-adverse, getting financing is hard. The financial institutions have the responsibility to provide new solutions to benefit their customers.

The quality of demand is becoming more careful over time thanks to the simplification and digitization of documents and processes, to industrial digitization and logistics, and to new technological potential to renew the services offered or to improve product and process control. This transformation occurs in particular through the use of portals, risk management tools, advance payment systems, document management, and countless utilities related to security.

In a global ecosystem, the development of international trade relations leads, as consequence, to the increase of international trade payments that need to be handled in a more agile, secure, and fast way. This context has to be managed in line with the wider digital transformation impact. An interesting development is the need for collaboration between financial institutions and fintech organizations. The fast development of the latter is allowing the birth of a new ecosystem that replaces the traditional one according to digital rules related to the accessibility, speed, and use of data analytics and sharing.

In the international market, using of new solutions with the possibility to exploit Big Data and analytics and the simplification and digitization of procurement documents allow to have a more transparent and secure procurement finance. Innovative actors enter in the market, new tools spread with disruptive impacts on processes and services, business models change pervasively, reaching the idea according to which digital is revolutionizing completely the financial sector.

The financial institutions need to deal increasingly with the requests of secure and integrated services for the digital transactions. They are stimulated to intensify the research and use of new solutions.

Regarding the payment market, the financial institutions are still considered as relevant liquidity providers. They are also valuable sources of information and advice on currency issues, where they can apply ever-changing restrictions. To do this and to keep up with the new digital era and competitive context, financial institutions are investing increasingly in new solutions and payments management. The technological trends underlying these financial institutions decisions are to be found in mobile payments and real-time payments. The financial institutions' world is called to master the digital transformation by opening to innovation and using tools for the simplification and digitization of processes, a more conscious and valuable asset management of internal and external data, to advanced transactional systems. The innovations in progress and those still on the horizon lead financial institutional actors to change their way of operating in the market.

The advances in new solutions are very rapid. An efficient commercial ecosystem, in terms of innovation, is increasingly necessary. It is useful to understand if the innovations are able to improve the transactions processing from an end-to-end perspective. Over the next few years, it will be essential to realize that the new instruments based on the platforms will be the basis of an intense competition. It is important to integrate them in a consolidated vision.

Once taken the digital path, the transformation is continuous and progressive. New solutions continue to develop, and the opportunity to create innovative services continues to expand in an increasingly global ecosystem.

Notes

1. Claessens, S., Glaessner, T. C., & Klingebiel, D. (2002). *E-finance in emerging markets: is leapfrogging possible?*. Blackwell Pub, Hobokien, NJ.
2. Nicoletti, B. (2017). *The Future of FinTech: Integrating Finance and Technology in Financial Services*. Springer.
3. Digital Banking Report. *2017 Retail Banking Trends and Predictions*. December 2016. Accessed 31 March 2018.
4. Nicoletti, B. (2014), *Mobile Banking: Evolution or Revolution*, Palgrave Macmillan, Houndsmill, UK (also translated in Chinese).
5. www.finextra.com/surveys/thankyou.aspx?surveyguid=ab766e49-17ce-4157-a462-073a95f1e712. Accessed 31 March 2018.
6. Mirsch, T., Lehrer, C. & Jung, R. (2016). Channel Integration Towards Omnichannel Management: A Literature Review. *20th Pacific Asia Conference on Information Systems (PACIS)*, Chiayi, Taiwan.
7. Yang, T., Guo, W., & Hou, H. Y. (2014). Review of Straight Through Processing (Stp) In Financial Services. *Journal of Investigative Medicine*, 62(8), S114–S115.
8. Dapp, T., & Slomka, L. (2015). Fintech reloaded–Traditional banks as digital ecosystems. *Publication of the German original*.

   Nicoletti, B. (2017). The Future: Financial Services as Platforms. In *The Future of FinTech* (pp. 261–274). Palgrave Macmillan, Cham, Switzerland.

9. resources.lloydsbank.com/international-trade-portal/, Accessed 12 February 2018.
10. www.worldbank.org/en/news/press-release/2017/07/12/vietnam-ministry-of-finance-world-bank-launch-trade-portal-to-improve-ease-of-doing-business, Accessed 12 February 2018.
11. www.businesswire.com/news/home/20160406005078/en/SAP-Ariba-Teams-PrimeRevenue-Transform-Financial-Supply, Accessed 26 December 2017.
12. www.prnewswire.com/news-releases/primerevenue-finds-90-percent-of-suppliers-agree-to-term-extensions-when-offered-supply-chain-finance-300688691.html. Accessed 01 August 2018.
13. www.crunchbase.com/ Accessed 12 February 2018.
14. www.thesundayleader.lk/2018/06/07/dfcc-iconnect-cutting-edge-payments-and-cash-management-solution/, Accessed 7 June 2018.
15. www.dfcc.lk/en/. Accessed 28 July 2018.
16. Neef, D. (2001). *E-procurement: From strategy to implementation.* FT Press, London, UK.
17. Turban, E., Outland, J., King, D., Lee, J. K., Liang, T. P., & Turban, D. C. (2018). Business-to-Business E-Commerce. In *Electronic Commerce 2018* (pp. 123–166). Springer, Cham, Switzerland.
18. Ramachandran, L. L., Sebastian, M. P., & Pillai, R. R. (2018). Harnessing the Digital Marketplace in India: Revolutionary Growth, Challenges and Opportunities. *Digital Marketplaces Unleashed*, 839–853. Springer, Berlin, Germany.
19. Wilber, L. (2018) Industry Marketplace surge. *Compass*, 13.
20. www.statista.com/statistics/261245/b2c-e-commerce-sales-worldwide/. Accessed 22 August 2018.
21. liquidx.com/, Accessed 12 February 2018.
22. liquidx.com/marketplace-in-action/ Accessed 27 December 2017.
23. supplychaininsights.com/sciwiki/index.php/Risk_Management. Accessed 31 March 2018.
    Hubbard, D. (2009). *The Failure of Risk Management: Why It's Broken and How to Fix It.* John Wiley & Sons, Hoboken, NJ.
24. Hallikas, J., Karvonen, I., Pulkkinen, U., Virolainen, V. M., & Tuominen, M. (2004). Risk management processes in supplier networks. *International Journal of Production Economics, 90*(1), 47–58.
25. Sæstad, M. (2017). *Risk-Based Thinking in Quality Management, an ISO 9001: 2015 Requirement: A case study to identify underlying elements enabling risk-based thinking in organizations* Master's thesis, Universitetet i Agder, Agder, Norway.
26. www.abe-eba.eu/media/azure/production/1546/mapping-the-supply-chain-processes-and-finding-the-opportunities.pdf, Accessed 28 December 2017.

27. www.abe-eba.eu/media/azure/production/1546/mapping-the-supply-chain-processes-and-finding-the-opportunities.pdf, Accessed 28 December 2017.
28. Zsidisin, G. A., Panelli, A., & Upton, R. (2000). Purchasing organization involvement in risk assessments, contingency plans, and risk management: an exploratory study. *Supply Chain Management: An International Journal*, *5*(4), 187–198.
29. Berger, A. N., & Udell, G. F. (2003). Small business and debt finance. In *Handbook of entrepreneurship research* (pp. 299–328). Springer, Boston, MA.
30. Dean, J. (2014). *Big data, data mining, and machine learning: value creation for business leaders and practitioners.* John Wiley & Sons, Hoboken, NJ.
31. www.enterpriseinnovation.net/article/dbs-adopts-big-data-analytics-cut-trade-anomalies-545131553, Accessed 12 February 2018.
32. www.riskshield.com/en/news/page/sia-and-inform-sign-agreement-to-fight-frauds-on-digital-payments, Accessed 12 February 2018.
33. www.swift.com/news-events/press-releases/swift-announces-new-payment-controls-service-to-bolster-customers_fraud-and-cyber-crime-controls, Accessed 12 February 2018.
34. www.thomsonreuters.com/en/press-releases/2016/october/thomson-reuters-launches-trac-to-combat-trade-based-money-laundering.html, Accessed 12 February 2018.
35. www.thomsonreuters.com/en.html. Accessed 03 August 2018.
36. Rejda, G. E. (2011). *Principles of risk management and insurance.* Pearson Education India, Bengaluru, India.
37. www.iso.org/iso-31000-risk-management.html, Accessed 3 July 2018.
38. International Organization for Standardization. (2009). *ISO 31000: Risk Management: Principles and Guidelines.* ISO, Geneva, Switzerland.
39. www.procurementjourney.scot/risk-management-process Accessed 03 February 2018.
40. Haimes, Y. Y. (2015). *Risk modeling, assessment, and management.* John Wiley & Sons, Hoboken, NJ.
41. Nicoletti, B. (2016), Resilience and Outsourcing, *PMWORLD*, 2, 16.
42. ec.europa.eu/invest-in-research/pdf/download_en/risk_management.pdf. Accessed 31 March 2018.
www.pwc.nl/nl/assets/documents/pwc-supplier-relationship-management.pdf. Accessed 31 March 2018.
43. Dig, D., & Johnson, R. (2006). How do APIs evolve? A story of refactoring. *Journal of software maintenance and evolution: Research and Practice*, *18*(2), 83–107.
44. https://www.nexmarkets.com/products-and-services/data-and-analytics/ebs-live-ultra. Accessed 20 August 2018.

45. The Innovators, *Trade Finance*. June 2017. www.gtb.unicredit.eu/sites/default/files/awards/the-innovators-2017-trade-finance-1493310922.pdf. Accessed 29 June 2018.
46. newsroom.nex.com/news/01022017/ebs-live-ultra-to-provide-data-at-5ms-intervals?ref=Home
47. www.ciosummits.com/B2B_Payments_Supply_Chain_Finance_E-invoicing_Market_Guide_2015.pdf., Accessed 28 December 2017.
48. Jančíková, E. (2014). Bank Payment Obligation–New Challenge For Supply Chain Finance. *Financie A Riziko 2014 Časť 2*, *2*, 107.
49. fci.nl/about-factoring/the-bank-payment-obligation-bpo-a-new-start-for-supply-chain-finance.pdf
50. www.swift.com/sites/default/files/resources/swift_corporates_trade_market_adoption_201607.pdf, Accessed 31 March 2018.
51. Harvey, C. R., & Huang, R. D. (1991). Volatility in the foreign currency futures market. *The Review of Financial Studies*, *4*(3), 543–569.
52. www.fireapps.com/products/cash-flow/, Accessed 12 February 2018.
53. www.Fireapps.com, Accessed 12 February 2018.
54. The Innovators, *Trade Finance*. June 2017. www.gtb.unicredit.eu/sites/default/files/awards/the-innovators-2017-trade-finance-1493310922.pdf. Accessed 29 June 2018.
55. www.gfmag.com/topics/global-banking/the-need-for-speed, Accessed 12 February 2018.
56. Thoman, P., Dichev, K., Heller, T., Iakymchuk, R., Aguilar, X., Hasanov, K., & Fahringer, T. (2018). A taxonomy of task-based parallel programming technologies for high-performance computing. *The Journal of Supercomputing*, *74*(4), 1422–1434.
57. www.tdsecurities.com/tds/content/IB_ProductsServices?language=en_CA, Accessed 8 July 2018.
58. www2.swift.com/uhbonline/books/public/en_uk/s_cert_app_gpi_lbl_crtria_2018/con_690826483.htm. Accessed 8 July 2018.
59. www.swift.com/our-solutions/global-financial-messaging/payments-cash-management/swift-gpi/swift-gpi-for-banks/features. Accessed 8 July 2018.
60. clearbridgemobile.com/cambridge-global-payments-mobile-app-launch/. Accessed 12 February 2018.
61. www.theprocurement.it/dalla-redazione/soluzioni-per-il-capitale-circolante-american-express/. Accessed 17 February 2018.
62. https://www.napcp.org/page/WhatArePCards. Accessed 20 August 2018.
63. business.americanexpress.com/it/vpayment. Accessed 18 February 2018.
64. Nicoletti, B., in Lupi C. (2008): Processi aziendali e documenti: tra flessibilità ed esigenze di controllo, *Sistemi & Automazione*, N. 3, Mar. 2008, pp. 8–17.

65. Nicoletti, B., (2014), Lean e-procurement, *EPCC 2014*, Lisbon, Portugal.
66. https://www.cnbc.com/2015/04/30/7-years-on-from-crisis-150-billion-in-bank-fines-and-penalties.html. Accessed 21 August 2018.
67. www.bcg.com/publications/2016/digital-revolution-trade-finance.aspx, Accessed 31 March 2018.
68. financial.thomsonreuters.com/content/dam/openweb/documents/pdf/governance-risk-compliance/fact-sheet/world-check-risk-screening-fact-sheet.pdf, Accessed 31 March 2018.
69. www.bcg.com/publications/2016/digital-revolution-trade-finance.aspx. Accessed 31 March 2018.
70. www.bcg.com/publications/2016/digital-revolution-trade-finance.aspx, Accessed 31 March 2018.
71. Dab, S., Ramachandran, S., Chandna, R., Hanspal, R., Grealish, A., & Peeters, M. (2016). Digital Revolution in Trade Finance, www.bcg.com/publications/2016/digital-revolution-trade-finance.aspx, Accessed 12 June 2018.
72. An enterprise resource planning (ERP) is defined as the ability to deliver an integrated suite of business applications. ERP applications share a common process and data model, covering broad and deep operational and management end-to-end processes, such as those found in finance, HR, distribution, manufacturing, service all along the value network of the organization. Leon, A. (2014). *Enterprise resource planning*. McGraw-Hill Education, New York, NY.
73. financial.thomsonreuters.com/content/dam/openweb/documents/pdf/governance-risk-compliance/fact-sheet/world-check-risk-screening-fact-sheet.pdf, Accessed 31 March 2018.
74. financial.thomsonreuters.com/content/dam/openweb/documents/pdf/governance-risk-compliance/fact-sheet/world-check-risk-screening-fact-sheet.pdf, Accessed 31 March 2018.
75. www.swift.com/our-solutions/corporates/drive-trade-digitisation/mt-798. Accessed 08 July 2018.
76. https://www.ukpandi.com/fileadmin/uploads/uk-pi/Documents/2017/Legal_Briefing_e_bill_of_Lading_WEB.pdf. Accessed 21 August 2018.
77. Ho, T. (2016). *Bills of lading in international trade and the actual, potential and perceived pitfalls associated therewith-an analysis from an international trade law perspective focusing particularly on the United Kingdom jurisdiction* Doctoral dissertation, University of Southern Queensland, Toowoomba, Queensland, Australia.
78. Rizzo, P. (2015), Wave Brings Blockchain Trade Finance Trial to Barclays, www.coindesk.com/wave-blockchain-trade-finance-barclays/, Accessed 26 December 2017.

79. www.bcg.com/publications/2016/digital-revolution-trade-finance.aspx. Accessed 12 February 2018.
80. The Innovators, *Trade Finance*. June 2017. www.gtb.unicredit.eu/sites/default/files/awards/the-innovators-2017-trade-finance-1493310922.pdf. Accessed 29 June 2018.
81. Besnainou, J. (2017), Blockchain and Supply Chain Financing: A Conversation with Skuchain, www.cleantech.com/blockchain-and-supply-chain-financing-a-conversation-with-skuchain/, Accessed 26 December 2017.
82. www.investopedia.com/terms/s/spv.asp. Accessed 08 July 2018.
83. traydstream.com/. Accessed 12 February 2018.
84. Carillo, K. D. A., Galy, N., Guthrie, C., & Vanhems, A. (2018). How to turn managers into data-driven decision makers: Measuring attitudes towards business analytics. *Business Process Management Journal.*
85. Murphy, S. (2014). *Trade Finance Applications Technology Analysis Abstract*, CEB Tower Group, August.

CHAPTER 6

Fintech and Procurement Finance 4.0

Introduction

This chapter analyzes the future of procurement finance, in terms of potential organizational and technological developments, and defines it procurement finance 4.0.

There are essentially two ways to consider procurement finance 4.0. They are strictly connected with the role that procurement should play in an organization. The role could be either of support or primary, according to the definitions introduced by Porter in its value chain model.[1] If procurement has a support role, it is a function which supports the other primary and secondary functions. On the contrary, if procurement has a primary role, it would be seen as a primary contributor to adding value to the organization.

The two potential roles would be rather different in a procurement 4.0 vision.

In the support role, procurement 4.0 would be essentially a support to an Industry 4.0 initiative.[2] This is an initiative which stresses at the maximum connectivity and automation of all the resources in the organization, be them machines, infrastructure, products, operators, and so on. This is the vision of procurement finance 4.0 included in many pieces of the literature.[3]

The author of this book believes that procurement is essentially a primary function in Porter's value chain model.[4] Procurement could

B. Nicoletti, *Procurement Finance*,
Palgrave Studies in Financial Services Technology,
https://doi.org/10.1007/978-3-030-02140-5_6

contribute between 50 and 80 percent of the operating costs. This value-added contribution is among the largest in the functions of an organization. Under this vision, procurement 4.0, and hence procurement finance 4.0, is substantially different from the one with procurement in a support role. Industry 4.0 is essentially based on interconnection and on automation. Similarly, procurement finance 4.0 should be based on the same principle as a primary function in adding value to the organization rather than only to support an Industry 4.0 initiative.

Procurement 4.0 considers procurement as a platform. A platform is an organization based on enabling value-creating interactions between producers and consumers.[5] A platform is an evolving organization or meta-organization that[6]:

- federates and coordinates constitutive agents who can innovate and compete;
- creates value by generating and harnessing economies of scope in procurement and/or in demand;
- involves a modular solution composed of a core and a periphery.

This vision of procurement 4.0 sees the interconnection based on the model Industry 4.0 and the automation based on a technology which supports interconnection. This technology is blockchain.[7] The interconnection among the modules of the platform should be based on cloud computing which allows a cheap, flexible, and effective way to link all the components.

This chapter develops this concept and this model of procurement finance 4.0. Firstly, the development of the organizations is considered from the different aspects which are strongly impacting on them all over the world.

The following section analyzes the technological developments, on the basis of the organizational developments but also strongly influenced by them.

The combination of these two developments is the base for the future vision of the organizations and of the procurement finance processes.

Procurement Finance 4.0

One of the key paradigms of Industry 4.0 is the use of modern information and communication technology (ICT) integrated with automation.[8] ICT has supported procurement processes since a long time. The concept of electronic procurement (or "e-procurement") is well established.[9] The architecture of e-procurement has been defined.[10] Industry 4.0 pushes further the concept of digitization based on the characteristics of the initiative. The integration in this model requires a comprehensive approach combined with process re-engineering.[11]

Industry 4.0 has been compared with previous disruptive innovations: the so-called industrial revolutions. They have in common an initiation not based on a single technology but on the interaction of a number of technologies whose effect created new solutions.[12]

The widespread use of the telecommunication networks (and especially of the Internet) marked the start of another industrial revolution. The introduction of the Internet of Things and advanced software applications combined with the machine automation into the production environment has introduced the fourth industrial revolution.[13]

This new paradigm shift thanks to the web enables the communication between machines and humans or other machines or products in real time and at a very cheap cost.[14] This allows the use of what is known as "smart products and smart services" as well as the advanced digitization within and among the factories.[15] The smart factory enables to connect potentially all the components involved in the production processes, and even the products itself. It makes possible the application of concepts as adaptability, interconnectivity, efficiency, and ergonomics.[16]

The implementation of these solutions, transforming the factories into "smart factory", will take a medium/long time. It requires important investments and special education programs. The returns are a substantial improvement of the cost performance of the procurement, saving time, but especially providing flexibility and effectiveness to the organization.

The literature on procurement finance 4.0 is limited. Henke and Schulte (2015), for example, claim that procurement is the interface of vendors and production solutions. In this position, it can be the key driver of the Industry 4.0 development. These authors postulate a number of questions around this statement.[17] Other publications either have a more technical focus[18] or deal with specific aspects, such as the logistics integration.[19]

Industry 4.0

History

Industry 4.0 can be seen as the convergence of the ICT and automation.[20] The term Industry 4.0 stands for an advanced digitization within organizations, combined with the Web and with future-oriented technologies in the field of smart objects (machines and products). This enables and transforms industrial production systems in the direction of products controlling their own production processes.[21] Besides the focus on digitization and automation, Industry 4.0 is supported by several technological innovations whose combined quantitative effects allows the creation of new products, processes, ways of production, and business models.[22]

Procurement finance 4.0 adds an additional component to the base Industry 4.0: the simplification of the processes and the digitization of the financial flows connected with the operational processes of the organization.

This fourth industrial revolution supports two important developments. On the one hand, there is an application pull that induces a change in the operational model conditions and an application push. The first aspect leads to social, economic, and potentially political transformations. The most important of them are the following ones:

- Fast development and innovation cycles.
- Customized production and sales. This trend leads to an increasing customization of products. At the limit, it is the "one-unit lot" of production.
- Flexibility. Due to the characteristics of the current markets, flexibility is essential in the entire operations of an organization.
- Decentralization. The organization structure should be as flat as possible.
- Sustainability. There is a push to an economic and ecological efficiency in the production, due to the increase in the prices of the resources as well as a social awareness on ecological issues.

On the other hand, there is a technological push on other solutions, like the mobile phones, 3D printers, web, apps, and so on. In industrial practice, these innovative solutions are not yet widely used. The approaches of these technological innovations are:

- More technological support to the physical work as well as the adoption of more automatic solutions. Examples are the autonomous automated guided vehicles (AGV) with their routes programmed or "pulled" by another machine or by the product itself.
- New technologies as simulation, artificial intelligence, cybersecurity, or virtual reality are driven by the increasing simplification and digitization of all production and production-supporting tools. There is an increased networking of technological modules. The software allows to collect and analyze the sensor data, read from the tags attached to the products, and hence track products within the factory or even manage and maintain products in the customer premises.[23]
- Miniaturized devices with better performance can be installed in a small space. Nanotechnology is becoming more used. This makes possible new fields of application, especially in procurement.

In short, the term Industry 4.0 describes different digitization- and automation-driven transformation in the production systems and consequently in the procurement processes.[24] These developments have technological implications as well as process, organizational, and labor implications.[25]

Industry 4.0 investments are more on the basis of the entire value network. The conclusion is that organizations in all sectors should focus their investments on the optimization of the procurement finance, underlying the importance of the procurement management in this fourth industrial revolution.

Main Components

This book claims that procurement finance 4.0 can be characterized with the six Cs: cybernetics, communication, controllership, collaboration, connection, and comprehension (Fig. 6.1).[26]

The model considers first a division of the procurement finance 4.0 characteristics in hard and soft. The hard characteristics have an infrastructural base. The soft characteristics are based on software. For each one of them, it is possible to name a technological solution that can support the implementation of procurement finance 4.0. All these sets of characteristics require a strict governance (or command) that in its turn should be supported by specific tools.

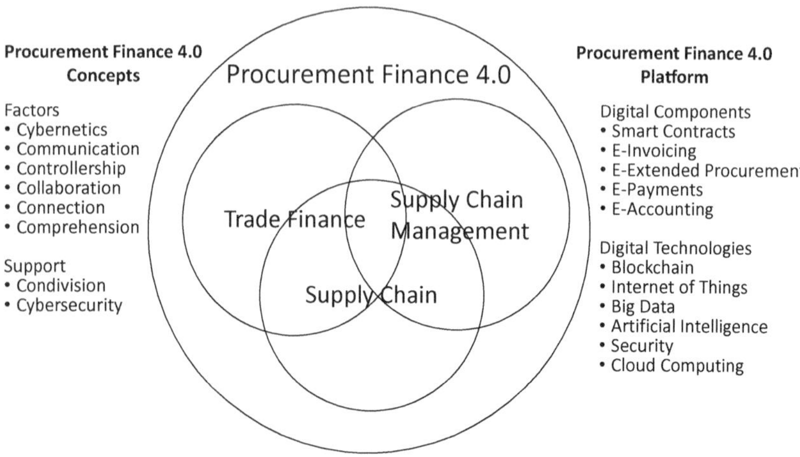

Fig. 6.1 Procurement finance 4.0

Hard

- Cybernetics refers to the use of computers, be they in a data center or distributed in the organization.[27]
- Communication refers to the need of linking together the computational devices and all the machines in a local area network (LAN) or in a wide-area network (WAN), normally based on the web.
- Controllership refers to the numerical control of the machines, essential to make them as much as possible autonomous of the need of human operators.

Soft

- Collaboration refers to the need to have all the machines, the robots, and the operators working together. Applications like enterprise resource planning (ERP) are useful to support in the most automated way all the management and operational processes.
- Connection is essential to support the integration of all the machines. The Internet of Things, or better the Internet of Everything,[28] allows also the humans to be part of the connected elements of the organization. Horizontal integration refers to the integration of the ICT systems in the different stages of the organization's processes as

inbound procurement, outbound procurement, production, and marketing and between different organizations (value network).[29] Procurement finance 4.0 pays attention to the procurement management pushing on communication and collaboration with the network of vendors (outbound procurement), the internal organization (inbound procurement), as well as the network of customers (outbound procurement). On the other hand, vertical integration refers to the integration of different hierarchical levels as corporate planning levels, production management, production, quality, and so on.
- Comprehension or knowledge is based on the intelligent use of the data. All the information systems, the sensors, and the numerical controls (all connected) generate Big Data. These data need to be analyzed. Big Data analytics is essential also in procurement finance 4.0. Big Data, analytics, data mining, and data distribution are critical issues due to the variety, the volume, and the velocity needed to process the data, for instance, in spend analysis.

The model should include also two other characteristics to assure the governance of the systems, the machines, and the processes:

- Condivision of the data and of the documents is important to support procurement finance 4.0 from the governance point of view. There are traditional and advanced tools that can assure such sharing not limited to the internal organization but also externally to connect with vendors, partners, intermediaries, and customers.
- Cybersecurity to assure the trust in the solutions through a very strict security, in accessing and in performance.

Platform Concept[30]

Some authors have written of the decreasing importance of traditional financial services offered by the financial institutions, especially corporate banks.[31] Financial institutions might decrease in importance but banking will not.[32] Banking is the interaction between providers of funds and users of the funds.

To retain market share, broaden revenue polls, and avoid disintermediation, financial institutions, in particular the ones operating with businesses, need to offer a more distinctive value proposition by drawing on their expertise, data, and strong relationships. There are four transformation levels for these financial institutions[33]:

- strengthen customer relationships with differentiated multichannel integrated coverage;
- digitize processes end to end;
- redefine the product offering;
- build an advanced analytics DNA.

To implement this transformation and reap the benefits of all these transformation levels, it is important to consider financial institutions as platforms rather than providers of services.[34] A platform is an organization based on enabling value-creating interactions between external producers and consumers.[35] A platform is an evolving organization or meta-organization that[36]:

- federates and coordinates constitutive agents which can innovate and compete;
- creates value by generating and harnessing economies of scope in procurement and/or in demand; and
- includes a modular solution composed of a core and a periphery.

The platform provides an open, participative infrastructure for these interactions.[37] It sets the governance conditions for them. The platform's main purpose is to create and operate interactions among participants. In this way, it facilitates the exchange of products, services, or social relationships. In this way, it enables value creation for all participants. A platform is particularly effective in the exchange of information, as exactly happens in the financial world.

A platform provides the infrastructure and rules for a marketplace bringing together producers and purchasers. The participants in a platform ecosystem fill four main roles but may shift rapidly over time from one role to another. Understanding the relationships both within and outside the ecosystem is central to define a platform strategy. It is even more important to understand the critical success factors of a platform and their business models.[38]

The players in a platform ecosystem are the four Ps (Fig. 6.2):

- The proprietors, or owners, are the controllers of the platform intellectual property. They decide who may participate and in which ways. The proprietor works on the innovation of the platform either modifying the business model or aggregating other business models.[39]

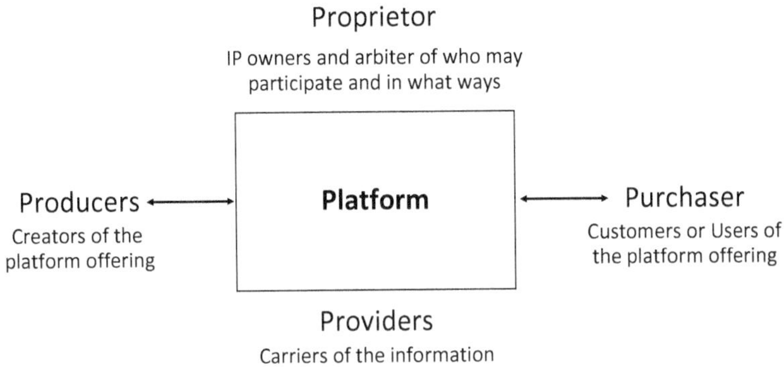

Fig. 6.2 The four Ps: the players in a platform ecosystem

- The providers make available the platform, from an infrastructural point of view.
- The producers are the creators of the platform's offerings.
- The purchasers, partners, or clients are the buyers or users of the offerings.

In the case of the procurement finance, the players are:

- The proprietor of the platform is the initiator and the owner of the platfom, which is not necessarily limited to a financial institution.
- The providers manage and make the infrastructure available.
- The producers are the financiers.
- The purchasers are the lenders.

The operations of a platform are not easy. Today's platforms, empowered by digital technology, are able to eliminate time and space constraints:

- they employ sophisticated solutions that connect producers and purchasers more precisely, speedily, and easily than ever before;
- a platform can produce results an especially business models not even imaginable some years ago.

The previous chapters have explored at length the first aspect. This chapter explores the platforms for the procurement finance 4.0. With them, there is an exchange of value, information, and feedbacks between the producers and purchasers. Though they come in many varieties, all platforms have an ecosystem with the same basic structure, including the four types of participants.

Platform organizations bring together producers and purchasers in a high-value exchange. Their main assets are information and interactions. Apple launched the iPhone and its operating system as more than a product a conduit for services.[40] It imagined them as a way to connect participants in two-sided markets—app developers on one side and app users on the other—generating value for both groups (and of course to produce value for the providers and the owner). As the number of participants on each side grew, that value increased. This is the so-called network effect.[41]

Platforms are a powerful solution for digital transformation. It is interesting to define an integrated architecture between the platform model and the DX digital transformation model defined by IDC (see Fig. 6.3).[42] The objective of the DX platform is to create an ecosystem of integrated proprietor, providers, producers, and purchasers that use (and contribute to pay for) the information and services available to them. In addition to this external focus, this platform requires an approach that aggressively modernizes legacy ICT environments to redefine processes and capabilities for both internal and external purposes.

In the new platform, everything is connected to everything else. Data comes into an organization through connected assets, employees, and

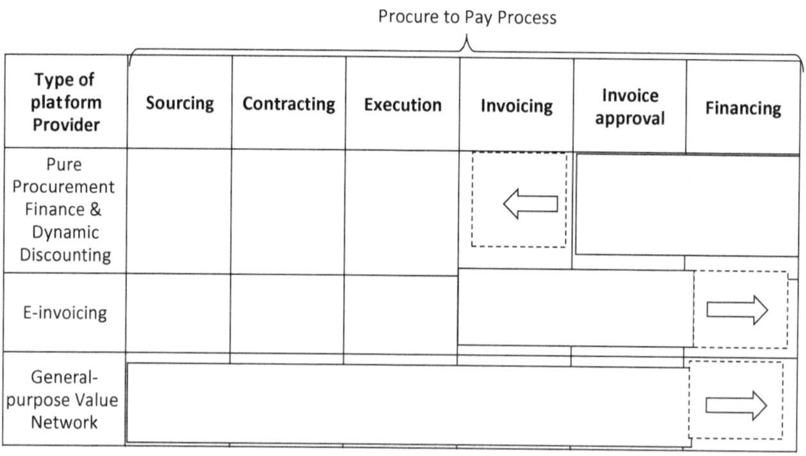

Fig. 6.3 Fintech and procurement finance

connected processes, or as other data streams through APIs. This data circulates through the intelligent core, the heart of the platform, where the algorithms, the code, and the models live to help organizations glean the insights and actions needed to improve internal processes. Data also comes in through ecosystem engagements. This data circulates through the intelligent core, which turns the data into actions to be taken when engaging with the ecosystem.

The DX platform provides and uses four different "types" of services including[43]:

- intelligent core;
- integration and orchestration services;
- platform as a service (PaaS) and developer services;
- engagement services.

Procurement Finance and Platforms

A typical example of a platform in the case of procurement finance is the marketplace lending. Credit is an important franchise of the financial industry. In the last few years, a growing number of fintech startups have taken a sledgehammer to that pillar.[44]

There are generally three ways financial institutions get into marketplace lending:

- build a proprietary platform in-house;
- form a referral partnership with a marketplace lender; or
- license a marketplace lender's platform.

The in-house option is normally the most expensive, time-consuming, and difficult to maintain. It offers an integrated control over underwriting and the customer experience. Referral partnerships, whereby financial institutions send potential borrowers to a marketplace lender's site and either purchase the resulting loans or receive referral fees, generate income and quickly fill product gaps. They often come with underwriting and user-experience risks. Platform licensing allows financial institutions to capitalize on white-labeled plug-and-play technology and non-traditional credit criteria. It is not free and the integration requires effort.

Procurement finance platform providers can be classified according to two discriminatory variables: flexibility and inclusiveness.[45] The first variable, flexibility, refers to the range of procurement finance instruments available on the platform and to the platform's market coverage. The latter is defined in terms of industries addressed. The second variable, inclusiveness, refers to the platform accessibility and its degree of operating efficiency throughout the life cycle of the financing process (users onboarding and audit, financing provision and follow-up). By mapping the providers, it is possible to acknowledge their relative positioning according to these two discriminatory dimensions.

Business Models for Platforms in Procurement Finance

Four recurrent business model's archetypes can be identified, based on a similar classification for supply chain finance: elite procurement finance platform, up-and-run procurement finance platform, one-stop procurement finance platform, and e-merchant procurement finance platform.[46]

1. Elite procurement finance platforms: procurement finance programs are normally endorsed by big financially solid and creditworthy organizations. They address the financing needs of a limited number of affiliated small and medium-sized enterprises (SMEs) (mainly vendors) characterized by long relationship history and poor variability in the transaction terms. Procurement finance programs are normally a plug-in service on the proprietary procurement platform used by the anchor organization to settle transactions with affiliated upstream/downstream organizations. In alternative, the procurement finance platform is a collaborative portal limited to a closed pool of big buyers. Procurement finance is normally limited to factoring/reverse factoring. These financial products are highly standardized.
2. Up-and-run procurement finance platform: procurement finance is provided on third-party-only procurement finance platform (such as B2B or invoice marketplaces) where users can access on-demand financing, limited industry coverage (single or few similar industries in such a way to standardize the process and ensure limited variability). Normally, the platform does an *a priori* selection of the core organizations endorsing the procurement finance program and joining the platform. The platform is characterized by low complexity

and timeliness in the financing process: one-time users' approval, on-demand online financing request, automated risk pricing, and fast financing release. Procurement finance is normally buyer-driven. The financing terms are moderately flexible.

3. One-stop procurement finance platform: procurement finance products are accessible by SMEs settling trade transaction with a cooperative core organization on the platform. The financial service is a value added of an e-procurement platform managing all the transaction stages (order settlement, storage, logistics distribution, and payment reconciliation). The platform relies on the traditional endorsement of the anchor organization but strengthens the value network perspective in the risk assessment through the integration of both upstream and downstream affiliated SMEs. The platform covers multiple industries (in many cases electronics, automotive, and manufacturing). The main diversification factor is the pressure for democratization as SMEs improve their value network compliance as a result of the provider's rigorous systems and processes. Normally, offline training and online-to-offline (O2O) tools are provided to facilitate procurement from SMEs thanks to the simplification and digitization process.
4. E-merchant procurement finance platforms: procurement finance is enabled by e-commerce platforms where vendors settling procurement transactions can access the financial service. The platforms' innovativeness relies on the breakthrough paradigm for the risk assessment. There is not any more reliance on the anchor organization. The focus is on the single organizations status in relation to multi-dimensional data generated on the platform. Dynamic customer relationship management (CRM) dynamically adjusts the offer for financing in response to detected events. This is possible due to the fact that all the relevant data for the decision-making are integrated and accessible during the whole financing life cycle. This solution is characterized by a high simplification and digitization of the financing processes (application, approval, financing terms definition, and release/collection) assuring timeliness and speed in the financing release.

Fabrick[47]

Fabrick is an independent and neutral ecosystem. It is based on the experience of a large Italian bank: Banca Sella.[48] It is based on the Fabrick Platform. This is the technological backbone which supports the connected ecosystem. It is a technological infrastructure, participative, and open since it is based on APIs, plug and play tools for the producers and the purchasers in the platform.

This ecosystem makes possible innovative business models and new ways of collaboration between all the players in the market. It converts complexity into simplicity, competition into virtuous cooperation, closure to aperture, and the impersonality of technology with a customizable solution.

The participants in this ecosystem are several:

- The purchasers, normally corporates and end customers, which can simplify their everyday routine thanks to the efficient and tailor-made solutions created starting with their needs. They open up to a new financial culture based on collaboration that generates a permanent value. They can cut their operational costs with the platform solutions. They can enhance and optimize their business due to improving the customer journey.
- The producers, normally the banks and other financial institutions. Fabrick allows them to grow their business thanks to the access to a vast ecosystem of quality services and to an easy and time/cost-effective compliance. They can share their APIs and use the other player APIs.
- The proprietors and providers, which are fintech organizations, system integrators, and developers which build new products and services thanks to the network effect that fosters collaboration and contamination among the best talents of the financial sector and not only. In this way, they can improve their time to market and create a long-term business plan based on their vision.

GT Nexus[49]

GT Nexus, based in Oakland, CA, started as a platform-based supply chain finance solution provider and evolved into a collaborative platform supporting large corporations in the control of the procurement finance on their global trade transactions.[50]

It is an online cloud platform. Large corporations join and submit the request for onboarding their intermediaries and buyers on the platform to manage their transactions. Any registered member can apply for financing. Its approval is conditional on the internal audit performed by the system.

Buyers and vendors access transaction data online and get real-time information on the transaction status. Buyers and vendors can access transaction data online. They receive event-based alerts in the case of purchase order changes.

GT Nexus targets SMEs, vendors, and distributors of the corporate customers, mainly located in the Asia-Pacific region (almost 85 percent of them are corporate vendors), in North America, and in Europe. GT Nexus manages USD 500 Billion in goods, 25,000 organizations, and 100,000 users on the platform.

Open Banking

The platform concept is based on open banking. Open banking can be defined as a collaborative model in which banking data is shared through APIs between two or more unaffiliated parties to deliver enhanced capabilities to the marketplace.[51] The benefits of open banking are substantial: improved customer experience, new revenue streams, and a sustainable service model for traditionally underserved markets.

Strictly connected with open banking, and on the basis of the platform concept, is the use of application programming interfaces (APIs). APIs are a set of functions and procedures that allow the creation of applications for bi-directional data feeds between application and other services. APIs have been leveraged in banking settings for years.[52] Given breakthroughs in advanced analytics and the market traction of several non-bank fintech organizations, APIs are considered as a means to enhance the delivery of financial services also for corporate customers.[53]

For an effective open banking, it is particularly important to standardize the data, the API, and the security.[54]

Open banking has challenges and opportunities in new relevant regulations such as PSD2 and GDPR. The revised EU Payment Service Directive (PSD2) caters for the possibility of third-party service providers having access to payment accounts held at other payment service providers, the so-called account servicing payment service providers.[55] PSD2 makes a distinction between two types of services: payment initiation services and account information services. The General Data Protection Regulation (GDPR) is a legal framework that sets guidelines for the collection and processing of personal information of individuals within the European Union (EU).[56]

UniCredit and CRX Markets[57]

UniCredit[58] and CRX Markets[59] collaborate in offering a procurement finance integrated platform. The collaboration between financial institutions and fintech organizations can be a profitable solution.[60] The two partners developed a solution to allow multiple organizations to be connected to several financial institutions and investors to obtain innovative solutions of financing. It is possible to exchange data without manual processing.

CRX Markets is an independent marketplace offering financial solutions. It includes different actors, that is, buyers, vendors, banks, and other financial institutions. It ensures a higher security of data and advanced technology. This allows participants to have access to versatile financing of working capital and clearer and efficient prices. One of the key features of the CRX Markets is the complete integration into the ERP systems[61] of the customers. This integration allows them to obtain the digitization of information exchanges between their ERP system and CRX, simultaneously.

CRX Markets provide solutions for[62]:

- dynamic discounting: through an ICT platform, the buyer proposes to the vendor an advance payment in return for a discount on the nominal value of the invoice, proportional to the days in advance;

(*continued*)

(continued)

- diversifying exposure to counterparty risk by doing financial institutions operations through multiple financial institutions;
- multi-investors financing or securitization: special vehicle through which it is possible to acquire credits and subsequently sell them, through the auction method, to financial institutions or investors in the marketplace.

CRX Markets provides financing through several channels; it allows the combination of these forms of financing and adapts them to the specific needs of each customer.

Organizational Developments

New solutions create also the need to develop the organizational structure and processes. A special but interesting case is connected with the extended supply chain. To deal with this case is not easy since procurement finance might require that evaluations must extend beyond the first tier of vendors and distributors to those whose overall financial status may not be visible. Providing financial support also to these second tiers of small and midsize organizations requires new risk assessment levels and new evaluation models that not all financial institutions have or are interested to adopt. This creates an opportunity for organizational developments that have a more entrepreneurial approach, fewer regulatory burdens, and the risk appetite to gain share in a potentially lucrative market.

EBRD[63]

EBRD (European Bank for Reconstruction and Development) is an international financial institution established in 1991 with the specific purpose of assisting the countries of Central and Eastern Europe and the republics of the Confederation of Independent States (CIS) in the process of transition towards the market economy. To carry out this mandate, the bank operates through direct investments and the

(*continued*)

(continued)
mobilization of international and local capitals in favor of the public bodies, financial institutions, and private organizations. Through its investments, the bank promotes the strengthening of the financial and legal system and the development of the infrastructure needed to support the private sector. The EBRD grants direct funding to private sector investment projects, restructuring and privatization, and the provision of infrastructure to support these activities.

In response to the 2008 financial crisis, EBRD launched the Trade Facilitation Program able to allow a greater number of trade exchanges. The Trade Facilitation Program has the aim of issuing guarantees to international confirming financial institutions to secure all or part of the commitments of local issuing financial institutions. In this way, the vendor has the potential to evaluate the commercial and political risk of non-payment by the local financial institution issuing the documentary credit.

EBRD guarantees can be used in support of different types of procurement finance, such as letters of credit, standby letters of credit, and advance payment guarantees. EBRD guarantees cover the commercial and political risk of non-payment by the issuing financial institution without posing any risk to the vendor or buyer.

For each transaction, the guarantee fee is negotiated and has to be paid by the financial institution that required the issuance by the EBRD.

Regarding the sustainability perspective, the EBRD has launched a "green" program of Trade Facilitation.[64] This program allows the financial institutions and their customers to support the export and import of technologies and green services provided according to the Green Economy Transaction.[65] In this way, it has been possible to reach a substantial energy saving, and a reduction of CO_2 emissions.

Fintech

The digital transformation is influencing the financial services. It is the holistic approach to assure procurement agility. The fusion of finance and technologies (fintech) creates new efficient models that are challenging the traditional financial services. The term fintech refers to all those organizations that exploit the digital technologies to provide innovative financial services. They also offer services in an easy, rapid, and transparent way internationally.

When the Internet became accessible to everyone and there was the possibility to use this new channel to improve services, the financial institutions failed to respond in full to the customer needs by exploiting the new opportunities. A certain number of fintech organizations responded to the customers' needs in a rapid and efficient way. The traditional financial institutions are now making some progresses. They are still not sufficient to cope with the rapid social and economic environment changes because there are still technological gaps with respect to the fintech organizations. After the financial crisis of 2008, there was a limitation of the traditional financial channels of providing funding. This situation led organizations to search for new financing channels. It led to an expansion of the application field by the alternative finance institutions (Fig. 6.4).[66]

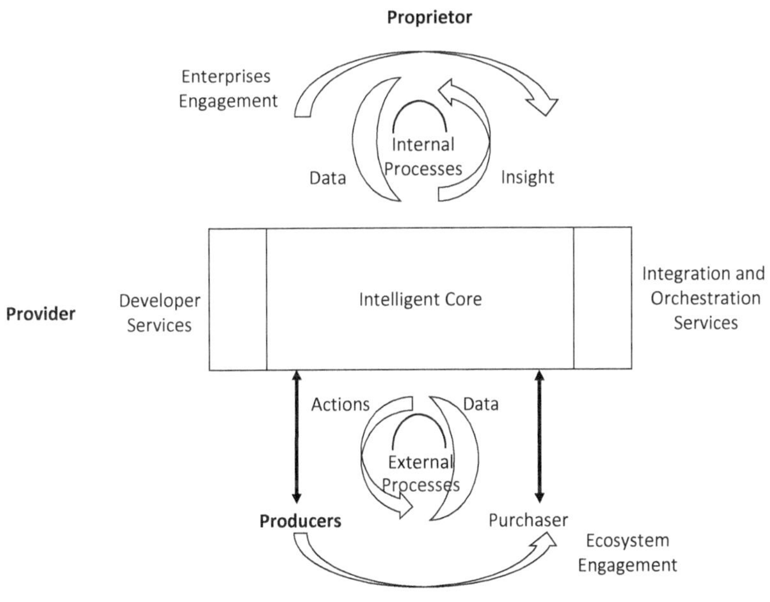

Fig. 6.4 Platform and digital transformation. (Adapted by the Author from *Alternative finance*. Cambridge Centre for Alternative Finance, Cambridge, UK)

The importance of technology and the entry of fintech organizations in the financial market can support the growth of procurement finance. It supports the simplification and digitization of the procure-to-pay and order-to-pay processes. In this way, it is possible to use platforms of a third party through which buyers and vendors can offer also financial services. It allows also an easy access to several providers of funding.[67]

The analysis carried out by the Osservatorio Supply Chain Finance of the Politecnico di Milano in collaboration with the Assifact (Italian Association for Factoring) examined the financing solutions for working capital brought by the main new organizations.[68] The survey covered over 100 international startups in the procurement finance area, of which 15 were Italian. The startups offer fast services based on digital platforms that reduce human interactions and accelerate the timing for the provision of advances on trade receivables. In this way, SMEs can optimize the liquidity within their value network.

This survey defines four distinctive business models in the fintech organizations.[69] The Cash Seeker startups bring together investors who are seeking non-traditional investment opportunities with organizations seeking alternative liquidity because they are having difficulty accessing the banking channel. The Cash Exploiters exploit excess liquidity in the value network for the benefit of small vendors who are struggling to access credit. Working capital brokers find financing alternatives to the traditional customer-vendor channels by bringing organizations in need of credit in contact with institutional investors. These organizations reduce information asymmetries along the value network and simplify the evaluation of creditworthiness or cash flow management.

The small business is the more exposed segment to change due to the insufficient financial institutions offer for them. Their relevant need is the management of cash flow. Especially, after the financial crisis, the traditional financial institutions have overlooked the small business segment. The same segment, on the contrary, has been a ground to exploit by the fintech organizations.

This small business segment produces over half of the global GDP and two-thirds of the world employment.[70] The obstacles to achieve the financing access are faced in both the developed and the emerging countries. In the emerging countries, the difficulty in accessing the credit is greater because there is a very small financial institutions' sector. The financial institutions have low interest in making business in these countries.

The traditional financial institutions get the benefits of the volume or scale thanks to a large number of customers. This aspect is changing because many customers are moving to the new digital offers. It is estimated that 75 percent of the millennials would be more interested in new financial services from the GAFA (an acronym for Google, Apple, Facebook, and Amazon) than from banks.[71]

The need of liquidity of SMEs can be satisfied by the fintech organizations through the digital invoice financing. This product is offered by the financial institutions at very high costs. It is necessary that the financial institutions start to be more agile compared to the changes in the surrounding environments. They need to understand which are the impacts deriving from alternative finance, which path they could take to grasp the opportunities that are coming from these innovations, and which services in their offering could be made more efficient.

Some fintech organizations are also combining financial services support to SMEs with activities of the type of business process outsourcing (BPO).[72]

The potential collaboration between financial institutions and fintech organizations would bring benefits to both parties, even if it is not easy to combine two completely different cultures.

Beesy[73]

Beesy is a digital financial management solution for small organizations and freelancers. It is an investment in Italy of FinLeap[74] supported by Fabrick[75] as lead investors. Beesy is a digital finance and consultant tailored to micro-enterprises. All functions are in a single portal.

SMEs can use this full-service fintech organization, Beesy, to move to paperless processes for accounting management and in full integration with their financial institutions and tax consultants. The portal offers them digital solutions for managing finances, with the addition of banking services, accounting tools, payment solutions, and analysis, but also tax advice thanks to a network of professionals in direct contact with customers through the platform.

Crossflow Payments[76]

Crossflow Payments is a UK fintech organization grown in turnover from £885k in 2016 to over £20 million in 2017: a growth of almost 2000 percent.[77] It is the fastest growing fintech globally, and also the closest to profitability, reporting a nominal loss of £401k.

Crossflow is active in supporting financial institutions to cost-effectively digitally support procurement finance. This market is huge:

- the supply chain finance market in the UK alone is estimated to be worth £46 billion;
- the market is expected to grow by around 15 percent;
- London is the fintech capital of Europe, with 53 percent of European fintech deals happening in the capital.

The supply chain finance sector is ripe for fintech disrupters, and the rapidly changing market represents a huge opportunity for fintech organizations in procurement finance, a market traditionally dominated by the banks.

Virtual Currencies

The virtual currency is a type of unregulated, digital money, which is issued and normally controlled by its developers. It is used and accepted among the members of a specific virtual community.[78] This chapter examines its potential uses in procurement finance.[79]

Defined as a virtual currency, Bitcoin is considered a digital asset.[80] Bitcoin is encrypted. It allows transacting money and payments in an anonymous form, without the need for a third party to act as a mediator. Bitcoin is a cryptocurrency, that is, its operation is based on a complex set of calculations that have to do with cryptography, so as guaranteeing its security. A Bitcoin is made up of bits, namely, numbers and mathematical operations. Thus, it is not a currency with a physical medium such as a financial banknote or coin.

Co-creators argue that Bitcoin provides a much cheaper and faster payment system that is available, especially for international transfers.[81] Bitcoin can be used wherever they are accepted as a valid form of payment. The Bitcoin transaction is transparent but it cannot be traced.

One of Bitcoin's major benefits over the most consolidated and conventional currencies is the total absence of the system of institutions, agencies, and intermediaries that make the financial system slow and expensive.

This lack of regulatory and traceability is useful for those who do not want to pay financial institution fees or pay taxes on their own capital. On the other side, it removes all the safeguards that these entities provide. A transaction in Bitcoin is, in fact, irreversible, that is, once the money is sent, if the buyer is not satisfied with the products purchased, or worse, it would not be sent, there will be no way to recover the money.

Bitcoin is not the only virtual currency available in the financial markets. The number of cryptocurrencies is growing, but only a few of them have reached an international importance. Some of the most relevant virtual currencies are Litecoin, Ethereum, and Ripple. They are classified on the basis of their capitalization.

Each cryptocurrency tends to have some special characteristic. For example difference of Litecoin from Bitcoin is that it occurs with greater speed in transaction confirmation, with a different script, and with more coins generated.[82]

Ethereum is a decentralized network in which smart contracts or intelligent contracts are launched (they are explained in depth later in this chapter).[83] It does not only become a way to exchange currency but also a way to transmit and exchange any assets. It is a solution able to facilitate some processes related to money exchange or services, making them reliable, secure, and almost impossible to attack. This feature is nowadays highly appreciated.

Ripple is a digital currency with the aim to significantly lower the cost of transactions normally held by third parties (financial institutions, credit cards, and so on) for each transaction.[84] Bitcoin looks like a digital currency, while Ripple looks like a network of transactions that also contains a digital currency, Ripple. In addition, Ripple can trace movements of any asset, so Ripple can track movements of any currency.

Bitcoin Cash[85]

An important obstacle in the use of Bitcoin is the speed of its transactions. It takes more time to approve the various movements, as the daily volume of operations is increasing. An innovative solution to this problem is Bitcoin Cash.

This new version of virtual currency is a new configuration of the Bitcoin itself. It was launched in the market as a sort of alternative to the classic Bitcoin. It was born following the work of some Bitcoin developers to have a more efficient, quicker, and in a way even more flexible cryptocurrency. The aim is to respond to the need for growth of the virtual currency market and make the Bitcoin a widely used currency all over the world. The effort is also to make a virtual currency no more than niche and no longer reserved for the speculators and specialists, but open to the entire customer market. The new cryptocurrency can process up to 8M transitions in 10 minutes, multiplying the system speed with respect to the classic Bitcoin.[86]

Crowdfunding

One of the more relevant examples of alternative finance is crowdfunding. Crowdfunding is a collective fundraising process to fund or to provide capital to projects, organizations, or startups.[87] Crowdfunding platforms are websites that are designed to help meet the demand for funding by those who promote projects or need procurement funds. They can be[88]:

- generalists: when they collect funding for any area of interest;
- vertical: specializing in specific sector projects or initiatives.

Crowdfunding allows the fundraiser to raise money from a large number of scopes through online platforms. The difference between the traditional financing and crowdfunding is that the first one consists of big amounts coming from one or few sources, while the second one consists of many small sums funded by a large number of investors.

Crowdfunding is mostly used by startups or expanding organizations as a means to access alternative finance. The "crowd" can look at the entrepreneurial projects proposed by the organizations. They can choose to support them with different forms of remuneration, which in practice can become forms of alternative financing with respect to the financial institutions.[89]

Crowdfunding can also be a way to gather a community around the offer to support an initiative. Thanks to the strength of the online community, it is possible to gain valuable knowledge of the market and reach new customers.

The characteristics of crowdfunding are[90]:

- open access to credit;
- community participation;
- social approval;
- centrality of the individual.

Classification of Crowdfunding Models

There are different models of crowdfunding[91]:

- Reward-based is fundraising that in return for cash donations provides a reward, such as the product for which the "crowd" is financing, or recognition, such as public thanks on the site of the new startup. Examples are platforms like Kickstarter or Indiegogo,[92] where startups raise pledges and in return offer buy-in incentives for anything they produce.
- Donation-based is a model used primarily by nonprofit organizations to fund nonprofit initiatives. In this model people donate money to an initiative. In return, backers may receive token rewards that increase their prestige as the size of the donation increases; for small sums, the provider of the funds may receive nothing at all.
- Lending-based is a model corresponding to a peer-to-peer money loan. It refers to non-brokerage loans for both organizations and private individuals, where the cash-settled individual chooses to allocate it. It includes the microcredit, such as P2P (peer-to-peer) and P2B (peer-to-business). This model rewards the lenders with the accrued interest rate on loan capital. The organizations are increasingly resorting to lending crowdfunding to overcome the tightening of the access to financial institutions credit. This situation has led to the emergence of the online platforms that no longer operate in the traditional context of private lending but have also expanded the scope of action to finance organizations.
- Invoice trading is a new form of crowdfunding loan that helps SMEs to finance the working capital by disintermediating financial institutions. The need of liquidity for SMEs can be satisfied by the advance payment of invoices, which is normally very expensive when offered

by traditional financial institutions. It represents an evolution of the new tool because in this case, the organizations obtain credit surrendering trading invoices. Everything is done through online platforms that contact SMEs that have invoices to offset to finance their business with more or less professional investors.

- Equity-based represents a classical financing by individuals who invest their money into shares in an organization. Equity crowdfunding development is leading to enlargement and democratization of financial tools access. It represents a good alternative to the capital search of newly born organizations. This opening to the new capital search has been made possible thanks to the efficiency and globalization of the digital platform. It is relative both to the capital and the financing of the research in the organizations. Seedrs is an example of an equity-based crowdfunding platform in the UK.[93]
- ICO (initial coin offering): Regarding the possible relation between crowdfunding and virtual currencies, ICO is a new form of crowdfunding that allows promoters of an initiative to raise funds against the issuance in a virtual currency. The issuer is normally a startup that intends to fund the development of a service or a product. As in a crowdfunding rewarding campaign, money is being rewarded in return for money. In this case, rewards consist of virtual "tokens", each of which represents a unit of a virtual currency. The uniqueness and authenticity of such tokens are guaranteed by an authentication system based on blockchain.[94] Normally, with the token purchased, the supporter can use the services offered by the startup that issued them.

The web offers different platforms which have fundamentally changed the nature of funding. They are no longer in the hands of big investors. With crowdfunding, the same users invest, "from below", in projects.

Compared to traditional fundraising platforms, the benefits that crowdfunding offers are[95]:

- rapidity in project promotion;
- possibility to reach a large audience;
- potentially endless budgets;
- reducing transaction costs and regulatory complexity;
- exponential expansion through sharing the initiative on social networks.

For financial institutions perspective, the development of crowdfunding is the sign that customers expect easier, transparent, and traceable financing methods. By allying to the platforms, financial institutions seek to meet these needs.

Crowdfunding and Social Networks

Crowdfunding can be seen as a bottom-up fundraising, but it is preferable to define it as a "social financing". The scoring process and the acceptance of loan request are based on the ability of a person to get trusted relationships among their contacts in the social networks.[96]

Social networks are born and raised for purposes entirely different from business applications. They could become a key tool for what is termed social value network, namely, the combination of social media with ICT tools and manufacturing, logistics, business processes, and interaction with vendors. These tools allow building direct relationships that were unthinkable in the past.

Crowdfunding is strongly based on the concept of social networks and the linkage between the latter and the procurement function. The procurement sector processes involve mainly dealing with relationships and access to information. Through a constant presence in the social network environment, the procurement function has the ability to expand their network and sources. In this digital environment, there is a possibility to create in a fast way relationships between who works in the procurement sector in the organization, who supplies that organization, and who uses the supplied services and products. Thanks to these digital relationships, the organization can have a response from both the internal side and the external side in real time. In addition, if the organization has the need to have a specific supply, it can use its own social network to reach the specific needed vendors in a very fast way.

Crowdfunding allows funding new projects, new organizations, and startups, or simply responds to the need to find capital, where traditional financial institutions offer partial and imperfect solutions and sometimes no solution at all. Private individuals, willing to support a project, make good use of their money, employing them as values, such as participation, proximity, trust, and even passion. In this way, crowdfunding satisfies a need. It responds to increasingly market social trends, such as collaborative, transparent, and horizontal consumption. This phenomenon is affected by the large influence and power of the web and of the social networks. It has its strengths in simplicity and low operating costs.

Regarding the financial sector and the current volatile and dynamic world, timing is all. The web and social networks can help in this. Thanks to the general digitization of social and business relations, the financial world but also wealthy individuals are able to exploit digital channels efficiently. It is considered one of the most beneficial sectors of the virtual world.

The financial crisis of 2008 has led to shrinking traditional financial institutions channels for obtaining financing. The startups have been particularly affected by this situation, looking for alternative ways to obtain financing. Financial institution credit is much harder to get for these startups due to the lack of guarantees and uncertain future profitability but also because the cost of servicing small organizations is relatively large.

CrowdFundMe[97]

CrowdFundMe is an Italian portal to support equity crowdfunding. It is based on creating contacts among a large number of investors with startups and SMEs in search of financing. In equity crowdfunding, the entrepreneurs propose their projects on the platform, offering potential investors the capitalization of their startup.

Before the publication, the project has to be approved by the CrowdFundMe team: the entrepreneurs can forward their ideas to the staff by email, specifying all the details. Once the evaluation process has ended, the project is published on the portal for a certain period agreed with the entrepreneur. If the minimum target is not reached, the organization shares are given back to the investors. Once the project is published, the entrepreneur is obliged to raise funds exclusively on the CrowdFundMe platform.

Crowdfunding is a key opportunity for startups because it also allows funding from small investors: CrowdFundMe starts at a minimum of 250 euros of funding from the single investor.

The portal also integrated in the same period a new investment procedure in startups looking for financing. It is called Click & Invest. It is approved by the Consob, the Italian equity funding authority.[98] Click & Invest allows users to invest any amount by doing everything directly from their computer with a few clicks, in a fast way.

Monzo[99]
Monzo is an English startup founded with the idea of being the first mobile financial institution launching a crowdfunding campaign to reach a million pound. It has been the fastest crowdfunding campaign in history. It opened the campaign on Crowdcube,[100] the UK's largest platform, and in 96 seconds reached its target capital.

Borsa del Credito[101]
Borsa del Credito is a digital lending crowdfunding platform serving Italian SMEs. It is a very simple to use: going to the site, filling out a form, and having direct access to investment or credit search.

The benefits are no paper, all digital. The cases are examined within 24 hours, and if successful money is on the account in 48 hours.

Value Chain Finance

Value chain finance[102] (or for generalization value network finance) refers to financial products and services that flow to or through any point in a value network. They enable investments that increase actors' returns and the growth and competitiveness of the chain.[103]

Financial transactions within a value chain are not new. Several emphases distinguish a value chain finance approach. These include improving finance at specific points in the value network to increase the competitiveness of the entire value chain and involving multiple actors and leveraging relationships to lower or mitigate the risks. A value chain approach involves the consideration of the risks and returns of the finance vendor along with the risk and returns of the value network actor demanding finance. Value chain actors themselves, financial institutions, microfinance institutions, other non-bank or government/regional financial institutions, or a combination of these actors can provide or facilitate financing to a value network. These actors may participate in a value chain financing arrangement for different reasons. These reasons determine the ways in which they are willing to facilitate financing for a value network upgrading investment.

Value chain finance can be grouped into three main types of instruments[104]:

- the provision of credit, savings, guarantees, or insurance to or among value network actors;
- the creation of strategic alliances through financing extended by a combination of value network actors and financial institutions;
- the offering of tools/services to manage price, production, or marketing risks.

Rural and agricultural organizations commonly have the greatest difficulty in accessing financial services from traditional providers. This makes any demand for financing a challenge. It can limit the value network development and growth. Many of the financial innovations which comprise the procurement finance were developed specifically to bridge this financial gap by lowering costs and risks of financing for value network upgrades. A stocktaking of rural financial innovations revealed that the most effective mechanisms were structured to address financial gaps that are broader than a specific value chain financing requirement.[105]

The Fluent Network is a blockchain-based financial operating network that, for instance, streamlines value chain finance.[106]

Technological Developments

Blockchain

The model of procurement finance 4.0 is based on the six Cs: cybernetics, communication, controllership, collaboration, connection, and comprehension. There are two additional aspects that are relevant for the procurement finance processes. They are two other Cs: condivision and confidence (trust). An emerging solution could support both of them. It is called blockchain.

The initiatives related to the blockchain jumped in 2017 by 73 percent worldwide. The announcements of new projects jumped 273 percent by companies in large part to be finalized. In the first five months of 2018, global venture capital has invested 1.3 billion dollars in blockchain start-ups, already exceeding 900 million dollars in 2017.[107] International Data Corporation, a global market intelligence company, estimates that spending on blockchain software is 1.79 billion euros in 2018. It will rise at a compound annual rate of 81 percent, hitting 7.7 billion euros in 2021.[108]

Blockchain as a New Solution

A blockchain solution is an open ledger in which every transaction on the network is recorded and available for all participants to see and verify.[109] It is a kind of a secured dataset. It sits in the cloud and multiple involved parties can access it. It can also be seen as a "digital trust", in the sense that it is a dataset trusted since it is based on consensus.

From a technical point of view, a blockchain is a database that runs across a global network of independent computers.[110] By providing a shared view, a blockchain solution eliminates the need to transfer information between organizations through such objects as files, messages, web services, emails, spreadsheets, direct network connections, and phone calls. It helps to eliminate differences in data between vendors, buyers, and financial institutions. For example, blockchain solutions are used to handle such things as vendor quality certificates, proof of ownership, vendor quotes, contracts, and purchase orders. It helps organizations quickly resolve delivery discrepancies by retrieving data collected end to end throughout the procure-to-pay process.

The blockchain can be categorized at data management (DM) 4.0, in the sequence:

- DM 1.0 dataset or files in one application
- DM 2.0 database in the Data Base/Data Communication (DB/DC) architecture
- DM 3.0 relational databases
- DM 4.0 blockchain in the cloud

The first use of a blockchain solution has been with Bitcoin, a digital currency that was launched on a public blockchain solution.[111] The creator, Mr. Satoshi Nakamoto, invented and released it as the underlying technology of the new digital currency. He wanted to create a system where the transfer of money was possible, secure, and independent from a central authority or an intermediary such as a central bank. To achieve this objective, two things are needed:

- ensure a secure transaction;
- decentralize the system.

The first point is addressed by using cryptography and the use of a digital signature through private keys, which enables a transaction to be authentic. The second point is based on building a distributed database (public ledger) where it is possible to register in a time sequence a series of encrypted transactions impossible to modify. Prerequisite for the recording is the establishment of the so-called public consensus. At first impact, this system might not seem very different from what happens today when people want to send information in a secure way. In fact, by using the digital signature and encryption, individuals, organizations, and institutions can digitally sign their digital documents to ensure the authenticity of the sender, integrity, and permanency, encrypt the documents, and so on. They can ensure that only somebody who has the corresponding private key can access the same content. Normally, digital signature and encryption have been centralized. Nakamoto tried to find a secure mechanism, a technology that could make real to get the public consensus and validate an operation in a peer-to-peer system without the presence of a central authority. In the protocol he invented, one of the problems he wanted to solve was to avoid the risk of the double spending. This is a type of fraud. A user could attempt to spend the same money twice, sending the same payment to two different recipients. This could happen because with virtual currencies there is the absence of a central authority that controls and validates transactions and that, hence, guarantees that a certain amount is not spent more than once.

Before the advent of blockchain, a trusted third party (for instance, a financial institution) was necessary to assure that a certain amount of data was sent or received, so that it could not be used fraudulently twice.[112] With blockchain the trust on third parties is eliminated and with it also the double-spending problem.[113] In fact, each account and the amount owned by this account are both linked to a public key. When the network validates a transaction that contains a transfer of funds, the block containing the transaction is added to the chain and the funds are automatically transferred from the sender to the recipient.

The blockchain is a chain of blocks that gathers and validates with a cryptographic process transaction made by unknown parties inside a network. This peculiarity is what makes the blockchain a trustless technology.[114] The validators, also called miners, by solving complex algorithms validate the pending transactions that are then incorporated in a block represented by a timestamp. It is not possible to modify or edit a block. To do so, it is necessary to perform another transaction. This means that transactions can be registered in a chronological order that is practically unmodifiable. So, the history of the legal affairs pertaining to a certain asset remains recorded on the blockchain. It cannot be edited or counterfeited unless the majority of the network (say the 51 percent) performs a new transaction that modifies the previous one. This statement is partially true because according to the blockchain solution and protocols used, there are mechanisms to alter the ledger. They are very difficult to implement and run.

A blockchain solution enhances the transparency and privacy of the operations performed. There are multiple copies of the same ledger. Users can verify each record. A record that is shared has a high degree of transparency. This allows a regulatory body or an independent body to check that the content of a data record has not been modified in any fraudulent way. In this way, a blockchain-based platform allows performing a transaction without the involvement of an intermediary or third party since the disintermediation and decentralization of all transactions are its main features.[115] Any form of assets, both tangible and intangible, can be registered, tracked, and transacted on it.[116] Hence, it allows performing commercial operations without a third-party certification body, with a cryptographic reporting (distributed ledger) that the network simultaneously verifies and updates.

The global blockchain solution market is expected to grow at a compound annual growth rate (CAGR) of 42.8 percent and would be worth USD 13.96 billion by 2022.[117]

Blockchain solutions are being used in the banking, financial services, and insurance segment for financial transactions and cross-border payments and often for a community of user organizations (an ecosystem).[118] This market is expected to exhibit swift growth owing to less time consumption and transaction costs. Despite its forecasted upward trajectory, there is still a lack of awareness and other regulatory problems that hinder the growth and adoption of this technology. Nonetheless, the blockchain solution market has the potential to create value and help also customers and financial institutions.

The recipient is identified and chosen by its public key. Public keys are not linked to the identity of the owner. Although a transaction can be audited, it cannot disclose information of the physical or juridical person that performed that transaction.[119] The sender authorizes the transaction by signing it with its private key, which is like a personal password. Then the network, so the peer-to-peer system, authorizes or denies the pending transaction according to the consensus mechanism used by the network.

A useful distinction to better understand this technology is the distinction between public and private blockchain. Public systems have the feature that each server, with its software, can view and write data on the registry. In private systems, however, those who are part of the network are known a priori and have a particular permission to make changes to the registry.

From a governance perspective, the blockchain can be arranged into:

- Permissioned blockchain is the private version of a blockchain solution. Here participants know each other, and an approval to join the network is necessary.[120] There is just one entity, which is the authority that centralizes the system and sets, which can join, perform transactions, and participate to the consensus mechanism.
- Un-permissioned blockchain is the public version of a blockchain solution. Here anyone can join the network and validate transactions by participating in the consensus mechanism.[121] Transactions are public, there is no central authority responsible for the running of the system and participants can have a pseudonym or can also be anonymous. This kind of distributed ledger is characterized by a high level of security of the data that increases with the number of participants as well as the computational power and processing time for the validation of a transaction.
- Blockchain consortium is a hybrid version with some elements in common to public and private blockchains. Organizations all over the world that decided to cooperate and work together towards gaining benefits by using the blockchain solution have started to use it.[122] Several consortia have been established, mainly in the financial sector. They are spreading also across other industries such as the procurement and the logistics sectors. For instance, 16 Dutch logistics operators announced to have created a consortium to explore the potential benefits of distributed ledger technologies.[123]

Blockchain and Digital Trust

This chapter focuses in more detail on the concept of trust, since it is a key element addressed by the blockchain solutions. To instill cooperation and create partnerships among players of the value network of an organization, trust is a prerequisite.[124] Its importance stems from the fact that its presence can cut the costs related to the drafting, monitoring, or non-breaching of contracts compliance.[125]

Trust can be defined as the belief by a party that the other subject with whom it is involved in a relationship will fulfill its obligations and maintain the words given.[126] Trust can also be defined as the extent to which the members of an organization believe that the members of another organization will perform their obligations and behave fairly.[127] Trust can be conceived as the willingness to rely on another party in whom someone has trust.[128] It is possible to give a definition of trust as the expectation of a behavior that is not negative by a counterparty, inside a context characterized by uncertainty.

Trust is a key feature of the relationship between parties inside the procurement processes.[129] Given its importance, it is worth to try to examine also the nature of trust, that is, where does it come from. It is not credible to state that trust is something that is born naturally. It is possible to distinguish[130]:

- Calculative trust, such as advantages and disadvantages analysis, which is an action when a party in the procurement processes believes to be the best choice not to cheat because of a rational utility maximization reasoning.
- Predictive trust, based on the ability to forecast the behavior of the other party. For this kind of trust, information availability is of primary importance because otherwise the forecasting is not reliable. In addition, the mutual sharing of information helps all the parties involved to feel less vulnerable.

The benefits of trust have been documented.[131] In fact, it was shown how it can cut transaction costs and improve the flow and sharing of information across the whole value network which is not only the cause of trust but also its effect.[132] Other authors have ascertained the same results, adding that another benefit brought by the increased trust is the information asymmetry reduction.[133]

Trust is an essential requirement for long-lasting relationships that are pivotal for building a competitive advantage in procurement. Procurement finance can benefit from an increased trust since the information is shared and there is no single entity in possession of it. The literature also points out that today each transaction requires a kind of trusted party, or intermediary, in addition to some kind of contracts and degree of trust.[134] If, for example, one considers a financial transaction between two parties, unless one exchanges cash hand by hand, a bank or another kind of intermediary is required.

Blockchain solutions make the altering of transactions nearly impossible because each block is linked to the previous one. Unless the network is hacked, transactions are tamper-proof. If one compares the example of a blockchain-based transfer of money (unless it is a transfer performed in a permissioned situation with the existence of a single authority) with an intermediary-based transfer, it is possible to note how in this last case it is sufficient only to corrupt the third party, which is the guarantor, to make an illegal transaction. What emerges from these examples is the fact that a blockchain solution may be able to ensure a security level greater than one centralized authority, since the network attacks are nearly impossible or, at least, more difficult to do if compared to a centralized system (single point of failure).

The fact that organizations can operate on a more secure network is itself a factor that can increase the trust of the parties. The sharing of information across the network can bring bigger trust among members of a value network. This is due to the reciprocal effects between information flow and trust in the relationships within a value network.

The features of the trust in a blockchain solution are[135]:

- All network participants have a log of all available transactions.
- Exploitation of network participants to verify and validate transactions, for example, to prevent multiple transactions being carried out more than once through a process called consensus.
- Adoption of security mechanisms to track transactions and prevent related ledgers from being modified.
- It contains time markings, so that traceability and transaction verification can be simpler.
- It is programmable. Writing operations can only be realized when certain predetermined conditions occur.

The potential benefits of a blockchain solution consist in the reduction of process management costs, the dissemination of the information, and the more efficient market functioning mechanisms.

Several financial institutions' sector's representatives have expressed their interest in deepening this solution. There are several participants, including through national and international collaborative initiatives, in the experimentation and development of applications, in proofs of concept, or prototypes. The common objective is to make processes more efficient, but also to allow the development of new products and services that best fit the digital economy.

The blockchain solution could have some potential risks[136]:

- Lack of legislative oversight. In the distributed peer-to-peer system, there seems to be no room for a regulatory organization. Not always it is acceptable that systems can operate without legally managed standards.
- Technical skills gap. In any organization, new technologies can create confusion and slowdown in the learning processes. Employees struggling to adopt new technologies can threaten security and slow down business initiatives.
- Incompatibility with existing ICT systems. This technology requires radical changes and a remarkable investment when deciding on its adoption.

- Lack of standardization. There are efforts to introduce standardization. This is, for instance, the case of the Blockchain in Transport Alliance (BiTA). This is a consortium of the foremost leaders in the trucking industry forging a path towards industry standards in blockchain use.[137] All organizations within BiTA share a unified mission of developing a standards framework, educating the market on blockchain applications, and encouraging the use of said applications through exemplary implementation;
- Control, security, and privacy. Although blockchain solution is based on an advanced encryption system, the sharing may be subject to security hurdles and threaten the confidentiality of the information and in the extreme cases open to frauds.

Tradle[138]

Tradle is a British startup. It can store information with high resilience to potential hackers and cyber-attacks.[139] It manages a platform to try to compensate for the blockchain limitations, such as low transaction throughput, high data storage limits, absence of transactional semantics, and high cost of computations.

Trust in Motion (TiM) is Tradle's app on this platform.[140] It allows users to start a secure line of communications and go on-the-record to exchange confidential documents, verifications, attributions, and agreements. The resulting records are stored securely and irrevocably with global permission-less access and high resilience to hackers, spying, and takedown demands.

In this way, it allows, for instance, a partner financial institution to share data of their customers. The partner organization of the financial institution can offer a very quick and streamlined process for subscribing to a product without asking data already available in possession of the financial institution.

The Use of Blockchain

There are several potential uses of the blockchain solutions. The following sections present some uses relevant to procurement finance.

Blockchain and Procurement

Procurement is substantially changing in the last decades. In fact, the spread of globalization and the change in the global markets led to the expansion of the organization's value networks: More and more they are crossing the national borders.[141] In the past, frequently there was an arm-length and sometimes adversarial relationship between vendors' and buyers' organizations.[142] In the 1990s, continuing through the 2000s, organizations have been more willing to focus on their core activities and outsource the remaining ones.[143] This evolution of the procurement, also called "extended enterprise", implies and requires the concept of cooperation between vendors and buyers. As a consequence, trust is its founding and essential value. All the parties in the value network know that to stay competitive and survive need to strengthen their relationships and cooperate. The overall performances improve, both in cost and quality, through cooperation rather than competition.[144] Some inputs are required to create these new synergies, such as[145]:

- trust;
- commitment;
- risk sharing.

Both trust and commitment are at the basis of procurement finance and long-lasting partnerships.[146] Partnerships and strategic alliances in the value network do not grow on their own. They need some inputs, and trust is one of the most important.[147]

Blockchain solutions can support this need of trust, thanks to their characteristics. This is one of the reasons why blockchain solutions are considered in the value network and particularly in the procurement applications.

The blockchain is a powerful support to the digital transformation of the procurement.[148] It is the best technological solution to implement the platform concept for procurement 4.0. A shared database can support the various stakeholders associated with the procurement processes: the organization, its customers, the vendors, the partners, and, whenever necessary, the regulators. It can manage a portfolio of vendors, their administration, sourcing, and the resolution and management of any complaints. The blockchain is able to provide visibility of shared data. It can provide a seamless, reliable, and uninterrupted service to support an ecosystem of an organization's procurement. As a consequence, it allows increasing the effectiveness, efficiency, economy, and ethics of this ecosystem. It is a method to facilitate the availability and exchange of data among many parties involved in the procurement processes.

Figure 6.5 shows the typical high-level process of the procurement. The blockchain can be used throughout the entire cycle.

In using the blockchain solutions in procurement, it is important to consider a framework (Fig. 6.6).

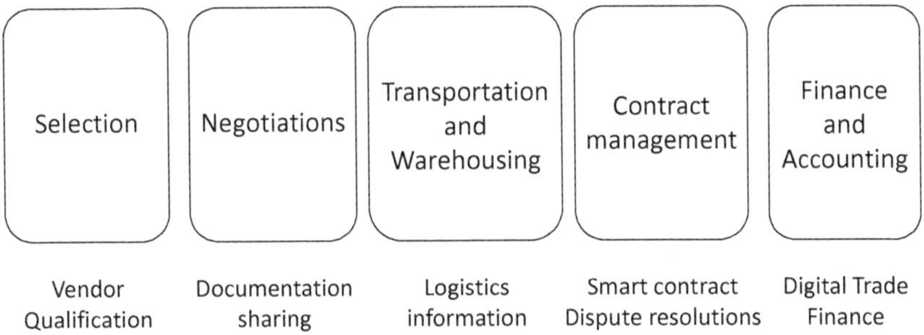

Fig. 6.5 Blockchain and the procurement processes

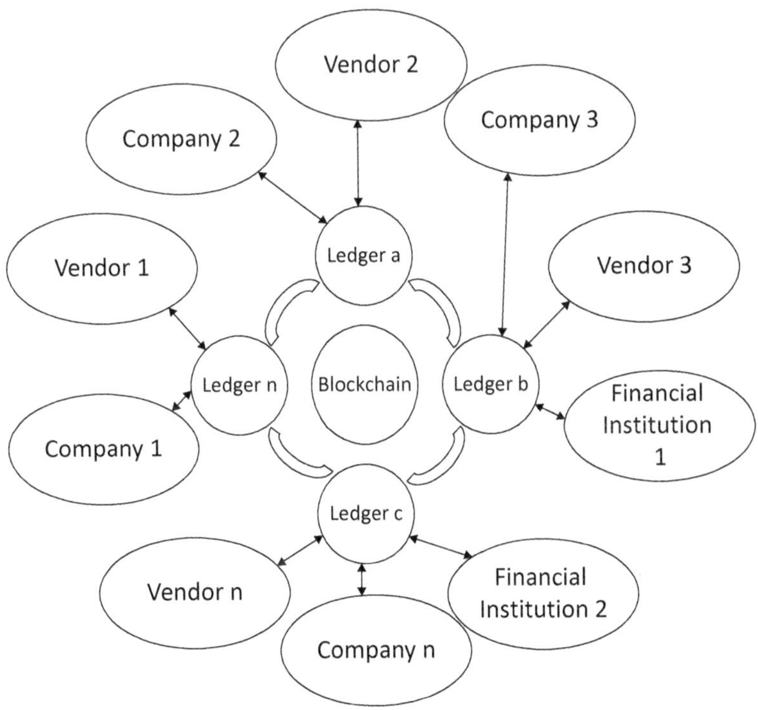

Fig. 6.6 Blockchain model procurement finance

Walmart[149]

Like most merchants, the world's largest USA retailer, Walmart, struggles to identify and remove food that has been recalled or gone beyond its expiration date. When a customer gets sick, it can take days to identify the product, shipment, and vendor. With the blockchain, Walmart is able to obtain critical data from a single receipt, including vendors, details on how and where food was grown and who inspected it.[150] The blockchain solution can include information from the pallet to the individual package, entered by the organization and its vendors.

With blockchain, Walmart can do timely removals. It can get more trust from consumers and its vendors.

Blockchain and Finance

The digital transformation occurring in the financial sector, favored by the introduction of blockchain solutions, can change substantially the rules of the financial system. It creates an open system to which everyone can access and participate. The certification process is distributed between the nodes of the system. It would not be in the hands of one party or dependent on the communication between parties.[151]

The blockchain solutions support the collaboration and the trust among network participants. They validate the transactions by the interaction of all nodes and not by an intermediary or central entity. There is no need for a central entity to verify data congruence and validity. This occurs through the consensus of the network: the distributed ledger. The elimination of intermediaries allows making money transactions more secure, rapid, and cheaper.

Blockhain is a revolutionary technology able to govern transactions in the online finance. It allows the transfer of trust from the hands of a classic broker to a network of computers connected to each other. Blockchain solutions have a future as an ally of financial institutions since they limit brokering in trading, guarantee compliance, integrity, and traceability. This technology is able to switch to a large-scale collaborative economy by reducing transaction costs due to the disintermediation and facilitation of exchanges between users around the world. This model would make quicker and more fluid transitional payments.

The Academy of Information and Communications Technology, a scientific research institute under China's Ministry of Industry and Information Technology (MIIT), and China's Tencent Holdings' report includes eight core conclusions on the blockchain solutions in the financial sector.[152] The report states that blockchain solutions will further enhance the transparency of financial transactions, strengthen the flexibility of system operation, and automate processes. In this way, it will affect the record keeping, the accounting, and the payment settlement methods of financial services.

Blockchain for Procurement Finance

The characteristics of the blockchain solutions can play a big role in the fields of payment and settlement, supply chain finance, securities trading, insurance, and credit reporting. It is necessary that blockchain solutions for financial applications should be legally regulated.

Blockchain solutions are an interesting application for cross-border payments, as through using the distributed ledger, the alignment of information between the parties is guaranteed. This technology can cut the infrastructure costs of financial institutions related to international payments, securities trading, and compliance.

Blockchain solutions have a global reach. The current transfer system employs a large number of intermediaries, adding costs and delays to settle the transactions. Blockchain solutions can eliminate these structural inefficiencies. They allow making money transfers instantly and cheaply. The central element in the transfer of money is the trust of all the parties involved in the transaction, especially in the case of cross-border transfers. Each intermediary involved in the transfer must carry out a series of operations in a timely and coordinated way often with the presence of the other intermediaries. The blockchain solutions allow having an alternative to this situation allowing to make the transactions more rapid and cheaper.

Blockchain solutions eliminate the need of a central counterparty. In the procurement finance context, the two financial institutions involved would not need to resort to third-party intermediaries. They use decentralized digital ledgers to communicate with each other and validate credits and charges on the liquidity provider account.

Eliminating the need of the matching financial institution reduces a whole range of risks[153]:

- the credit risk connected with the corresponding financial institution becoming insolvent, putting at risk the sums it should pay to the counterparts in the payment;
- the liquidity risk that the counterparts do not have enough money to settle a payment at some point in time;
- the operational risks and external events that may interrupt or delay the settlement process.

Despite these benefits, in the international trade context, some risks remain related to the use of the blockchain solutions. There is still a lack of a linkage between this new technology and a regulatory framework. There is no uniform legislation among the countries able to establish counterparties' rights or obligations in the field of money transfers made through the exploitation of the blockchain solutions.

Several projects have already been launched by many big financial institutions, with the aim of exploring the potential capabilities of the blockchain solutions and how to exploit them.

Alfa-Bank[154]

Alfa-Bank is the major Russian private bank.[155] It is one of the most important financial institutes to have already started working with Ethereum's blockchain to build a prototype for financial messages called Masterchain, a ledger able to provide instant data confirmation and guarantee security in financial transactions.

S7 Airlines made the first payment through the intelligent agreement of Ethereum's blockchain,[156] thanks to Alfa-Bank. The agreement was made between the airline and its counterparty by using a letter of credit (LoC) through Alfa-Bank.

Deloitte acted as an airline consultant, providing technical support on the operations of the blockchain solution and legal support to the project.

Smart contracts helped register on the Ethereum blockchain the financial institution opening and execution of the LoC. Legally this transaction meets all the requirements of a LoC as the financial institution's liquidation form. It demonstrates the potential of smart contract applications under the Russian law.

Two smart contracts were used simultaneously, one to open the LoC and one to close it. The two Ethereum smart contracts helped improve visibility, reduce any code errors, and automate the transactions.

Bank of America[157]

Microsoft Corp. and Bank of America Merrill Lynch[158] collaborate in using Microsoft Azure-based blockchain as a service. This collaboration aims to change the way that some transactions in procurement finance are processed. Normally, the use of standby letters of credit requires high costs and time. The blockchain solution can facilitate the use of them and make them cheaper.

This experimentation was the first collaboration-based blockchain solution between a financial institution and a treasury organization.

Standard Chartered[159]

The collaboration between Standard Chartered, the Development Bank of Singapore, and Infocomm Development Authority of Singapore has launched the first procurement finance blockchain platform developed by financial institutions relative to the trading invoices. This platform is called TradeSafe. Its aim is to reduce the risks of invoices duplications in the trade operations and to monitor the invoices guaranteeing the confidentiality of the customers. Through this platform, the invoices can be changed into digital form within a distributed ledger. The access to the customers is open. They can take part and check the correctness of the financed trade documents.

Standard Chartered has also launched in Hong Kong a proof of concept to verify the distributed ledger applications (DLTs) useful in procurement finance.[160] Standard Chartered has collaborated with four important financial institutions forming the DLT procurement finance working group.

The aim of this proof of concept is reducing the fraud cases for buyers and vendors involved in procurement transactions. This solution allows the upgrading of data in real time and their visibility from all the stakeholders. In this way, the buyer has the benefit of reducing the risks of non-payments by the buyer.

Deutsche Bank[161]

Deutsche Bank has a strong interest in the blockchain solutions. This financial institution has collaborated with other big financial institutions on several blockchain initiatives. Deutsche Bank, BNY Mellon, Santander, and UBS decided to join forces to bring about an innovation project on blockchain. The aim was to get a solution that can handle business and financial transactions on the blockchain.[162]

The motivation of this initiative is to identify the possibility of a platform that can handle more financially and more securely all back-office activities related to financial transactions. Transactions between large financial institutions and other financial institutions are a very large number. They are time-consuming and require financial institutions to have costly back-office structures. Transaction management through a blockchain network promises to ease back-end office workloads and speeding up all the procedures.

IBM, Natixis, and Trafigura[163]

IBM, Natixis, and Trafigura collaborate for making the crude oil sector in step with the current digital transformation. This initiative is based on the digitization of a blockchain solution of the transactions related to the oil sector.

The solution includes one distributed ledger accessible to all the participants in the transaction, such as the buyer, the vendor, and the financial institutions. All these actors have the same information of the transactions, since the data of the transactions are shared in a distributed solution, throughout the entire phase of the procurement operations.

The new trading platform provides several functionalities, such as the sharing of trading and shipping documents and their updates in one shared register: using this platform. The results are the reduction of transaction access and processing times and the elimination of the duplication of documents and of their authentication processes among all commercial partners. These transactions traditionally require complex workflows and processes based on paper. This solution provides a greater visibility, efficiency, economics, and security.

Commonwealth Bank of Australia and Wells Fargo[164]

The collaboration between the Commonwealth Bank of Australia and Wells Fargo regards the cotton sector.

The collaboration aims at experimenting the use of a blockchain solution in the global trade of cotton through open-account transactions. The core feature of this collaboration is the linkage among blockchain, smart contracts, and the Internet of Things (IoT). The operation involves a letter of credit performed with the use of digital smart contracts recorded on a distributed ledger.

This solution allows releasing payment of transactions through an automatic way, digitally, when the shipping has arrived at its destination. Normally, the reference financial institutions of the actors use letters of credit. The blockchain solution allows the organizations to be informed in real time of the shipping and its possible modifications. In this way, it is possible to make a faster exchange of guarantees of payments. All actors are involved in a unique distributed ledger. This solution provides the capability to see every change in the transactions immediately. This blockchain solution assures more visibility and security in the relations between buyers and vendors because of their financial institutions.

UniCredit[165]

One of the biggest problems for financial institutions is the inability to track cross-border payments in real time. The purpose of the Swift's global payment innovation (GPI) project is to overcome this disadvantage.

GPI aims to define a new qualitative standard for cross-border payments. This test phase is born thanks to the collaboration of Swift with the major financial institutions such as the Italian bank UniCredit.

The initiative aims to help financial institutions address challenges in monitoring and managing the international accounts of their customers. This is important to support cross-border payments. In this way, the financial institutions can have information on their liquidity in the organizations in real time to manage in a better way funds during the day.

Operating Solutions in Procurement Finance

Blockchain can greatly simplify, digitize, and make more agile and secure the procurement finance transactions among organizations and financial institutions. This application aims to make domestic and cross-border procurement transactions easier especially for SMEs. This is achieved thanks to the capabilities of the distributed ledger solution. It is intended to seamlessly connect the parties involved in a trade transaction (that is, buyer, buyer's financial institution, vendor, vendor's financial institution, logistics operators, and other interested parties, such as the customs), online and via mobile devices. This product simplifies procurement finance processes for SMEs by addressing the challenges of managing, tracking, and securing domestic and international trade transactions.

Blockchain provides a solution to two problems in the case of procurement finance (Fig. 6.7).[166] First, it ensures that the same unit of the asset cannot be sent to more than one place (a "double spend"). Second, it must be impossible for anyone to create new units of the asset on a whim ("forgery"). Any entity able to do either of these things could steal large value from the system. A blockchain solution is a completely digital solution that reduces substantially times, checks, paper, back-office, operational risks, all the ugly, inefficient, and heavy procedures that are behind the traditional financial institutions' processes.

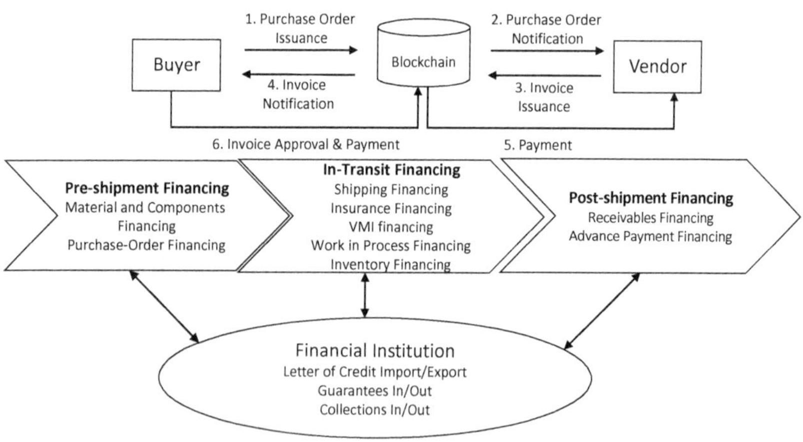

Fig. 6.7 Procurement finance model with blockchain

Larger organizations use documentary credit as a way of reducing the risks involved in doing business. The documentary credit is not always suitable for SMEs or for organizations that prefer open-account solutions. The secure records on these blockchain-based applications accelerate the order-to-settlement process and decrease significantly the administrative paperwork. A platform of this type helps also in end-to-end visibility. This can provide SMEs' trust to open trade opportunities with new partners in their home market or especially in foreign markets. By pooling expertise and resources, the participants to this blockchain application can jointly exploit the benefits of a digitized and lean procurement network.

Procurement finance leverages the buyer's creditworthiness to improve the vendor's cash flow.[167] It can help in several ways. For instance, it can support the credit transfer, if the buyer's rating is strong enough to finance not only the vendor but also the vendor's vendor and possibly beyond (the tier 2+ vendors). Procurement finance can help also to support the cost pressure over the buyer's entire upstream value network.

Unlike highly customized procurement finance systems, the design of blockchain solutions is decentralized and collaborative. Adding new participants (such as the tier 2 and 3 vendors in the example before) is relatively straightforward. It may be relatively easy by authenticating participation with a digital signature (with an associated public key).

The systems to implement what is described in the previous paragraphs exist today. There are blockchain-based procurement finance platforms. They have varying degrees of sophistication in terms of workflow, customizability, and linkages with standard ICT systems.

In particular, a blockchain solution can also help the cash flows associated with procurement: finance. The blockchain solution could record the different transactions between the parties. It would allow authorized customers to track and refine transactions securely and fast in paperless mode.[168] All parties would be able to verify immediately the status of their reconciliation. The blockchain allows a seamless connection between the parties involved in a transaction, simplifying management, monitoring, and settlement of domestic and international transactions. The financial transactions would be recorded on the blockchain, speeding up the processes with full visibility and security.

In addition to reducing or eliminating bureaucracy, the blockchain solutions ensure visibility end to end of the entire process, reducing the barriers of distrust that often hinder especially small organizations when it comes to operating in new markets.

The visibility and auditability that are characteristics of the blockchain solutions allow financial collaboration across the extended value network, including potential vendors, financial institutions, partners, and customers. According to some estimates, of the annual global trade expenditure of USD 18 trillion, procurement finance 4.0 could address USD 255–280 billion with existing procurement finance 4.0 instruments.[169]

The potential of blockchain solutions in procurement finance 4.0 is only now starting to be analyzed and especially implemented. For instance, most of the value network solutions described above are mainly supported by fintech startups. Traditional procurement finance applications are only slowly considering modifications to allow these new solutions.[170]

The use of blockchain solutions can be further improved in combination with other advanced technological solutions. Advanced predictive Big Data analytics can support complex decision-making scenarios based on a variety of performance tests, in different and critical market conditions. Such business simulations can support the design and redesign of procurement finance operations.[171] For example, by simulating different market and competitor scenarios, the use of blockchain and open data can help in assessing business agility and resilience of a given vendor or risk.

Another example of the use of blockchain is Ethereum, also a global network of computers.[172] Examples of what this network can register and monitor are:

- debts;
- delivery promises.

we.trade[173]

we.trade was established by Deutsche Bank, HSBC, KBC, Natixis, Nordea, Rabobank, Santander, Societe Generale, and UniCredit to address the expectations of their customers to make cross-border trade more straightforward.[174] The consortium has succeeded in meeting each bank's internal governance and procedures requirements to make this innovation a reality.[175]

we.trade is an example of the solutions for procurement finance 4.0:

- it combines a blockchain solution to share the data in the procurement finance ecosystem;

(*continued*)

(continued)

- each external partner can connect to data feed we.trade using application programming interfaces (APIs), based on agreed and efficient standards;
- it hosts smart contract which allows the automation of the contract clauses and their full reliability on the side of the parties of those smart contracts.

we.trade operates on the IBM Cloud. It is designed to link the parties of a commercial transaction online and through mobile devices. In this way, it is possible to streamline procurement finance processes by addressing the challenges of managing, tracking, and securing business transactions globally. Addressing the financial gap of SMEs, which are not using documentary credit and prefer to rely on an open account, this solution aims to open new opportunities for improving margins, start new business relationships, and promote business growth. This platform improves access to finance, providing international procurement transactions with accountability and visibility. This highly scalable platform is able to support the customers of financial institutions. It helps in providing the SMEs with the information necessary to start trading with new partners across Europe. With we.trade, SMEs have access to an easy-to-use platform that can provide a consolidated view of their procurement finance transactions.

Accounting transactions are recorded on distributed databases, based on a blockchain model, speeding up the process in full visibility. Only organizations authorized by participating financial institutions may access we.trade. we.trade is available across 11 European countries: Belgium, Denmark, Finland, France, Germany, Italy, the Netherlands, Norway, Spain, Sweden, and the UK. we.trade is expanding into additional markets in Europe and globally as further financial partners come on board.

we.trade is a solution, apparently technical. It is the base to create real collaboration across multiple actors in a procurement ecosystem. This solution demonstrates how a new solution can help the procurement ecosystem to gain efficiencies and provide greater transparency in live transactions. It is a disruptive model that has the potential to reshape the future of global procurement finance.

Barclays[176]
The bill of lading (BOL) is a document issued by carriers containing details about a shipment, generally the type of product carried, their quantity, and their destination. It gives the title of property to a certain party. Barclays, in partnership with an Israeli startup, conducted on September 2016 the first trade transaction using blockchain for dematerializing the BOL. This transaction guaranteed USD 100,000 in dairy exports from a cooperative in Ireland to a Seychelles trading organization. In this way, it is possible to transfer procurement documentation, cutting processing times from ten days to less than four hours. It is also possible to cut the costs of the procurement finance.

BBVA[177]
Spain's BBVA has become the first global bank to issue a loan using the distributed ledger technology. BBVA carried out the entire process for a €75 million corporate loan—from negotiating terms to signing the loan—on a mutually distributed ledger that kept both the financial institution and the borrower up to date on the loan's progress. The process cuts the negotiation time for the loan from "days to hours", and BBVA hailed it as a significant advance in the exploitation of distributed ledger technology not just in banking but in the way private and public blockchains can interact.

The main benefit of a blockchain solution over existing processes is its ability to speed up and simplify complex transactions by making changes and updates visible immediately to all parties. A single blockchain-based system is cheaper to maintain than a large number of systems and storages that financial institutions use for managing the transactions of this type. In the lending market, blockchain solutions have more potential in corporate and syndicated loans than in consumer loans, because corporate and syndicated lending is more complex and records need to be accessed by a broader range of organizations than the single borrower normally involved in consumer loans. For its pilot project, BBVA used a private blockchain for the negotiation and completion process. Finally, it registered the completed contract on an Ethereum's public blockchain.

Smart Contracts

Blockchain solutions can support several types of transactions including the so-called smart contracts.[178] Szabo envisioned many years ago the possibility of translating contractual clauses in smart contract codes that were embedded in a software that was responsible for their execution.[179] In this way, it is possible to release the signatory parties from using intermediaries and reducing the percentage of errors in the execution of a contract. These contracts are deterministic, in the sense that all possible outcomes are coded in advance when inserted in the blockchain. The chance of having random results is then not possible.[180] In addition, their presence in the blockchain makes auditing easier. Each user of the network receives all the history of a contract's code operations in real time as they are performed. The parties who want to control some events related to the execution of the contract can do it in real time.

A smart contract can be defined as a code that performs the logic of a contract agreed upon by the parties.[181] This type of contract acts as a kind of independent third party in complying with the terms and conditions of the agreement, coded in the blockchain solution (Fig. 6.8). It is possible to establish all the possible outputs *a priori*.[182] This feature improves efficiency and transparency in the execution of several types of contracts by reducing excessive paperwork and monitoring as well as all risks and costs related to such operations.[183]

Smart contracts are one of the means by which the blockchain solution changes the way organizations work. They extend the fields of application of this solution without being only restricted to the use in the financial sector.[184] They are not just paper contracts "translated" on a software.

A possible classifications of smart contracts is the following one[185]:

- Smart contract code, intended as a code that is run on a blockchain. This kind of contract is recorded on the blockchain and executed by it when certain pre-established conditions are met. In addition, it can transfer assets, such as virtual currencies.
- Smart legal contracts, intended as a legal paper contract translated and executed on a software. While the previous kind of contract is somehow more simple and straightforward because it is something coded and set on a software, smart legal contracts face the issue of having so many facets and categories around the world, according to the jurisdiction, so to translate them on a software tends to be much more complex.

Fig. 6.8 Procurement process intelligence

The key features of a smart contract are[186]:

- Digitization
- Self-execution (enforcement)

Figure 6.9 resumes the concepts mentioned.[187]

There are many interesting features in the smart contracts.[188] Smart contracts have the characteristic of being also decentralized for the simple reason that they are not on a single server since they are distributed across the entire network. The smart contract has the responsibility of executing some actions when some events are triggered in the contract.[189] It is up to the peer-to-peer network of users to check that the actions performed by

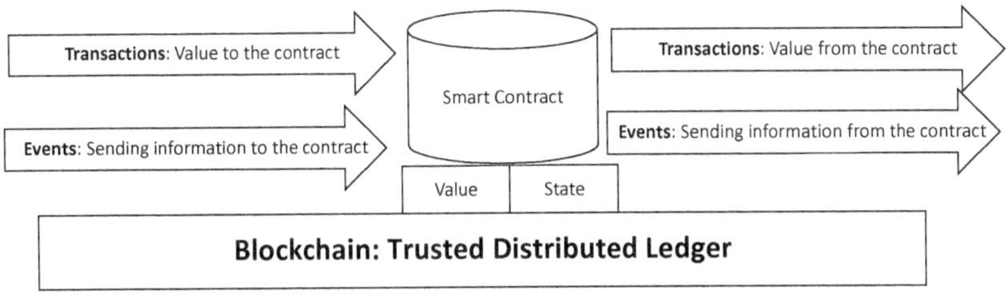

Fig. 6.9 Schema for the smart contracts

the parties correspond to those that have established during the drafting of the contract. The network does it through the consensus mechanism. The network allows the execution thereof and updates the status of the smart contract on the distributed ledger.[190]

From a technological point of view, smart contracts inherit the characteristics of the blockchain solution. They enhance the level of security and prevent fraudulent practices from happening. To reach effectiveness for this kind of contracts, a computing system that executes them is required, such as a distributed ledger technology (DLT).[191] Smart contracts (SC) and DLT are two distinct but complementary technologies,[192] in the sense that a distributed ledger is a platform that makes the execution of a smart contract possible and concrete. A smart contract code can be embedded in the blockchain. Once activated, it self-executes, so the parties involved do not need to start a case before a court since smart contracts are self-enforcing.[193] They also allow the replacement of legal paper contracts and the decrease of manual work due to their digitization bringing an improvement in the efficiency, productivity, and growth.[194]

Smart contracts inherit many of the benefits of which the blockchain is characterized. In fact, the digitization and self-execution attributes can bring cost savings since they cut the involvement of operators and intermediaries. Transactions are faster, more accurate, and secure.[195] The human role in the implementation of the contracts is drastically reduced. As a consequence, the percentage of human errors and the costs related to the use of operators and intermediaries' shrink. Besides, the resolution of issues related to the performance of a contract is leaner and faster. It is more efficient. The self-execution of contracts means that there is no room for parties to breach the contract and the terms and conditions set in it.[196]

The application of this type of contracts is large. Procurement finance can benefit from the use of these contracts since the blockchain solutions began to develop in finance (Figs. 6.10 and 6.11).

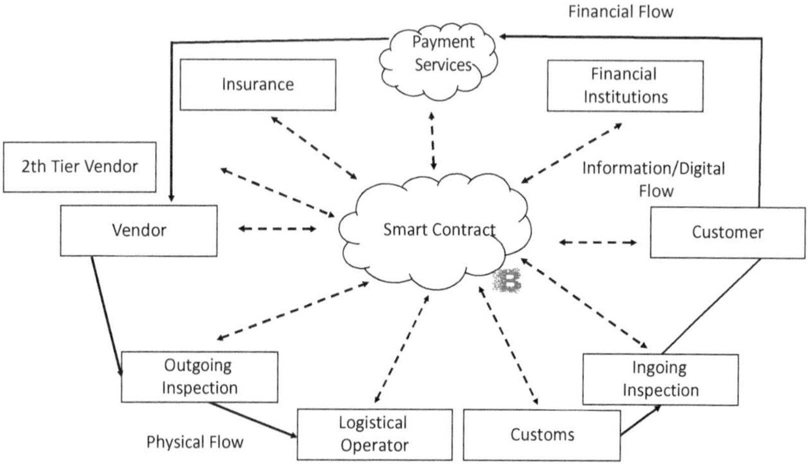

Fig. 6.10 Smart contracts and procurement finance

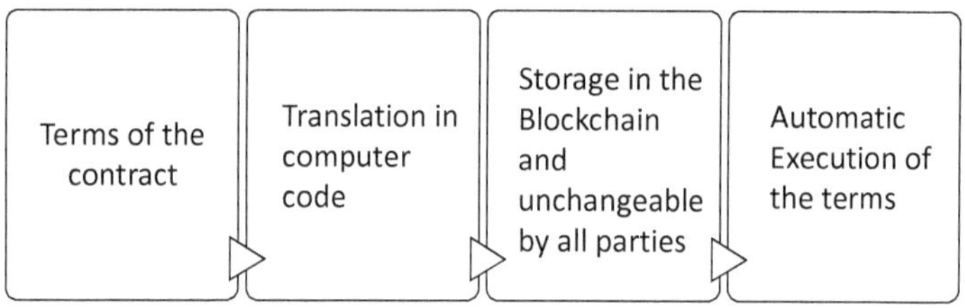

Fig. 6.11 Smart contracts

Despite the several benefits, smart contracts have some limitations that may reduce their application and, therefore, the scope of their benefits. They rely on the data virtually present on the blockchain. Regulations in this sector of smart contracts and blockchain solution are non-existent or limited. Some people argue of the feasibility of a real-world enforceability before a court for this kind of contracts.[197] Another issue stems from their flexibility. In real life, even when legal contracts are drafted as precise as possible, some unforeseen events can take place. Since smart contracts produce outputs according to the inputs used in their drafting, some mechanisms should be put in place for the parties to face this kind of problems also for a contract that runs on a blockchain.[198]

Another issue with smart contracts is the compliance with the legal systems. Each jurisdiction has its own regulations. The fact of having a peer-to-peer system where new types of contracts are executed without the need for intermediaries poses questions for the government authorities. An example is the taxations of the parties in these contracts.[199] In a more globalized world, the audit of the accounts for the application of VAT becomes more complex as happened in the case of online platforms for organizations like Airbnb. New tax reporting methods should be put in place.[200] In the light of the deep impact that the blockchain and smart contracts could bring into the *modus operandi* of the organizations, it is necessary that government agencies have to change and update the traditional legal systems.[201]

The City of Kouvola[202]

Not only startups are pushing the innovation boundaries in the value network field. The Finnish city of Kouvola has received €2.4 million of European funding to develop a project called SmartLog that applies the blockchain and smart contracts to shipping containers. The city is a hub for trade between the EU, Russia, and Asia. Its region is hosting around 700 logistics organizations.

R3[203]

The US enterprise software company R3 and the procurement finance technology company TradeIX[204] work together for an initiative focused on the overhaul of open-account procurement finance infrastructure. The initiative is a joint undertaking between R3, TradeIX, and 12 financial institutions including Bangkok Bank, Barclays, BBVA, Bladex, BNP Paribas, Commerzbank, CTBC Bank, ING, Intesa Sanpaolo, Shinhan Bank, Royal Bank of Scotland, and Wells Fargo.

R3, TradeIX, and the participating financial institutions are developing an end-to-end open-account procurement finance business network powered by TradeIX and R3's Corda distributed ledger platform. The prototype is customized to meet the needs of participants across multiple geographies. It supports the continued growth of open-account trade while making it more secure and simpler.

(*continued*)

(continued)

This initiative includes a robust suite of trade specific APIs and technology tools, an advanced rules engine, and an open, standard core infrastructure for procurement data, contracts, and transactions.

This solution allows financial institutions to automate pre- and post-shipment financing and risk mitigation for corporate buyers and vendors around the world. With it, corporate buyers and vendors get access to a light and flexible API-driven technology solution. This approach helps simplify procurement finance by improving visibility into trade flows, and providing access to the credit and risk mitigation services at critical points in the procurement lifecycle. This infrastructure enables a high degree of interoperability. It is designed to integrate with existing platforms as well as R3 and other ecosystems.

The business network improves access to open-account procurement finance for the global ecosystem of financial institutions, buyers, vendors, technology providers, insurers, and other parties, such as logistics organizations or customs, that are critical to facilitating global open-account procurement flows.

The development phase involves creating standard procurement finance smart contracts on a distributed ledger infrastructure.[205] This provides secure and automated financing of value network using a single record for critical procurement data including identities, purchase orders, invoices, shipping and logistics information, trade assets, financing activity, credit risk, and more.

Cloud Computing

Cloud computing is a new way of using and deploying information and communication technology (ICT) services where the users only use the ICT services rather than having the ICT infrastructures which provide the service. Users are not interested in how they are built or the technologies that they are using to support or where the applications are processed if they are secure.[206]

Cloud computing promises access to hardware and software resources that provide on-demand services massively scalable and distributed over the web. A third-party provider makes available the cloud computing with the on-demand formula. The users only pay for what they consume in terms of resources, usage time, number of transactions, and so on. This model applies the principles of mass production to ICT transforming it into a commodity.

The NIST (National Institute of Standards and Technology) defines cloud computing as[207]:

> Cloud Computing is a model enabling convenient and on-demand access to a shared pool of configurable computing resources that can be quickly obtained and released with minimal management effort and a limited interaction with the service provider.

From this definition, it is possible to clarify the cloud computing's five essential characteristics. They specify which functionalities a cloud computing service should provide to its users[208]:

- Self-service: The user must be able to request services independently, without the intervention of infrastructure managers or service providers.
- Global accessibility: Services must be accessible from multiple devices, from multiple locations, and at all times. Cloud computing needs to provide different accesses: personal computers, mobile, tablet, small desktop, or large server.
- Resource pooling: ICT resources (storage, processors, virtual machines, and so on) are grouped. They need not be isolated. In this way, it is possible to make dynamic possible servicing for a large number of users according to their needs.
- Immediate elasticity: Resources can be acquired and released elastically, in some cases even automatically, to quickly move outward and inside the specific application in relation to its demand. To the customer, the resources available should appear unlimited and available in any quantity and at any time.
- Service measurability: Every service needs to be monitored transparently so that it can be measured in terms of resource consumption. In this way, it is possible to apply the pay-per-use model.

In addition, there are three basic models of service[209]:

- Infrastructure as a Service (IaaS): Hardware infrastructure, network, and storage are made available as services. The customer controls the processing, storage, network, and computing resources. The customer does not have the management or control of the underlying cloud infrastructure. He/she can change the configuration and overall capacity of the system within predetermined limits.

- Platform as a Service (PaaS): The customer can develop and deploy their applications on the platform provided, within the limits allowed by the vendor. The customer has no control over the underlying infrastructure, but he can control applications and he/she configures the application environment.
- Software as a Service (SaaS): It is a web-based application software distribution model. Accessing SaaS applications directly from a web browser eliminates the need to purchase, install, maintain, and upgrade hardware or software. The SaaS provider deals with the entire infrastructure management, and the customer always has the latest version of the application. The application becomes a service available on request.

There are four models of deployment:

- Public cloud computing services are provided to customers via a network made available to the public. Public clouds offer efficiency and affordable costs, and they are often multi-tenants, that is, the vendor manages the service in a shared environment.
- Private cloud computing services are provided by the organization, or by an external provider, only to the organization and its various units (on-premise). What matters is the use of the services. The infrastructure can be managed by the organization itself or by an external provider. The property can be internal or external. The services must be the sole property of a single organization. It offers the highest level of security and control.
- Community cloud computing services are delivered by an organization or service provider to a small group of organizations that share some features, for example, security levels, legal norms, objectives, and so on. The infrastructure can be managed by one of the organizations in the group or by an external provider.
- Hybrid cloud services are built on hybrid infrastructure that uses private mode for some aspects (such as data retention) and public mode for others (such as access interfaces).

Cloud computing is not just a technology. It is an architectural revolution involving all levels of ICT: software that people use every day, reading email, servers that distribute business application, or the configuration of the entire ICT infrastructure. In all these areas, cloud computing is able to improve existing technologies, to cut acquisition costs, to increase agility, to improve service efficiency, and to enable innovative processes. It is a transformation not only to large or very large organizations, rather than for anyone using computer tools. It is particularly useful for SMEs and startups since it cuts their processing costs, but especially it allows to move from capital costs to variable costs, to cut setup times and costs, and to increase flexibility.[210]

Cloud computing is a set of interacting solutions. The peculiarity of these solutions is the absence of physical contiguity between the technologies used to implement the solutions. Cloud computing allows the movement of part or all of the needed features outside from the local network (which can be the only existing computer in a small business).

The needs that cloud computing is able to satisfy are:

- Sharing the information and data among the various devices and users in a totally transparent, simple, and fast way.
- Integrating such information and data with other information and data that may come from other services or from other external sources.
- Better pacing of work because the organizations can ignore the infrastructure management aspects that allow them to enjoy the services. They only need to use a device that connects to the Internet, a connection, a browser, or a small customer software (such as an android or an iOs app).
- Provisioning flexibility, since cloud computing services are highly flexible and easily scalable, the organizations are able to change fast, reducing efforts and issues.

Against these benefits, cloud computing has several criticalities. The most important issues are the difficulty of integrating a public cloud computing environment with the existing infrastructure in the organization (hybrid computing). There is also the immaturity of supply and services, followed by regulatory compliance issues, the difficulty in quantifying costs and benefits deriving from the use of the provision ways "as a Service".

With cloud computing, it is essential to pay particular attention to problems related to security and privacy.

Cloud Computing in the Procurement Finance

Regarding the international context, in an increasingly globalized world, the number of cross-border transactions increases. This increase underlines the need to allow the transactions take place fast. In a cross-border transaction, there is the need to receive and deliver financial services located in different countries and to make and receive related payments and payment confirmations in real time. Cloud computing makes all this possible and at a relatively small cost.

There are several profitable connections between cloud computing and procurement finance.[211] Cloud computing allows organizations to innovate products and solutions in multiple locations and to easily reach new markets. SMEs become able to access global markets using digital platforms to connect with customers and vendors from other countries.

In procurement finance, cloud computing is able to connect several and different vendors and financial services globally and in real time. It no longer refers to a precise location, but it allows connection with the vendors' markets around the world providing solutions to the current challenges of the financial sector, such as compliance, security, and vendors' communication.

Digital procurement finance gains a relevant role in trade agreements. Regulatory authorities are seeking greater control over privacy-related issues, server locations, and access to information and online services. With the ever-growing push for simplification and digitization of information and procurement, these issues should be considered and remediated.

Cloud computing transfers the power to process applications from individual physical computers to a global network of linked structures. In this way, it creates a truly capable platform for deploying and accessing any kind of services, among which procurement finance, anywhere in the world.

Globalization and the possibility of moving data internationally, across borders, are changing the concept of the global procurement. Organizations can use digital platforms for imports and exports. Cloud computing provides useful opportunities to reach customers at a global level using the several services provided by these digital platforms, such as smart contracts and online payments.

The cloud computing solutions related to the exchange of information, payments, and foreign exchange can cut the operating costs, to guarantee efficiency, and to reduce risks, especially in the international trade.

In addition, the integration between blockchain and cloud computing is able to transform the management of trade transactions on more efficient digital platforms, allowing to move out of paper-based documents in procurement finance.

Simplification and digitization involve countless types of services. The security of information systems is critical. With the cloud computing solutions, organizations rely on third parties for interaction activities or for managing digital resources, such as money, online purchases, personal data, and so on. These third parties could be victims of hacking or loss of data. Blockchain solutions come into play to solve such problems, through its revolutionary potentials to allow securely checking an executed transaction anytime and practically in real-time. This can be achieved without compromising the privacy of the users involved.

Organizations and financial institutions require increasing cloud computing. The first reason is the cost and the increasing importance attributed to data. In the current financial world, data is generated and is stored in great quantities. Keeping track of all activities in a timely manner is important, both to serve in the best way customers and to comply with increasing stringent regulations. All of these data, if appropriately processed, represent a valuable source of monetization.

The financial sector needs more flexibility. It must take more action to meet market needs. It needs to move to an ICT infrastructure that is simpler and more secure to access and use.

Financial institutions today have to face an ever-increasing competition by fintech organizations and cope with the growing expectations of people on customer experience. The opening up of financial institutions outwardly can be seen through their progressive reliance on cloud computing. Relying on the cloud computing provides, in addition to a higher degree of security, obtained by the availability of security experts in the cloud computing organizations, greater agility in service delivery, better collection and access to data, and thus better service to all users.

The Lloyds Banking Group[212]

The Lloyds Banking Group signed with IBM one of the most important cloud transformation agreements in the financial services sector. Through this strategic partnership, which will last ten years, IBM provides cloud computing services hosted in both Lloyd and IBM data centers in the UK, managing the migration of applications to the cloud. This initiative enables the banking group to develop innovative products and to offer better service to its customers.

IBM solutions for financial institutions use analytics and cloud computing to help financial institutions in evolving rapidly, increasing customer profitability, improving operational efficiency, and managing the most cost-effective risks.

IBM uses a platform called IBM Z, which aims to make all super-secure processes and allows for the implementation of emerging technology projects. Its strengths are the encryption capabilities that extend to all data, networks, external devices, and applications. In addition, capacity and performance enhancements make this platform a good environment for initiatives based on technologies such as blockchain.

Cloud B2B

An interesting variation of the distribution models of cloud computing is the so-called B2B cloud. This solution helps to address the very important aspect of cooperation and integration among organizations.

Cloud solutions can be leveraged intra-organization and inter-organization. Organizations that have an advanced approach to cloud computing tend to maximize their benefits through hybrid solutions. This allows them to effectively use cloud computing as a way of integrating information within the organization and also as a way of interacting effectively, efficiently, and in total visibility with their business partners.

In particular, procurement organizations can have a shared information environment on the cloud with their principal vendors. In this environment, they can exchange information and interact, using a B2B cloud for vendor's integration and collaboration.

The cloud B2B paradigm is the application of the cloud solution to create value for the organizations. They can leverage that benefit to create end customer value. The customer demands in a B2B cloud solution greatly differs from those of a B2C.[213] Cloud B2B makes available opportunities such as:

- the systems of different organizations can be linked in real time;
- the conventional access boundaries are easily eliminated;
- the functions are shared and transparent.

Organizations can use these opportunities to implement B2B clouds. This solution is interesting when:

- there is the need for frequent exchanges of information between the various organizations;
- organizations wishing to work are distant from the geographical point of view;
- standard formats are available for the connection of different solutions.

In this situation, it is possible to implement a partnership B2B outsourcing and management of a community in support of procurement. This solution can support the collaboration process due to the possibility of securely communicating via the network. Even more important, organizations can improve their connections with their partners, be them customers, dealers, vendors, research centers, or academic centers.

The best solution might be, at least initially, a hybrid B2B. This would allow the organization to connect directly with their most important and demanding partners. At the same time, the organization may use a cloud B2B to connect with the remaining partners. The cloud makes easy also to build a social network to improve collaboration between partners.[214]

Artificial Intelligence and Business Intelligence

There is no universally accepted definition for artificial intelligence (AI). It is an evolving field. It is possible to say that AI is the ability of a computer to perform reasoning and functions that are typical of the human mind. De Mauro in his dictionary defines AI as[215]:

> Set of studies and instruments that tend to make machines, especially computers, capable of solving problems and reproducing human intelligence.

The AI is the science that deals with how to create intelligent machines. It does that using the possibilities offered by the information and communication technology.

There are a number of technologies included in the term artificial intelligence. These include machine learning (ML) and deep learning (DL)—also called deep neural networks—natural language processing and natural language understanding (NLP and NLU), and computer vision. AI technology systems—the combination of various AI technologies and the essential raw material of data—include robotics, autonomous vehicles, and virtual agents.

Computer science is the area in which more AI solutions have been experimented. Progress over the last few years in the ability to keep thousands of computers working together, and the vast amount of data available over the web have been critical for the evolution of AI to increasingly intelligent systems.

A survey underlines that AI in procurement can have the most impact in alerting the enterprise and vendors to the value network disruption (44 percent), recognizing and flagging vendor compliance issues (39 percent), and quickly identifying instances of fraud (37 percent).[216] Two of the biggest areas flagged by respondents as having the greatest potential for automation is invoice processing (51 percent) and approval of proposed purchases (35 percent). Banking industry expects USD 450 billion in AI impact, which is a 25 percent reduction of the traditional cost base.[217] Some of the experimental results show that the probabilistic neural network (PNN) is particularly suitable to support enterprise risk management, especially in the case of SMEs.[218]

The artificial intelligence market is growing. There is an increased number of startups and organizations that are investing in artificial intelligence systems. It is a pervasive market because it is cross-sectoral in many areas. Many startups now use this technology. Its applications seem infinite and able to radically modify the so-called user experience of business applications.

Regarding the financial sector, automated learning capabilities and ability to formulate forecasts are key elements of this sector. The idea is to use AI to create a "thinking and learning" system that conducts simple procurement operations and intelligently adapts to market conditions in a skillful and fast way.

The collaboration between finance and procurement can get a big support from organization and technology changes. Machine learning is becoming the password in almost every sector today. Finance is not an exception. Automatic learning depends on real-time activity and large data that is integrated throughout the organization. Digital finance solutions, incorporating automated learning capabilities, can greatly speed up transactional activity and bring teams closer to the virtual reduction initially, and elimination over time, of the manual administrative tasks. Financial professionals can increase time dedicated to strategic priorities by automating back-office processes such as procure-to-pay and order-to-cash. Machine learning programs use predictive algorithms to unleash large amounts of data, working at a much higher speed than traditional human-dependent processes.

AI can support procurement finance.[219] AI can bring concrete benefits in efficiency and performance. Procurement can look at AI as a technology that reduces the efforts until now dedicated to low value-added activities. In this way, it is possible to focus the efforts of the procurement professionals on the search and collaboration with vendors and in streamlining costs. If the procurement office were AI-enabled, it would be able to optimize the costs of documentation processing and delivery. This would be in addition to the ability to recognize, automatically and in real time, some of the unnecessary costs and cut them.

Procurement finance strategies that exploit AI are the future. The human mind has always been the same for the past many years. Traditional methods are no longer enough to handle the amount of information produced by the global economy.[220]

Machine learning can help support transactions and reduce errors in activities that require human input. Its technologies can handle, through high data volumes, financial relationships at an exponentially faster pace than human work. AI can help also in progressing into voice interaction with the computers. This could be useful for the operators to analyze the story behind the numbers and assessing whether certain patterns or anomalies may be cause for concern. The benefits of the collaboration between humans and intelligent machines are the reduction of fraud and the increase in network security.

As financial departments are embracing digital solutions for storing and managing financial data, both on the spot and in the cloud, ICT security is becoming a concern for CFOs. They must ensure that access to such information is monitored and regulated. Once again, machines have the ability to go through massive data and transaction data groups, identifying abnormal patterns or unique access behaviors.

From a financial institution perspective, AI enables financial institutions to discover and analyze the intentions and desires of their customers. It is possible for financial institutions to improve the customer interactions through the implementation of immediate and efficient user interfaces. By using digital solutions, financial institutions can also make a significant reduction in operating costs towards an increasingly sustainable financial institution model.

One of the next advances of AI is in OCR enhanced with machine learning. This solution automatically transfers paper-based content into back-end fields. It can screen documents for consistency and compliance and feeds data into issuance systems. Thanks to machine learning, the automation can increase over time. For a financial institution that serves both ends of a transaction, the marginal transaction cost could decrease substantially.

IBM[221]

IBM launched a new program, called BizBang, to offer to startups up to 120,000 euros in funding. This offer includes Bluemix, IBM's cloud platform, and over 150 Watson services. Watson is the IBM data analysis system based on AI. It is the innovative computer system able to answer questions expressed in natural languages. This solution represents an advanced application of natural language processing, information retrieval, knowledge representation, automated reasoning, and automatic learning technologies.

BizBang is a program that seeks to seize the innovative startup boost by providing them with Watson's cognitive capabilities. Innovation serves as a growth accelerator of the company. IBM helps startups understand in a better way the market and its customers. It can make fundraising campaigns smarter.

The BizBang portal is divided into two sections: the first one collects all the products on which startups have access; the second focuses on services, from technology to financial ones.

Big Data and Artificial Intelligence

According to a survey conducted by KPMG and *The Economist*, about four percent of organizations still have little or no tier 1 vendor visibility.[222] Several organizations have woken up to the fact that maintaining close vendor relationships will benefit them in the medium-long run. This can be clearly seen from the fact that about 49 percent of organizations have some amount of visibility into their tier 1 and tier 2 vendors. However, 32 percent of organizations know everything of their tier 1 and tier 2 vendors. Leading the race are nine percent of organizations which have complete visibility on the vertical side.

The most agile organizations are aiming at finance as a way to bring additional value in terms of analytics and insight. As the amount of data increases, integrated finance governance provides a way to gain insights. There are organizations moving towards the center of excellence models where finance professionals, skilled in analytics, valuations, mergers, or treasury, are co-located where they can serve as a repository of knowledge for outlying offices. This is an effective way to gain strategic leverage.[223]

The automated analyses that financial institutions need to perform for payments are only possible thanks to AI, allowing for inclusion of devices and locational analysis. Probing such large amounts of data manually could not be done as quickly or reliably by the humans alone.

The time to start using and investing in AI is now. No matter how big or small the organization, virtually any financial services organization can solve some daily difficulties with the support of AI. There is a very large volume of data available in financial institution systems. Being able to have a global picture of what is occurring, by making sense of data, is one of the most important actions to take. The real value is not just in providing simple answers to operational questions because the organization has the data. It is about providing insights on which immediate action to take.

Artificial Intelligence and Risk Management[224]

Risk management has the largest opportunity for incorporating and strengthening the use of AI. Without strong, sound risk practices, financial institutions leave interesting margins and have their reputation vulnerable. With AI, risk modeling and pricing are more advanced and optimized without the need for the traditional rate sheet.

Amazon and other intermediaries are implementing dynamic pricing, with real-time adjustments personalized on a customer-level basis.[225] Today's financial institutions' pricing models largely tend to be suboptimized. Instead, profitability could be defined on a relationship level which could benefit both the financial institution and the customer.

AI is very useful also in support of procurement finance risk management. It is possible to use a support vector machine to classify the risk of value network finance of small- and medium-sized organizations. It is possible to obtain results in a very effective way.[226] Experiment results show that AI is promising. It can be used for comprehensive evaluations, sequencing problems, and other multi-classification problems.

AI can be beneficially applied to fraud detection and prevention in procurement finance. AI fraud preventing tools are more effectively mining data to uncover meaningful patterns, which then translate to information that operators from the financial institutions can use. Being able to identify accounts, customers, or transactions with unusual characteristics can expedite the consideration of anomalies and verify suspicions to the likelihood that fraud is taking place.[227]

AI and Operational Efficiency

Many areas in operations can begin to be automated through AI.[228] Whether it is leveraging something like robotics, analyzing details about existing customers, or leveraging chatbots to improve the customer experience, there are tremendous opportunities to make operations more efficient through AI.

At the heart of procurement finance, there are critical systems and processes driving operations across functions including product management, distribution, customer service, and resource management. The continuous testing, refinement, and optimization of the many variables, behaviors, and configurations that drive the outputs of these systems could lead to a significant competitive advantage, productivity improvements, and cost savings.

The biggest challenge for any organization looking to optimize any one of these operations has been the breadth and complexity of the effort.[229] Manually modeling and optimizing every variable within multidimensional systems outruns the time, budget, and skillset of many development teams. It is possible to leverage internal skills and expertise to develop AI models to improve prediction accuracy and real-time decision support, resulting in greater operational efficiency from these advanced back-office systems.

Procurement Process Intelligence

One of the best ways to obtain an agile procurement finance is to use the so-called procurement process intelligence. The high volatility of information that characterizes the current environment leads the organizations to consider the need to increase their agility in such a way to be able to handle the information and to apply the agility within one of the most relevant sectors in the organizations, the procurement sector. The problem is to manage the volatility of the information and the large amount of them in procurement. The question is how this sector can improve its agility managing in an optimal way this amount of information. The traditional business intelligence (BI) assumes a strategic importance in the organization, especially in the procurement finance. The business intelligence (BI) is "a stack of theories, methodologies, processes, architecture, and technologies which change raw data into meaningful and useful information for business purposes".[230] The BI is able to manage in an optimal way the information to obtain strategies of success and to reach a competitive advantage making decisions knowingly and in a very rapid time necessary to face unpredictable situations.

The procurement process intelligence is an innovative approach able to measure and to manage the processes of procurement.[231] The optimization of the value that this sector provides to the organization is important. It is innovative because, unlike the traditional model focused mainly on the analysis of the information, this new approach focuses on the processes. Through the use of tools of collaboration and expert systems, the business process intelligence makes it possible to operate continuously, directly, and rapidly the processes, incrementing over time the agility of the organization. It is oriented to the optimal management of the procurement. The procurement process intelligence can support different components of the procurement processes (Fig. 6.8).

Regarding the first three components in Fig. 6.8 clockwise (Marketing & forecasting, Strategy setting, and Planning), their integration with the BI into a unique solution is useful. To obtain it, a collaborative platform that provides analytics and planning capabilities is necessary. The innovative aspect of the collaborative platform of procurement process intelligence is that the collaboration is focused on processes, information, and documents and not only on people. The objective of this new approach is to have a platform able to provide collaborative and executive capabilities of procurement finance processes simultaneously to the information and relevant documents in a way that it makes possible the increase of the organization agility against the rapid and constant changes. Procurement process intelligence is flexible, easy to use and to implement. These elements allow an organization to increase the level of reactivity, to support the decisions at every level of the organization, and to identify and to analyze critical indicators in a real-time. In this way, the value of the procurement finance within the organization increases.

The procurement business intelligence makes the sector of procurement finance more agile against the rapid changes of the economic environment. Having become more agile thanks to the application of BI inside it, this solution is able to exploit the opportunity of the market getting competitive advantages and adapting to the rapid changes of the market.

Procurement processes need to be standardized. In the field of procurement finance, one standard is particularly important for processes. ISO 20022—universal financial industry message scheme (which used to be called "UNIFI")—is the international standard that defines the ISO platform for the development of financial message standards.[232] Its business modeling approach allows users and developers to represent financial business processes and underlying transactions in a formal but syntax-independent notation. These business transaction models are the "real" business standards. They can be converted into physical messages in the desired syntax. At the time ISO 20022 was developed, XML (eXtensible Markup Language) was the preferred syntax for e-communication. Therefore, the first edition of ISO 20022, published in December 2004, proposed a standardized XML-based syntax for messages. The second edition of the standard, published in May 2013, included the possibility to use ASN.1 as well. The standard was developed within the Technical Committee TC68—financial services of ISO—the International Organization for Standardization.

The first focus of ISO 20022 is on international (cross-border) financial communication among financial institutions, their customers, and the domestic or international market infrastructures involved in the processing of financial transactions. It is also possible to use ISO 20022 for the development of new domestic financial messages, thereby streamlining and standardizing several communications in the financial institutions.

Smart Finance: Autonomous Value Network

Smart Finance is the research and development in the intersection of business intelligence (Big Data analytics and data science) and new finance (fintech, P2P lending, crowdfunding, procurement finance, e-invoicing, and e-payment systems).[233]

The value networks are increasingly characterized by the speed of logistical processes (for instance, same-day delivery), higher shipping volume, and a growing number of partners. Between the physical and financial flows, there is a growing gap in the value network. This gap leads to inefficiency and additional costs. The transfer of monetary values in the field of B2B is mostly based on invoice-driven transaction processes.

Due to the dynamical technological developments, more ICT services are available in the fields of physical and financial flows. The efficient and secure handling of the information is challenging, and gets more complex due to the growing amount of data, or is completely missing in the B2B area.

Procurement finance 4.0 provides many opportunities for the development of new processes that are more efficient and flexible in the business networks.[234] An interesting concept is the one of Smart Finance. It is the contribution to the harmonization of financial and physical flows. The simplification and digitization are the basis for Smart Finance. It supports the contribution of different technologies such as Big Data, e-invoices, blockchains, and smart contracts. It takes into account also the integration of fintech organizations and service platforms in the management of the value network. Digitized processes, in combination with key technologies, provide more visibility. At the same time, there is the need for more decentralization and autonomy in the value networks. With the integration of financial flows into the planning and controlling of objects in the value networks, cyber-physical systems are equipped with financial information. They can contribute to the holistic decisions in the value networks.

With operations largely automated, finance support to procurement will increase on business insights and service.[235] The skills required by finance professionals will change as a new combination of technology and human workforces collaborates in the workplace. Procurement partnering will shift upstream from budgeting and reporting to include advanced forecasting, integrated planning, and more joint visibility. Teams of finance and procurement could work together to focus on the most complex procurement decisions, moving around the organization as needed. Finance will have a bigger role in how decisions get made in procurement.

The benefits of adopting an approach of Smart Finance are[236]:

- increasing effectiveness and sales through new services;
- increasing efficiency through process optimization;
- economics optimization of working capital, liquidity, and process costs in the value networks;
- improvement of decision quality and speed;
- faster service provision and reduction of reaction time;
- digitization of paper-based transaction processes.

Procurement and finance professionals will change the type of work from routine activities to exception-based and insight-driven activities, supported by simplification, digitization, and blockchain solutions.[237] This work is investigative in nature. No more copying and pasting values from a contract, invoice, or other documents into an ERP system. Organizations are designing and selecting automation tools to do this work.

Loans processing and settlement creates opportunities for process efficiency through intelligent automation. Organizations are far from realizing the full support from intelligent automation. The proportion of organizations with full-scale intelligent automation implementation of the business processes in procurement finance is around 11 percent, but it is growing.[238] Apart from cost reduction, intelligent automation brings also more revenues. A survey has shown these benefits: faster time to market to launch new products 31 percent, improved cross-selling efforts with customers 25 percent, improved targeting of new customer groups 16 percent, a competitive advantage over peers 12 percent, higher customer loyalty 10 percent, and increased business by being accessible longer hours 6 percent.[239]

SOFiA Project[240]

The German Fraunhofer Institut[241] works on a research project called SOFiA (Smart Objects and Smart Finance Approaches).[242] This project addresses relevant Industry 4.0-based management approaches for the self-control and self-organization of logistics, production, and the respective tasks for payment processing and procurement finance. This research project is part of the funding initiative "Service Innovation through Digitization" of the German Ministry of Education and Research. The objective of this project is to improve process handling in complex production and logistics networks by integrating smart objects and digital B2B Smart Finance approaches.

The ICT infrastructure developed in SOFiA consists of a cloud-based central component and a network of decentralized control units (DCU). The cloud-based components connect the several stakeholders involved in a value network via a smart contracting service. This service bridges the gap between financial and physical/digital flows in the value network. It also provides security and fraud tolerance. It serves as the enabling connector to run smart payment methods

(*continued*)

(continued)

(automated and invoice-independent transactions) between smart objects and smart financial services based on smart contracts. The service is based on a blockchain solution.[243] This private blockchain solution guarantees a shared and trusted ledger of transactions that every consortium partner can access. No one can control or change transactions at a later point in time.[244] The smart contract services, which are implemented as web applications, connect the contracting parties, so they are able to negotiate contract details and create digital agreements. The blockchain solution stores this information transparently for every contract partner. The smart contract service is able to analyze, monitor, and verify all the events in terms of examining whether all contract components and requirements are fulfilled or not. Additionally, the smart contract is empowered to automatically trigger a financial transaction after an on-time delivery with no defect.

To connect the smart contract service with the payment cloud, write-and-read permissions are assigned by open-source technologies such as the MultiChain.[245] The MultiChain consists of different streams. Every stream provides specific information related to the entire contracting process. The extent of the permissions given to the contracting parties is defined by the business community. It varies between full access on data, reading-permission only, or the complete refusal of all information. This procedure ensures that only a verified party can add data or change status. It also simplifies the traceability in case of data abuse. When a contract component or requirement is fulfilled, the DCU transfers the information of completion to one of the related blockchains. Subsequently, the smart contract triggers the authorized payment. The cloud-based system can integrate the payment cloud, and additional smart B2B services, like financing or insurance service. The central component of the SOFiA architecture integrates with the ERP systems of the participant parties.

These systems provide the initial plans on how to execute the negotiated logistical services—either by using a manual disposition process or utilizing an OTD-NET-[246] based simulation of the value network to come up with a suitable set of actions and schedules for all involved parties and objects.[247]

IBM Center for Blockchain Innovation[248]

IBM established the first IBM Center for Blockchain Innovation in Singapore. In the first collaboration of its kind with the Singapore Economic Development Board (EDB) and the Monetary Authority of Singapore (MAS), IBM researchers work with government, industries, and academia to develop applications and solutions. They are based on organization blockchain, cybersecurity, and cognitive computing technologies. The center uses the expertise in the Singaporean talent pool and that of the IBM research network. It engages with SMEs to create new applications and grow new markets in finance, trade, and procurement.

The center explores the use of blockchain and cognitive technologies to improve business transactions across several different industries. The cloud computing services make these technologies more accessible. Managers from all industries can be alerted on the deep and disruptive implications in a range of settings including finance, financial institutions, IoT, healthcare, value networks, manufacturing, and procurement finance. The first projects for the center focused on solutions using blockchain to improve the efficiency of multi-party procurement finance processes and transactions.

IBM also works with the PSA Singapore Terminals, the world's largest container transshipment port, and others to create a trade ecosystem to connect emerging financial technologies with the physical world of global trade and logistics. This leads to new business models.

The Innovation Center delivers a number of technology pilots across the finance and trade industries. These projects build on IBM's work with the Linux Foundation Hyperledger. Hyperledger is a consortium of providers that are promoting cross-industry initiatives in blockchain solutions.[249] Hyperledger has been growing its membership—numbering 200+ organizations across the value network, finance, manufacturing, and technology. The platform is building interest as an open-source effort designed to promote blockchain applications across industry sectors.

Conclusions

This chapter underlines the importance of (near) future solutions, analyzing their importance for procurement finance. The most likely hypothesis is that there will be a growing importance of platforms, meant as the integration of finance and technology and not as only new organizations. There will probably be a complete transformation of financial services through the intense and advanced use of innovative solutions. The primary driver is the customer satisfaction, and if possible delight, trying to satisfy its stated and implied needs with an increasing effectiveness, efficiency, economics, and ethics in handling data and information. Almost all of the transactions processing in the new solutions can satisfy in real time the increasing need of rapidity in this current dynamic context.

Although the new solutions introducing alternative financing instruments are varied, in parallel a change in the financial culture of the organization to select and to access them is essential. In terms of new organization solutions, fintech organizations are the most relevant ones. Although fintech organizations are a major innovation, financial institutions should see them as potential partners rather than competitors. Traditional financial institutions have the experience and deeply embedded relationships. Fintech organizations have plenty of technological innovations. By working together with traditional financial institutions, they can revolutionize also procurement finance, making it faster, more secure, and cheaper for everyone involved.

Some of the most interesting new technological solutions are blockchain, cloud computing, and artificial intelligence (AI).

Blockchain solutions are a new paradigm for organizing activities, with less waste and greater accessibility, efficiency and security, rather than a purely technological solution. This characteristic is not simply linked to the fact that clockchain solutions are a way that can exploit the resources of the web. Above all, they enable the implementation of scalable global operating models.

Blockchain is an innovative solution enabling transparent, tracked, and secure transactions, and avoiding or reducing the need for human or organization intermediary.[250] This disruptive innovation could eventually affect the implementation and processing of procurement finance solutions, often based on net operating working capital (NOWC) financing.[251] This promising solution could enable secure processing of the financial flows and of the receivables, greatly reducing the back-office paperwork of financial institutions.

Blockchain can play an important role in preventing fraud during procurement finance solution implementation and reverse factoring in particular.[252] Blockchain solutions can enable complete track-and-trace of factored or not factored invoices and invoice status, preventing fraudulent organizations from extracting funds from multiple financiers by using the same invoice.[253]

Blockchain is interesting when the following conditions are present[254]: the central authorities are part of the current process or need to be trusted; there is the involvement of multiple organizations; the information exchange needs to be trustworthy and it has a value; multiple regulations are applicable; the processes are auditable; processes have not yet been automated; the server uptime and redundancy has substantial costs.

The application of blockchain solutions helps in solving the procurement finance needs for traceability and real-time visibility on the status of invoices.

Until now, the applications of blockchain solutions within procurement finance programs are limited. They represent a key challenge and opportunity for the near future.

Cloud computing is playing an important role in the digital era. Cloud computing represents the beginning of an evolution in the field of information and communication technology that will affect the whole economy over the next decades.

As information grows and the financial access becomes easier, the analytic capacity has also been increasing, demonstrated by the development of AI solutions. With this tool, the algorithms become increasingly powerful. The speed increases. The quality of analysis becomes more precise. These improvements change radically the entire business models of all the stakeholders in procurement finance.

These innovative solutions are just a few of the many innovative phenomena that are carrying overwhelming transformations into the financial and economic system. They are redesigning the relationship between finance and the other functions, in a process that also seeks the financial institutions becoming increasingly digitized and innovative.

The key takeaways for the financial institutions are that procurement finance is becoming a tough business for them. It is getting tougher for those that do not embrace the digital transformation. They find themselves offering services that are more expensive, slower, and less secure than those of their tech-savvy competitors. Financial institutions seeking a long-term future in procurement finance must go more and more digital. Three aspects should guide them[255]:

- Deliver new value-adding functions on the full procurement finance processes but especially in the front end for documentary trade and financing.
- Pay attention to the increasing importance of best practices. It is possible to get an increased effort in OCR, machine intelligence, and digital compliance while at the same time obtaining lower costs and increased agility and speed of service.
- Experiment to stay well ahead of the technology curve. Financial institutions can decide if to push MT798, BPO, electronic bills of lading (eBOLs), blockchain, or whichever new solution is available. It is important to use the relevant opportunities in the simplification and digitization of procurement finance and as a consequence to change how it works. Financial institutions that explore this and collaborate with innovative partners and key vendors and customers come out ahead rather than risk to be left behind when the digital transformation becomes more common practice.

The final message of this chapter is to consider procurement finance as a platform in an ecosystem. This revolutionizes procurement and makes it more ready for procurement finance 4.0. This is a must in a world of an expanding Business 4.0.[256]

Notes

1. Christopher, M. (2016). *Logistics & supply chain management.* Pearson, London, UK. Porter, M. E. (2008). *Competitive advantage: Creating and sustaining superior performance.* Simon and Schuster, New York City, NY
2. Lasi, H., Fettke, P., Kemper, H. G., Feld, T., & Hoffmann, M. (2014). Industry 4.0. *Business & Information Systems Engineering*, *6*(4), 239–242.
3. Glas, A. H., & Kleemann, F. C. (2016). The impact of industry 4.0 on procurement and supply management: A conceptual and qualitative analysis. *International Journal of Business and Management Invention*, *5*(6), 55–66.

   Weissbarth, R., Geissbauer, R., & Wetzstein, J. (2016). Procurement 4.0: Are you ready for the digital revolution?. PWC.

Batran, A., Erben, A., Schulz, R., & Sperl, F. (2017). *Procurement 4.0: A survival guide in a digital, disruptive world.* Campus Verlag.

4. Nicoletti, B. (2017), *Agile Procurement.* Volume I: Adding Value with Lean Processes, Springer International Publishing, London, UK. ISBN 978-3-319-61082-5.
5. Van Alstyne, M. W., Parker, G. G., & Choudary, S. P. (2016). Pipelines, platforms, and the new rules of strategy. *Harvard Business Review*, *94*(4), 54–62.
6. Gawer, A. (2014). Bridging differing perspectives on technological platforms: Toward an integrative framework. *Research Policy*, 43(7): 1239–1249.
7. Pilkington, M. (2016). 11 Blockchain technology: principles and applications. *Research handbook on digital transformations*, 225.
8. Lasi, H., Fettke, P., Kemper, H. G., Feld, T., & Hoffmann, M. (2014). Industry 4.0. *Business & Information Systems Engineering*, *6*(4), 239–242.
9. Brenner, W., & Wenger, R. (Eds.). (2007). *Elektronische Beschaffung: Stand und Entwicklungstendenzen.* Springer-Verlag, Heidelberg, Germany.
10. Nicoletti, B., (2013), A Model and Best Practices of e-procurement in cloud computing, in *e-Public procurement in Europe: public management, technologies and processes of change*, Amazon Books, Dedham, MA.
11. Nicoletti, B. (2014), Lean and Digitize e-procurement, paper presented at the *e-Public procurement in Europe: public management, technologies and processes of change,* Lisbon, Portugal, 27 May.
12. Schmidt, R., Möhring, M., Härting, R.-C., Reichstein, C., Neumaier, P., & Jozinović, P. *Industry 4.0—Potentials for creating Smart Products: Empirical Research Results.* Germany: Springer. Heidelberg., Germany.
13. Kagermann, H., Helbig, J., Hellinger, A., & Wahlster, W. (2013). *Recommendations for Implementing the strategic initiative INDUSTRIE 4.0: securing the future of German manufacturing industry; final report of the Industrie 4.0 working group.* Forschungsunion, Essen, Germany.
14. Domingo Galindo, L. (2016). *The Challenges of Logistics 4.0 for the Supply Chain Management and the Information Technology,* Master's thesis, NTNU, Trondheim, Norway.
15. Stock, T., & Seliger, G. (2016). Opportunities of sustainable manufacturing in Industry 4.0. *Procedia CIRP*, *40*: 536–541.
16. Lasi, H., Kemper, H. G., Fettke, P., Feld, T., & Hoffmann, M. (2014, 6 19). Industry 4.0. *BISE Journal.*
17. Henke, M., & Schulte, A. T. (2015), Einkauf und die 4. Industrielle Revolution, *Beschaffung Aktuell*, 62(3): 20–21.

18. Sundermann, F. (2013), Einkauf 4.0: Einsparungen durch Zusammenarbeit von Einkauf und Technik, *Pool4Tool*, (11): 24–28.
19. Aslanbas, M. (2014), Emporias Survey Procurement Finance 4.0: Significance and Future Challenges for the Logistical Integration of Vendors, in Emporias Management Consulting (Ed.), *Emporias*, Quarterly 3 Munich, Germany: 10–14.
20. Schwab, K. (2017). *The fourth industrial revolution*. Penguin UK, London, UK. www.bmbf.de/pub/HTS_Broschuere_eng.pdf, Accessed 24 April 2017.

    Herman, M., Pentek, T., and Otto, B. (2015). *Design Principles for Industrie 4.0*. Dortmund, Germany. Internet Plus (Chinese: 互联网+), similar to Information Superhighway and Industry 4.0, is proposed in China's Government Work Report on March 5, 2015 so as to keep pace with the Information Trend. China unveils targets for 2015: Li Keqiang's speech as it happened South China Morning Post, March 5, 2015
21. Schwab, K. (2017). *The fourth industrial revolution*. Penguin, London, UK.
22. Domingo Galindo, L. (2016). *The Challenges of Logistics 4.0 for the Value network Management and the Information Technology*, Master's thesis, NTNU, Trondheim, Norway.
23. Nicoletti, B. (2009), Sintesi Seminario RFID per l'Impiantistica, *L'Impiantistica Italiana*, N. 6, Nov.-Dic.: 1–7.
24. Schmidt, R., Möhring, M., Härting, R. C., Reichstein, C., Neumaier, P., & Jozinović, P. (2015). Industry 4.0-potentials for creating smart products: empirical research results. In *International Conference on Business Information Systems*. Springer International Publishing, New York City, NY: 16–27.
25. Lasi, H., Fettke, P., Kemper, H. G., Feld, T., & Hoffmann, M. (2014). Industry 4.0. *Business & Information Systems Engineering*, *6*(4), 239.
26. Nicoletti, B. (2018). The Future: Procurement 4.0. In *Agile Procurement* (pp. 189–230). Palgrave Macmillan, Cham, Switzerland.
27. Lyytinen, K., & Yoo, Y. (2002). Ubiquitous computing. *Communications of the ACM*, *45*(12): 63–96.

    Saha, D., & Mukherjee, A. (2003). Pervasive computing: a paradigm for the 21st century. *Computer*, *36*(3): 25–31.
28. Porter, M. E., & Michael; ilustraciones Gibbs. (2001). Strategy and the Internet.
29. Group, R. F. (2013). *Acatech*. www.acatech.de/de/publikationen/stellungnahmen/kooperationen/detail/artikel/recommendations-for-implementing-the-strategic-initiative-industrie-40-final-report-of-the-industr.html. Accessed 28 January 2017.

30. Nicoletti, B. (2017), *The Future of Fintech*, Springer International Publishing, London, UK. ISBN 978-3-319-51414-7.
31. Eckermann, S., Heidegger, H., Röhrig, M., Santos, S., Zahn, C. (2016), Building the Corporate Bank of the Future, www.mckinsey.com/industries/financial-services/our-insights/building-the-corporate-bank-of-the-future. Accessed 1 May 2018.
32. Bill Gates said: "the world needs banking not banks". Ferrari, R. (2017). *Fintech Era: Digital Revolution in Financial Services.* FrancoAngeli, Milano, Italy.
33. Eckermann, S., Heidegger, H., Röhrig, M., Santos, S., Zahn, C. (2016), Building the Corporate Bank of the Future, www.mckinsey.com/industries/financial-services/our-insights/building-the-corporate-bank-of-the-future. Accessed 1 May 2018.
34. Nicoletti, B. (2017). *The future of FinTech: Integrating finance and technology in financial services.* Springer, Berlin, Germany.
35. Van Alstyne, M. W., Parker, G. G., & Choudary, S. P. (2016). Pipelines, platforms, and the new rules of strategy. *Harvard Business Review*, *94*(4), 54–62.
36. Gawer, A. (2014). Bridging differing perspectives on technological platforms: Toward an integrative framework. *Research Policy*, 43(7): 1239–1249.
37. Parker, G. G., Van Alstyne, M. W., & Choudary, S. P. (2016). *Platform Revolution: How Networked Markets Are Transforming the Economyand How to Make Them Work for You.* WW Norton & Company, New York City, NY.
38. Saebi, T., & Foss, N. J. (2015). Business models for open innovation: Matching heterogeneous open innovation strategies with business model dimensions. *European Management Journal*, *33*(3), 201–213.
39. Moser, D. J., & Gassmann, O. (2016, June). Innovating Platform Business Models: Insights from Major Tech-Companies. In *ISPIM Innovation Symposium* (p. 1). The International Society for Professional Innovation Management (ISPIM).
40. Burgess, J. (2012). The iPhone moment, the Apple brand, and the creative consumer: From "hackability and usability" to Cultural Generativity. In *Studying Mobile Media* (pp. 36–50). Routledge, London, UK.
41. Moser, D. J., & Gassmann, O. (2016, June). Innovating Platform Business Models: Insights from Major Tech-Companies. In *ISPIM Innovation Symposium* (p. 1). The International Society for Professional Innovation Management (ISPIM).
42. www.idc.com/getdoc.jsp?containerId=prUS43543618. Accessed 22 August 2018.

43. www.idc.com/getdoc.jsp?containerId=prUS43543618. Accessed 22 August 2018.
44. Orem, T. (2016). Platforms and partners. *American Bankers Association. ABA Banking Journal, 108*(4), 32.
45. Di Gioia, S. (2018). Supply chain finance in China: an investigation on the business models of platforms' providers. *Master Graduation Thesis. Politecnico di Milano*, Milano, Italy.
46. Di Gioia, S. (2018). Supply chain finance in China: an investigation on the business models of platforms' providers. *Master Graduation Thesis. Politecnico di Milano*, Milano, Italy.
47. www.fabrick.com. Accessed 8 July 2018.
48. www.sella.it. Accessed 8 July 2018.
49. Di Gioia, S. (2018). Supply chain finance in China: an investigation on the business models of platforms' providers. *Master Graduation Thesis. Politecnico di Milano*, Milano, Italy.
50. www.gtnexus.com. Accessed 22 July 2018.
51. Brodsky, L., & Oakes, L. (2017). Data sharing and open banking. *McKinsey & Company*.
52. Brodsky, L., & Oakes, L. (2017). Data sharing and open banking. *McKinsey & Company*.
53. Chang, J. F. (2016). *Business process management systems: strategy and implementation*. Auerbach Publications.
54. The Open Banking Working Group (2016). The Open Banking Standard. Retrieved from www.scribd.com/doc/298569302/The-OpenBanking-Standard Uk Competition. Accessed 7 July 2018.
55. www.thepaypers.com/expert-opinion/access-to-payment-accounts-under-psd2-which-accounts-are-in-scope-/763682. Accessed 8 July 2018.
56. Tankard, C. (2016). What the GDPR means for businesses. *Network Security, 2016*(6), 5–8.
57. blog.moorgategroup.com/2017/05/04/unicredit-named-as-global-finance-innovator-in-trade-finance-2017/, Accessed 12 February 2018.
58. www.unicredit.it/. Accessed 08 July 2018.
59. www.crxmarkets.com/. Accessed 05 August 2019.
60. Arner, D. W., Barberis, J., & Buckley, R. P. (2015). The evolution of Fintech: A new post-crisis paradigm. *Geo. J. Int'l L., 47*, 1271.
61. ERP (Enterprise Resource Planning): Systems and software used by organizations to handle day-to-day operations of their own business as procurement, production, accountability, gathering data from different part of organization providing a unique and central collection of data.

62. The Innovators, *Trade Finance*. June 2017. www.gtb.unicredit.eu/sites/default/files/awards/the-innovators-2017-trade-finance-1493310922.pdf. Accessed 29 June 2018.
63. www.ebrd.com/. Accessed 8 July 2018.
64. The Innovators, Trade Finance. June 2017. www.gtb.unicredit.eu/sites/default/files/awards/the-innovators-2017-trade-finance-1493310922.pdf. Accessed 29 June 2018.
65. www.europarc.org/wp-content/uploads/2015/03/2014-pp-Nature-and-its-role-in-the-transition-to-a-Green-Economy-OPERAs-Patrick-ten-Brink.pdf. Accessed 8 July 2018.
66. *Alternative finance refers to financial channels and instruments that have emerged outside of the traditional finance system such as regulated banks and capital markets*. Definition by Cambridge Judge Business School: Cambridge Centre for Alternative Finance, Cambridge, UK.
67. McKinsey&organization (2015). *McKinsey on payments. Vol.8 n.22*
68. www.assinews.it/03/2018/fintech-factoring-convegno-supply-chain-finance-15-marzo-milano/660049966/. Accessed 07 July 2018.
69. www.osservatori.net/it_it/osservatori/comunicati-stampa/il-supply-chain-finance-opportunita-ancora-da-sfruttare. Accessed 07 July 2018.
70. Ferrari, R. (2016). *L'era del Fintech. La rivoluzione digitale nei servizi finanziari,* FrancoAngeli, Milano, Italy.
71. Deloitte (2017). *Bank of the Future*. Monitor Company, Cambridge, MA.
72. Scardovi, C. (2017). Transformation in Investment Management. In *Digital Transformation in Financial Services*(pp. 105–125). Springer, Cham, Switzerland.
73. /www.finleap.com/press/press-releases/167661-venture-in-italy-finleap-becomes-even-more-international-with-beesy/. Accessed 26 July 2018.
74. www.finleap.com/. Accessed 26 July 2018.
75. www.platfr.io. Accessed 26 July 2018.
76. markets.businessinsider.com/news/stocks/crossflow-becomes-the-fastest-growing-fintech-globally-with-turnover-growth-over-2-000-1027392793. Accessed 25 July 2018.
77. www.crossflowpayments.co.uk/. Accessed 25 July 2018.
78. European Central Bank (2012). 1. *Virtual Currency Schemes*. European Central Bank, Frankfurt am Main. Germany. 5.
79. Trautman, L. J. (2014). Virtual currencies; Bitcoin & what now after Liberty Reserve, Silk Road, and Mt. Gox?, *Richmond Journal of Law and Technology*, 20(4).
80. Glaser, F., Zimmermann, K., Haferkorn, M., Weber, M., & Siering, M. (2014). Bitcoin-asset or currency? revealing users' hidden intentions.

https://papers.ssrn.com/sol3/papers.cfm?abstract_id=2425247. Accessed 05 August 2018.

81. Meiklejohn, S., Pomarole, M., Jordan, G., Levchenko, K., McCoy, D., Voelker, G. M., & Savage, S. (2013, October). A fistful of bitcoins: characterizing payments among men with no names. In *Proceedings of the 2013 conference on Internet measurement conference* (pp. 127–140). ACM.
82. litecoin.org/. Accessed 05 August 2018.
83. www.ethereum.org/. Accessed 05 August 2018.
84. ripple.com/insights/10-things-need-know-xrp/. Accessed 05 August 2018
85. www.bitcoincash.org/. Accessed 8 July 2018.
86. www.telegraph.co.uk/technology/2017/08/01/bitcoin-cash-everything-need-know-bitcoins-hard-fork. Accessed 8 July 2018.
87. Adhikary, B. K., Kutsuna, K., & Hoda, T. (2018). *Crowdfunding: Lessons from Japan's Approach*. Springer, Berlin, Germany.
88. Gerber, E. M., Hui, J. S., & Kuo, P. Y. (2012). Crowdfunding: Why people are motivated to post and fund projects on crowdfunding platforms. In *Proceedings of the International Workshop on Design, Influence, and Social Technologies: Techniques, Impacts and Ethics* 2(11).
89. Belleflamme, P., Omrani, N., & Peitz, M. (2015). The economics of crowdfunding platforms. *Information Economics and Policy*, *33*, 11–28.
90. Méric, J., Maque, I., & Brabet, J. (Eds.). (2016). *International Perspectives on Crowdfunding: Positive, Normative and Critical Theory*. Emerald Group Publishing Limited.
91. www.thecrowdfundingcenter.com/?page=report. Accessed 12 June 2018.
92. thecrowdfundingformula.com/2015/11/13/kickstarter-vs-indiegogo-2/. Accessed 05 August 2018.
93. www.seedrs.com/, Accessed 20 March 2017.
94. Swan, M. (2015). *Blockchain: Blueprint for a new economy*. O'Reilly Media, Inc., Sebastopol, CA.
95. Valanciene, L., & Jegeleviciute, S. (2013). Valuation of crowdfunding: benefits and drawbacks. *Economics and Management*, *18*(1), 39–48.
96. Ferrari, R. (2016). *L'era del Fintech. La rivoluzione digitale nei servizi finanziari*, FrancoAngeli, Milano, Italy.
97. www.crowdfundme.it. Accessed 08 July 2018.
98. www.consob.it. Accessed 08 July 2018.
99. monzo.com/. Accessed 08 July 2018.
100. www.crowdcube.com. Accessed 08 July 2018.
101. www.borsadelcredito.it. Accessed 08 July 2018.
102. www.marketlinks.org/good-practice-center/value-chain-wiki/value-chain-finance. Accessed 31 March 2018.

103. - (2017). *Value Chain Finance Guide: Tools for Designing Project Interventions that Facilitate Investment in Key Value Chain Upgrades.* ACDI/VOCA, FHI 360 and USAID.
104. www.marketlinks.org/good-practice-center/value-chain-wiki/value-chain-finance. Accessed 31 March 2018.
105. *Rural and Agricultural Finance: Taking Stock of Five Years of Innovations.* microReport 181. USAID. December 2011.
106. bravenewcoin.com/news/fluent-unveils-blockchain-based-global-supply-chain-software-platform/, Accessed 25 April 2017.
107. mobapp24.ilsole24ore.com/art.php?testata=S24&issue=20180814&artid=4.1.677279978. Accessed 14 August 2018.
108. www.idc.com/getdoc.jsp?containerId=prUS43526618&pageType=PRINTFRIENDLY. Accessed 22 August 2018.
109. Crosby, M., Pattanayak, P., Verma, S., & Kalyanaraman, V. (2016). Blockchain technology: Beyond bitcoin. *Applied Innovation*, *2*, 6–10.
110. Mainelli, M., & Smith, M. (2015). Sharing ledgers for sharing economies: an exploration of mutual distributed ledgers (aka blockchain technology).
111. Vigna, P., & Casey, M. J. (2016). *The age of cryptocurrency: how bitcoin and the blockchain are challenging the global economic order.* Palgrave Macmillan, Houndsmill, UK.
112. Swan, M. (2015). *Blockchain: blueprint for a new economy*, O'Reilly Media, Sebastopol, CA.
113. Back, Adam, et al. Enabling blockchain innovations with pegged sidechains. URL: www.opensciencereview.com/papers/123/enablingblockchain-innovations-with-pegged-sidechains (2014).

    Pilkington, M. (2016). Blockchain technology: principles and applications. *Research Handbook on Digital Transformations*, 225
114. medium.com/@preethikasireddy/eli5-what-do-we-mean-by-blockchains-are-trustless-aa420635d5f6. Accessed 23 February 2018.
115. Swan, M. (2015), *Blockchain: blueprint for a new economy*, O'Reilly Media, Sebastopol, CA.
116. Manav, G. (2017), *Blockchain for dummies*, John Wiley&Sons Hoboken, NJ.
117. www.researchonglobalmarkets.com/global-blockchain-technology-market-2014-2022.html. Accessed 31 March 2018.
118. B. Wang, B., Zhu, X., Q. He, Q., & Gu, F. (2018). The forecast on the customers of the member point platform built on the blockchain technology by ARIMA and LSTM, *2018 IEEE 3rd International Conference on Cloud Computing and Big Data Analysis (ICCCBDA)*, Chengdu, China 589–593. doi: https://doi.org/10.1109/ICCCBDA.2018.8386584

119. Pilkington, M. (2016). Blockchain technology: principles and applications. *Research handbook on digital transformations*, 225.
120. Deshpande, A., Stewart, K., Lepetit, L., & Gunashekar, S. (2017). Distributed Ledger Technologies/Blockchain: Challenges, opportunities and the prospects for standards, *BSI*, 2
121. Bogart, S., & Rice, K. (2015). *The blockchain report: Welcome to the Internet of value*. Needham & Company LLC. New York City, NY.
122. Gratzke, P., Schatsky, D., & Piscini, E. (2018). *Banding together for blockchain Does it make sense for your organization to join a consortium?* Deloitte Insights, New York City, NY.
123. www.globaltrademag.com/global-logistics/dutch-logistics-consortium-explore-blockchain-technology?utm_campaign=shareaholic&utm_medium=twitter&utm_source=socialnetwork. Accessed 12 February 2018.
124. Johnston, D. A., Mccutcheon, D. D., Stuart, I. F., & Kerwood, H. (2004). Effects of vendor trust on the performance of cooperative vendor relationships. *Journal of Operation Management,* 22(1), 23–38. doi: https://doi.org/10.1016/j.jom.2003.12.001
125. Vieira, L. M., Paiva, E. L., Finger, A. B., & Teixeira, R. (2013). Trust and Vendor-buyer Relationships: An Empirical Analysis, *BAR—Brazilian Administration Review*, 10 (3).
126. Schurr, P. H., & Ozanne, J. L. (1985). Influences on Exchange Processes: Buyers' Preconceptions of a vendor's Trustworthiness and Bargaining Toughness, *Journal of Consumer Research*, 11(4), 1 March, 939–953, doi.org/10.1086/209028
127. Zaheer, A., McEvily, B., & Perrone, V. (1998). Does trust matter? Exploring the effects of interorganizational and interpersonal trust on performance. *Organization Science*, 9 (2), 141–159.
128. Moorman, C., Zaltman, G., & Deshpandé, R. (1992). Relationships between Providers and Users of Market Research: The Dynamics of Trust within and between Organizations. *Journal of Marketing Research (JMR)*, 29(3) (August 1992): 314–28.
129. Handfield, Robert & Bechtel, Christian. (2002). The Role of Trust and Relationship Structure in Improving Supply Chain Responsiveness. Industrial Marketing Management—*Ind Market Manag*. 31. https://doi.org/10.1016/S0019-8501(01)00169-9
130. Williamson, O. E. (1993). Calculativeness, Trust, and Economic Organization, *The Journal of Law and Economics*. 36(1), Part 2, 453–486.
131. Kramer, R. M., & Carnevale, P. J. (2003). Trust and intergroup negotiation. *Blackwell handbook of social psychology: Intergroup processes*, 431–450.

132. Dyer, J. H., & Chu, W. (2003). The Role of Trustworthiness in Reducing Transaction Costs and Improving Performance: Empirical Evidence from the United States, Japan, and Korea. *Organization Science*, 14(1), 57–68. JSTOR, JSTOR, www.jstor.org/stable/3086033
133. Zaheer, A., McEvily, B., & Perrone, V. (1998). Does trust matter? Exploring the effects of interorganizational and interpersonal trust on performance. *Organization Science* 9 (2), 141–159.
134. Manav, G. (2017). *Blockchain for dummies*, John Wiley & Sons, Hoboken, NJ. www.cognizant.com/whitepapers/blockchains-smart-contracts-driving-the-next-wave-of-innovation-across-manufacturing-value-chains-codex2113.pdf (Accessed 03 March 2018)
135. Deloitte (2016), *Blockchain. Enigma, Paradox, Opportunity*, Deloitte White Paper.
136. Heires, K. (2016). The risks and rewards of blockchain technology. *Risk Management, 63*(2), 4.
Koens, T., & Poll, E. (2018). *The Drivers Behind Blockchain Adoption: The Rationality of Irrational Choices*, White Paper of the Radboud University, Nijmegen, The Netherlands.
137. bita.studio/. Accessed 18 June 2018.
138. tradle.io/, Accessed 28 March 2017.
139. Grisoni, A. (2016), Se anche le assicurazioni guardano alla blockchain, *AziendaBanca*, Mar., 66–67.
140. www.startupbootcamp.org/alumni/tradleinc/, Accessed 11 April 2017.
141. MacDuffie, J. P. (2011). Inter-organizational trust and the dynamics of distrust. *Journal of International Business Studies, 42*(1), 35–47.
142. Sahay, B. S. (2003). Understanding trust in supply chain relationship, *Industrial Management & Data Systems*, 103, 553–563
143. Daugherty, P. J. (2011). Review of Logistics and Supply Chain Relationship Literature and Suggested Research Agenda, *International Journal of Physical Distribution & Logistics Management,* 41(1), 16–31
144. Chee Yew, W. C., Boon-Itt, S., & Wong, C. W. Y. (2011), The contingency effects of environmental uncertainty on the relationship between supply chain integration and operational performance. *Journal of Operations Management* 29.6 (2011): 604–615.
145. Sahay, B. S., & Maini, A. (2002). Supply chain: a shift from transactional to collaborative partnership. *Decision, 29*(2), 67–88.
146. Lee, H. L., & Corey Billington, C. (1992). Managing supply chain inventory: pitfalls and opportunities. *Sloan Management Review* 33.3 (1992): 65.
Morgan, R. M., & Hunt, S. D. (1994). The commitment-trust theory of relationship marketing. *The Journal of Marketing*, 20–38.

147. Zsidisin, G. A., & Ellram, L. M. (2001). Activities related to purchasing and supply management involvement in vendor alliances. *International Journal of Physical Distribution & Logistics Management*, 31(9), 629–646. doi: https://doi.org/10.1108/09600030110408143
148. Camerinelli, E. (2016). Blockchain in the Value network, *CSCMP Hot Topics*, Jun.
149. www.walmart.com. Accessed 08 July 2018.
150. www.bloomberg.com/news/articles/2016-11-18/wal-mart-tackles-food-safety-with-test-of-blockchain-technology, Accessed15 April 2017.
151. Jøsang, A., Ismail, R., & Boyd, C. (2007). A survey of trust and reputation systems for online service provision. *Decision support systems*, *43*(2), 618–644.
152. www.caict.ac.cn/xwdt/ynxw/201807/t20180724_180737.htm. Accessed 25 July 2018.
153. Institute of International Finance (2015), *Banking on the Blockchain*. www.iif.com/system/files/blockchain_report_-_november_2015_-_final_0.pdf. Accessed 07 July 2018.
154. cointelegraph.com/news/s7-airlines-and-alfa-bank-test-blockchain-for-b2b-payment-in-russia. Accessed 08 July 2018.
155. alfabank.ru/. Accessed 08 July 2018.
156. Ethereum is a public blockchain platform, and it is the most advanced in terms of code writing and smart contract processing. Buterin, V. (2014). A next-generation smart contract and decentralized application platform. *White Paper*.
157. Microsoft Azure is a collection of cloud services that are constantly evolving. It is an application platform to provide developers with useful services—accessible on the net—for creating applications and data storage. A distributed Blockchain as a service (BaaS) of Microsoft Azure provides organizations with a fast, low-cost, low-risk, and time-to-error response platform to collaborate, by experiencing new business processes, supported by a cloud environment with the largest portfolio for the industry conformity. Marston, S., Li, Z., Bandyopadhyay, S., Zhang, J., & Ghalsasi, A. (2011). Cloud computing—The business perspective. *Decision support systems*, *51*(1), 176–189.
158. www.bankofamerica.com/?page=corp. Accessed 07 July 2018.
159. www.opengovasia.com/articles/8129-singapore-exploring-use-of-blockchain-to-link-national-trade-platform-to-trade-platforms-in-other-countries. Accessed 8 July 2018.
160. av.sc.com/hk/content/docs/hk-dlt-trade-finance-eng-final.pdf. Accessed 07 July 2018.

161. http://www.cib.db.com/insights-and-initiatives/flow/trade_finance_and_the_blockchain_three_essential_case_studies.htm. Accessed 08 July 2018.
162. steemit.com/blockchain/@lighthouse7/ubs-santander-deutsche-bank-and-bny-mellon-are-working-on-bitcoin-for-banks. Accessed 31 March 2018.
163. www-03.ibm.com/press/us/en/pressrelease/51951.wss. Accessed 9 July 2018.
164. http://fortune.com/2016/10/24/commonwealth-bank-well-fargo-blockchain/. Accessed 8 July 2018.
165. www.coindesk.com/unicredit-white-paper-explores-blockchain-uses-for-bank-payments-post-trade-processes/. Accessed 08 July 2018.
166. Greenspan, G. (2018). Where Blockchains Add Real Value. *Innovations: Technology, Governance, Globalization*, *12*(1–2), 58–69.
167. www.sdcexec.com/article/12247812/supply-chain-finance-on-the-blockchain-enables-network-collaboration, Accessed 25 March 2017.
168. www.finextra.com/newsarticle/29288/bank-consortium-creates-block-chain-process-to-replace-letters-of-credit, Accessed 14 March 2018.
169. Camerinelli, E., & Schizas, E. (2014), A Study of the Business Case for Supply Chain Finance, Acca/Aite Group, www.accaglobal.com/ab111, Accessed 25 April 2017.
170. Pilkington, M. (2016). 11 Blockchain technology: principles and applications. *Research handbook on digital transformations*, 225.
171. Groves, A., Rickelman, C., Cassarino, C., & Hall, M. J. (2012). Are you ready for agile learning design? *T+D (USA)*, 66(3): 46–50.
172. Marino, B., & Juels, A. (2016). Setting Standards for Altering and Undoing Smart Contracts. *International Symposium on Rules and Rule Markup Languages for the Semantic Web.* Springer International Publishing, Heidelberg, Germany: 151–166.
173. www.natixis.com/natixis/upload/docs/application/pdf/2017-01/digital_trade_chain_mou_release_120117_001_-_ve.pdf, Accessed 10 April 2018.
174. https://we-trade.com/article/we-trade-blockchain-platform-completes-multiple-real-time-customer-transactions, Accessed 16 August 2018.
175. The Innovators, Trade Finance. June 2017. www.gtb.unicredit.eu/sites/default/files/awards/the-innovators-2017-trade-finance-1493310922.pdf. Accessed 29 June 2018.
176. Ketterer, J. A. (2017). *Digital Finance: New Times, New Challenges, New Opportunities.* Inter-American Development Bank, Washington, DC.
177. www.ft.com/content/8c5a44e8-4878-11e8-8ae9-4b5ddcca99b3. Accessed 30 April 2018.

178. Nakamoto, S. (2010). Transactions and Scripts: *Bitcointalk*, June 17. bitcointalk.org/index.php?topic=195.msg1611#msg1611. Accessed 24 June 2018.
179. Szabo, N. (1997). The Idea of Smart Contracts, szabo.best.vwh.net/smart_contracts_idea.html, Accessed 31 March 2018.
180. Christidis, K., & Devetsikiotis, M. (2016). Blockchains and Smart Contracts for the Internet of Things. *IEEE Access*, 4, 2292–2303.
181. Nicoletti, B. (2016), Open Data and Procurement, *Proceedings of the Third Interdisciplinary Symposium on Public Procurement*, Belgrade, Serbia, 29–20 Set.
182. Christidis, K., & Devetsikiotis, M. (2016). Blockchains and Smart Contracts for the Internet of Things. *IEEE Access*, 4, 2292–2303.
183. www.cognizant.com/whitepapers/blockchains-smart-contracts-driving-the-next-wave-of-innovation-across-manufacturing-value-chains-codex2113.pdf. Accessed 14 February 2018
184. Ream, J., Chu, Y., & Schatzky, D. (2016). *Upgrading blockchains: smart contract use cases in industries*, Deloitte Press University, New York City, NY.
185. Stark J., 2016, www.coindesk.com/making-sense-smart-contracts/. Accessed 31 March 2018.
186. Clack, C., Bakshi, V., & Braine, L. (2016). Smart Contract Templates: foundations, design landscape and research directions. arXiv:1608.00771v3 [cs.CY].
187. Elaboration of the Author from Blockchain solution and its potential in taxes, Deloitte, 2017.
188. Swan, M. (2015). *Blockchain: blueprint for a new economy*, O'Reilly Media, Sebastopol, CA.

Clack, C., Bakshi, V., & Braine, L. (2016). Smart Contract Templates: foundations, design landscape and research directions. arXiv:1608.00771v3 [cs.CY].
189. www.cognizant.com/whitepapers/blockchains-smart-contracts-driving-the-next-wave-of-innovation-across-manufacturing-value-chains-codex2113.pdf. Accessed 31 March 2018.
190. Delmolino, K., et al. (2016). Step by step towards creating a safe smart contract: Lessons and insights from a cryptocurrency lab. In: *International Conference on Financial Cryptography and Data Security*. Springer, Berlin, Germany: 79–94.
191. Walport, M., www.gov.uk/government/uploads/system/uploads/attachment_data/file/492972/gs-16-1-distributed-ledger-technology.pdf, 2015, pp. 18. Accessed 31 March 2018.
192. Linklaters, www.isda.org/a/6EKDE/smart-contracts-and-distributed-ledger-a-legal-perspective.pdf, 2017, pp.8. Accessed 31 March 2018.

193. Linklaters, www.isda.org/a/6EKDE/smart-contracts-and-distributed-ledger-a-legal-perspective.pdf, 2017, pp.9. Accessed 31 March 2018.
194. Walport, M. (2015). www.gov.uk/government/uploads/system/uploads/attachment_data/file/492972/gs-16-1-distributed-ledger-technology.pdf, pp.24. Accessed 31 March 2018.
195. Ream, J., Chu, Y., & Schatzky, D. (2016). *Upgrading blockchains: smart contract use cases in industries*, Deloitte Press University, Brussels, Belgium.
196. medium.com/legalthingsone/smart-contracts-3-limitations-of-a-self-enforcing-agreement-257cfbabeff5. Accessed 12 March 2018.
197. www.bbvaresearch.com/wp-content/uploads/2015/10/Digital_Economy_Outlook_Oct15_Cap1.pdf. Accessed 24 March 2018.
198. www.bbvaresearch.com/wp-content/uploads/2015/10/Digital_Economy_Outlook_Oct15_Cap1.pdf. Accessed 24 March 2018.
199. www.bbvaresearch.com/wp-content/uploads/2015/10/Digital_Economy_Outlook_Oct15_Cap1.pdf. Accessed 14 March 2018.
200. www.theguardian.com/business/2017/aug/10/airbnb-faces-eu-clamp-down-fair-share-tax. Accessed 14 March 2018
201. Deloitte (2017). *Blockchain technology and its potential in taxes*, Deloitte White Paper.
202. www.coindesk.com/finnish-city-wins-2-4m-blockchain-shipping/, Accessed 15 April 2017.
203. www.r3.com/blog/2017/09/26/r3-and-tradeix-develop-open-account-trade-finance-dlt-business-network/, Accessed 26 December 2017.
204. Tradeix.com. Accessed 06 August 2018.
205. Witthaut M, Deeken H, Sprenger P, Gadzhanov P, & David M (2017). Smart Objects and Smart Finance for Supply Chain Management. *Logistics Journal*, Vol. 2017.
206. Nicoletti, B., (2013), *Cloud Computing and Financial Services*, Palgrave Macmillan, Houndsmill, UK (also translated in Chinese). There are might be legal issues connected with the localization of the ICT services. See Van Eecke, P. (2013). Cloud computing legal issues. *Pozyskano z:* http://www.isaca.org/Groups/Professional-English/cloud-computing/GroupDocuments/DLA_Cloud% 20computing% 20legal% 20issues.pdf. Accessed 06 August 2018.
207. Pell Mell, T. G. (2011), *The NIST Definition of Cloud Computing*. NIST Tech Beat, Boulder, CO.
208. Harris, T. (2009). Cloud Computing-an overview. *Whitepaper, Torry Harris Business Solutions,* January.
209. Harris, T. (2009). Cloud Computing-an overview. *Whitepaper, Torry Harris Business Solutions,* January.

210. Nicoletti, B., (2013), *Cloud Computing and Financial Services*, Palgrave Macmillan, Houndsmill, UK (also available in Chinese).
211. Nicoletti, B., (2013), *Cloud Computing and Financial Services*, Palgrave Macmillan, Houndsmill, UK (also available in Chinese).
212. /www-03.ibm.com/press/us/en/pressrelease/52548.wss. Accessed 7 July 2018.
213. Kruger, C. P., & Hancke, G. P. (2014, July). Implementing the Internet of Things vision in industrial wireless sensor networks. In *2014 12th IEEE International Conference on Industrial Informatics (INDIN)*: 627–632.
214. Zincir, O., Ünal, A., & Erdal, M. (2017). Lean and Digital: A Case Study on Procurement and Supply Chain Professionals' Online Social Network. In *Key Challenges and Opportunities in Web Entrepreneurship*. IGI Global, Hershey, PA: 79–102.
215. www.internazionale.it/opinione/tullio-de-mauro/2016/12/23/il-nuovo-vocabolario-di-base-della-lingua-italiana, Accessed 31 March 2018.
216. info.ivalua.com/forrester-enabling-smarter-procurement-2018. Accessed 7 June 2018.
217. next.autonomous.com/augmented-finance-machine-intelligence/. Accessed 15 June 2018.
218. Huang, X., Liu, X., & Ren, Y. (2018). Enterprise Credit Risk Evaluation Based on Neural Network Algorithm. *Cognitive Systems Research.*
219. Bahrammirzaee, A. (2010). A comparative survey of artificial intelligence applications in finance: artificial neural networks, expert system and hybrid intelligent systems. *Neural Computing and Applications*, *19*(8), 1165–1195.
220. Poole, D. L., & Mackworth, A. K. (2010). *Artificial Intelligence: foundations of computational agents.* Cambridge University Press, Cambridge, UK.
221. www-01.ibm.com/easytools/runtime/hspx/prod/public/X0027/PortalX/page/pageTemplate?s=34bd033d8881483899158bfca10b61d8&c=34bd033d8881483899158bfca10b61d8. Accessed 08 July 2018.
222. www.mypurchasingcenter.com/purchasing/industry-articles/managing-vendor-risk-predictive-analytics/. Accessed 28 March 2018.
223. www.kpmg.de/docs/GlobalManufacturingOutlook.pdf, Accessed 28 March 2018.
224. thefinancialbrand.com/69154/ai-banking-financial-artificial-intelligence-trends-uses/?edigest
225. Kephart, J. O., Hanson, J. E., & Greenwald, A. R. (2000). Dynamic pricing by software agents. *Computer Networks*, *32*(6), 731–752.
226. Chen, Y. (2012). Research on risk of supply chain finance of small and medium-sized enterprises based on fuzzy ordinal regression support vector machine. *International Journal of Business and Management*, 7(8), 115.

227. Singleton, T. W., & Singleton, A. J. (2010). *Fraud auditing and forensic accounting* (Vol. 11). John Wiley & Sons, Hoboken, NJ.
228. Burgess, A. (2018). AI in Action. In *The Executive Guide to Artificial Intelligence* (pp. 73–89). Palgrave Macmillan, Cham, Switzerland.
229. Northouse, P. G. (2018). *Leadership: Theory and practice.* Sage publications. Thousand Oaks, CA.
230. Evelson, B., Moore, C., Kobielus, J., Karel, R., & Nicolson, N. (2008). The Forrester wave: Enterprise business intelligence platforms. *Forrester Research.–2010.*

Uçaktürk, A., Uçaktürk, T., & Yavuz, H. (2015). Possibilities of Usage of Strategic Business Intelligence Systems Based on Databases in Agile Manufacturing. *Procedia-Social and Behavioral Sciences, 207*, 234–241.
231. Nicoletti, B. (2013). *Lean procurement. Come migliorare gli acquisti, la logistica e la supply chain con l'approccio del pensiero snello,* FrancoAngeli, Milano.
232. www.iso20022.org/faq.page, Accessed 31 March 2018.
233. International Summit on Smart Finance (2016). 45.32.20.160/ISSF/about.html. Accessed 12 June 2018.
234. www.iml.fraunhofer.de/en/fields_of_activity/einkauf_finanzen_supply_chain_management/services/financial-supply-chain-management/smart-finance.html, Accessed 30 December 2017.
235. www2.deloitte.com/us/en/pages/finance-transformation/articles/finance-digital-transformation-for-cfos.html?id=us:2em:3na:crunchtimeV:awa:con:072418&sfid=0031O000032T3RBQA0. Accessed 25 July 2018.
236. www.iml.fraunhofer.de/en/fields_of_activity/einkauf_finanzen_supply_chain_management/services/financial-supply-chain-management/smart-finance.html, Accessed 30 December 2017
237. www2.deloitte.com/us/en/pages/finance-transformation/articles/finance-digital-transformation-for-cfos.html?id=us:2em:3na:crunchtimeV:awa:con:072418&sfid=0031O000032T3RBQA0. Accessed 25 July 2018.
238. www.capgemini.com/wp-content/uploads/2018/07/Report2.pdf. Accessed 28 July 2018.
239. www.capgemini.com/wp-content/uploads/2018/07/Report2.pdf. Accessed 28 July 2018.
240. Witthaut, M, Deeken, H, Sprenger, P, Gadzhanov, P, & David, M (2017). Smart Objects and Smart Finance for Supply Chain Management. *Logistics Journal*: referierte Veröffentlichungen, Vol. 2017. Accessed 31 March 2018.
241. www.fraunhofer.de, Accessed 31 March 2018.
242. www.sofia-projekt.de/, Accessed 31 March 2018.

243. Watanabe, Hiroki; Fujimura, Shigeru; Nakadaira, Atsushi; Miyazaki, Yasuhiko; Akutsu, Akihito; Kishigami, Jay: Blockchain Contract: Securing a Blockchain Applied to Smart Contracts. 2016, ieeexplore.ieee.org/stamp/stamp.jsp?arnumber=7430693&tag=1, Accessed 31 March 2018.
244. Schlatt, Vincent; Schweizer, André; Urbach, Nils; Fridgen, Gilbert: Blockchain White Paper: Grundlagen, Anwendungen und Potentiale. Fraunhofer FIT, 2016.
245. Kerbache, L., & Smith, J. M. (2004). Queueing networks and the topological design of supply chain systems. *International Journal of Production Economics*, *91*(3), 251–272.
246. The Order-To-Delivery-NETwork simulator (OTD-NET) has been continuously developed and used in studies and projects in various fields of application at the Fraunhofer IML for two decades. The focus of the simulator is the discrete production with particular focus on processes in the automotive industry. A unique feature is the detailed illustration of comprehensive planning processes. In this way, handling processes can be analyzed starting from the forecast, over the specific incoming order, the scheduling and production up to the delivery to the customer. OTD-NET can be used in the search of a weak point analysis, the evaluation of current processes and also to validate and evaluate target concepts. https://www.iml.fraunhofer.de/en/fields_of_activity/supply_chain_engineering/products/otd-net.html. Accessed 06 August 2018.
247. Liebler, K., Beissert, U., Motta, M., & Wagenitz, A. (2013, December). Introduction OTD-NET and LAS: Order-to-delivery network simulation and decision support systems in complex production and logistics networks. In *Simulation Conference (WSC), 2013 Winter* (pp. 439–451). IEEE.
248. www-03.ibm.com/press/us/en/pressrelease/50163.wss, Accessed 10 February 2018.
249. automotivelogistics.media/intelligence/digitalisation-quicker-off-blocks. Accessed 31 March 2018.
250. www.osservatori.net/ww_en/osservatori/executive-briefing/the-scf-market-and-technology-potential-in-europe-and-italy, Accessed 26 December 2017.

Beije, A., & Jullens, J. (2016). *A lead* via *Blockchain technology*. Position paper on a digital Port of Rotterdam (Concept).
251. Brigham, E. F., & Ehrhardt, M. C. (2013). *Financial management: Theory & practice*. Cengage Learning, Boston, MA.
252. Hofmann, E., Strewe, U. M., & Bosia, N. (2017). *Supply Chain Finance and Blockchain Technology: The Case of Reverse Securitisation*. Springer, Berlin, Germany.

253. www.scfbriefing.com/event-report-scf-market-and-technology-potential-in-europe-and-italy/, Accessed 31 March 2018.
254. www.osservatori.net/ww_en/osservatori/executive-briefing/the-scf-market-and-technology-potential-in-europe-and-italy. Accessed 5 April 2018.
255. www.bcg.com/publications/2016/digital-revolution-trade-finance.aspx. Accessed 5 April 2018.
256. Gilchrist, A. (2016). *Industry 4.0: the industrial internet of things*. Apress, New York City, NY

CHAPTER 7

Procurement Finance for the Small and Medium-Sized Enterprises

Introduction

This chapter analyzes the importance of procurement finance for the small and medium-sized enterprises (SMEs) in the current globalized economy. It underlines their differences with the multinational enterprises (MNEs).

In the case of procurement finance, with the word SME, it is possible to refer to buying or selling organizations, or to small financial institutions. This chapter deals mainly with selling organizations. Similar considerations apply also to the other two typologies.

This chapter considers the digital transformation and the application of innovative procurement finance solutions to the SMEs. These solutions are currently applied mainly in large multinational organizations. This limited use of innovative procurement finance solutions in SMEs is one of the factors that explains the difficulty in accessing to the credit for the SMEs. The traditional financial institutions consider them risky customers. This is another reason to apply innovative methods of procurement finance also in SMEs.

The financing of SMEs is normally featured as "small, frequent, and fast".[1] SMEs are sensitive to the market. Once they find business opportunities, they need credit quickly. Due to their situation in funding, they need to ask financial institutions to offer them loans as soon as possible to organize materials and realize transactions in time without losing the customer. However, commercial financial institutions have to follow strict procedures

B. Nicoletti, *Procurement Finance*,
Palgrave Studies in Financial Services Technology,
https://doi.org/10.1007/978-3-030-02140-5_7

and operational standards before issuing loans. This would not satisfy SMEs' needs for quick financing.

To be successful and competitive, procurement in SMEs should take into account the specific characteristics of this sector and its differences from the large organizations. Those features and dissimilarities include the following:

- lower level of available funding and their need for short-term financial results[2];
- longer cash-to-cash cycle;
- lack of time for the management to implement changes[3];
- dependence on core customers and their ways of interaction in the value networks[4];
- lack of knowledge or resources for an effective implementation of key procurement functions[5];
- need of flexible procurement services and fixed cost reduction in times of crisis, making customer demand even more volatile and harder to forecast.[6]

Difficulty of Credit Access by SMEs

A SME can be defined as "a formal enterprise with annual turnover, in U.S.A. dollar terms, of between 10 and 1000 times the mean per capita gross national income, at purchasing power parity, of the country in which it operates".[7]

Sourcing equity and debt financing are the two main barriers to success that SMEs face.[8] In general, SMEs lack finance. This fact imposes severe restrictions on their development.[9] Financial capital is needed to acquire other resources. It is the most common form of financial resources.[10] The lack of finance prevents SMEs from investing in new solutions, innovations, and so on. As such, SMEs are less likely to invest in procurement finance information systems and therefore ascertain the associated benefits.[11] It is a vicious circle, which needs to be broken.

The economic and financial features that characterize SMEs and the failure to reach a contractual power equal to that of a large multinational enterprise makes the financial institution-company finance ratios more complex and appealing, resulting in difficulty in finding cover for their financial needs.[12] The extreme variability of the profits, lifespan, and development of SMEs, compared to MNEs, generates specific financing issues. The main reason that

SMEs often encounter difficulties in obtaining funding is the fact that financial institutions and traditional lending institutions believe that SMEs are risky organizations.[13]

SMEs tend to be relatively heavily indebted and their debt is concentrated with financial institutions. The high level of indebtedness over the years and the poor diversification of funding sources make SMEs very vulnerable and subject to financial strains. In this high debt system, payment times, especially among the organizations themselves, have considerably lengthened. Less liquidity for organizations, therefore more credit requirements. This is another vicious circle.

Regarding the provision of loans, financial institutions are asking for greater communication and visibility from their customers. They require clear and reliable data on the organization's situation. Because SMEs do not always have the right tools to analyze and communicate their financial situation, this request from financial institutions creates a barrier between financial institution and organizations that again hampers access to credit.[14]

SMEs are opaque with respect to MNEs. Their ability to do business is more difficult to evaluate because their budgets offer less information. Their credit histories are generally shorter. In addition to these features, there are higher fixed costs of external evaluation and monitoring. All this means for SMEs higher transaction costs, both in percentages and in absolute value with respect to their assets, especially for those transaction with lower visibility from financial institutions (this is the so-called informational asymmetry).

It is somewhat unavoidable that, during the economic downturns, credit sources for SMEs tend to drain more quickly than for large organizations, hindering their activities and investment considerably.

From the point of view of risk management by financial institutions, it can be partly understandable that financial institutions adopt a more selective approach to credit supply in a recession period to preserve asset quality in their financial statements. Overall, the credit crunch is very hard for SMEs, because financial institutions consider them to be more likely to default than large organizations, and because SMEs are often unable to shift from financial institution credit to other sources of external financing. As a result, SMEs, compared to large organizations, are more likely to be affected by excessive financial institution risk aversion and hence by credit rationing. The difficulty of obtaining credit, which affects not only their ordinary administration but also their ability to grow, can easily transform liquidity problems into insolvency risk leading to bankruptcy.

MNEs and SMEs

Procurement finance is mainly developed in the USA, followed by Europe, particularly in the UK and Germany.[15] Asia is gaining momentum, especially in India and China. These countries are becoming the fastest growing markets in procurement.[16] The industries in which procurement finance programs are prevalent are retail, manufacturing, consumer products, automotive, agriculture, chemicals, and pharmaceuticals.[17] There are three common attributes of organizations in those industries that make them good candidates for better procurement finance. Firstly, they are all multinational organizations, which normally do operations and procurement worldwide. Their presence in a number of countries ensures that their products and services can reach their customers. Secondly, all of them have extensive value networks. They are involved in fast and rapid changes in the demand and supply worldwide. The volume of transactions involved is huge.[18]

SMEs represent a high percentage of organizations in many national economies. There are nearly 30 million small organizations in the USA.[19] Development reports issued by the China State Administration for Industry and Commerce in 2014 show that SMEs contribute more than 60 percent of the Chinese GDP. They contribute more than 50 percent of tax revenue to finance and contribute more to economic development than large state-owned enterprises.[20] SMEs provide more than 80 percent of employment in cities and towns in China.[21] They provide a high percentage of employment since they generate a large part of new working places in the economies of the countries of the Organisation for Economic Co-operation and Development (OECD).[22]

SMEs have specific strengths and weaknesses that require the implementation of appropriate policies. New solutions and globalization have reduced the importance of economies of scale in many activities, while the potential capabilities of small organizations have been strengthened. However, many of the traditional problems facing SMEs are[23]:

- lack of financing;
- difficulty in exploiting new solution;
- limited managerial skills;
- poor productivity;
- difficulties in complying with regulatory constraints.

These problems are more critical in a globalized system and a technology-dominated environment.[24]

These differences between MNEs (large organizations) and SMEs could determine how financial institutions deal with them. A distinctive element of SMEs is represented by the access to credit. It means the availability of financial institutions to issue loans to SMEs. More than half of SMEs needed credit to purchase equipment, 35 percent to purchase inventory, and 28 percent to help them expand into new markets.[25]

The solutions of procurement finance, used normally in MNEs, are still often unknown by SMEs. These solutions of procurement finance could be profitable also for SMEs.[26] In addition, the development of procurement finance is able to make up for the credit absence of SMEs as well as to reduce the information asymmetry of the credit market. SMEs with procurement finance can cut the cost of funds through the income sharing contracts and the repurchase contract and other means so as to alleviate the financing constraints they face.[27]

In times of rigid constraints on financial institution credit, an element of relief is the ability of organizations to replace financial institution credit with alternative sources of financing. The first cause is to be found in the pervasive digitization that is pushing the financial services sector to become increasingly online. The second one is in the closure of credit access that directs organizations to alternative channels for finding financial resources. The third one is that in some jurisdictions some procurement finance instruments do not impact on the creditworthiness of the organization. Therefore, the use of the new fintech platforms has grown along with the awareness of the business world of the benefits of the new instruments made available by alternative finance.[28]

The procurement finance is the set of solutions that enable organizations to finance their working capital (credits, debts, and inventories) by leveraging on the role they have in the value network in which they operate and on the relationships with other actors in the network. It can represent a new opportunity for collaboration.

It is important to consider procurement finance for two structural elements. The first one is the long payment times for commercial debts. The second one is the important role that SMEs have in the economic context and their difficulty on the credit access. Therefore, alternative tools of access to liquidity are needed. In this regard, procurement finance is a concrete and available opportunity, especially for SMEs.

A key element of procurement finance's most innovative models is the use of digital technologies, enabling extended service delivery to SMEs as well, managing customers, documentation, and information more quickly and more rapidly to activate financing and to improve risk evaluation. Through specific digital platforms, customers and vendors can create efficiency in adopting traditional solutions, innovative solutions, or initiating collaborative solutions between value network partners.

To have a more precise idea of the risks and potential of an organization, it is necessary to look at its relations with vendors and customers, that is, the role that it plays in its value network. If these relationships are in a structured digital form, it is possible to analyze them, having a more precise idea of the level of risk.

Digitizing procurement processes facilitates access to credit. The financial sustainability of an organization is shifted towards digital relationships that allow to analyze and to monitor more accurately the role of each actor in the procurement processes from vendors to customers.

The trade is increasingly becoming global, and procurement finance value networks become increasingly international. Procurement finance innovative solutions can support SMEs. The large organizations are the best customer of financial institutions for procurement finance because they are less risky, more financially stable, and able to create long-term relationships with financial institutions. By contrast, the access to procurement finance for the SMEs is necessary to extend their international trade transactions and thus to stimulate the economic growth due to their important role in the national economies.

The participation on international trade can present risky challenges for SMEs. This participation is important considering SMEs as an important economic growth engine. The financial institutions have difficulty to support the financial needs of SMEs customers. In this situation, the procurement finance innovative solutions are instruments which can facilitate the financing access for them. Many procurement finance providers are starting to consider SMEs vendors as strategic actors for the international value networks and thus need to support the development of SMEs.

Use of Procurement Finance in Multinational Organizations

The procurement processes can be divided into three flows: the information/digital flow, the physical flow, and the financial flow. Figure 7.1 represents these three flows and their directions.

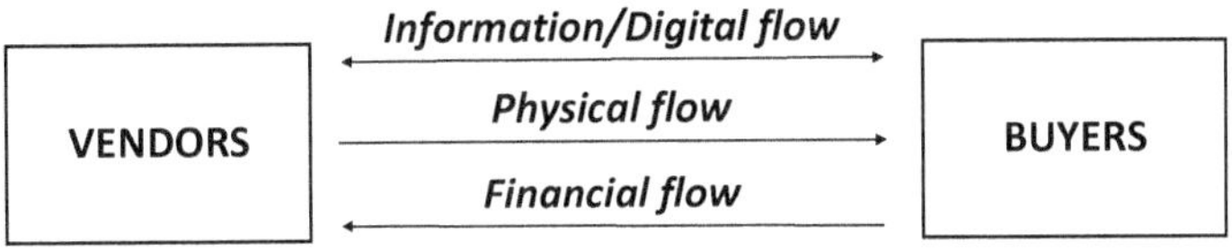

Fig. 7.1 The three flows in procurement

Over time, the financial flow has assumed a relevant role. Particularly important is the management of the financial flow throughout the entire value network, allowed by the procurement finance solutions. Procurement finance is able to provide opportunities of easier credit access. It allows the creation of financial collaboration between two or more procurement organizations including third-party vendors. This is possible through financial flows planning, governance, and control at an inter-organization level. Procurement finance is able to provide better access to credit at a lower cost of financing, by addressing the issue that value network weaknesses may become a risk for all other actors involved in the cycle. On the other side, the procurement finance application has a relatively high level of complexity and competence.

Procurement finance solutions are more used in MNEs. To understand the success of these solutions in large organizations, it is useful to report the results of an empirical study, relative to the procurement finance application in six European large organizations.[29] This empirical study helps in understanding how procurement finance applications should work from a vendor-buyer organization perspective. It emphasizes that some of its important parts are still relatively not completely explored.

It is important to underline that this study focused only on European large organizations because they are under the same or very similar regulatory and socio-economic context. In addition, the authors decided to apply their work to large organizations because several of these organizations have already applied procurement finance solutions, despite their complexity.

The challenging feature of this empirical study is that it is focused on the adoption of procurement finance from an upstream innovation perspective. Being a process innovation, procurement finance that includes vendors in its adoption is not aimed mainly to downstream customers but to add value to the entire innovation process. This innovation is based on the supply phase of the buyer-vendor organization. In this way, the direct vendors of the buyer organization become the target customers of this innovative process.

In this context, there is an increasing interconnection between financial and logistics aspects. It is possible to assume that, with the application of procurement finance, the handling of upstream cash flow can improve the vendor position related to financial restrictions. While procurement finance is getting better, as a consequence, it improves also the physical flow in the value network.

The organizations that decide to adopt procurement finance focus mainly on improving their working capital and their liquidity management. Both of them have a central role within an organization. Procurement finance allows having solutions not only from a short-term perspective but also from a medium/long-term one. Procurement finance can cut the total amount of liquidity that is necessary for the value network. This is reached with a coordinated financial flow throughout the value network.

Relatively to the phase of the adoption decision of procurement finance, a large organization that decides to adopt procurement finance is considering a medium-long-term efficiency improvement in line with simultaneous structural adjustments. It is important to have a good credit evaluation to guarantee favorable conditions to the participants in procurement finance.

Benefits of Procurement Finance Applications

The financial benefits are certainly the main incentive to adopt procurement finance solutions. There are other important benefits as well. Large organizations that have adopted procurement finance solutions claim the improvement of cash-to-cash, better access to credit with a reduction in the cost of financing, and improvement in the financial flexibility through a managerial approach to operating working capital and liquidity management. Better financial management of the procurement function produces economic impacts on the organization. Customer-vendor relationships, thanks to the improvements in the revenues and costs, reach a base of more solid procurement finance. This also means better procurement efficiency and better internal operations. It reduces the default risk of strategic partners since it creates long-term relationships based on visibility, trust, and collaboration.

The empirical study mentioned before pointed out that the credit rating is an important element for credit access.[30] Credit rating is still mainly limited to financial information pertaining to a single organization, rather than information on value network relationships. On respect to a traditional rating, an operating rating based on the entire value network could more accurately estimate the probability of default of an organization.

One of the benefits of the procurement finance is to be able to extend access to credit to more organizations. It is able to allow access to credit even to organizations that, in the absence of collaboration with other actors in the value network, would not be able to finance through external channels.

Economic benefits are determined by lower financial charges and discounts on the procurement costs of products and services.

An important element in the most innovative procurement finance models is the use of innovative digital solutions. They enable faster document and information processing to activate financing solutions and monitor risks. This results in a potential base for effectiveness and efficiency both in the customer-vendor relations and in the relations with the financial institutions.

The study reported before shows clearly that many large organizations have already applied procurement finance or they intend to do so in the short term.[31] Their focus is now how the adoption can become a routine.

Opportunities and Challenges for SMEs

Financial decisions stem from the need to provide adequate coverage of financial needs undertakings. The financial problem has uniform characteristics in the various organizations, although its criticality and the supply, production, and distribution processes are different. They vary based on the size of the organization, the solutions assigned to it, as the financial channels that can be used are not the same for small, medium, and large organizations.

In a crisis context, above all, the management of the net working capital is very important. Managing the working capital and liquidity has a strategic importance especially for the SMEs. Succeeding in its optimization is one of the few levers available to the entrepreneur to free liquidity in a relatively short period without an invasive and structural restructuring program. In the management of the working capital, there are significant potential financial resources that the entrepreneurs, sometimes, do not completely perceive. The lesser is the lifetime of the operating cycle, for instance as a result of a commercial policy, a decrease in inventories or the orientation to maintain a level of trade receivables low (resulting from the same amount of revenue from a lower credit collection time), the lower is the use of the financial assets for carrying out the operating activities. A longer payment delay, always at equal purchases, allows an increase in supply debts and, consequently, less dependency from financial institution debts.

The dynamics of working capital largely influence the net financial position of an organization by[32]:

- An extension of payments to vendors frees liquidity. As a consequence, it reduces the debts.
- The opposite phenomenon, or a delay in customer receipts, typical in a crisis period, deteriorates the indebtedness.

The impact of the changes in the net working capital on cash flows, and therefore on the net financial position, depends on many factors (Fig. 7.2)[33]:

- Sales performance: an increase in sales generates working capital growth (more inventories, higher receivables). This results in larger

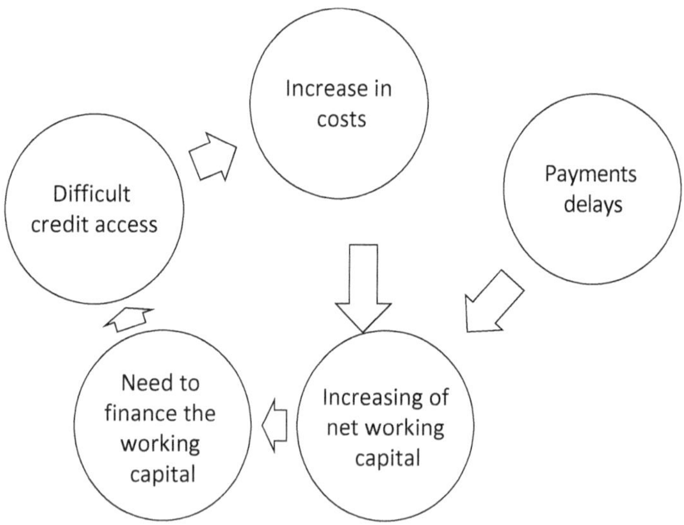

Fig. 7.2 Vicious circle for SMEs

financial need. A contraction of sales does not necessarily mean a reduction in the working capital. It may create problems such as managing and disposing of non-marketable inventories in the market.

- Business model (for instance, serial production for the warehouse compared to commodity production) and seasonality of demand are variables that affect the inventory levels.
- Payment and collection policies for debts-credits and the type of customer-vendor are the main drivers for the evolution of trade payables/receivables and the quality of the latter.
- Competitive scenario: the organizations must make choices that impact on the net working capital to compete in the market.

The importance of basic working capital management is equal for small and large organizations. The main difference lies in the financial channels. Financial institutions are not often equipped to provide financial resources at competitive costs and with the speed and efficiency needed to meet the needs of SMEs. The consequences are missed development opportunities for the organizations and as a consequence for the economic system. Alternative finance in these cases can help. There is a need for large-scale standard financial products for SMEs. There is also the need for niche products and specialists specially adapted to the diverse needs of smaller organizations.

The financial needs of SMEs are complex. The delivery of consistent services is not sustainable without the support of solutions that optimizes operating costs. For this reason, finance and technology linkage is spreading in segments as loans, procurement finance, marketplace lending, and alternative finance. What is common to them is the optimization of the processes to identify the right lender and instrument for the organization's specific needs. Then the services should be provided in an intuitive, quick and relatively simple way.

To capture the best opportunities in the procurement finance, fintech organizations should place themselves in the market space left by the traditional operators. A cornerstone of procurement finance most innovative models is the use of digital technologies. They would enable complex services to be extended also to SMEs by managing customers, documentation, and information more quickly, improving the risk evaluation and assessment, and activating financing solutions.

In this current globalized and dynamic ecosystem, the larger financial institutions present limits especially related to provide financing based on credit rating.[34] This leads to problems, especially for SMEs. The attention is focused on risk management methods to protect financial institutions from excessive exposures. The most widespread applications have weaknesses. They give too much importance to the budget/business plan data, by the old and static definition. The qualitative component is often deficient, weak, and not representative. Progress data evaluation is limited to the single part of the relationships that define the health status of an organization.

There is a need to outline better risk management models. This includes, in addition to the information already assessed by financial institutions, typical value network variables, to have a right vision about risks and the potentiality of an organization. It is not sufficient to consider the single organization. It is useful to consider its relationships with its customers and vendors, namely, the role that such organizations have in the value network. It helps if these relationships are digital. Procurement finance solutions exploit the digital transformation of processes in a way through which it is possible to have more transparent data related to relationships with vendors and customers, making possible in this way a more realistic risk evaluation.[35]

A joint financial and operational rating management has relevant important benefits for the vendors. This is true especially for small vendors, which could get a credit risk more aligned with their operations. In this way, they could get more liquidity at a lower cost. At the same time, the financial institutions could benefit from it, due to a lower probability of bankruptcy and the ability to become a financial partner able to advise and anticipate customers' needs through greater visibility and sharing of information.[36]

It is useful to have a collaborative approach in such a way that SMEs are increasingly involved in accessing innovative procurement finance solutions. The collaboration along the value network allows SMEs to gain more visibility throughout the value network. This helps in becoming more flexible and improving service levels.

If an actor of the value network becomes weak, this weakness influences the entire value network.

The increased use of technology that makes improvement in the procurement finance solutions and that results in online procurement finance creates real benefits for SMEs but also challenges (Table 7.1).[37] The online trading platforms allow collecting data about financing, management, and

Table 7.1 Benefits and challenges for SMEs in procurement finance

Benefits	*Challenges*
Collecting data along the entire value network	Low potential cost reduction
Collaboration between financial institutions and all the organizations of the value network	Not easy implementation
Improvement in credit access	Reduced cost
Increased attention to risk management	Structure and mechanisms intermediation

capital information of upstream and downstream organizations of the entire value network. This highlights the need for more collaboration between financial institutions and all organizations along the value network, involving SMEs and logistics organizations.[38] This collaboration can reduce the problem of credit access of SMEs because the financial institution provides the financing to SMEs based on the real transactions along the value network thanks to the online and clear information exchange. It increasingly improve the attention to risk management. These solutions require an enforcement on the mitigation of the financial institution credit risks, through forecasting and evaluating the potential growth of the organizations, and on finding all the potential risks in a rapid and efficient way.

The benefits and challenges for SMEs from the use of new solutions are summarized in Table 7.1.

The benefits of the new solutions for the SMEs consist in reduced informational asymmetries over large organizations, by having greater access to capital, customers, and potential partners.

ING[39]

The Dutch ING Bank partnered with USA-based fintech startup Kabbage[40] to serve SME customers in Europe. Kabbage's easy-to-use interface and novel risk management algorithms allow delivering decisions on loan applications in a matter of minutes. As a startup, Kabbage had a distinctive new capability but lacked capital and customer relationships. ING brought to the partnership its deep reserve of capital and its relationships with prospective SME customers.

IBM[41]
An example of new solutions used for SMEs involvement is the digital trade chain of IBM. It is a platform based on blockchain solutions for the management and regulation of business transactions, mainly import-export, of SMEs. The objective is to avoid the use of documentary credit or other forms of credit insurance. These processes are complex and economically difficult to sustain. Blockchain solutions increase the visibility of the transactions and simplify exchanges between SMEs, both domestically and internationally. Blockchain should reset the time and cut transaction costs.

Facing the financial gap of SMEs, a traditionally not much considered market segment, this solution aims to help open new opportunities for revenues, start new business relationships, and promote commercial growth.

Ideabank[42]
Ideabank and ING have extended into banking adjacencies by providing services like accounts-receivable management, factoring, accounting, and cash flow analysis to SME customers.[43]

Innovation in SMEs

Digital Credit

One of the most important innovations in the case of SMEs is connected with innovative solutions labeled digital credit.[44] Procurement finance can support SME financing focused around purchase orders, invoices, receivables, and pre- and post-shipment processes between buyers and vendors along the value network. Triggers from the physical supply chain activate financial events. Cloud-based digital procurement platforms can gain insights into complex trade flows by digitizing documents and transactions and applying data analytics to make credit decisions. They also leverage the financial stability and strength of bond-rated large corporations

Digitization	Simplicity	Scalability	Agility
• Timeliness • Traceability of transactions • Efficiency • Integration with financial institutions systems • Automatic messaging	• Open and user friendly access for all involved actors • Flexible connection • Low level of training for trade actors	• Extension of offered products • Flexibility for financial products • Business growth without constraints	• Flexibility • Continuous improvement • Rapid response to customer and vendor markets

Fig. 7.3 Critical success factors of digital credit

(often large department store chains or manufacturers) buying SME products or services, to offer faster and cheaper SME financing.

There are several platforms which provide digital credit to SMEs. For all, simplification and digitization provide more efficient SME lending for vendors, accelerate approval, increase SME credit access, reduce the chance of vendor or procurement fraud, and sometimes lower the cost of financing for SMEs. Figure 7.3 presents the critical success factors for an initiative of digital credit. Some examples are Kickfurther, Tungsten, Basware, Tradeshift, and Kinara Capital.[45] Many of these models work by digitizing the value network, allowing for such innovations such as contracts that trigger immediate payments and loan disbursements when they are delivered and scanned.

Hong Kong Monetary Authority[46]

Hong Kong's de facto central bank went live in August 2018 with a blockchain-backed procurement finance platform set to link up with 21 financial institutions, including HSBC and Standard Chartered. The launch of the system is one of the first and largest examples of a government-led project aimed at upgrading the USD 9 trillion global trade finance industry.

(*continued*)

(continued)

This blockchain solution is expected to cut the time and paperwork needed to push through routine procurement finance transactions by making it easier to verify each step of the complex process and confirm the credentials of the parties involved. This solution allows small companies greater access to procurement finance. SMEs around the world are often denied access to banking services due to the increasing costs of due diligence required to sign up new customers. The blockchain solutions are able to extract a wide range of organization data, at a low cost, to evaluate potential customers. This allows the procurement finance platform to take on more small organizations. This technology is expected to innovate procurement finance by cutting the amount of documentation and resources needed to process transactions. It also reduces the amount of time needed for some transactions from a couple of weeks down to one day. Fraud is also easier to detect. Organizations often request more financing from financial institutions than what is needed to fund the trade. Once trades are logged in the blockchain, all parties will be able to view the level of financing requested and reduce the ability to acquire excess funds.

Technology Acceptance Model

It is interesting in the case of procurement finance for SMEs to analyze a model developed for evaluating the acceptance of new solutions (technology acceptance model, TAM).[47] A number of studies have adopted this model to study the acceptance of the Internet and related technologies, such as m-payments, online banking, digital insurance, and m-commerce.[48] The base of the evaluation of TAM is on the hypothesis that the important determinants of the adoption and use of new technologies are:

- The perceived usefulness (PU), which is the degree to which people think that using a particular system enhances their performance. The measures of PU include performance increase, productivity increase, effectiveness, overall usefulness, timesaving, and increased job performance.
- The perceived ease of use (PEOU), which is the degree to which a person believes that using a particular system requires little effort.

The measures for PEOU include ease of control, ease of use, simplicity, clarity, and flexibility of use. This has a significant and direct effect on the intention of SMEs to adopt procurement finance.

These two beliefs create a favorable disposition or intention towards the use of a technology and consequently affect its use.

There are other factors to take into account when considering procurement finance with respect to the basic TAM. Despite the unique benefits of procurement finance, overcoming trust issues is, for instance, a major challenge to the adoption of procurement finance. In the case of the SMEs, a study extended the TAM to include also the theory of planned behavior.[49] It examined the influence of several other potential factors.[50] Taking into account this and other studies, it is possible to generalize the TAM.[51]

A complete TAM should include (Fig. 7.4)[52]:

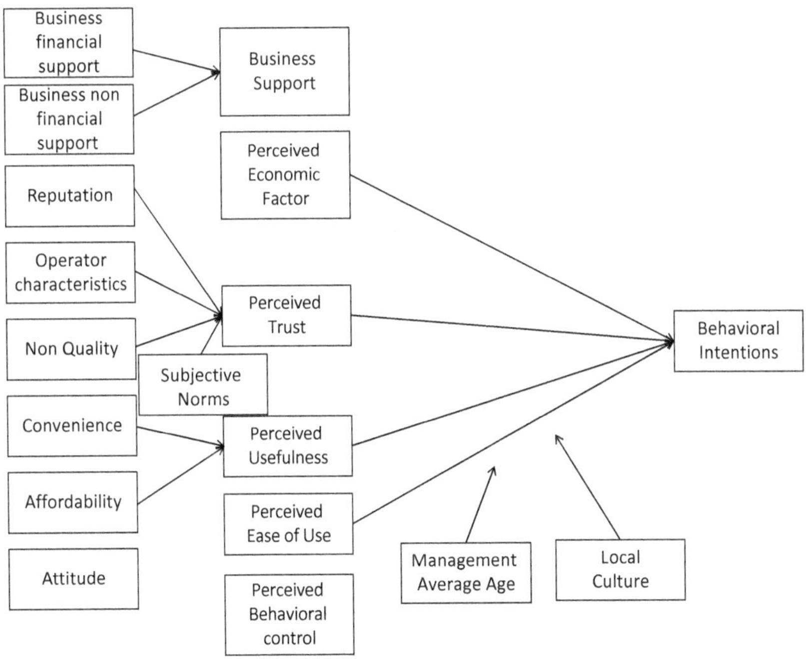

Fig. 7.4 Technology acceptance model

- Behavioral intentions (BI) of adopting procurement finance, which is the propensity to adopt a new solution.
- Perceived economic factor (PEF), which has a significant and direct effect on the intention of SMEs to adopt procurement finance.
- Perceived usefulness (PU), which has a significant and direct effect on the intention of the customer to adopt new technology services. It is determined by the level of convenience (CON) and affordability (AFF) derived from procurement finance.
- Perceived trust (PT), which has a significant and direct effect on the intention of SMEs to adopt procurement finance.
- Digital operator (DO) characteristics.
- The non-quality (NQ) of the service provided by the financial institutions.
- The awareness and knowledge (AK) is having or showing realization, perception, or knowledge of a situation or fact.
- The business support can be divided into two sections: (1) financial support such as property loan, working capital, and grant and (2) non-financial support such as courses, advisory, management, distribution, research, and development.[53]
- The reputation (RE) is based on perceptions of the reliability, credibility, social responsibility, and trustworthiness of the organizations.[54]
- The attitude towards the procurement finance (APF) refers to the SME's favorable or unfavorable evaluations of the behavior.[55]
- The subjective norms refer to the perceived social pressures (SP) which influence an individual's behavioral intention.[56]
- The perceived behavioral control (BC) refers to the perception of ease or difficulty to perform the behavior of interest.[57]

Innovation in the Procurement Processes

For the procurement finance innovation to be effective, it is important to adapt the structure of the organization to the innovation. This is achieved through different steps[58]:

- redefining the innovation or restructuring of the organization;
- clarifying the organization;
- diffusing the innovation;
- arriving at steady state (routine) for the innovation.

Regarding the redefinition of the innovation, this process consists in an adjustment rather than an entirely new approach. This adjustment is relative not only to the way through which the implementation of procurement finance can satisfy the needs of the organizations. It is necessary to consider also the increasing importance attributed to vendors and to the relationships with them. For this assignment, some organizations have sought not only to meet their needs but to provide a high degree of flexibility to the vendors through the provision of more visibility to the procurement flows and to the invoices issuing.[59] This has been provided to satisfy the vendor needs through the implementation of procurement finance. The survey, examined in this chapter, found three different fields regarding the innovation redefinition, namely, the simplification and digitization level of transactions, the assignment of benefits, and the extent of use of the procurement finance by the vendors.[60]

The restructuring process consists of a complete change of the organization. It has been evident how in an increasingly globalized ecosystem a new collaboration between different sectors of an organization is necessary, namely, finance and procurement sectors, to make the procurement finance innovations effective. An upstream innovation of the organizations in which the vendors assume a relevant role is important. To implement this type of innovation, the collaboration and a strong communication with the vendors are necessary. The term restructuring is important because this new collaboration leads the experts of the procurement function to carry out tasks that have not been assigned to them in the past. In particular, they need to market procurement finance upstream of the organization or its vendors. These tasks are instead normally executed by the marketing experts towards the downstream customers.

The survey shows as the redefining and restructuring can be inventory beneficial to each other.[61] The internal restructuring of the organization is not sufficient without understanding the importance of the vendors' involvement. Considering the redefinition of procurement finance, these are possible only with a restructuring of organizations. The latter is possible only with necessary feedbacks derived by redefining the innovation. For instance, in some organizations, the adjustment of performance evaluations and the new collaboration between finance and procurement functions allow both redefining and restructuring the processes. The functions have to be in line, namely, adjusted, towards the same objective: the effective adoption of procurement finance. At the same time, this alignment is possible with the restructuring process. Having to be conveyed towards the same objective, the functions need considering procurement finance adoption as a tool able to improve the organizations' performances. On the other side, the finance managers have to evaluate the potential challenges before deciding how procurement finance has to be applied.

Regarding the vendors' involvement, some organizations have understood that, besides alignment, the involvement of vendors is necessary for attempting to redefine the organization considering the vendors' needs. This involvement not only allows a simpler redefinition of the processes. It also facilitates the alignment of the different functions, possible thanks to the communication with the vendors.

The survey confirms that this involvement has facilitated the linkage between restructuring and redefining and it has not directly improved the procurement finance effectiveness.[62]

After the redefining and the restructuring process, procurement finance adoption is able to become a routine for the organization. Some organizations have already applied procurement finance solutions. They are working converting this adoption into routine. To do it, the organizations need to convince all procurement managers of the effectiveness of procurement finance adoption, a phase called clarification.

Another important phase is called upstream dissemination. This phase consists of making the diffusion of innovation increasingly rapid in the upstream organization, namely, spreading this innovation among vendors. In this action of spreading procurement finance, the finance managers, which are responsible for the procurement finance of selling organizations, play an important role. These actors should be in direct communication with the value network managers of the buying organization in such a way to have more awareness of the financial decisions allowing a direct spread among vendors. There is a linkage between these two phases: without clarifications, the diffusion would not be possible.

The benefits that a buyer organization can provide to the vendors are several. They represent a tool for the procurement finance leverage. These benefits depend on the credit evaluation of the buyer organization and on the procurement finance structure. The leverage of the buyer organization influences the capability to diffuse the procurement finance. This diffusion depends on an important element: the trust. Through trust, the vendors are able to accept the procurement finance adoption. Some organizations have tried to create a strong trust with vendors using a direct communication with them through their financial institutions. A modern way to create trust is the use of blockchain solutions.[63]

Another important element for the diffusion of procurement finance is the power of the position of the procurement organizations towards their vendors. Some organizations have the power to impose procurement finance adoption. The power of the buyer-vendor relationship assumes a relevant role. The procurement finance leverage, the power of relations, and the trust are an important element for buyer organizations that want to adopt procurement finance.

To sum up, this empirical study shows which variables influence the procurement finance adoption and how buyer organizations can spread its diffusion.[64] The authors clarify that procurement finance adoption is different from the traditional business innovation. In this new type of innovation, the procurement finance redefinition needs the involvement of the vendors. This is made possible through a restructuring process able to align different sectors as procurement and finance sectors. Making these two sectors convey towards the same objective, namely, the effective adoption of procurement finance, is a new concept for many organizations. The challenge of this innovation is not only an internal challenge but also an external one since it requires an involvement of the vendors also in the initial phases of the procurement. The increasingly anticipated involvement of vendors is necessary because the more vendors adopt procurement finance, the more this adoption can become a routine.

The problem is that organizations want tools able to make the extension of payment terms providing liquidity to their vendors at the same time possible. The procurement finance can be one of the potential solutions to this problem. In addition, the financial managers no longer have a secondary role because they should operate in line with procurement managers to convince vendors to adopt procurement finance.

The large organizations are in the right position to promote the procurement finance sustainability. The value of these procurement finance solutions often revolves around the initiative of a large lead-chain organization that not only optimizes its position among vendors and customers but also facilitates the continuity of its vendors from a financial point of view. If the large organizations expand the perspective of value network's members, the benefits are risk sharing in return for more reliable revenues and a more stable procurement.

This empirical study has some limits, for instance, the focus on only a few European large organizations cannot make sense of a wider international application under different regulatory and business contexts.

While this analysis is based on a survey on large organizations, it is applicable also to smaller organizations. For the latter ones, the benefits could be even more since they have bigger problems in accessing to the credit.

Conclusions

This chapter has underlined the important role of the SMEs for the economic growth of the organizations and the economy of a nation. At the same time, the difficulties to access credit for the SMEs push to evaluate possible innovative solutions. Procurement finance solutions look like an innovative approach able to satisfy the need of the organizations, especially for the SMEs. The new form of alternative finance allows SMEs to see a possibility to get financing and as a consequence the possibility to grow.

The constant development of new solutions has interesting benefits for the SMEs. The traditional financial institutions aimed at richer customers. New solutions allow a more democratic access to financial services.

A summary of the benefits of procurement finance applications for SMEs is[65]:

- agreements between financial institutions and large organizations for the implementation of financial value network solutions allow also smaller organizations to enjoy more favorable and less costly conditions than traditional credit;
- reduction of the risk of financial bankruptcy of virtuous but financially weak vendors which may affect the whole value network;
- greater efficiency in processes both in the value network and in the relationships with financial actors;
- mitigation of risks using transactional data allowing a better credit rating.

The key concepts of procurement finance are integration and collaboration. The business world, as it is today, sees both potential customers and vendors dispersed at a global level. To be competitive, it is useful to look at the global market by getting value for money that can be aligned with the global offer. To do this, it is necessary to evaluate vendors not only locally but globally as well.

Considering the increasingly globalized ecosystem and taking into account the role of the focal organization, the role of vendors, and the role of the financial institutions, the integration and collaboration concepts emerge as particularly important. Procurement finance not only includes specific financial solutions, but it focuses on the collaboration throughout the extended value network.[66]

Procurement finance allows a reduction in overall financial requirements thanks to collaborative management that cuts working capital or redistributes it optimally based on the financial capabilities of the various players in the value network. It can improve the financial performances of the entire value network and mitigate its risks.

An empirical study of the procurement finance applications in large organizations underlines the challenges of implementing procurement finance. It focuses on the increasing important role of financial flows and the attention to the roles of the actors in the value network as well as their mutual relationships. This new intersection between different functions as procurement and finance creates new tasks for financial institutions and providers of financial services. The different sectors in an organization should collaborate increasingly. This important change can be reflected in a transformation of the business background creating benefits, especially for SMEs.

From these important concepts of integration and collaboration and from the need of credit access for SMEs, it is clear how a global and integrated vision related to the linkage between granting credit and procurement field is important.

Procurement finance is developing into a clear concept for the boardroom of organizations since a good system of procurement can contribute to a higher EVA™.[67] Standard theories of finance and management accounting might contribute to the development of new approaches in procurement, as well as to the integration of value network management and procurement. There are a lot of possibilities to connect the different ERP systems in the different organizations in the extended value network with electronic data interchange (EDI) or similar technologies (such as blockchain).[68] A point of attention is still on how to divide the lower costs of value network finance and the value network performance. Business models have to be developed between partners to share the gain of lower costs.[69] Besides the technological solution, the collaboration among organizations and their managers, and to share the so-called "win-win" situations with each other, is important.

Procurement finance is adding value to control by adding value to the organization (lower working capital, reduction of the cash cycle, sharing the benefits of interest arbitrage, and reduction of risks). Procurement finance adds value also through the collaboration with other departments in the organization to integrate their processes: value network management, procurement, marketing, finances, and ICT.[70]

It is necessary to help SMEs with the introduction of procurement finance instruments. Procurement finance is not only about reverse factoring and dynamic discounting. It is a paradigm shift about collaboration in the value network. It creates value by having better liquidity and working capital management (lower working capital, because of sharing forecast in the value network, lower interest rates, and a shorter cash cycle). This paradigm shift is also on the fact that departments as control (or finance), value network management, production, marketing and sales, and ICT need to cooperate more tightly together. This might be also a shift in an organization culture especially for small- and medium-sized organizations.

Procurement finance presents a win-win-win situation, for buyers, vendors, and financial institutions. Large organizations are, and should be even more, concerned of the financial health and the continuity of their vendors. Big buyers need to pay attention to financially supporting their small vendors. In a global market that evolves rapidly and in an economic context in constant change, the large organizations should devote even more attention on usable ways able to strengthen the partnerships with their strategic vendors. Procurement finance is a relevant tool to help in this subject. Many large organizations have already applied the procurement finance, and some of them are already in the steady state. The procurement finance application is profitable also for SMEs. They are able to reach benefits through the new way to consider the value network as collaborative chain and the new way to focus on potential alignment among different sectors of the organization and their vendors considering the latter a new cultural change of their ecosystem (Table 7.2).

The collaboration approach along the value network can create trust relations between organizations and SMEs. The financial institutions can consider this situation as the possibility to extend the financing to SMEs. This is possible since procurement finance solutions allow financial institutions to evaluate in a better way the real credit rating of the organizations with the possibility to mitigate the risks of financing them. This scenario is developing and improving increasingly thanks to the continuous development of new solutions for procurement finance.

Table 7.2 Objectives of the parties

Buyer	*Vendor*	*Financial institution*
Improved cash flow	Improved cash flow	Mitigated risks
Optimized working capital	Optimized working capital	Optimized working capital
Mitigated risk	Mitigated risk	Reduced cost
Reduced cost	Reduced cost	Shorter duration
Lower interest rates	Lower interest rates	Self-liquidating financing tools
Freed-up credit lines	Stable payment policy	Expanded business volume
Automated processes	Automated processes	Automated processes
Extended DSO	Reduced DSO	Improved liquidation management
Discounted price from vendors	Faster and secure access to cash	More opportunities with other customers
Improved delivery	Enhanced distribution network	Cross-selling opportunities
Lower risk on vendor innovation	Additional income from financing	
Debt-free balance sheet	Cross-selling opportunities	
Cross-buying opportunities		

In policy terms, small- and medium-sized banks should be encouraged to develop procurement finance operations for SMEs, thus creating synergies.[71] It can not only break the credit monopoly of large financial institutions. It can also help small and medium sized financial institutions and fintech organizations to establish longer-term credit relationship with SMEs.

Notes

1. Duan, H., Han, X., & Yang, H. (2009). An analysis of causes for SMEs financing difficulty. *International Journal of Business and Management*, *4*(6), 73.
2. Wagner, M., & Franklin, J. (2008) Why LSPs don't leverage innovations. *CSCMP's Supply Chain Quarterly*, 4, 67–71.
3. Brau, J. C., Fawcett, S. E., & Morgan L. (2007) An empirical analysis of the financial impact of supply chain management on small firms. *The Journal of Entrepreneurial Finance*, 12 (1), 55–82.
4. Arend, R., & Wisner, J. (2005) Small business and supply chain management: is there a fit? *Journal of Business Venturing*, 20, 403–436.

Quayle, M. (2003) A study of supply chain management practice in UK industrial SMEs. *Supply chain management: An International Journal*, 8 (1), 79–86.

5. Soinio, J., Tanskanen, K., & Finne, M. (2012) How logistics-service providers can develop value-added services for SMEs: A dyadic perspective. *International Journal of Logistics Management*, 23 (1), 3149.
6. Dybskaya, V. V., & Vinogradov, A. B. (2018). Promising Directions for the Logistics Service Providers Development on the Russian Market in Times of Recession. *Transport and Telecommunication Journal*, *19*(2), 151–163.
7. Gibson, T. & Vaart, H. J, (2008). Defining SMEs: A less imperfect way of defining small and medium enterprises in developing countries, www.brookings.edu, Accessed: 08 August 2018.
8. Storey, D. J. (1994). *Understanding the Small Business Sector*, Routledge, London, UK.
9. Kumar, R. S., & Subrahmanya, M. B. (2010). Influence of subcontracting on innovation and economic performance of SMEs in Indian automobile industry. *Technovation*, *30*(11–12), 558–569.
10. Dollinger, M. J. (1999). *Entrepreneurship: Strategies and Resources.* Prentice-Hall, Upper Saddle River, NJ.
11. Levy, M., Powell, P. & Yetton, P. (2002) 'The dynamics of SME information systems', *Small Business Economics*, 19, (3), pp. 341–354
12. Abbasi, W. A., Wang, Z., & Alsakarneh, A. (2018). Overcoming SMEs Financing and Supply Chain Obstacles by Introducing Supply Chain Finance. *HOLISTICA–Journal of Business and Public Administration*, *9*(1), 7–22.
13. www.ccsenet.org/journal/index.php/ijbm/article/download/26253/16989, Accessed 31 March 2018.
14. Lovelock, P., & Ure, J. (2002). The new economy: Internet, telecommunications and electronic commerce? http://citeseerx.ist.psu.edu/viewdoc/summary?doi=10.1.1.125.913. Accessed 21 July 2018.
15. Price water house Coopers Co., L. (2014). Managing risk: Supply chain finance, *PWC White Paper*, (June)
16. Salecka, L. (2009). Accelerating supply chain finance, (September). www.gtreview.com/news/global/accelerating-supply-chain-finance/. Accessed 05 May 2018.

    Price water house Coopers Co., L. (2014). Managing risk: Supply chain finance, *PWC White Paper*, (June)
17. Salecka, L. (2009). Accelerating supply chain finance, (September). www.gtreview.com/news/global/accelerating-supply-chain-finance/. Accessed 05 May 2018.

    Price water house Coopers Co., L. (2014). Managing risk: Supply chain finance, *PWC White Paper*, (June).

18. Salecka, L. (2009). Accelerating supply chain finance, (September). www.gtreview.com/news/global/accelerating-supply-chain-finance/. Accessed 05 May 2018.

Price water house Coopers Co., L. (2014). Managing risk: Supply chain finance, *PWC White Paper*, (June).

19. thefinancialbrand.com/72541/community-bank-credit-union-small-business-banking-lending-trends/, Accessed 31 May 2018.
20. Luo, S., Zhang, Y., & Zhou, G. (2018). Financial Structure and Financing Constraints: Evidence on Small- and Medium-Sized Enterprises in China. *Sustainability*, *10*(6), 1774.
21. Luo, S., Zhang, Y., & Zhou, G. (2018). Financial Structure and Financing Constraints: Evidence on Small- and Medium-Sized Enterprises in China. *Sustainability*, *10*(6), 1774.
22. www.oecd.org/cfe/smes/31919286.pdf, Accessed 31 March 2018.
23. Bouazza, A. B., Ardjouman, D., & Abada, O. (2015). Establishing the factors affecting the growth of small and medium-sized enterprises in Algeria. *American International Journal of Social science*, *4*(2), 101–115.
24. Beck, T., & Demirguc-Kunt, A. (2006). Small and medium-size enterprises: Access to finance as a growth constraint. *Journal of Banking & Finance*, *30*(11), 2931–2943.
25. La Cour, M. (2018). Saxo Payments' Virtuous Circle. *Fintech Finance*, issue 9, 16–19.
26. Jansen, J. (2016). Supply Chain Finance. *Vestnik (Chelyabinsk State University)*.
27. Feng, X.; Moon, L., & Ryu, K. Supply Chain Coordination under Budget Constraints. *Comput. Ind. Eng.* **2015**, *88*, 487–500.
28. Liu, C. (2019). Finance Strategies for Medium-Sized Enterprises: FinTech as the Game Changer. M. Vemić (Ed.), *Strategic Optimization of Medium-Sized Enterprises in the Global Market* (pp. 162–184). Hershey, PA: IGI Global. https://doi.org/10.4018/978-1-5225-5784-5.ch008.
29. Wuttke, D. A., Blome, C., Foerstl, K., & Henke, M. (2013). Managing the innovation adoption of supply chain finance—Empirical evidence from six European case studies. *Journal of Business Logistics*, *34*(2), 148–166.
30. Wuttke, D. A., Blome, C., Foerstl, K., & Henke, M. (2013). Managing the innovation adoption of supply chain finance—Empirical evidence from six European case studies. *Journal of Business Logistics*, *34*(2), 148–166.
31. Wuttke, D. A., Blome, C., Foerstl, K., & Henke, M. (2013). Managing the innovation adoption of supply chain finance—Empirical evidence from six European case studies. *Journal of Business Logistics*, *34*(2), 148–166.
32. Hubbard, R. G. (1997). *Capital-market imperfections and investment* (No. w5996). National Bureau of Economic Research, Cambridge, MA.

Vuorikari, M. (2012). *Optimizing working capital management from processes perspective*. Master's Thesis. Saimaa University of Applied Sciences.
33. Devereux, M., & Schiantarelli, F. (1990). Investment, financial factors, and cash flow: Evidence from UK panel data. *Asymmetric information, corporate finance, and investment* (pp. 279–306). University of Chicago Press, Chicago, IL.
34. Pilbeam, K. (2018). *Finance & financial markets*. Macmillan International Higher Education, London, UK.
35. Grover, V., Chiang, R. H., Liang, T. P., & Zhang, D. (2018). Creating Strategic Business Value from Big Data Analytics: A Research Framework. *Journal of Management Information Systems*, *35*(2), 388–423.
36. Hyder, S., & Lussier, R. N. (2016). Why businesses succeed or fail: a study on small businesses in Pakistan. *Journal of Entrepreneurship in Emerging Economies*, *8*(1), 82–100.
37. Indjikian, R., Branch, E. C., & Site, U. (2002). E-finance for SMEs: global trends and national experiences. *Journals of Electronic Commerce*, *1*, 1–38.
38. Hong, L. I. N. (2017). Research on the Risk Management of the Online Supply Chain Finance. *DEStech Transactions on Economics, Business and Management*, (eced).
39. www.mckinsey.com/business-functions/digital-mckinsey/our-insights/six-digital-growth-strategies-for-banks?cid=other-eml-alt-mip-mck-oth-1804&hlkid=7ed527cde8a246d0aed2a94896dfadca&hctky=9204549&hdpid=ba15e788-b1c2-4c5c-a208-4cf937008f35. Accessed 31 March 2018.
40. www.kabbage.com. Accessed 08 August 2018.
41. www.linkedin.com/pulse/ibm-consortia-smes-trade-finance-william-laraque/. Accessed 8 July 2018.
42. www.ing.com/Newsroom/All-news/How-do-you-like-my-idea.htm. Accessed 8 July 2018.
43. www.mckinsey.com/business-functions/digital-mckinsey/our-insights/six-digital-growth-strategies-for-banks?cid=other-eml-alt-mip-mck-oth-1804&hlkid=7ed527cde8a246d0aed2a94896dfadca&hctky=9204549&hdpid=ba15e788-b1c2-4c5c-a208-4cf937008f35. Accessed 31 March 2018.
44. Owens, J. (2018). Responsible Digital Credit. http://www.centerforfinancialinclusion.org/storage/Responsible_Digital_Credit_FINAL_2018.07.02.pdf. Accessed 14 July 201\8.
45. https://issuu.com/centerforfinancialinclusion/docs/responsible_digital_credit_final. Accessed 08 August 2018.
46. www.ft.com/content/f2cacb86-85a3-11e8-96dd-fa565ec55929. Accessed 16 July 2018.
47. Davis, F. D. (1989). Perceived usefulness, perceived ease of use, and user acceptance of information technology. *MIS Quarterly*, 13(3): 319–340.

48. Kim, Y., Park, Y. J., & Choi, J. (2016). The Adoption of Mobile Payment Services for Fintech. *International Journal of Applied Engineering Research*, 11(2): 1058–1061.

Chen, M. C., Chen, S. S., Yeh, H. M., & Tsaur, W. G. (2016). The Key Factors Influencing Internet Finances Services Satisfaction: An Empirical Study in Taiwan. *American Journal of Industrial and Business Management*, 6(06): 748–762.

49. Ajzen, I. (1991). The Theory of Planned Behaviour. *Organizational Behaviour and Human Decision Processes*, 50(2), 179–211.

50. Bin, M. A., Pyeman, J. B., Ali, N. B., Abdul, N. B., & Khai, K. G. (2018). Determinants Of Supply Chain Finance Adoption Among Malaysian Manufacturing Companies: A Proposed Conceptual Framework, *International Journal of Education and Research*, 6(4), 237–248.

51. Nicoletti, B. (2017). The Future: Financial Services as Platforms. In *The Future of FinTech* (pp. 261-274). Palgrave Macmillan, Cham, Switzerland.

Bin, M. A., Pyeman, J. B., Ali, N. B., Abdul, N. B., & Khai, K. G. (2018). Determinants Of Supply Chain Finance Adoption Among Malaysian Manufacturing Companies: A Proposed Conceptual Framework, *International Journal of Education and Research*, 6(4), 237–248.

52. Schierz, P. G. et al. (2010). Understanding customer acceptance of mobile payment services: an empirical analysis, *Electronic Commerce Research and Applications*. 9(3): May–June: 209–216.

Nicoletti, B. (2014). *Mobile Banking*, Palgrave Macmillan, Houndsmill, UK.

53. Yusoff. M. N. H. & Yaacob, M. R. (2010). The Government Business Support in the New Economic Model, *International Journal of Business and Management*, 5 (9), 60–7.

54. Fombrun, C. J. (1996). *Reputation: Realizing Value Form The Corporate Image*, Boston, MA: Harvard Business School Press.

55. Ajzen, I. & Fishbein, M. (1980). *Understanding Attitude and Predicting Social Behaviour*, Prentice-Hall, Englewood, Cliffs, NJ.

56. Ajzen, I. (1991). The Theory of Planned Behaviour. *Organizational Behaviour and Human Decision Processes*, 50(2), 179–211.

57. Ajzen, I. (1991). The Theory of Planned Behaviour. *Organizational Behaviour and Human Decision Processes*, 50(2), 179–211.

58. Zafar, A., & Kantola, J. (2018). Relationship Between Firm's Performance and Factors Involved in the Selection of Innovation Providers. In *International Conference on Applied Human Factors and Ergonomics*, 194-205. Springer, Cham, Switzerland.

Wuttke, D. A., Blome, C., Foerstl, K., & Henke, M. (2013). Managing the innovation adoption of supply chain finance—Empirical evidence from six European case studies. *Journal of Business Logistics*, *34*(2), 148–166.

59. Nicoletti, B. (2013), *Lean Procurement*, FrancoAngeli, Milano, Italy.
60. Wuttke, D. A., Blome, C., Foerstl, K., & Henke, M. (2013). Managing the innovation adoption of supply chain finance—Empirical evidence from six European case studies. *Journal of Business Logistics, 34*(2), 148–166.
61. Wuttke, D. A., Blome, C., Foerstl, K., & Henke, M. (2013). Managing the innovation adoption of supply chain finance—Empirical evidence from six European case studies. *Journal of Business Logistics, 34*(2), 148–166.
62. Wuttke, D. A., Blome, C., Foerstl, K., & Henke, M. (2013). Managing the innovation adoption of supply chain finance—Empirical evidence from six European case studies. *Journal of Business Logistics, 34*(2), 148–166.
63. Nicoletti, B. (2017), *Agile Procurement*. Volume II: Designing and Implementing a Digital Transformation, Springer International Publishing, London, UK, ISBN 978-3-319-61085-6.
64. Wuttke, D. A., Blome, C., Foerstl, K., & Henke, M. (2013). Managing the innovation adoption of supply chain finance—Empirical evidence from six European case studies. *Journal of Business Logistics, 34*(2), 148–166.
65. Song, H., Yu, K., & Lu, Q. (2018). Financial service providers and banks' role in helping SMEs to access finance. *International Journal of Physical Distribution & Logistics Management, 48*(1), 69–92.
66. Jansen, J. H. (2016). Is supply chain Finance ready to be applied in small and medium-sized enterprises? *Вестник Челябинского государственного университета*, 14 (396).
67. Jansen, J. (2016). Supply Chain Finance. *Vestnik Chelyabinsk State University*. Chelyabinsk, Russian Federation.

    Osinski, M., Selig, P. M., Matos, F., & Roman, D. J. (2017). Methods of evaluation of intangible assets and intellectual capital. *Journal of Intellectual Capital, 18*(3), 470–485.
68. Xiong, L., & Wu, Y. (2017). Discussion on the Future Development Direction of Electronic Data Interchange Logistics Systems in China. *American Journal of Industrial and Business Management, 7*(01), 40.
69. Jonker, J. (2012). *New Business Models: An explorative study of changing transactions creating multiple value(s)*. Jab management consultants bv. Doetinchem, The Netherlands.

    Osterwalder, A., & Pigneur, Y. (2010). *Business model generation: a handbook for visionaries, game changers, and challengers*. John Wiley & Sons, Hoboken, NJ.
70. Jansen, J. (2016). Supply Chain Finance Is SCF ready to be applied in SMEs?. *Vestnik*. 14 (396). 135–154.
71. Luo, S., Zhang, Y., & Zhou, G. (2018). Financial Structure and Financing Constraints: Evidence on Small- and Medium-Sized Enterprises in China. *Sustainability, 10*(6), 1774.

CHAPTER 8

Conclusions on Procurement Finance

The main themes emerging from this book are the deep inter-relationships between financial services and innovative solutions for the organizations. These relationships are substantial and increasing in particular in the procurement area. They are consistent with a vision of the financial institutions as platforms.[1]

Procurement and financial services develop and innovate. This book examines the reasons why the innovation in procurement is so important especially now. This book develops the idea that the procurement sector is a strategic sector for the organizations. It should not be concerned only with cost saving but with value adding. It should focus on supporting the customer delight, improving the financial results of the organization, and mitigating the risks, especially in the current volatile, dynamic, and globalized ecosystems. Procurement needs to extend its attention to the entire extended value network not focusing only on its mere basic sourcing functions. It needs to consider the value it can provide to the customer and to the organization. The importance attributed to these aspects is due to the possibility for the procurement function to have a full internal vision of the organization. It is a point of contact with the outside environment, handling the increasingly dispersed and different vendors. For this reason, procurement is one of the most important drivers of the organization innovation. This book demonstrates how the development of intelligent and collaborative approaches in the procurement field is useful for changing the entire organization. This can be obtained by considering and implementing innovative solutions.

B. Nicoletti, *Procurement Finance*,
Palgrave Studies in Financial Services Technology,
https://doi.org/10.1007/978-3-030-02140-5_8

In the procurement transactions more and more international and with notably long payment terms, the concept of procurement finance can handle in the best way the financial relationships. It is necessary to introduce new solutions able to ease the procurement transactions. It is necessary to overcome limits and risks related to them. For instance, procurement finance can help minimize the risks related to payments.

This book demonstrates that the digital transformation is engaging more sectors, even those who have traditionally never or little experiences in advanced solutions. The application of innovative solutions to the procurement finance sector is the first step towards the development of innovative business models that, thanks to the web, introduce and launch a whole series of new financial services and products for the entire organization.

From a procurement perspective, one of the first challenges can be related to globalization that has led to the need for flexibility and of being able to manage complexity, spreading information and risks around the world. The globalization and a complex combination of sourcing and outsourcing has led to the creation of global supply and distribution networks, leading to an increase and diversification of the number of stakeholders.

Global and competitive trade is intended to evolve increasingly. The key words that must be taken into account are flexibility, innovation, simplification, disintermediation, and collaboration. Innovative solutions have to take place. The digital transformation assumes an important role to reach these objectives.

This scenario underlines the importance of the platform concept for procurement finance. Emerging models like the ones of the fintech organizations compete with traditional financial institutions stimulating them to consider innovative solutions. It is necessary to seize the great benefits of the digital transformation. The leaning and digitization of processes should support end to end the processes involving customers and vendors: from the search and choice of organization partners (customers and vendors) to the definition of a contract, from sending an order to managing the logistics, and later the delivery, billing, and payment. Between the beginning and the end of these processes, there is often an important organizational distance, characterized by multiple steps within different functions and with third parties outside the organization. These steps involve frequent interactions with the counterparts. The collaboration is essential.

This innovative approach consists of adopting advanced processes and digital platforms for managing and optimizing the entire flow of transactions ranging end to end from order to payment. For each step, it is possible to add value to the customers and the organizaiton, and to get savings (time and digitization of documents), greater control, and, from the financial side, better solutions for buyers and vendors. The financial institutions should exploit the digital transformation inserting their financing and operational processes along the entire organization's value network, supporting all actors, also the weaker ones.

In improving procurement, it is essential to take into account all four Es: effectiveness, efficiency, economics, and ethics. The last aspect is important. It is growing in complexity and areas of actions, due to the increasing importance of regulations. The regulations should be always respected. Often, procurement finance needs to take into account several different jurisdictions all over the world. The best way for guaranteeing compliance is through collaboration. The end-to-end process underlines the need of the collaboration of the organizations with their vendors in a way through which it is possible to have a global approach to the procurement.

Procurement finance is an important opportunity to create benefits for all actors involved. This is true especially for the weaker actors in procurement, namely, the small and medium-sized enterprises (SMEs), through the exploitation of this new vision of collaborative value network. If the financial institutions consider SMEs riskier than large organizations, it is useful to find ways to ease the access to the credit to those smaller organizations by working to cut the risks by adopting advanced solutions also of procurement finance. An effort of this type has an important role for the growth of the economy. Procurement finance can provide a lower credit cost because it allows access to more quality information. This helps to calculate risk ratings more accurately and cut the operating risks and costs on which financing is assessed. Exploiting the positions of the SMEs in procurement financing, the credit rating becomes more realistic and precise on the basis of the digital relationships among physical, financial, and information/digital flows along the value network.

To respond effectively, efficiently, economically, and ethically to the new challenges posed by the market, it is possible to push procurement to become innovative, agile, and dynamic. Available data, global relationships, and international markets blurry the contours of the organization, which are today potentially in continuous connection with information from products, services, and affiliate partners. It is imperative the governance of the digital information flows connecting it and making it one with the largest ecosystem in which it operates and is part of. Simplification and digitization can increase efficiency in the processes across the ecosystem and in the relationships with the financial actors. The visibility can also improve ethics and with the right approach it needs to implement agility in the organizations.

Finally, there is a last E which is of growing importance after effectiveness, efficiency, economics, and ethics. It is environment savvy. Procurement needs to take more into account environment sustainability.[2]

To reach these targets, it is indispensable to apply agile, innovative, and effective procurement finance instruments. Due to the increasingly international scenario, collaboration and integration are key concepts and opportunities.

The concept of procurement finance aims proposing an integrated vision considering different perspectives with the same relevance such as the financing of international trade, the optimization of the working capital, the management of liquidity, and the best handling of payments. From this perspective, the digital transformation can stimulate this integration, especially by adopting some of the innovative solutions such as blockchain. This solution is the ideal for cross-border payments, allowing the alignment of information among all the actors involved, the reduction of the infrastructure costs of the financial institutions related to global payments, securities trading in the case of crowdfunding, and compliance. In addition, its elimination or reduction of intermediaries allows making money transactions more secure, rapid, and cheaper. Regarding cloud computing, its contribution can be important especially for the SMEs because it can make easier the access to global markets using digital platforms, based on the clouds, to connect with customers and vendors from other countries.

The potential of the new solutions presented in this book (such as the concept of procurement finance platforms supported by blockchain solutions) is being proven more and more in procurement finance.[3] It is attracting more interest. In a few years, new solutions applied to procurement finance will become more available. These solutions have the potential not only to cut costs through simplification and digitization but also to increase speed, flexibility, and security: in one word, to make procurement more agile. It is possible to expect a paradigm shift in procurement finance.

The globalization of the economy and the increasing of financial inclusion necessarily requires the full digital development of financial services in the procurement area. The mantra becomes: either procurement innovate or the organization will disappear.

Notes

1. Nicoletti, B. (2017). The Future: Financial Services as Platforms. In *The Future of FinTech* (pp. 261–274). Palgrave Macmillan, Cham, Switzerland.
2. Arnold, M. (2017). Fostering sustainability by linking co-creation and relationship management concepts. *Journal of Cleaner Production*, *140*, 179–188.
3. Dai, J., & Vasarhelyi, M. A. (2017). Toward Blockchain-Based Accounting and Assurance. *Journal of Information Systems*, *31*(3), 5–21.

Glossary[1]

Abusive Draw It is a drawing on a standby letter of credit when no violation of the underlying contract has occurred.

Acceptance It constitutes an unconditional obligation on the part of the accepting party to pay the draft at maturity. A draft accepted by a financial institution is called a banker's acceptance. Once accepted by an organization, it is called a trade acceptance.

Account It is a record of financial transactions for an asset or individual, such as at a financial institution, brokerage, credit card organization, or retail store. In general, it is an arrangement between a buyer and a vendor in which payments are to be made in the future.

Account Party It is the party for whom a letter of credit is opened. Account party and applicant are the same. Sometimes one party agrees with the issuing financial institution to make all payments under a letter of credit showing the name of another party (as in the case of affiliated companies). Banks may refer to one of these parties as the applicant and the other as the account party.

Accounts Payable They are legally enforceable liabilities to a creditor recorded in the balance sheet, normally arising from the purchases of products and services. It is based on a received invoice due to be paid within an agreed timeframe.

Accounts Receivable They are the accounts for which payment is still to be received. These include invoices, bills, and promissory notes. Such items can be sold to a factor or used as collateral in securing a loan.

B. Nicoletti, *Procurement Finance*,
Palgrave Studies in Financial Services Technology,
https://doi.org/10.1007/978-3-030-02140-5

Accrued Debts They are the debts that have accumulated during a given period.

Advance It is an extension of credit by means of a loan. Advance is often a synonym for a loan.

Advance Against Inventory It is financial instrument provided to a buyer or vendor involved in a value network for the holding or warehousing of products (either pre-sold, un-sold, or hedged) and over which the finance provider normally takes a security interest or assignment of rights and exercises a measure of control.

Advance Against Receivables It is a financial instrument for procurement finance made available to a party involved in a value network on the expectation of repayment from funds generated from current or future trade receivables. It is normally made against the security of such receivables. It may be also unsecured.

Advance Payment It is a payment made by the buyer to the vendor prior to the shipment. It is customary to only pay an agreed percentage of the value of the products with the remainder paid after shipment.

Advance Payment Bond Bond, guarantee, or standby letter of credit given by a vendor receiving an advance payment (or contract) to the buyer to assure that the funds are returned if the products are never delivered or the services are not performed.

Advance Ratio It is the maximum percentage of the value of an asset or assets by reference to which factor is prepared to make an available fund.

Advances on Debtors Outstanding They are funds advanced by a factor or a receivable financier (prepayments) to an assignor against debtor balances. It is also referred to as a current account, utilization, or drawing. This is the actual currency advance at a certain moment in time.

Advising Bank It is a bank that receives a letter of credit from the issuing financial institution for authentication and delivery to the beneficiary. The advising financial institution is normally a correspondent of the issuing financial institution located in the same country as the beneficiary.

After Sight It is a term used in a bill of exchange to show the period for which the bill is to be computed from the date the drawer presented it to the drawee for acceptance.

Agency Factoring Sometimes, it is also called bulk factoring. It is a service which enables the customers to retain the collection function, which is disclosed to the debtor.

Agile Methodologies They are agile development values, principles, and methods used to increase flexibility and responsiveness of development or transformation teams in an organization.

Agile Team It is an autonomous cross-functional team following an agile methodology.

Agile Vendor It is an organization that embraces agile project methodologies that are more supportive towards changes, for instance, scrum.

Agility It is a metric to measure how quickly a solution responds, as the load changes, by allocating additional or fewer resources to the activity.

Airway Bill It is a document signed by an airline to show receipt of products for air transportation from and to the airports shown in the document.

Amortization It is the liquidation of a debt over a period of time.

Anchor Party It is a party, normally a large buyer, who facilitates a buyer-led procurement finance program for its vendors and whose credit risk is the economic basis of the finance provided. It is also used to describe a large vendor, which orchestrates a program of receivables.

Ancillary Guarantee It is a guarantee instrument where the guarantor joins with one of the parties to the contract and agrees to fulfill that party's obligations if necessary, effectively co-signing the contract. Differently from an independent or demand guarantee, under an ancillary guarantee the guarantor also acquires rights under the contract and may resort to terms in the contract to dispute claims against the guarantee. It should be noted that financial institutions in the USA are generally prohibited by law from issuing ancillary guarantees. Financial institutions in other countries, which are not. USA financial institutions, issue demand guarantees or standby letters of credit.

Anti-Money Laundering Policy It is a policy put in place to help detect and report suspicious activity including the predicate offenses to money laundering and terrorist financings, such as securities fraud and market manipulation.

Any Safe World Port It is the delivery to any safe world port at the buyer's choice.

App It is short for application. It is a program or piece of software, especially as downloaded by a user into a mobile device.

Applicant It is the party requesting to open a letter of credit.

Application It is a software program that uses the basic software, middleware, and network environments to achieve a specific function related to the purposes of the organization.

Application Programming Interface (API) It is the interface used by software components to communicate with each other. Its specifications include a set of requirements that define how two pieces of software can interact with each other. It allows moving data between applications. An API may include specifications for routines, data structures, object classes, and variables. These are important because they enable other programmers to use components of existing software, allowing for faster and more reliable software development.

Approval, Documents Sent on It is the treatment of letter of credit documents where the negotiating financial institution does not certify that the documents meet the requirements of the letter of credit but rather forwards the documents to the issuing financial institution with a request that it examines the documents, obtains waiver of any discrepancies, and pays, or, in the case of time drafts, accepts the drafts, if drawn on them, or authorizes acceptance by the paying/drawee financial institution.

Approved Payables Finance It is a synonym for payables finance.

Asset-Based Lender It is a lender providing asset-based loan (ABL) facilities.

Asset-Based Loan (ABL) It is an agreement between an organization (customer) and a financial organization in which the latter provides the customer with a structured facility combining secured loans and revolving credits. The customer may pledge/assign as collateral any combination of assets used in the conduct of its business (for instance, receivables, inventories, plants and machineries, properties, brands, and so on). ABL instruments are normally complex structures combining revolving credit lines based on current assets with amortizing loans based on fixed assets. ABL is used for larger customers, normally in a restructuring or management buyout (MBO) situation. Syndication between ABL organizations for very large facilities is common.

Assets It is anything owned, whether in possession or by a right to take possession, by a person or a group acting together, for instance, an organization. The value of an asset is normally expressed in monetary terms. Assets may be classified in many ways. The principal distinction, normally made for business purposes, is between fixed assets and current assets. Fixed assets are purchases for continued and long-term use in earning revenues in an organization. Examples are land, buildings, machinery, and so on. Current assets are assets continually turned over in the course of an organization during normal business activity. Examples are accounts receivable, inventory, cash, and work in progress.

Assignable It is a receivable which can be assigned without any legal constraints.

Assignee It is the entity for which a receivable is assigned.

Assignment It is the transfer of all rights to the receivables from the assignor to the assignee.

Assignment Clause It is a written notification to the debtor/buyer that the accounts receivable have been assigned and are payable to the designed factoring organization.

Assignment of Proceeds It is a legal mechanism by which the beneficiary of a letter of credit may pledge the proceeds of future drawings to a third party. Assigning proceeds involves giving the letter of credit to a financial institution, which holds the letter of credit until drawn upon, along with irrevocable instructions to the financial institution to disburse proceeds, when generated, in a specified way (such as pay 40 percent of each drawing to XXX Corporation). The financial institution acknowledges the assignment to the assignee. It does not have any obligation to pay any funds to the assignee unless the letter of credit is drawn upon by the beneficiary and payment is received from the issuing or confirming financial institution. An assignment of proceeds is not an assignment or transfer of the letter of credit and the assignee acquires no rights to perform under the letter of credit in order to generate funds.

Assignor It is the entity disposing of an asset by an assignment.

Atomic Swap It is the exchange of cryptocurrencies from two different chains without the need for a trusted third party. It is based on a concept called hash time-locked contracts that ensure that both parties are fulfilling their part of the deal. It requires certain functions to be implemented on each blockchain solution involved.[2]

Audit It is the process by which financial records, organization's processes, and information systems are independently verified by an internal or external auditor.

Audit and Compliance It is the ability to collect, audit, and verify compliance information.

Authentication It is the verification of the identity of a user by a system or service.

Authorization It is the procedure to check whether a customer or another person inside or outside the organization has the right to do a certain action, for instance, to transfer funds or access sensitive data.

Automated Clearing House (ACH) It is a network capable of handling and processing digital payments in significant volume. Most nations have at least one ACH which provides a fully automated way of collecting and settling payments. The ACH provides a secure digital network to allow banks and financial institutions exchange of information.

Availability It is the metric which measures the percentage, normally computed over a periodical basis (such as a month) and net of planned or unplanned service downtimes of service coverage. In procurement finance, it is the amount of money that is available for drawing to the assignor. This would be the value of all approved receivables multiplied by the pre-agreed prepayment percentage less any amounts already paid to the assignor.

Aval It is a guarantee added to a debt obligation, evidenced by a financial instrument by a third party who is not the payee or the holder. The latter ensures the payment if the issuing party default. The debt obligation could be a promissory note, bill of exchange, draft, note, or bond. The third party providing the aval is normally a financial institution.

Avalized Draft It is a trade acceptance to which an aval has been added.

Back-to-Back Documentary Credit When a vendor obtains an ordinary documentary credit from the buyer's financial institution, he/she can use this as security with its own financial institution. With this documentary credit serving as collateral, the vendor's financial institution can then issue a second documentary credit in favor of the vendor's vendors.

Back-to-Back Factoring It is the provision of factoring services to a debtor to provide security for the approval of the debtor's indebtedness arising from the sales of another customer.[3]

Bacs It provides the system for the clearing and settlement of UK automated payment methods, including direct debit and Bacs (previously known as Bankers' Automated Clearing Services) direct credit payments. Payments sent via this method take three working days to clear.

Bad Debt It is an unpaid account that will likely remain uncollectible. It must be written off.

Balance Sheet It is an itemized statement that lists how much an organization owns and owes at a given moment in time. It is called a balance sheet because the value of what the organization owns must equal to the total of its debts and its net worth. In many jurisdictions, it is a compulsory document by law.

Ban on Assignment It is a clause in a contract between a vendor and a buyer which prevents the vendor from assigning the related receivables. It can make ineffective any assignment of the receivables arising out of the contract. In some legal environments, the factoring agreement may overrule the ban on assignment.

Bank It is a regulated financial institution licensed to receive deposits and undertake a range of activities such as the ones of commercial, retail, and investment financial institutions.

Bank Comfort Letter It is a letter issued from the buyer's financial institution to the vendor. This letter states that the buyer has sufficient funds to cover the cost of the order. A financial institution comfort letter is one of the first pieces of documentation that a prospective buyer must provide to a vendor in order to negotiate a deal. It is not an agreement to pay the vendor anything, nor does it make the financial institution liable in any way.

Bank Guarantee It is a financial instrument issued by a financial institution on behalf of its customer for the benefit of another party to whom the financial institution's customer has a contracted financial obligation. In the event that the financial institution's customer does not pay on a contract, the beneficiary of the financial institution guarantee can draw on the financial institution guarantee and be paid.

Bank Guarantee 100% (BG 100%) It is a type of bank guarantee which meets several conditions. It must be issued or guaranteed by 1 of the top 25 world financial institutions and be irrevocable, confirmed, and transferable. It must also cover the entire amount of the contract. It must be payable on sight upon presentation of authentic shipping documents.

Bank Identifier Code (BIC) This is often referred to as a Swift code or Swift address as Swift owns and administers the BIC system.

Bank Payment Obligation or Order (BPO) It is an inter-financial instrument to secure payments against the successful matching of trade data. The BPO offers the benefits of a letter of credit in a digital environment, without the drawbacks of manual processing associated with the traditional trade finance instruments. Using Swift's trade services utility (TSU) or an equivalent transaction matching program, a BPO is an irrevocable undertaking given by one financial institution to another financial institution that payment will be made on a specified date after a specified event takes place.

Banker's Acceptance It is a time draft that has been drawn on and accepted by a financial institution. In a large and active market, investors purchase and sell bankers' acceptances at rates similar to, and often below, LIBOR. Rates are low due to the low risk of default on the part of a financial institution and the fact that there is generally an underlying trade transaction, the proceeds of which are pledged to cover the acceptance when it matures.

Basel III/IV It is a comprehensive set of reform measures, developed by the Basel Committee on the supervision of the financial institutions to strengthen the regulation, supervision, and risk management of the financial institutions' sector.[4]

Baseline It is a term within the BPO rules defining the criteria (for instance, a dataset including a purchase order) required for a successful data match in a transaction matching application (TMA).

Basic Qualification Requirements They are the technical, quality system, and organizational requirements that, for each merchandize group, the companies must have to obtain the qualification. Normally, it includes also the legal, sustainability, and economic-financial requirements regarding the company as a whole.

Benchmarking It is the comparison of processes and/or measures to other processes and/or measures implemented by well-organized entities or a large number of them.

Beneficiary It is the party in whose favor a letter of credit is issued, who is entitled to present documents required by the letter of credit and receive payment.

Bid Bond It is a bond, guarantee, or standby letter of credit that accompanies a bid, issued for an amount that is forfeited if the bidder wins the bid but reneges.

Big Data It is an all-encompassing term for any collection of datasets so relatively large and complex that it becomes difficult to process it by using traditional data processing applications. Big Data has the five V characteristics: volume, velocity, variety, veracity, and value.

Bill Discounting It can be used as a synonym for forfeiting or for the discounting of any bill of exchange, for example, arising under a letter of credit. It can also be a variation of receivables discounting.

Bill of Exchange It is an unconditional written order by one party, the drawer, requiring another party, the drawee, to pay the drawer or a third party (the payee) a specified sum of money on demand or at a predeterminable future date.

Bill of Lading (BOL) It is a document setting out the terms of the contract between the vendor of the products and the carrier, under which the freight is to be transported from the port of shipment to that of destination. The BOL serves as a document of title, a contract of carriage, and a receipt of products. Its holder has the right to gain possession of the shipped products. There are two main types of BOL: the straight bill of lading and the shipper's order bill of lading.

Bitcoin It is a cryptocurrency for sending funds without any third party involved. It has been introduced in 2008.[5]

Block A number of transactions (on the blockchain) or other data grouped together.[6]

Blockchain Solution It is a trustless distributed data structure exchanging and storing data in blocks and linking each block to the previous block, using the hash of the previous block.[7]

Bond It is a debt issued for a period of more than one year. A bond investor is effectively lending money. The vendor of the bond agrees to repay the principal amount of the loan at a specified time. Interest-bearing bonds pay interest periodically.

Borrower It is the party to whom a lender makes a loan.

Borrowing Base It is the amount of money a lender loans to a borrower based on the value of the collateral or security that the borrower pledges. The borrowing base is normally determined by margining, where the lender determines a discount factor that is multiplied by the value of the collateral. The result is the amount that is loaned to the organization.

Budget It is an estimate of the revenues and costs for a future period of time, normally 12 months.

Business Intelligence (BI) It is a broad category of the applications and technologies for gathering, storing, analyzing, retrieving, and providing access to data to help users make better decisions. BI applications include the activities of decision support systems, querying and reporting, online analytical processing, statistical analysis, forecasting, and data mining. Analytics has generalized and extended business intelligence components.

Business Model Canvas It is a strategic management and entrepreneurial tool. It allows one to describe, design, challenge, invent, and pivot business models.[8]

Business Plan It is a document prepared for the purpose of determining the technical feasibility (that is, if a project is possible using a proper complement of specific resources, methods, machines, and equipment) and financial viability (that is, will earn margins) of planned activities or business transactions.

Business Process Management It is the management of processes to improve them substantially.

Business Process Outsourcing or Business Process Optimization It is the outsourcing of business processes for their optimization.

Business Process Re-engineering It is the re-engineering of business processes to improve them drastically.

Buyback Agreement or Guarantee It is an agreement between a buyer and a vendor in which the vendor agrees to repurchase products or property from the buyer if a certain event occurs within a specified period of time. The buyback price is normally set out in the agreement.

Buyer It is an entity procuring products and services, issuing orders, and making payments to the vendors. Together with the vendors and the customers, it represents the extended value network.

Buyer's Credit It is a financial arrangement by which a financial institution or an export credit agency (ECA) in the nation of the vendor extends a loan, either directly to the foreign buyer of the products or indirectly through a financial institution in the buyer's country acting on its behalf. The credit is meant to enable the buyer to make payments due to the vendor under the contract. It is normally a medium-to-long-term loan. It can also be considered financing that is put in place by a buyer to purchase products or services or provided for its benefit by a third party, such as an ECA.

Buyer-Centric It is a description of a procurement finance transaction where the origination normally takes place through a relationship with a buyer, sometimes referred to as the anchor party.

Buying Forward It is the act of buying foreign currency for a future value date at a price quoted at the present.

Cable for Authority to Pay It is a request for permission to pay a letter of credit draw, even if there might be discrepancies. It is sent digitally by the negotiating financial institution to the issuing financial institution.

Capital They are resources that will yield benefits and create wealth over time. The term is normally related to investments. It may be divided into physical and financial, fixed and working, and so on.

Carriage and Insurance Paid to (Named Place of Destination) It is a shipping term included in a contract of sale (abbreviated as CIP). Its meaning is that the vendor agrees to arrange and pay for the transportation and cargo insurance over the products to the named destination. Such costs are included in the price of the products. All risks of loss of or damage to the products, as well as any additional costs due to events occurring after the time the products have been delivered to the carrier, are transferred from the vendor to the buyer when the products have been delivered into the custody of the carrier.

Carriage Paid to (Named Place of Destination) It is a shipping term included in a contract of sale (abbreviated as CPT) meaning that the vendor agrees to arrange and pay for the transportation of the products to the named destination. Such costs are included in the price of the products. Insurance is not included. All risks of loss of or damage to the products, as well as any additional costs due to events occurring after the time the products have been delivered to the carrier, is transferred from the vendor to the buyer. At that point, the buyer must arrange for cargo insurance if so desired.

Carrier It is any person who, in a contract of transportation, undertakes to perform, or to procure at its own responsibility the performance of, transportation by rail, road, sea, air, waterway, or a combination of such modes of transportation.

Case-of-Need It is an agent of the exporter located in the country of the buyer who is to be notified by the presenting financial institution under a draft collection of any difficulties in collecting payment. The case-of-need may be given the power to change the collection instructions or even the draft amount, or may just be expected to make arrangements to store the products and find an alternate buyer. Whatever authority the case-of-need has should be specified in the collection instructions letter.

Cash Against Documents It is a collection procedure where the vendor asks its financial institution to forward the organization's shipping documents to the buyer's financial institution with instructions to release the products upon payment of the invoice.

Cash Flow It is the flow of cash payments to or from an organization during a given period of time. Expenditures are sometimes referred to as "negative" cash flows.

Cash Flow Statement It is a document that reflects the amount of cash that comes in (for instance, equity, loan proceeds, cash collection on receivables, sales, or other revenues) and goes out (capital expenses, production expenses, selling and administrative expenses, payment of dividends, or other expenses) of an organization. It analyzes how much cash is needed and when that money is required by the organization within a period of time.

Cash in Advance It is a type of sale in which the full amount of the purchase price of an order must be paid up front. It is not a standard procedure in the trading industry. It is not advised that any buyer pays upfront for products that have not yet been shipped or accepted. e-Commerce has changed substantially this statement.

Central Bank A central bank, reserve financial institution or monetary authority, is a financial institution granted the exclusive privilege to lend a government its currency. Like a normal commercial financial institution, a central bank charges interest on the loans made to borrowers, primarily the government of whichever jurisdiction the financial institution exists in, and to other commercial financial institutions, normally as a lender of last resort.

Certificate of Origin It is a document that is required in certain jurisdictions. It is a signed statement as to the origin of the export item. The certificates of origin are normally signed through an official organization, such as a local chamber of commerce, or can simply be a statement signed by the manufacturer or exporter as to the source of the products.

Change Agents They are figures considered benchmarks within the project team. They have the task of introducing, motivating, and supporting changes within the organization. These figures have essentially two tasks. On the one hand, they identify priorities that characterize the different areas, giving reasons for the choices made and organizing the necessary technical and operative support. On the other hand, they speed up the implementation of the changes, such as agile procurement finance, to avoid unnecessary extensions in the use of resources.

Clean Bill of Lading It is a bill of lading that bears no clause or notation which expressly declares a defective condition of the products and/or the packaging.

Clean Draft It is a draft which is not accompanied by documents.

Clean Letter of Credit It is a letter of credit that calls for the presentation of nothing more than a draft to trigger the payment.

Clearing House Automated Payment System (CHAPS) It is normally used for making high-value transactions where same day guaranteed payment is required. Payments are guaranteed to be processed same day providing instructions are received by a certain time (for instance, 2 pm on a specified time zone) on a working day. Banks may charge a fee for CHAPS transfers. They are only used to make bank-to-bank fund transfers in the local currency.

Client It refers to a customer. In some cases, the word client indicates the access device. In this latter meaning, there is always in this book a specification (such as a thin client). Legally, it is the contracting authority of the contract.

Cloud It is a metaphor for a global network or synthetic for cloud computing. It refers normally to the Internet.

Cloud Computing It is a computing capability that provides convenient and on-demand network access to a shared pool of configurable computing resources. These resources can be rapidly provisioned and released with minimal management effort or vendor interaction. Cloud computing has six essential characteristics: pay-per-use, self-service, broad network access, resource pooling, rapid elasticity, and measured service. In general terms, cloud computing enables three possible modes: Infrastructure as a Service (IaaS), Platform as a Service (PaaS), and Software as a Service (SaaS). It can be public, private, or hybrid.

Collateral It is an asset pledged as security for a credit, lease, or other commitment or liability and forfeited to the lender if the borrower fails to honor its obligations. They include marketable properties, such as real estate, chattel, inventories, and financial institution deposits.

Collecting Bank It is any financial institution other than the remitting financial institution involved in the collection of a draft and/or documents.

Collection It refers to the general (cash) collection function of an organization operating to collect funds for all outstanding invoices before they become overdue, by means of digital payments, checks, cash, documentary credits, and collections and other means of payment. Sometimes, it is used shortly for documentary collection.

Collection Only It is an arrangement in which the factor is required to pay the purchase price on the collection date only (that is, with no prepayments). Often goes with non-recourse facility.

Collection Turnover It is the average time it takes an organization to receive payments for receivables.

Commercial Bank It is a financial institution that provides a wide variety of financial institutions services, including procurement finance, accepting savings and demand deposits, buying and selling foreign currency, and lending money against business security or property.

Commercial Finance It is a generic term for a range of asset-based financial instruments which include factoring, invoice discounting, international factoring, reverse factoring, and value network-based lending facilities.

Commercial Invoice It is a bill for the products from the vendor to the buyer. These invoices may be used by governments to determine the true value of products when assessing customs duties.

Commercial Letter of Credit It is a letter of credit intended to act as an instrument of payment for products sold by one party to another.

Commercial Risk It is a risk that the buyer of products cannot or does not pay the vendor when payments are due.

Commission Charge It is a charge made by a factor for services rendered including receivables management and collection and/or credit protection services. The commission is normally computed as a percentage of the total assigned turnover.

Commitment to Pay It is an obligation made by a party such as a financial provider to make a payment to meet a specified obligation at a future date.

Committed Facility It is a credit facility that is committed to being available for a stated period.

Commodity It is a raw material, for instance, foodstuff, metal ore or refined product, crude oil or oil product, for which there are normally liquid markets and which represent attractive collateral for the provision of finance.

Commodity Exchange It is an association which governs the rules of commodity trading in a jurisdiction.

Commodity Finance It is a super-category or umbrella term used by finance providers to describe the business financing lines, organizational units, and activities. Commodity finance is oriented towards the specialized market segment of commodity traders and processors. It combines the use of procurement finance and a variety of other, often customized, financial services to meet their needs.

Company It is a contractor, vendor or service provider, legal person, including craft companies, trade, cooperative, temporary grouping of companies, consortium, consortium companies, and European Economic Interest Groups (EEIG), which offers on the market, respectively, the realization of works or structures, the supply of products, or the provision of services.

Compliance It is the respect for the internal and external compulsory rules of the organization.

Concentration It describes to which percentage one buyer represents on the vendor's total accounts receivable. It is normally expressed in percent.

Confirmed Letter of Credit It is a letter of credit to which the advising financial institution has added its own, independent undertaking to honor the presentation of the required documents, that is, pay the beneficiary at sight or at maturity, as specified by the letter of credit.

Confirmed or Confirmation It is the confirmation by one party to another that an obligation or contract has been accepted and will be discharged. In the case of a letter of credit, upon request by the issuing financial institution, the advising financial institution adds its confirmation to the letter of credit, meaning that it commits itself to honor the payment in case the issuing financial institution fails to fulfill its obligation.

Confirmed Payables It is a synonym for payables finance.

Confirming It is a variation of payables finance, normally provided in some countries under a local structure.

Confirming Bank It is a financial institution that has added its confirmation to a letter of credit. This term is also sometimes used loosely to refer to a financial institution that has issued a commitment to purchase letter of credit documents without recourse, a practice called silent confirmation.

Consensus It is a general agreement. In the case of distributed ledger technology, since the blockchain and its calculations are distributed, some methods to reach consensus about results are needed. Two common ways to reach consensus on whether to add blocks to the blockchain or not are Proof-of-Work and Proof-of-Stake.[9]

Consignee It is a party into whose possession products are to be delivered.

Consignment It is a term of sale where a vendor delivers products to the buyer but retains legal ownership of the products until they are used or re-sold by the buyer. The buyer is responsible for remitting payment to the vendor at the time of a resale.

Consortium It refers to consortia foreseen by law, with or without legal personality.

Consular Invoice It is a document that is required in some countries. It describes the shipment of products. It shows information such as the buyer and the vendor, and the value of the shipment. Certified by the consular officer of the foreign country stationed in the foreign country, it is used by the country's customs officials to verify the value, quantity, and nature of the shipment.

Consultation Class It is the set of economic/technical parameters evaluated on a yearly basis and correlated with the production capacity.

Consumption-Based Pricing Model It is a pricing model in which the vendor charges its customers based on the number of services the customer consumes, rather than on a time and material-based fee. For example, a cloud storage vendor might charge per gigabyte of data stored.

Continuous Linked Settlement (CLS) It is a settlement system run by CLS Bank International, a financial institution dedicated to settling foreign exchange trades.[10] CLS operates a multi-currency settlement system that mitigates risk for foreign exchange transactions through the provision of its payment versus payment settlement service, which has direct links to the real-time gross settlement (RTGS) systems of the 18 currencies it settles.

Contract It is a legally binding agreement between two or more parties.

Contract Monetization It is a synonym for pre-shipment finance. Contract monetization is used more widely as a financial instrument, outside the procurement finance and trade environment.

Contract Risk It is a risk that the buyer of products reneges on the contract (as opposed to simply being unable to pay).

Control It is the power to monitor, influence, or direct people or organizations or the course of events.

Corporate Customer It is a customer of a financial institution, which is an incorporated business entity of all kinds. It ranges in size from a multinational, large domestic corporation to a small- and medium-sized organization.

Corporate Performance Management It is the information system for the management of key business metrics.

Correspondent Factor It is a factor that acts as an import factor or export factor under the two-factor system.

Correspondent Financial Institution It is a financial institution that provides services on behalf of another financial institution. A correspondent financial institution can conduct business transactions, accept deposits, and gather the proceeds of procurement transactions on behalf of the other financial institution. Correspondent financial institutions are more likely to be used to conduct business in foreign countries and act as a domestic financial institution's agent abroad.

Cost and Freight (Named Port of Destination) It is a shipping term included in a contract of sale. It means that the vendor agrees to take full responsibility for delivering the products to the port of loading, clear the products for export, and arrange and pay for the transportation of the products to the named port of destination, such costs being included in the price of the products. All risks of loss of or damage to the products, and any additional costs due to events occurring after the time the products have been delivered on board the vessel, is transferred from the vendor to the buyer when the products pass the vessel's rail at the port of loading. It is up to the buyer to arrange marine insurance for the sea voyage and transportation from the port of destination.

Cost of Production It is the sum of the costs of materials, labor, and overhead that goes into the manufacture of products or fulfillment of a service.

Cost, Insurance, and Freight (Named Port of Destination) It is a shipping term included in a contract of sale (abbreviated as CIF) meaning that the vendor agrees to take full responsibility for delivering the products to the port of loading, clear the products for export, and arrange and pay for transportation and marine insurance over the products to the named port of discharge, such costs being included in the price of the products. All risks of loss or damage to the products, as well as any additional costs due to events occurring after the time the products have been delivered on board the vessel, are transferred from the vendor to the buyer when the products pass the vessel's rail at the port of loading. It is up to the buyer to arrange transportation from the port of discharge.

Counter-trading It is a situation where two trading parties are buying and selling products and/or services from/to each other, thus creating mutual obligations to settle invoices in both directions, or settle differences only.

Country Risk It is a risk incurred by a vendor of products that a buyer in a different country is not able to pay for the products due to political or economic conditions in its country. The two components of country risks are the political risk and the transfer risk.

Credit It is another word for debt. Credit is given to customers when they are allowed to make a purchase with a promise to pay later. A financial institution gives credit when it lends money.

Credit Approval It is given when the factor accepts the credit risk assumed by taking a debt from a customer without recourse to that customer in the event of a payment default.

Credit Control It is the system and procedures used by an organization to manage its sales ledger and make certain that it extends credit only to customers who are able to pay and that customers pay on time.

Credit Enhancement It is a method by which a finance provider is entrusted with additional rights, such as collateral, insurance, or a third-party guarantee, to secure payment by a borrower.

Credit Insurance It is the insurance purchased by an organization to insure payment of sums due in relation to credit extended to trade debtors. It may be used as a form of credit enhancement to protect finance provider providing receivables finance.

Credit Limit It is the maximum amount of outstanding debts which a factor is prepared to approve with regard to a specific debtor.

Credit Note It is an accounting document which cuts the value of an outstanding invoice or debtor account.

Credit Protection It is a service offered by a factor or a receivable buyer or an insurance company where the factor accepts the risk of non-payment in the event of the inability of the debtor to repay the debt.

Credit Rating It is an evaluation of the creditworthiness of a debtor, an organization, or a government. The evaluation is made by a credit rating agency of the debtor's ability to pay back the debt (both short-term and long-term) and the likelihood of default. A rating is normally reflected in a grading range such as AAA to B.

Credit Risk It is a risk incurred by a vendor of products that the buyer cannot or does not pay for them. See also the commercial risk, the contract risk, the financing risk, the political risk, and the transfer risk.

Credit Risk Insurer It is an entity which offers to insure credit and, normally, political risks in relation to one obligor, transaction, portfolio, or continuing line of specified trade transaction or obligors. Such entities may be either private organizations or public or semi-public institutions such as ECAs.

Creditor It is an entity that is owed money, sometimes being the vendor of products and services.

Creditworthy It is an entity in which the risk of default on a debt obligation is evaluated low.

Cross-Border Payments They are transactions that occur between accounts based in different countries (that is, non-domestic payments). Normally, cross-border payments are made via an incumbent correspondent financial network, which involves the fund traveling between multiple organizations, resulting in the process to be slow and costly.

Crowdfunding It is the practice of funding a project or venture by raising money from a large number of persons. This takes place often via online platforms. It can also happen through mail-order subscriptions, benefit events, and other methods.

Cryptocurrency A digital currency operating independently of any central bank, which uses cryptography to regulate the creation of new units of the currency and to verify the transfer of funds.[11]

Cumulative Revolving Letter of Credit It is a revolving letter of credit that permits the vendor to carry over any amounts not drawn into successive periods.

Currency It refers to the money used in exchanges, which has an assigned value and normally is authorized by law.

Current Assets They are valuable resources or property of an organization that will be turned into cash within one year, or used up in the operation of the organization within one year. They include cash, government bonds, marketable securities, notes, and accounts receivable, inventories, and prepaid expenses.

Current Liabilities It is any liability which must be honored within one year (for instance, dividends, taxes, accounts payable, or payroll).

Customer It is an organization, he, or she who pays for the product, service, or activity. It is not necessarily the user of the product or the process or activity. It can be external or internal to the organization. In the latter case, unless there is a system of internal prices, the internal customer does not pay the product or service or activity but uses it. Customers should be seen as a reason for the existence of the organization and not just as a result of the receptors of the products or services.

Customer (Vendor) A vendor business which has a contractual relationship with a factor or an asset-based lender.

Customer Experience It is the set of relationships, products, and services that enable customers to be successful with the products evaluated. In particular, it includes the ways customers receive technical or account support. This can also include ancillary tools, customer support programs (and the quality thereof), availability of user groups, service-level agreements, and so on.

Customer Value Proposition They are the benefits a product or service holds for a customer. They are the reasons why a customer might purchase that product or service.

Cycle Time This term can be used in different situations. The cycle time gives the idea of the time it takes for a product/service from its beginning phase to delivery. In the case of production, the cycle time is the time that elapses between the arrival of the raw materials and the payment of the finished product. If one evaluates the cycle time from the point of view of the end customer, the cycle time can be defined as the total time that the customer must wait to receive and accept a product/service after ordered it.

Data Collection It is the process of collecting the data to generate information that can be used for making decisions. In the case of a manual data collection, check lists are used to collect information and provide for their initial classification.

Data Governance and Compliance It defines who is responsible for what and the policies and procedures that persons or groups need to follow. Data governance requires governing the organization's own infrastructure and the infrastructure that the organization does not totally control. Data governance has two key components: understanding compliance and risk, and organization performance objectives.

Data Match or Matching It compares submitted data or datasets with a baseline or criteria and declares a match or non-match in a chosen environment, for instance, a matching engine or a trade services utility (TSU).

Database or Dataset It is a collection of data normally from a common source and assembled for a particular organization or another purpose. The term is used generally to define data that could historically have been brought together in a document. In an automated process, the data are transmitted as a dataset. Under the rules of the BPO, datasets must be matched prior to when a payment obligation becomes due.

Days of Grace It is the number of days the acceptor of a draft may go past due before being judged in default and triggering any guarantor to pay on the acceptor's behalf. When an avalized draft is sold to a forfeiter, the forfeiter imputes the days of grace into the financing period.

Days Payable Outstanding It is the average number of days an organization takes to pay its vendors.

Days Sales Outstanding It is an efficiency ratio that measures the average number of days an organization takes to collect the proceeds of invoices due from its customers, that is, its average collection period.

Debenture It is a fixed-interest bond secured against the issuing organization's assets. It may consist either of specific assets of the organization or of its assets in general. Debenture bonds are distinct from ordinary bonds, the latter being unsecured. Debentures are paid whether the issuing organization makes a profit or not. In case of liquidation, debenture holders have priority over ordinary bondholders on the organization's remaining assets. Debentures can be bought and sold on a stock exchange.

Debt It is a duty or obligation to pay money, deliver products, or render services. The use of debt to finance an organization's activity implies the repayment of principal and interests. Because the interest paid on debt can be written off as an expense, debt is normally the cheapest type of long-term financing.

Debt Collection It is a service offered by a factor (or a receivables buyer) where the factor or the receivables buyer collects the receivables on behalf of the assignor. It may also include all actions aimed at collecting the due amounts from insolvent debtors.

Debtor (Buyer) It is an organization that has been supplied with products or services by a vendor and is obliged to make payment for them. It is also referred to as the buyer of products or services supplied by a vendor whose credits have been assigned/sold to a factor.

Debt-to-Equity Ratio It is the proportion, expressed in percentage, that shows how much of the total organization funds are supplied by creditors. This is determined by dividing total debt by total asset.

Decentralized Application There is no exact definition because of the novelty of the area. It can be said to be an application without any single point of failure, which runs on many different nodes.[12]

Default It is the failure to pay loan interest or loan principal on schedule. When a borrower defaults on its loan obligation, its loan account is said to be delinquent or in arrears.

Deferred Payment It is a payment at a set time after the shipment or the presentation of shipping documents, as opposed to immediately or at sight. A distinction is drawn between a letter of credit that is available for deferred payment and one that is available for acceptance of time drafts in that no drafts are involved under a deferred payment letter of credit. Without accepted drafts, the beneficiary's ability to sell, or discount, its right to payment to another lender or investor is restricted.

Deferred Reimbursement It is an arrangement under a letter of credit where the issuing financial institution agrees up front with its customer, the applicant, to pay the beneficiary upon presentation of the documents required in the letter of credit but to defer charging the applicant until a later date. In this way, the financial institution finances the purchase of products under the letter of credit. Ideally, the delay would be for the expected time the applicant needs in order to use or re-sell the products.

Deferred Tax It is a liability of an organization resulting from income that has already been earned from an accounting perspective, but it is not yet considered for tax purposes.

Delinquency It is the failure to make payment on a loan obligation on the due date.

Demand Guarantee It is a type of guarantee that is payable immediately upon presentation of the specified documents, without regard to the validity of the documents or compliance with the underlying contract, as opposed to an ancillary guarantee. It is also called an independent guarantee. Although there are separate rules of practice for demand guarantees and letters of credit, both of them are considered letters of credit under USA law.

Destination Control Statement It is an item which appears on the commercial invoice and sea or air waybill of lading to notify the carrier and all parties that the item can be exported only to certain destinations.

Digitization It is the automated handling of information, applications, and services. It can be measured by the percentage of requests to the vendor handled without human intervention.

Dilution It is every situation that legally allows the buyer to cut the value of an outstanding invoice, except the default of the debtor.

Direct Collection It is a service for handling export draft collections in which the exporter's financial institution provides the forms that bear the financial institution's own letterhead for mailing documents to the buyer's financial institution for collection. To the buyer's financial institution, it appears that the documents were sent from the exporter's financial institution. By bypassing unnecessary processing at the exporter's financial institution, it is possible to save time and expenses.

Direct Export Factoring It is export factoring without the use of a correspondent factor. Export factor covers the risk of a counterparty in another country (normally backed up by an insurance policy). It is similar to domestic factoring, except that the buyers are abroad.

Directive on Payment Services (or Payment Service Directive) (PSD) It is an European Union (EU) legislation that provides the legal foundation for the creation of a single market for payments across the Eurozone, and the necessary legal platform for the Single Euro Payments Area (SEPA).[13] The introduction of PSD made cross-border payments easier and faster with SEPA payments being used to make transfers across the majority of countries in Europe. Another key objective for the PSD is to improve competition by opening up payment markets to new entrants, providing greater efficiency and cost reduction to end users.

Disclosed or Undisclosed It is when a finance provider undertakes a transaction such as a receivables purchase which may or may not be advised to or disclosed to the underlying debtor. Undisclosed might be described as confidential or non-notification as in confidential or non-notification factoring.

Discount It is the amount of money that is deducted from the face value of a negotiable instrument. It is expressed as a percentage of the face value of the instrument. The individual or institution that discounts negotiable instruments is called discounter.

Discount Rate or Charge It is when a buyer purchases a bill of exchange or an accounts receivable from a vendor, the rate at which it is paid (discounted relative to its face value) prior to its maturity date.

Discounting of Promissory Notes They are synonyms for forfeiting.

Discrepancies It describes deviations between the documents presented and requirements set in the letter of credit or inconsistencies among the documents themselves.

Dishonor It is the failure or refusal by the drawee/payer to accept a draft presented for acceptance or to pay a draft presented for payment.

Dispute Notice It is a written notification to the customer from the factor informing the customer of a dispute.

Disruptive Innovation It is an innovation that completely changes the way people do something (for instance, e-commerce versus physical in-store shopping). It describes innovations that improve products or services in unexpected ways. This innovation changes both the way things are done and the market. The smartphone is an example of a disruptive innovation. It changes completely the way in which users connect to the computer services and among themselves.

Distributed Ledger Technology (DLT) It is a shared database that is updated by consensus and records time-stamped data with unique cryptographic signatures leading to a secure and auditable history of the transactions.[14]

Distribution or Third-Party Distribution It is a general term for the various methods of selling or sharing financial risks (both funded and unfunded) in an underlying financial transaction with investors such as another financial provider, insurer, or other parties. Typical examples are syndication and sub-participation.

Distributor It is a person or entity that supplies products on a wholesale basis to retail outlets or organizations. It may be a manufacturing entity, an arm of a manufacturing entity, or an independent entity.

Distributor Finance It is a financial instrument where a finance provider provides financing for a distributor of a large manufacturer to cover the holding of products for resale and to bridge the liquidity gap until the receipt of funds from receivables following the sale of products to an intermediary or end customer.

Documentary Collection It is the handling by financial institutions of documents in accordance with instructions received to obtain payment and/or acceptance, or to deliver documents against payment and/or against acceptance, or to deliver documents on other terms and conditions, if subject to internationally recognized rules of practice issued by the International Chamber of Commerce (ICC). ICC's current publication is called Uniform Rules for Collections (URC 522).[15]

Documentary Credit Arrangement It is a method of financing procurement by which a financial institution (the issuing financial institution), acting on the request of a customer, is instructed to pay, accept, or negotiate drafts following certain terms and conditions agreed in the draft.

Documentary Draft Collection It is the process for collecting payment in a sale of products where a legal demand for payment from the buyer is made by a financial institution acting as a collecting agent for the vendor. Demand is made by presenting a draft. The collecting financial institution is also entrusted with documents to deliver in accordance with accompanying instructions, normally, once the draft is either paid or accepted. These documents are generally needed by the buyer to show title to the products before they are released by a freight forwarder and customs.

Documentary Letter of Credit It is an irrevocable undertaking by an institution (the issuing financial institution) to the beneficiary of the documentary letter of credit on behalf of their customer to pay the stated amount at sight or at a determinable future date or to accept a draft and effect payment at maturity subject to the presentation of compliant documents as stated in the terms and conditions of the letter of credit. They are normally subject to internationally recognized rules of practice issued by the International Chamber of Commerce (ICC). ICC's current publication is called Uniform Customs and Practice for Documentary Credits (UCP) 600.[16]

Documentary Trade Finance It is a term that covers a large element of the traditional trade finance market relating to tools such as documentary credits, documentary collections, and guarantees. They are normally governed by rules published by the International Chamber of Commerce (ICC) (e.g., UCP 600 for the letters of credit (or later version) or URC 522 for Collections or URDG 758 for guarantees).[17] Although not procurement finance instruments in their own right, these tools can be incorporated into procurement finance transactions or used alongside procurement finance instruments.

Documents Against Acceptance It is a term for documentary draft collection instructions requesting the presenting financial institution to deliver documents only upon acceptance of the draft by the drawee/buyer.

Documents Against Payment It is a term for documentary collection instructions requesting the presenting financial institution to deliver documents only upon receipt of payment from the drawee/buyer.

Domestic Factoring It is a form of factoring in which both assignor and debtor are based in the country of the factor.

Double-Financing or Double-Pledging It is the fraudulent practice of raising funds more than once on the same receivable or other assets.

Draft It is a written demand for payment of a specified amount addressed to a named party, called the drawee, and signed by the drawer. A draft may demand payment immediately upon presentation (at sight) or on a specified maturity date. It must also specify a party to be paid (the payee). Most drafts are negotiable, meaning the payee's right to payment can be transferred by the payee to another party by endorsement and delivery of the draft.

Draft Collection It is the process for collecting payment in a sale of products where a legal demand for payment from the buyer is made by a financial institution acting as collecting agent for the vendor. Demand is made by presenting a draft.

Draft Contract (DC) It is an initial contract which is drawn up and sent from the vendor to the buyer. The buyer has the opportunity to make amendments and send it back to the vendor for consideration. This process continues until both parties are satisfied with the terms of the contract.

Drawee It is a party to whom a draft is addressed and from whom payment is demanded, or, in a documentary collection with no draft, a party from whom payment is requested in exchange for delivery of documents.

Due Date It is the date on which a payment is due to be made.

Due Diligence It is an investigation into the facts connected with an organization, an initiative, or a process, normally in respect of the customer or prospective customer. It can be part of the know-your-customer (KYC) process. In existing agreements, it is normally applied to a portfolio of debtors to check the outstanding invoices.

Duty It is a tax imposed by the customs authority of a country on imported or special products.

Dynamic Discounting It describes a number of methods through which early payment discounts on invoices awaiting payment are offered to vendors and funded by the buyer. The service is dynamic in the sense that the earlier the payment, the higher the discount.

Early Payment It is a payment done before it is due.

Early Payment Discount It is one form of procurement finance and a way for organizations to obtain a discount on a vendor's invoice in exchange for paying the vendor or the financial institution earlier with respect to when it is due.

Ecosystem It is a complex network or interconnected system.

Ecosystem Participants They are a set of organizations or individuals that can work together to gain synergies.

Electronic Commerce (e-commerce) It is a web solution for accomplishing organization's transactions to include an email or messaging, other web solutions, digital bulletin boards, purchase, payments, digital funds transfers, and digital data interchange.

Electronic Data Interchange It is the computer-to-computer exchange of an organization's documents in a standard digital format between parties.

Electronic Funds Transfer (EFT) It refers to any transfer of funds initiated digitally, including card payments, automatic teller machine (ATM) withdrawals, point-of-sale (POS), and debit transfers without requiring the intervention of a financial institution staff. These transactions can take place within the same organization, or across accounts spread between one or more financial institutions in the financial network.

Electronic Invoicing or e-Invoicing It is the exchange of the invoice document between a vendor, a buyer, or a financial institution wholly in an integrated digital format or dataset. Traditionally, invoicing, like any heavily paper-based process, is manually intensive. Manual invoices are subject to human errors resulting in increased costs and processing lifecycles for the organizations.

Eligibility It is the proof of the existence of the qualification requirements: concerning technical and operational (availability of appropriate means of design and manufacturing resources and, where applicable, professional staff, means of testing and inspection, as well as management systems for the realization of the products of organization's interest), legal, and economic-financial official documentation (for instance, profitability reports, balance sheets, and so on).

E-Money Directive It is a currency that is digitized to be stored on, and used via, mobile phones, prepaid cards, or online accounts. The second E-Money Directive is a revised set of regulations introduced to benefit organizations, customers, and the wider economy.[18] It aims to enable secure e-money services, to provide market access to new organizations, and to foster heavy competition between all participants.

Encumbrance It is a claim against a property held by another party. An encumbrance can take several forms: mortgages, claims by other parties, court judgments, pending legal action, unpaid taxes, restrictive deed or loan covenants, easement rights of the neighbors, or zoning ordinances. An encumbrance normally impacts the transferability of the property.

Endorsement It is a legal term that refers to the signing of a document which allows for the legal transfer of a negotiable instrument from one party to another.

Enterprise Resource Planning (ERP) It is the extension of the Manufacturing Resource Planning II to the remaining functions in the organization, such as engineering, finance, and personnel administration and management. It consists of a software package with a single data model that facilitates the horizontal and vertical integration of all inter-organizational processes and improves process efficiency.[19] It supports the monitoring of processes through special key performance (or process) indicators (KPIs) according to quality, economic values, service levels, and timeliness. Some components of an ERP are accounting, industrial accounting, payrolls, sourcing, warehouse management, production, project control, sales, distribution, and facility maintenance.

E-procurement (Electronic Procurement) It is a tool for managing the procurement with the integration of the vendors in a business-to-business (B2B) relationship. It integrates the procurement processes, cuts transaction costs for buyers, and simplifies the workflows for vendors and the access to the market. The e-procurement includes a set of technologies, processes, operations, and organizational procedures for the acquisition of products and services online through the opportunities offered by the development of the web and e-commerce.

Equity In accounting, it is ownership interest or claim of a holder of common stock (ordinary shares) and some types of preferred stock (preference shares) of a company. On a balance sheet, equity represents funds contributed by the owners (shareholders) plus retained earnings or minus the accumulated losses. It can also be the net worth of a person or organization computed by subtracting total liabilities from the total assets. In the case of cooperatives, equity represents members' investment plus retained earnings, minus losses.

Escrow Account It is an account held in a financial institution or other trusted third party, outside the location of a debtor, through which a portion of its revenues is retained to cover future debt-servicing payments. The beneficiaries of the escrow accounts are the creditors who can obtain in this way extra security for their loans and priority in debt servicing.

Ethereum It is a blockchain specifically designed to be a platform for smart contracts.[20]

EURO1 It is a large-value payment system for same-day euro transactions at a Pan-European level, which processes transactions of high priority and urgency and primarily of a large amount at a domestic and cross-border level on a multilateral net basis.[21] Currently, EURO1 processes in excess of 250,000 payments per day, with an overall value of approximately €210 billion. EURO1 is based on a messaging and ICT infrastructure provided by Swift.

European Committee for Standardization It is a public standards organization whose mission is to foster the economy of the European Union (EU) in global trading and the welfare of European citizens and the environment by providing an efficient infrastructure to interested parties for the development, maintenance, and distribution of coherent sets of standards and specifications.[22]

European Federation for Factoring and Commercial Finance (EUF) It is the representative body for the factoring and commercial finance industry in the European Union (EU). It comprises national and international industry associations that are active in the EU.[23]

Evergreen Letter of Credit It is a letter of credit with an initial expiration date but containing a clause that states that it is automatically extended for additional periods unless the issuing financial institution provides notice to the beneficiary stating otherwise.

Ex Quay It is a contract for the sale of products where the vendor bears all the costs, consisting of duties, taxes, freight, and other charges, incurred in the course of delivering the products. It also includes the costs of loading and unloading products from the quay at the port of destination to the road vehicles. The buyer assumes all subsequent charges.

Ex Ship It is an Incoterm that denotes the vendor's obligation to deliver the products to the buyer at the named port of destination.[24]

Ex Works (Named Place) It is a shipping term included in a contract of sale meaning that the vendor fulfills its obligation to deliver when he has made the products available at its premises (that is, works, factory, warehouse, and so on) to the buyer. In particular, the vendor is not responsible for loading the products for export, unless otherwise agreed. The buyer bears all the costs and risks involved in taking the products from the vendor's premises to the desired destination.

Expiry Date It is the last date on which documents may be presented or corrected in order to comply with a letter of credit. The presentation must be made to the financial institution shown in the letter of credit.

Export Credit Agency (ECA) Finance It is a form of trade finance provided by ECA.[25] It includes guarantees, loans, and credit insurance to promote exports by removing the risks.

Export Credit Guarantee It is an assurance normally provided by a government agency that safeguards financial institutions against losses that could arise from financing export transactions. It facilitates vendors' access to pre-/post-shipment credit from a financial institution. It is a powerful incentive to exporting. Export credit guarantees do not involve the actual provision of funds to the vendors.

Export Credit Insurance It is a policy to cover some of the riskier areas faced by vendors in exporting their products/services, that is, non-payment due either to the insolvency of the buyer (commercial risk) or political events (political risk). Export credit insurance is frequently mentioned in connection with export credit guarantees. While guarantees cover financial institution export loans, insurance policies are issued directly in favor of the vendors. In many emerging countries, this type of insurance is either not available or is very expensive. Several types of export credit insurance are available. These differ from country to country according to the needs of the local organization community. The most widely used types of export credit insurance include the following: short-term export credit insurance, medium- and long-term export credit insurance, investment insurance, external trade insurance, and exchange risk insurance.

Export Factor It is the factor, normally located in the vendor's (or vendor's) country, with whom the vendor has a factoring agreement or contract.

Export Factoring It is a form of factoring in which the assignor, normally based in the country of the factor, assigns/sells receivables due by debtors based in another country.

Export Letter of Credit It is a term used by an exporter to describe a commercial letter of credit in its favor or by a financial institution other than itself. The same letter of credit is called an import letter of credit by the vendor, the buyer, and the issuing financial institution.

Exports It refers to all products leaving a country that are properly cleared by customs.

Face Value It is the principal or redemption value of a financial instrument or claim.

Factor It is a financial institution that purchases accounts receivable at a discount. The factor can administer the receivables, purchase them outright, and advance cash payment before collection.

Factorable Receivables They are receivables that are free from lien. They are assignable and collectible.

Factoring It is the service of assuming the credit risk of another party's sales, generally including collecting payment when due. Factors often provide or arrange limited-recourse financing against the accounts receivable they are guaranteeing referred to as purchasing receivables.

Factoring Agreement It is the agreement between the finance provider (factor) and a customer setting out the terms on which a factoring arrangement is made available, including scope, charges, operational procedures, and security to be taken.

Factors Chain International It is a global association that facilitates two-factor cross-border international factoring in a structured environment under the General Rules for International Factoring.[26]

Faster Payments It is a UK payment system which allows transactions to be made 24/7, 365 days a year. Originally the network was restricted to established incumbent banks. It has begun to open up, allowing new entrants access to the network.

Feasibility Study It is a detailed examination of the comparative costs and benefits of an initiative proposed for funding. It ascertains the initiative's potential for commercial success before a loan is approved.

Fed Funds Rate It is the interest rate at which financial institutions in the USA lend each other dollars for next-day repayment (overnight loans).

Finance Provider It is a bank, financial institution, or other regulated or non-regulated provider of finance and related services.

Financial Institution It is a provider of financial services in the broad sense, normally referring to financial institutions and other regulated entities such as insurance organizations, investment dealers, and trust organizations. It includes a range of non-bank financial institutions.

Financial Instrument It is a tradable asset of any kind, either cash, evidence of an ownership interest in an entity, or a contractual right to receive or deliver cash or another financial instrument. In forfeiting, the rights under the financial instrument are normally independent of the underlying transaction which gave rise to the financial instrument, since they rely on the legal obligations created by the legal status of the financial instrument itself.

Financial Supply Chain It is the chain of financial processes, risk and liquidity management decisions, events, and activities that provides financial support to the physical supply chain and interfaces with data to the information supply chain flow.

Financial Viability It is the earning capacity of a project to generate acceptable returns to service its debt on time and in full.

Financier It is a general expression for any person or entity that provides finance in various forms.

Financing Margin It is a margin built into an interest rate or discount rate charged to a customer to cover risk and a level of margin for the finance provider.

Financing Risk It is the term used to describe the increasing uncertainty that the buyer of products has the capacity to pay when payment is due the longer the time period he or she is given to make payment.

Finished Products Inventory They are products for sale that are held in inventory.

Fintech It is an innovative organization creating products or services offered by combining new solutions, often technological, with financial instruments.

Fixed Asset It is a term indicating tangible assets such as real estate, buildings, land, plant, and machinery, bought by the organization for long-term use rather than for resale or immediate consumption. Fixed assets include intangible assets such as patents, trademarks, brands, intellectual properties, and customer recognition. Fixed assets are retained in the organization for long periods. A portion of their original cost is written off (amortized) against revenues to reflect their diminishing value over time. In an organization's balance sheet, fixed assets are therefore normally shown at cost, less depreciation charged to date. Certain fixed assets, such as property, can appreciate or lose in value.

Floor Plan Finance It is a synonym for distributor finance specifically relating to finance of vehicles and machinery placed for sale on the sales floor of a dealer.

Foreign Exchange (FX/Forex) It is the exchange, or conversion, of one currency into another currency. Foreign exchange also refers to the global trading markets by which currencies are virtually exchanged around the clock, with the largest centers being based in London, New York, Tokyo, and Singapore. The term foreign exchange is frequently abbreviated to "forex" as well as "FX".

Foreign Exchange Fee They are the charges to mark up to the mid-market (also known as interbank) rate. The midpoint between the purchase and the sale prices of the two currencies on the global currency markets determines this rate. Providers that process FX payments often add a high commission to this rate in order to make a margin from the transaction and cover its risks. Fees may also be added when a transaction has to pass through multiple correspondent financial institutions to reach the recipient.

Foreign Exchange Rate It is the rate at which a unit of one nation's currency is converted into another nation's currency.

Foreign Exchange Risk It is the probability of the loss occurring from an adverse movement in foreign exchange rates. It can affect both buyers and vendors as well as investors and financiers.

Forfeit (or Forfait) It is the purchase of negotiable instruments, most often avalized drafts, without recourse. The forfeiter assumes the credit risk of being able to collect payment when due.

Forfeit (or Forfait) Discounting It is the method of discounting without recourse, where the vendor sells its receivables to a forfeiter who takes over the risk of non-payment.

Forfeiter or Forfaiter It is a provider of forfeiting services, either a bank or a non-bank financial institution.

Forfeiting It is a form of receivables purchase, consisting of the without recourse purchase of future payment obligations represented by financial instruments or payment obligations, at a discount or at face value in return for a financing charge.

Forfeiting Agreement Under the Uniform Rules for Forfeiting,[27] it is the agreement between the initial vendor and the primary forfeiter

Formal (Final) Contract It is a formal contract drawn up and signed by both parties when the negotiation stages of the draft contract are complete and both parties are satisfied.

Forwarder's Cargo Receipt It is a document issued by a freight forwarder or freight consolidator showing that the products have been received from the vendor and are being held on behalf of the buyer. Goods are generally received in the vendor's country, and the forwarder/consolidator arranges shipment to the buyer based on the buyer's instructions.

Four-Corner Model It is a situation where two trading parties are using the services of separate financial institutions or service providers and use their services acting on an interoperable basis.

Free Alongside Ship It is an export contract that makes the vendor responsible for the cost of delivering the products to the quay at the port of shipment but not for the cost of loading them onto the ship.

Free Carrier (Named Place) It is a shipping term included in a contract of sale meaning that the vendor fulfills its obligation to deliver when he or she has handed over the products, cleared for export, into the charge of the carrier, freight consolidator, or freight forwarder named by the buyer at the named place or point.

Free on Board (Named Port of Shipment) (FOB) It is, under this term, the price of the products quoted by a vendor including transport, insurance, and loading costs incurred until the merchandize is loaded onboard the vessel. The vendor fulfills its obligations when the products are boarded at the named port of shipment. The buyer has to bear all costs and risks of loss or damage arising from the point of loading. The term FOB can only be used for sea or inland waterway transport. When the ship's rail serves no practical purpose, such as in the case of roll-on/roll-off container traffic, the term "free carrier" is more appropriate. FOB values also serve as a reference for import and export valuation shipment, all costs of inland transportation and loading being included in the price of the products. The buyer has to bear all costs and risks of loss of or damage to the products from that point.

Freely Negotiable Letter of Credit It is a letter of credit that shows it is available with any financial institution by negotiation. By including this wording, the issuing financial institution authorizes the beneficiary to present the documents to the financial institution of its choice for examination and collection of payment.

Freight Forward It is a shipment where the freight is payable at the port of destination.

Freight Forwarder It is an organization that, as an agent for the logistics operator, arranges transportation for products. Many freight forwarders offer additional services such as preparing export documentation, arranging for products to be packed into shipping containers, arranging for products to clear customs, and so on.

Front-End Fees They are fees charged by financial institutions for the services rendered in assessing a loan application or opening the loan account. These fees are normally deducted from the loan proceeds upon disbursement.

Full Corporate Offer It is a proposal issued by the vendor after the preliminary stages of negotiation are complete, such as a letter of intent having been issued by the buyer and a soft discovery having been conducted on their accounts by the vendor. A full corporate proposal is a document which outlines the terms and conditions of the sale.

Full Set They are all the signed originals of a document. For example, bills of lading are often issued in three originals, all having the same validity for claiming products at the place of delivery.

Full-Service Factoring It is a form of factoring in which the factor provides the assignor with all the following services relative to the receivables assigned: an advance of a percentage of the amount of receivables assigned, receivables management, collections, and credit protection.

Funding Limit It is the maximum value available to a customer against its assigned receivables.

Funds in Use It is the total number of funds advanced to the customer prior to the collection by the factor.

General Rules for International Factoring They are the rules which the members of Factors Chain International (FCI) agree to adopt when transacting two-factor cross-border factoring.

General Terms and Conditions for Payment Method It is the offered payment method. It can greatly affect the price offered by the vendor; the more secure the payment, the cheaper the price. Vendors are looking for more security in payment and because of a high percentage of dropouts paying by ordinary documentary letter of credit. Very few vendors offer this payment option any more. The minimum payment option is an irrevocable letter of credit (IRDLC) revolving for one month's shipment value. For larger contracts, the vendor is looking for one month's shipment value held by the vendor as surety against the buyer dropping out. In the past, a buyer would contract a quantity say up to 12 times more than the quantity they actually required; they pay for one or two shipments and drop out, after having obtained the benefit of a price offered for a much larger quantity. Buyers would drop out of a contract because they had since found a vendor at a cheaper price.

Payment options can vary with the commodity, such as sugar, where payment may be mandatory by a financial bank guarantee with some vendors.

Global Procurement Portal It is the section of the organization portal dedicated to the vendors.

GOST Certification It is the system of quality certification valid in Russia (this can also be called GOST-R).[28] GOST certification is very important for Russian companies and exporters to Russia and has the same sense of ISO 9000 certificates for Western societies. GOST certification is not only committed to the quality management of the organization subject but also carried the products thereof. That is to say, to obtain certificates, test samples are required. These tests are conducted on accredited laboratories. Based on these tests, certificates are presented to the organization that requested them.

Governance It refers to the controls and processes that make sure of the effectiveness, efficiency, economics, and ethics (and possibly environment sustainability) of a sector. The sector might refer to the entire organization or to an organization unit, a process, systems, or data.

Grace Period In the context of a loan, it is the period during which no repayments of principal (sometimes principal plus interest) are due from the borrower to the lender.

Green Clause It is a clause inserted in the letter of credit requiring the vendor to provide some form of guarantees, such as a warehouse receipt or warrant, evidencing the existence of the products being pledged in favor of the financial institution.

GRIF They are the General Rules for International Factoring, which the members of the Factors Chain International (FCI) agree to adopt when transacting two-factor cross-border factoring.[29]

Guarantee It is a promise or assurance by a person or institution to pay a loan in the event that the borrower fails to meet its obligation. With a guarantee cover, the lender's risks are minimized.

Hedging They are activities undertaken to eliminate exposure or minimize losses that may arise as a result of fluctuations in foreign exchange rates.

Hurdle Rate It is the minimum return on investment necessary to cover all costs associated with an initiative. If the expected rate of return is below the hurdle rate, the initiative is abandoned or should be modified to increase returns.

Hyperledger The Hyperledger project is an open-source initiative to create blockchains for organization use which the Linux Foundation launched it in 2016 together with 30 founding corporate members. Currently, there are nine different blockchains being developed by the project. The focus is not to have specific chains, which are to be used by the members, but to collaboratively develop code bases and frameworks that can be implemented by those organizations who are interested.[30]

Import They are all products entering into the seaports or airports or by land from another nation properly cleared through customs or remaining under customs custody, whether such products are for direct consumption, for trading, for warehousing, or for further processing.

Import Factor It is a correspondent factor, normally located in the country of the debtor, who is responsible for the collection and/or credit risk by sub-assignment of the debts.

Import Factoring It is a form of factoring in which an export receivable is managed and collected by an import factor normally based in the same country of the debtor.

Import Letter of Credit It is a term used by a buyer to describe a commercial letter of credit he or she has asked a financial institution to issue or by a financial institution to describe a letter of credit it has issued. The same letter of credit is called an export letter of credit by the exporter.

Incoterms Incoterms or International Commercial Terms are a series of international sales terms, published by the International Chamber of Commerce (ICC).[31] They standardize international trade practices, facilitate trade, and minimize misunderstandings over commercial terminology. They are therefore widely used in international commercial transactions. They divide transaction costs and responsibilities between buyers and vendors. In particular, they define which parties incur the costs and at what specific point the costs are incurred.

Indirect Payment It is a payment made to the customer by a debtor.

Ineligibility It is the proof of the non-existence of the following qualification requirements concerning technical and operational (availability of appropriate means of design and manufacturing resources and, where applicable, professional staff, means of testing and inspection, as well as management systems for the realization of the products of organization interest), legal, and economic-financial (for instance, profitability, balance sheet, and so on).

Information and Communication Technology It is the combination of computers, storage, network, applications, and similar devices that provides integrated computer-based services.

Initial Coin Offering (ICO) It is similar to an initial public offering in that it is used to raise capital for organizations in the blockchain domain. If the organization offers a blockchain service that has a native cryptocurrency, it can raise capital by selling this cryptocurrency, where investors hope that the coin will gain value as the service increases in popularity.[32]

Initial Vendor (Forfeiting) It is the person who first sells a payment claim or receivable to a primary forfeiter or creates a receivable or payment claim and transfers it to the primary forfeiter.

Input It is a resource introduced into the system or consumed in its operations which helps in getting a result or output.

Insolvency It is a situation when an entity can no longer meet its financial obligations with its creditors when debts become due.

Inspection Certificate It is a document that is required by some purchasers and countries in order to attest to the specifications of the products shipped. It is normally performed by an independent third party that inspects the products for conformity.

Installment Letter of Credit It is a letter of credit calling for multiple shipments within specified date ranges.

Insurance Certificate It is a document signed and issued by an insurance organization stating the amount and type of insurance coverage.

Integration It is the process of combining components or systems into an integrated entity.

Interest It is a charge paid by a borrower to a lender for the use of the lender's money. It is expressed as a percentage rate over a period of time.

Interest Rate It is the amount of interest charged for borrowing a particular funding over a specified period of time.

Interfactor Agreement It is an agreement between correspondent factors by which they mutually agree to act as import and export factors in accordance with a code of practice.

International Bank Account Number (IBAN) It is an account number written in a standardized and internationally recognized format which is used to identify an individual account, making it faster and easier to process cross-border transactions across Europe. An IBAN is made up of a code that identifies the country the account belongs to, the bank the account belongs to, followed by the account number.

International Chamber of Commerce (ICC) ICC provides a forum for the organizations to examine and better understand the nature and the significance of the major transformation taking place in the world economy. It offers an influential and respected channel for supplying the organization's leadership to help governments manage those transformations in a collaborative manner for the benefit of the world economy.

International Commercial Terms They are internationally recognized standard trade terms used in sales contracts.[33] They are used to make sure buyers and vendors know: who is responsible for the cost of transporting the products, where the products should be picked up from and transported to, and who is responsible for each step of the transportation process.

International Factoring It is a variation of factoring, in which the buyer (debtor) is located in a country different from the vendor. Country-specific rules or regulations may apply due to the international character of the debt. These rules could affect the relationship between the finance provider, the buyer, and the vendor. For these reasons, often two factors are involved, one in the buyer's country (known as the import factor) and one in the vendor's country (known as the export factor). The two factors establish a contractual relationship to serve the buyer and the vendor, respectively (called the "two-factor system"). Normally, the two factors use the established frameworks provided by either Factors Chain International (FCI) or International Factors Group (IFG).[34]

International Factoring Organization It is an organization that acts as a trade association for factoring organizations. It normally manages international rules for the conduct of international factoring transactions.[35]

International Factors Group It is a global association for factoring providers.[36]

International Finance Corporation (IFC) It is a member of the World Financial Institution Group. It is the largest global development institution focused exclusively on the private sector in emerging countries.[37]

International Organization of Factoring It is a network of organizations acting as factors whose common aim is to facilitate international trade through factoring and to act as trade organizations representing the industry.

Internet of Things It is a development of the Internet in which objects have network connectivity, allowing them to send and receive data. Internet of Things (IoT) has the ability to record, receive, and send data. This covers Internet-connected machines, vehicles, devices, switches, sensors, and everything in between. It is based on using the Internet to communicate between objects, machines, and other non-humans.

Interoperability It is concerned with the ability of systems to operate in multiple environments.

Inter-Organizational Collaboration (IOC) It is the case of multiple parties collaborating on, for instance, a common procurement solution. This kind of collaboration could include organizational alliances (partnerships), vendors, customers, and even competitors. They all interact in order to create a common end delivery. In some countries, IOC can become formalized in a temporary association of companies:

Introductory Letter It is a letter sent by the vendor to each of its debtors to advise them that the customer has entered into a factoring agreement.

Inventory Finance-Borrowing Base It is a variation of loans and advances against inventory, by which the amount of finance is made available against a computed market value of the products (which could be of more than one type) being financed at a margin which varies according to the quantity or quality of the products.

Inventory Finance-Repo It is a variation of the inventory finance, by which the finance provider enters into a sale and repurchase agreement for the products being financed.

Inventory Finance-Tolling It is a variation of loans and advances against inventory, in which the finance is provided to allow raw materials or components to be submitted to a third-party refining or manufacturing processes prior to onward sale.

Invoice It is a document, or a digital version of the document, addressed by a vendor of products and services to a buyer recording and describing a transaction for the supply of products and services, requesting payment by a specified due date, and setting out any applicable taxes to be collected and remitted to a tax authority.

Invoice Discounting It is a synonym for receivables purchase. It is also used as a variation of factoring. The term is therefore subject to different uses.

Invoice Trading Platform It is an alternative to factoring. The online platform allows vendors to place individual invoices for auction. Investors or buyers can then bid for the invoice resulting in an advance payment to the vendor.

Irrevocable Confirmed Letter of Credit It is a letter of credit which is confirmed by another financial institution, normally one in the beneficiary's jurisdiction. A confirming financial institution is one which undertakes to make payment on the letter of credit on behalf of the issuing financial institution at such time as the beneficiary meets the terms and conditions outlined in the letter of credit.

Irrevocable Corporate Purchase Order (ICPO) It is a document drawn up by commercial buyers. It contains the quantities of products required, the type of products required, and other conditions that the buyer wants the sale to proceed under. Once submitted to the vendor, it is deemed to be binding and the corporation is obliged to complete the sale.

Irrevocable Letter of Credit (IRDLC) It is a document issued from the buyer's financial institution to the vendor which guarantees payment upon the presentation of the agreed documentation. As an irrevocable document, it cannot be canceled. The buyer's financial institution is legally obligated to make payment at such time as the beneficiary fulfills the terms set out in the letter of credit.

Islamic Trade Finance It refers to financial services which comply with the Islamic (Sharia) law.[38] Interest cannot be charged. Instead, the finance is structured using service charges, discounts, sale/lease, profit participation, or repurchase agreements. It may be involved in procurement finance transactions.

Issuing Bank It is a bank that has issued a letter of credit. The issuing financial institution is obligated to pay if documents are presented that comply with the letter of credit requirements.

Just-in-Time Method It is a manufacturing system that minimizes inventories by arranging that components and parts to be delivered as they are needed in the production process.

Key Performance Indicators or Key Process Indicators (KPIs) They are the metrics (or measures) used within corporations to measure the performance of one department or process against another one with respect to revenues, sales lead conversion, costs, customer support, and so on.

Know Your Customer (KYC) It is a mandatory banking regulation designed to protect the integrity of the financial system by reducing the likelihood of financial institutions becoming vehicles for money laundering, terrorist financing, and other unlawful activities. To mitigate risks, financial institutions perform KYC checks by obtaining sufficient information that can be used for developing a comprehensive profile of the customer, such as proof of address, photographic identification, or historical behavior.

Knowledge-Based Authentication (KBA) It is a security measure that seeks to prove the identity of a user who is attempting to access an online service, by asking them to answer at least one secret question. KBA is generally used as a component in multifactor authentication (MFA) and for self-serve password retrieval.

Large Value It is a high monetary value of the items to be financed. Such large value may result from either a large volume of items and specifically triggers considerations related to credit and risk concentration.

Large Volume It is a high number of individual items or transactions that normally calls for automated (or straight-through) processing and a technical and operational infrastructure capable of handling such volume.

Large-Value Payment System It refers to real-time gross settlement (RTGS) systems, such as CHAPS, TARGET2, and country-specific equivalents. Payments via this method are sent securely, in real time, with complete certainty that the payment will settle.

Lean and Digitize It is the method used to make the processes at the same time simple and automated.[39]

Lender It is the party, normally a financial institution or a financial entity, who lends money to a borrower.

Letter of Credit (L/C) It is a financial instrument issued by a financial institution at the request of a buyer (applicant) to a vendor (beneficiary). It guarantees payments to the vendor if the terms and conditions specified in the L/C are fulfilled. It normally contains a brief description of the products, the documents required, a shipping date, and an expiry date after which payment will no longer be made. There are different types of L/C, according to the level of security they grant to the beneficiary (the vendor): irrevocable letter of credit; revocable letter of credit, confirmed irrevocable letter of credit; irrevocable unconfirmed letter of credit; revolving letter of credit, documentary letter of credit, and negotiable letter of credit.

Letter of Guarantee It is the undertaking, normally on the part of a financial institution, either to fulfill the obligations of another party or to pay a specified amount of money upon presentation of specified documents stating that the party is guaranteed from defaults on certain obligations. One must be careful to discern which type of guarantees one is dealing with as they both require presentation of documents but work very differently thereafter. USA law forbids financial institutions from providing guarantees. They use letters of credit to accomplish the same goal.

Letter of Intent It is a document issued from the buyer to the vendor which shows that the buyer would like to enter into negotiations with the vendor with the intent to purchase a product or a service. The letter of intent is not legally binding. It provides a starting point for the negotiations.

Liability It is an amount owed (that is, payable) by an individual or entity for products or services received, expenses incurred, assets acquired, and amounts received but not yet earned.

LIBOR Acronym for the London Interbank Offered Rate.[40] It is the interest rate at which financial institutions in London, UK, place Eurocurrency/Eurodollar deposits with each other for specified, fixed periods of time, most commonly six months. It is used also by financial institutions in other nations.

Lien It is a legal claim against an asset that is used to secure a loan and must be removed before the property is sold.

Line of Credit It is the commitment of a financial institution to a borrower to extend credits under certain conditions up to an agreed amount for a specified period of time. It is renewable at the discretion of the lender.

Liquidity It is an organization's ability to meet its current obligations (or debts that must be paid within one year) using its current assets.

Liquidity Coverage Ratio (LCR) It is the ratio of current assets to current liabilities. It is an essential component of Basel III regulation. LCR shows if a financial institution has an adequate stock of unencumbered high-quality liquid assets (HQLA) that can be converted into cash easily and immediately in private markets to meet its liquidity needs for a 30-calendar-day liquidity stress scenario.

Loan It is making available money to another party in exchange for future repayment of the principal amount plus interest or other finance charges. A loan may be for a specific, one-time amount or can be available as a variable credit line or overdraft up to a specified ceiling amount. It is also possible to make loans of actual real and financial assets.

Loans Outstanding It is the unpaid balance of loans as of a certain date.

Lock-in It is the guarantee of a specific interest rate and/or points for a specific period of time. Some lenders will charge a fee for locking in an interest rate

Long Warranties They are warranties in respect of products and services that are long-lasting and may over time affect the value of receivables purchased or discounted.

Low Value It is a lower monetary value relating to the individual items to be financed. For economic reasons, low-value items are likely to be processed as a large-volume business.

Low Volume It is a lower number of individual items or transactions that allows for manual and individual processing on an item-by-item basis.

Management Process It is a method to optimize the organization as a system, determining which processes need improvement and/or control, define priorities, provide leadership to initiate and support efforts to improve processes, and manage the information obtained as a result of these processes.

Margin It the percentage margin added to the cost of funds or a base rate to establish the interest rate or discount charge.

Marine Cargo Insurance It is the insurance covering loss of or damage to products in the course of international transportation. The term is used for all types of transportation, be it via air, land, or sea.

Market Risk It is the risk that the value of an investment will decrease due to moves in market factors. The four standard market risk factors are equity risk, interest rate risk, currency risk, and commodity risk.

Marketable It means fit for sale and in demand from buyers.

Markets in Financial Instruments Directive (MiFIR/MiFID II Directive) It is the EU legislation that regulates providers of services that are linked to "financial instruments", such as shares, bonds, investment schemes, and derivatives, and the venues where these instruments are traded.[41] In April 2014, the European Parliament approved an updated version of the law, MiFID II, which expands the scope of the rules to cover more organizations and products.

Maturity Date It is the date on which a receivable becomes due and payable.

Maturity Factoring It is a form of factoring in which the assignor receives the payment of the receivables on a certain and fixed date, normally pre-agreed on the basis of the average payment period taken by the debtor.

Merchandize Groups It is the merchandize category (materials, labor, or services) of interest to the organization and subject to the qualification/registration process.

Merchant It is an individual or company that conducts business either to provide wholesale or retail products to end users.

Metrics It is an index of the performance of an organization that shows whether or not an objective is reached.

Mining In the case of cryptocurrencies, it means carrying out the consensus algorithm that allows for the creation and addition of new blocks to the blockchain. A node carrying out the mining is called a miner. The exact process varies between chains. It basically includes verifying transactions and publishing blocks.[42]

Mobile Device It includes smartphones, feature phones, and tablet computers. The term mobile device is also used interchangeably with mobile handset.

Mobile Point of Sale (mPOS) It is a tablet, smartphone, or wireless device that performs the functions of a regular POS terminal. Any device can be transformed into an mPOS with the use of a dedicated app.

Mortgage It is a long-term loan that involves the pledge of an asset, such as real estate, as collateral for the loan.

MT 103 It is a Swift message format for making payments between financial institutions.

MT 760 It is a Swift message format of a bank guarantee. An account with the MT 760 capability allows financial institution-to-financial institution automatic verification of the account. It includes a blocked funds provision. It is a written guarantee honoring the commitments to a third party in certain circumstances, in the event that the buyer is unable to meet them. It is not a payment instrument. In the event of a default, the beneficiary can liquidate the said guarantee. The beneficiary would notify its demand via a free format MT 799 or MT 999. Upon receipt of the written demand, the financial institution would remit proceeds via Swift format MT 103. Since financial institutions try hard not to put their money at risk, the customer's funds are blocked by the financial institution and held by the financial institution as a security (collateral) for the issuance of the guarantee. The transfer MT 760, therefore, is more than just an inter-financial institution message. It is a full-blown cash-backed negotiable instrument.

MT 798 It is a format Swift message which offers to corporations a single channel for exchanging standardized corporate-to-bank trade data. It helps corporations to streamline their trade messaging. Using MT 798, a corporation can apply to its bank for a letter of credit or guarantee, and receive an advice of letter of credit back from its bank. The bank can then notify the issuance of a letter of credit or guarantee, or notify an amendment.

MT 799 It is a free format Swift message type in which a banking institution confirms that funds are in place to cover a potential trade. This can also be used as an irrevocable undertaking, depending on the language used in the MT 799. It is not a promise to pay or any form of financial institution guarantee in its standard format. The function of the MT 799 is simply to assure the vendor that the buyer does have the necessary funds to complete the transaction. The buyer's financial institution sends a proof of funds via MT 799 with full financial institution responsibility. In it, it states to be ready, willing, and able to perform the transaction with the vendor's financial institution. This pre-advice is to engage the transaction, and for the first tranche, only the MT 799 is incorporated as part of the contract and the wording to be approved by the vendor. The MT 799 is normally issued before a contract is signed and before a letter of credit or a financial institution guarantee is issued. After the MT 799 has been received by the vendor's financial institution, it is normally the responsibility of the vendor's financial institution to send a Proof of Product (POP) to the buyer's financial institution. At this point, the trade continues towards commencement. The actual payment method commonly used is a documentary letter of credit, which the vendor presents to the issuing or confirming financial institution along with the transportation documentation. Once the financial institution confirms the documentation, the vendor is paid. An alternative method is to use a financial institution guarantee in place of a letter of credit. It is at the vendor's discretion which method of payment is used.

Multilateral Institution It is a financial institution that provides advice and financing for national or regional development projects or programs. The institution is normally owned by governments. It provides a framework of cooperation in which borrowers and vendors of finance are represented.

Multimodal Bill of Lading It is the bill of lading covering shipment of products by more than one mode of transportation but including a sea leg. The two major forms of multimodal bill of lading are the combined transport bill of lading and the through bill of lading. In a combined transport bill of lading, the carrier signing the bill of lading (the contractual carrier) frequently subcontracts the various legs to other carriers (the actual carriers). It still takes responsibility for the delivery of the products to the place of delivery and for any damage that might occur during the transportation. In a through bill of lading, the carrier takes responsibility for the products only up to a specified point (still called the place of delivery) and passes responsibility to a second carrier for the transportation to the final destination.

Multimodal Transport It is the shipment of products by more than one mode of transportation with normally including a sea leg.

National Institute of Standards and Technology It is a USA Department of Commerce agency that also promotes the effective and secure use of cloud computing within organizations.[43]

Negotiability and Transferability In the case of products, commodities, property, and many financial assets, which are transferable from party to party, the general rule of law is that the transferor cannot transfer to the transferee title better than the transferor possesses. A negotiable instrument is an exception to this rule of law. The holder of a negotiable instrument, in the position of being a transferee, is not compromised by a fault in the title of the transferor or any other party.

Negotiable It is the characteristic of a document that enables it to transfer the ownership of money, products, or other items, of the value specified in the document, by endorsement and/or delivery of the document. Checks, drafts, promissory notes, bonds, stock certificates, bills of lading, and warehouse receipts are examples of documents often issued in negotiable form.

Negotiable Instrument It is a written order or an unconditional promise to pay a fixed sum of money on demand or at a future date. A negotiable instrument can be transferred from one party to another by endorsement. Once the instrument is transferred, the holder obtains full legal title to the instrument. Examples also include bills of exchange, promissory notes, checks, drafts, certificates of deposit, and negotiable bills of lading.

Negotiating Bank It is the bank to which letter of credit documents are presented by the beneficiary for the collection of the payment. The name derives from the fact that the negotiating financial institution is normally authorized by the issuing financial institution to negotiate documents. It may or may not choose actually to do so. Furthermore, realizing that this financial institution may be authorized to pay or accept drafts, rather than negotiate them, UCP500 now uses the term nominated financial institution rather than negotiating financial institution.[44] Unless otherwise instructed, negotiating financial institutions in North America generally examine the documents for discrepancies before forwarding them to the issuing financial institution. It is properly viewed as a service separate from negotiating and is not necessary when negotiating with recourse.

Net Stable Fund Ratio It is a significant component of the Basel III reforms. It requires financial institutions to maintain a stable funding profile in relation to their on- and off-balance sheet activities. In this way, it reduces the likelihood to lose a financial institution's liquidity position in a way that could increase the risk of its failure and potentially leads to broader systemic stress.

Node In this book, it is a computer running a blockchain protocol[45] and holding a copy of the blockchain.[46]

Non-Cumulative Revolving Letter of Credit It is a revolving letter of credit that does not permit the vendor to carry over any amounts not drawn upon in previous periods.

Non-Notification (or Confidential) Factoring It is a form of factoring in which the assignment has not been notified to the debtor. The vendor performs the sales administration and collects the receivables as an agent for the factor.

Non-Recourse Factoring It is a form of factoring in which the factor offers a credit protection service and therefore the credit risk of debtor failure remains with the factor.

Norms In this book, they are informal guidelines about what is considered normal (what is correct or incorrect) organizational behavior in a particular group or social units.[47] It is an alternative to the word compulsory standardization.

Notice of Acknowledgment It is a notice issued by a debtor to a finance provider in which the debtor acknowledges and recognizes that the debt (accounts payable) has been assigned to or purchased by the finance provider.

Notice of Assignment It is a notice which can be issued by the factor (or the invoice discounter) or by the assignor to a debtor and which informs the debtor that its related debts payable has been assigned to the factor.

Notify Party It is a party to be notified by the carrier of the arrival of the products or the delivery of the service at their destination. Normally the notify party is the buyer and/or the buyer's agent for clearing products through customs.

Novation It is the act of replacing one party in a contract with another, which may include the exchange of new debts or obligations for older existing ones with the consent of all the affected parties. Unlike an assignment, obligations and rights may be assumed or exchanged, depending on the jurisdiction.

Obligor It is a synonym for any debtor or creditor under a financial obligation. It is also more specifically employed as a term for a party which is obligated under payment facility such as a negotiable instrument. In forfeiting, such a party is also known as the primary obligor. The underlying obligation may be supported by guarantees and similar arrangements provided by other parties, which create other (secondary) obligors.

Obligor Bank In a bank payment obligation (BPO) transaction, the obligor financial institution is the issuer of a BPO and is obligated to settle it at maturity when the BPO conditions have been fulfilled through a data match.

Ocean Bill of Lading It is another term for the bill of lading. It refers to the transportation via ship when over an ocean.

Off-Balance Sheet It is a term used to describe an asset, debt, or financial transaction that is not reflected as such in the balance sheet of the obligor. Off-balance sheet transactions are subject to the local and then current accounting rules.

Open Account It refers to trade transactions between a vendor and a buyer where transactions are not supported by any financial institutions or documentary trade instrument issued on behalf of the buyer or vendor. The buyer is directly responsible for meeting the payment obligations in relation to the underlying transactions. Where trading parties supply and purchase products and services on the basis of open-account terms, an invoice is normally raised and the buyer pays within an agreed timeframe.

Opportunity Cost It is the potential benefit that is lost or sacrificed when the selection of one course of action makes it necessary to forgo an alternative course of action.

Order to Cash Cycle It represents the process steps and the time interval between receipt of an order, the manufacturing or fulfillment process, the delivery, and the receipt of cash from the customer.

Organization In this book, it indicates a company, a public institution, either central or local, a department, or a nonprofit entity.

Output It is the result of a product or system processes. The final output is normally a product, a service, or an initiative.

Outsourcing This term defines an operation by which an organization relies on an outside vendor for the management of a specific process or activity already operational within the organization (normally non-core processes or sub-processes such as the sourcing of indirect materials, administrative management, and so on).

Outstanding It is a receivable which has not yet been paid.

Packing Credit or Packing Finance It is a synonym for pre-shipment finance. It owes its origin to traditional trade finance practices by which a vendor is able to draw down funds under a letter of credit to prepare products for shipment.

Packing List It is an enumeration of the contents of a particular pack or crate indicating the quantity, weight, and measurements of the contents.

Party It is an entity that becomes engaged in a financial or commercial transaction, whether a natural or legal person such as an organization, corporation, financial institution, unincorporated organization or government organization, or not-for-profit entity.

Payables Finance It is a form of financial instrument provided through a buyer-led program within which the vendors in the buyer's value network are able to access finance by means of receivables sale.

Payback Period It is the length of time required for the recovery of an investment or a loan.

Payment It is a means of settlement for a commercial or another obligation, such as a digital credit transfer, direct debit, credit or debit card payment, wire transfer, automated clearing house (ACH) payment, check, or cash. The payment is completed when good funds are received by the creditor.

Payment Terms It is the specific term which determines which payments of an invoice are due. Normally, it is stated on each invoice or in the contract/order.

Peer-to-Peer Lending It is the practice of lending money to unrelated individuals, or peers, without going through a traditional financial intermediary, such as a financial institution or other traditional financial institution.

Performance Bond It is a bond issued at the request of one party to a contract in favor of the other party to the contract to protect the other party against loss in the event of default on the contract by the requesting party. The bonding agent may undertake to fulfill the contract or may simply undertake to pay a specific amount in monetary damages. A standby letter of credit or demand guarantee is often used as a performance bond with the latter characteristics.

Performance Risk It is the risk associated with a party's ability to meet its obligations under a contract, in particular, to procure, manufacture, and ship products, or provide services in a timely fashion according to quality standards.

Permission-Less Blockchain It is a blockchain that anyone can read, send transactions to, have their transactions included if valid and take part in the consensus process to add new blocks.

Physical Procurement It is a term used to describe the totality of the organizations, systems, people, activities, information, and resources involved in moving a product or service from a vendor to a buyer.

Platform In this book, a platform provides the infrastructure and rules for a marketplace. It is owned by a proprietor. It has a provider which provides an information and communication technology solution and its surrounding management, bringing together producers and purchasers. The participants in a platform ecosystem, such as the producers or the purchasers, may shift rapidly over time from one role to another.

Pledge It is an item of value that is given or held as security for the fulfillment of a debt or obligation.

Policy It is a guideline developed by an organization to govern its actions. It defines the limits within which decisions must be made.

Political Risk It is a risk in the sale of products that the government in the buyer's country may take some actions that prevents the buyer from paying. This covers possibilities such as foreign exchange controls and non-payment due to war or insurrection.

Port-to-Port Bill of Lading It is the bill of lading covering shipment by sea only. The shipper/vendor is responsible for transporting the products to the port of loading. The buyer is responsible for picking the products up at the port of discharge. Multimodal, rather than port-to-port, bills of lading should generally be used for containerized shipments and other shipments where the place of receipt and/or the place of delivery is inland.

Post-Dated Check It is a check bearing a date in the future that can only be cashed on or after that future date.

Post-Shipment Finance It is a generic expression denoting all the procurement finance instruments that are employed once the shipment has occurred. It normally includes all forms of receivables finance and the inventory finance.

Pre-export Finance It is a synonym for pre-shipment finance, where the products or services are destined for a buyer in an export market

Pre-export Financing It is a specific form of working capital lending in which the borrower is given funds to obtain or manufacture products that have been ordered by a buyer in another country. As such, financing is normally earmarked to individual sales, documentation of each sale must be provided to the lender, often in the form of a letter of credit with proceeds assigned to the lender.

Preferred Shares They are shares of an organization that have some priority over the other shares in terms of the payment of dividends or the distribution of assets upon liquidation.

Prepaid Expenses They are expenses for products or services that are paid in advance.

Pre-payment or Prepayment It is a payment in advance (prior to maturity) of all or part of the purchase price of the receivables assigned (the balance being paid when the debt is paid by the buyer). It is the repayment of a loan or financial obligation before its maturity date or the payment in advance for products or other contractual liability.

Presenting Bank In a draft collection transaction, it is the financial institution that contacts the drawee/buyer of products, for acceptance and/or payment.

Pre-Shipment Credit Cover It covers the cost of production for products and services in a procurement contract up to the maximum of the contract value.

Pre-shipment Finance It is the financing advanced to the vendor to support the costs of activities undertaken prior to the shipment of the products (that is, purchase of inputs and components, payment of salaries, wages and overhead, and so on) and to provide it with additional working capital. Pre-shipment financing may take the form of a short-term loan, an overdraft, a cash credit, and so on.

Primary Forfeiter It is the forfeiter which first purchases a financial instrument or claim from an initial vendor.

Primary Market It is the marketplace where issuers of debts or other financial obligations deal directly with finance providers to raise funds. This can be described as origination. It is contrasted with the secondary market where financial assets are traded and purchased by other finance providers or investors. This is a defined term in the Uniform Rules for Forfeiting.[48]

Prime Bank It is one of the top 25 world financial institutions. These are trusted financial institutions which are preferred (or in most cases even mandatory) in commodity trading.

Principal It is the party entrusting a draft and/or documents to a financial institution for the collection of the payment. Normally, it is the vendor of the products.

Private Blockchain It is a blockchain controlled by someone or something such as an organization.

Problem It is the cause that creates an incident. Incidents that cannot be resolved due to the lack of an available solution, as well as repeated incidents related to a known issue ("known problem/error"), pass through the process of problem management. A workaround could remediate the problem, before finding the root causes and resolving them completely.

Process It is a set of interrelated activities that transform a set of inputs on one or more results with a prefixed objective. Sometimes the process is identified with or supported by a system or outsourced to a third party.

Process Control It is the act of getting and keeping a process stable. In fact, the stability is not always a natural state for a process.

Process Improvement It is a continuous effort to learn the causes and effects in a process to reduce its complexity and its variations and cut its cycle time. The process gets better by removing the incorrect causes of waste.

Process Management It is a method used to optimize the organization as a system, to determine which processes need to be improved and/or controlled, to define priorities, and to encourage the leadership to initiate and sustain process improvement efforts.

Procurement In this book, it refers to the initiation, design, development, acquisition, logistics of products and services for the organization. Procurement generalizes further the management of the value network, also including strategic aspects, internal and external to the organization.

Procurement Finance It is the chain of financial processes, risk and liquidity management decisions, events and activities that provide financial support in part or in full to the procurement processes.

Procurement Transaction It is the procurement of products and services from external vendors. When accepted by the vendor, it forms the basis of a contract or an order binding on both parties. It is also called an order procurement transaction.

Procure-to-Pay Cycle or Process It represents the process steps and time interval between the issue of a purchase order, the delivery of products and services, the receipt of invoice, and the payment to the vendor.

Product Owner It is the person who is responsible to make the best use of the team's capacity working on the same process, by maximizing the process value. Responsibilities of the product owner include also maintaining and prioritizing the content of the items backlog.

Profit and Loss Statement (P&L) It is a financial statement that summarizes the revenues and costs incurred during a specific period of time, normally a fiscal quarter or 12 months. These records provide information that shows the ability of an organization to generate margin by increasing revenue and reducing costs. The P&L statement is also known as a "statement of profit and loss", an "income statement", or an "income and expense statement".

Program It is a set of projects with similar objectives. The improvement of systems installed in different subsidiaries of the same group is an example.

Progress Payment It is one in a series of payments made at stages in the performance of a contract. Examples are payments made during the various stages of a construction or the delivery of a service.

Promissory Note It is an unconditional written promise, issued and signed by the debtor, to pay on demand or at a fixed or determinable future date an agreed amount of money to the order of a specified person or to the note's bearer. Promissory notes are transferred by endorsement.

Proof of Funds It is a proof obtained by conducting a soft discovery on the buyer's accounts. A vendor might require a proof of funds before they will proceed with negotiating a product sale.

Proof-of-Stake It is a consensus algorithm that uses ownership of the blockchain's currency as a scarce resource to ensure security and integrity of the blockchain. This is also in limited supply, and for an actor to be able to make changes not following the rules of the chain, they would need to own more than half of the coins.

Proof-of-Work It is a consensus algorithm that uses work as a scarce resource. In the case of the Bitcoin, this means computational power and the proof is in the form of solving a hash puzzle. The nodes compete in solving this puzzle by finding a specific number, the nonce,[49] so that when one concatenates the block header and use the hash function on it, the value of the hash falls within a certain range.[50]

Protest In a draft collection transaction, it is the formal legal process of registering that payment or acceptance of the draft has been demanded by the drawee which has refused to pay or accept the draft.

Public Blockchain It is a blockchain that anyone can read.

Public-/Private-Key Cryptography It is the method by which a public identity is created with an associated private one. In the blockchain solutions, this is used for creating public addresses for sending currency and to verify signatures made by the private key. One needs to use the private key to make a transaction.[51]

Purchase Order It is a buyer-generated document or message that authorizes a purchase.

Purchase Order Commitment to Pay It is a commitment issued by a financial institution in favor of a vendor that once products relating to a specific purchase order have been received by the buyer, the vendor will be paid. It is a form of payment guarantee.

Purchase Order Finance It is a synonym for pre-shipment finance where reliance is placed on a purchase order issued by a reputable buyer.

Purchase Price It is the amount payable by a factor or a receivable buyer to an assignor for an assigned receivable.

Qualification of Vendors According to the American Society for Quality, the vendor qualification is "the process of demonstrating whether an entity is capable of fulfilling the specified requirement".[52] In the process, a vendor is evaluated to determine whether or not it meets the basic qualification requirements and the possible standards of the merchandize group. It is necessary to evaluate also if the vendor can provide the services required by the specific organization that is doing the evaluation.

Qualification Procedure It is the set of all the measures to be undertaken and the decisions to be taken—by the use of the procedure defined by the organization procurement—to collect and analyze information, assess the eligibility/ineligibility of the organizations seeking qualification, record and disseminate the outcome of the qualification process to the departments involved, and notify the applicant companies of this outcome. The process involves, for each organization, the assessment of the legal, economic-financial, organizational-managerial, technical-production, and sustainability aspects, as well as the payment of the qualification fee when required.

Quality The classical definition of quality is "fitness to use".[53] It is a concept not easily defined, because there are several variants, at times specified by an adjective or specification added to the name. In general, one can say that the quality is customer satisfaction profitably for the organization.

Quality Assurance It is the set of planned and systematic actions necessary to provide adequate trust that a product or service meets certain quality requirements.

Ready Willing and Able It is a document which is issued by the buyer's financial institution. With this document, the financial institution confirms that its customer has the sufficient funds in its possession and is willing and able to engage in the contract.

Real-Time Gross Settlement (RTGS) Systems They are fund transfer systems designed to move high-value and wholesale payments between financial institutions instantly. RTGS are usually controlled by the central bank of a nation. Payments made via the RTGS are settled as soon as they are processed, and once processed, payments are final and irrevocable. Since with these payments there are high values involved, they do not need to be netted or bundled, meaning that the transaction is settled on a one-to-one basis in real time.

Reassignment It is the transfer of an assigned receivable from the original assignee back to the original assignor.

Receivable It is the money owed by the customers to an organization that the organization expects to collect on some future date.

Receivables Discounting It is a form of receivables purchase, flexibly applied, in which the vendors of products and services sell individual or multiple receivables (represented by outstanding invoices) to a finance provider at a discount.

Receivables Finance It is a collective expression for the various instruments of receivables purchase and loan or advances against receivables. It is used as a synonym for such individual instruments.

Receivables Purchase It is a convenient intermediate category of procurement finance instruments, which includes procurement finance instruments such as receivables discounting, forfeiting, factoring, and payables finance. It has a number of synonyms and variations.

Receivables Purchase Agreement It is an agreement between a finance provider and a customer (vendor) to cover the purchase of individuals or a portfolio of receivables.

Recipient Bank It is the bank which receives a bank payment obligation (BPO) in its favor and which on meeting the conditions specified in the BPO is entitled to receive money from the obligor bank on behalf of a customer.

Recourse Factoring It is a form of factoring in which the credit risk on the debtor remains with the assignor. The part of the receivable retained by the factor covers specific risks such as dilution.

Red Clause It is a clause (originally typed in red) added to a letter of credit authorizing the advising/negotiating financial institution to make an advance payment to the beneficiary (vendor) before the actual shipment to the buyer. The advance may be up to 100 percent of the export contract value and may be used by the vendor to purchase the inputs or the activities necessary for manufacturing or shipping the products. The red clause credits are used primarily when the buyer has an agent in the exporting country. To finance its purchases, the buyer may arrange for the opening of a red clause letter of credit. Negotiations of red clause credits are limited to the financial institution making the advances to assure that revenues from the shipment are used to repay the advances made.

Reimbursing Bank In a letter of credit transaction, it is the financial institution with which the issuing financial institution maintains an account and which is authorized by the issuing financial institution to charge that account to pay claims received from the negotiating financial institution for documents that have been presented.

Remitting Bank In a draft collection transaction, it is the first financial institution in the chain of collection, the principal's or vendor's financial institution.

Reporting It consists of supplying and updating representative data and indicators whose degree of details tends to vary depending on the person or organization for whom or for which they are intended. Reporting can be based on the so-called triple-bottom line principle.[54] Such name is due to the metaphorical addition of environmental and social dimensions to the classic profit bottom line (economic dimension).

Request for Qualification It is the request accompanied by all the information and documentation necessary to demonstrate and specify that a vendor meets the qualification requirements.

Rescheduling It is the process of drawing up a new principal repayment schedule, thereby readjusting the terms of the loan, either by a reduction of interest rates and/or an extension of the duration of the loan.

Reserve/Retention It is the part of a receivable(s) retained by a factor to cover specific risks such as dilutions.

Restructuring It is the combined process of rescheduling and converting all or part of the existing loan into another type of financing facility.

Retention of Title It is a provision in a contract for the sale of products that the title to the products remains vested in the vendor until certain obligations (normally the payment of the purchase price) are fulfilled by the buyer. It is sometimes called a Romalpa clause in some jurisdictions. It is especially used in Germany.

Return on Equity It is the percentage of earnings on the capital invested by the owners.

Reverse Factoring It is a procurement financial instrument when a finance institution interposes itself between an organization and its vendors and commits to pay the organization's invoices to the vendors at an accelerated rate in exchange for a discount. This is a lower-cost form of financing that accelerates accounts receivable receipts for vendors. It is a synonym for payables finance.

Revised Directive on Payment Services (or Payment Services Directive II) (PSD2) It is built on the existing PSD and has been developed to make certain provisions in PSD clearer, as well as putting emphasis on further opening up the payments industry for third-party organizations and non-banks, to increase competition.[55]

Revocable Letter of Credit It is the letter of credit that can be amended or canceled at any time without notice to or consent of the beneficiary. A letter of credit that is subject to the UCP500 or to USA law is revocable only if it clearly states this on the letter of credit.

Revolving Facility It is a credit facility that allows an organization to finance its current needs by borrowing from the financial institution, on a short-term basis, up to a certain specified maximum amount. The borrower is privileged to borrow, repay, and borrow again during the specified period.

Revolving Letter of Credit It is the letter of credit that reverts to its original amount at specified intervals, thereby preventing drawing too much in any one period.

Risk It can be defined as "the threat or probability that an action or event will adversely or beneficially affect an organization's ability to achieve its objectives".[56] In simple terms, the risk is the uncertainty of outcome, either from pursuing a future positive opportunity or an existing negative threat in trying to achieve a current objective.

Risk Management It is an iterative process to identify, assess, remediate, accept, and control risks in a systematic, proactive, comprehensive, and cost-effective manner, taking into account the organization, costs, technical aspects, quality, and constraints.[57]

Risk Participation It is an unfunded sub-participation.

Sale and Repurchase (Repo) It is an alternative to a loan by which a finance provider enters into a sale and repurchase agreement for the products or financial assets being financed. The finance provider acquires title to the products or financial assets concerned at the commencement of the transaction and reverses the process at a future date. The parties may include a margin to protect against the diminution in value during the life of the transaction.

Sales Ledger It is a report of outstanding receivables, normally analyzed by debtor balance and debt aging.

Sales Ledger Management It is the process of management of a portfolio of accounts receivable including credit control. Under a factoring agreement, it is common for the factor to take responsibility for the sales ledger management.

Scrum Master It is the profile in an agile management which supports the team in incorporating scrum theory and practices. This role includes the responsibility of protecting the team towards unnecessary interactions with people external to the team.

Secondary Market It is the counterpart of the primary market. In a secondary market, financial assets are traded and purchased by other finance providers or investors, not involved in the primary origination of the transaction.

Securitization It is the process of taking an illiquid asset, or group of assets, such as a portfolio of receivables and, through financial intermediation, transforming them into a security or tradable financial obligation.

Security It is the financing or investment issued by an organization or government agency that denotes an ownership interest and provides evidence of a debt, a right to share in the earnings of the issuer, or a right in the distribution of a property. Securities include bonds, debentures, notes, options, shares (stocks), and warrants but not insurance policies. They may be traded in financial markets such as stock exchanges. Security defines also collaterals used to guarantee the repayment of a debt.

Security Interest It is an interest created by agreement or by operation of law over assets to secure the performance of an obligation. It is normally the payment of a debt. It gives the beneficiary of the security interest certain preferential rights in the disposition of the secured assets.

Security Margin It is a computed deduction from the stated or market value of an asset being financed to allow for the diminution of the value of the asset, while the finance provider is exposed to a borrower or obligor.

Self-Liquidating It is providing enough income to pay off the amount borrowed from financing.

Selling Forward It is the practice of selling foreign currency for a future value date at a price that is fixed and quoted at the present.

SGS Inspection Before the product leaves the port of sale, an inspection can be carried out by the Société Générale de Surveillance (SGS),[58] the world's most respected independent product inspection organization. SGS inspections provide peace of mind for the buyer who can be assured that the product is of a high quality if it is cleared by SGS inspectors.

Shipper's Export Declaration (SED) It is used to control exports and acts as a source document for official US export statistics. SEDs must be prepared for shipments through the US Postal Service when the shipment is valued over USD 500. SEDs are required for shipments not using other carriers, when the value of the commodities, classified under any single Schedule B number, is over USD 2500. SEDs must be prepared, regardless of value, for all shipments requiring an export license or shipped to countries restricted by the Export Administration Regulations. SEDs are prepared by the exporter, or the exporter's agent, and delivered to the exporting carrier (the post office, airline, or maritime organization). The exporting carrier presents the required number of SED copies to the USA Customs Service at the port of export.

Shipper's Indemnity It is the indemnity given by the beneficiary of a letter of credit to the negotiating financial institution to induce payment despite any discrepancies that may exist in the documents.

Shipping Terms It is that part of a contract between a buyer and a vendor that specifies who is responsible for each aspect of shipping the product. This may include responsibility for packing, arranging, and paying for transportation and insurance, clearing customs, and so forth.

Short-Term Loan It is a loan that comes due in one year or less.

Sight It is the time of presentation, as in a draft payable at sight or 90 days after sight.

Sight Draft It is the draft that demands payment at sight, or immediately, as opposed to a time draft, which may be payable for instance 90 days after sight or 30 days after bill of lading date.

Sight Letter of Credit It is a letter of credit that is payable on the sighting of both the letter of credit and necessary documentation as stipulated in the letter of credit.

Silent Confirmation It is the term used for a financial institution's commitment to negotiate documents under a letter of credit without recourse at a future date. A silent confirmation is not a confirmation in the true sense and does not use the word confirm. It is an equivalent form of protection for the beneficiary. The financial institution requires that the letter of credit be negotiable or payable by itself in order to be able to establish holder-in-due-course rights equivalent to those of a confirming financial institution.

Single Euro Payments Area (SEPA) It is a European payment initiative which was introduced in order to establish a single payment market; making it simple and less costly for customers (be them consumers and organizations) to make and receive payments across Europe.[59] SEPA payments are available in 35 countries, and provide cross-border bank transfer capabilities for organizations, vendors, and customers in a way which is equivalent to making a domestic payment.

Smart Contract It is a piece of code on the blockchain, using logical IF/ ELSE statements to stipulate conditions. The conditions are executed without any person or middleman involved. Smart contracts can also be used to transfer funds from one place to another if some criteria are fulfilled.[60]

Society for Worldwide Interbank Financial Telecommunication (Swift) It is a cooperative utility whose objective is to develop standardized messaging and processing of transaction services for financial institutions globally, making global cross-border transfers easier.[61] Swift is the network backbone of the international finance industry. It serves more than 200 countries and territories. Swift payments are a type of international transfer sent via the Swift network. Swift does not facilitate the transfer of funds. Instead, it sends payment orders via its secure and reliable network, which must be then settled by the correspondent accounts that institutions have with each other. When sending or receiving international payments, a Swift code is used to identify a specific bank.

Soft Probe It is a confirmation method used by financial institutions to verify funding for a vendor from a buyer, conducted by the vendor to the buyer's financial institution. Such a discovery is not recorded in the buyer's banking information. Normally, nothing but confirmation or lack of confirmation is recorded by the vendor.

Special Purpose Vehicle/Entity It is a bankruptcy-remote entity that is used to isolate or securitize assets. It has often held the off-balance sheet.[62]

Sprint In agile management, it is a predetermined timeframe of one week or more in which a certain number of activities from the process deliverables backlog are added to the sprint backlog and developed or produced during the sprint.

Standard It is an indication of voluntary or compulsory standardization.

Standby Letter of Credit As opposed to a commercial letter of credit, it is a letter of credit that does not cover the direct purchase of merchandize. It is called with the adjective "standby" since it is often intended to be drawn on only when the applicant for whom it is issued fails to perform an obligation. There is a type of standby letter of credit that is intended to be drawn on, referred to as a direct pay letter of credit. Standby letters of credit are based on the understanding that payment is made against presentation of documents: normally a statement from the vendor indicating that the buyer has not paid for the merchandize/ invoices on the due date.

STEP1 It is a payment service offered by the European Banking Authority (EBA), clearing for small and medium-sized banks for single euro payments of high priority and urgency, processing approximately 20,000 transactions on a daily basis.[63]

STEP2 They are processes for mass retail payments in euros which provide banks across Europe with one channel through which they can send and receive their SEPA credit transfers and SEPA direct debits.[64]

Stop-Supply Letter It is a letter from a vendor to a distributor informing it that supply of products will cease, as a method of protecting the vendor's interests in the event of a distributor being unable to meet its obligations

Structured Trade Finance It is a general expression for the provision of finance for trade, where a variety of structures and techniques, which may include procurement finance instruments, are incorporated into a bespoke transaction or a specific financing solution. Such solutions often involve security being taken over assets, commodities, or commercial off-take contracts

Sub-participation It is an agreement between a finance provider who has incurred or is to incur a financial exposure on, or lend funds to, a debtor or obligor and another finance provider under which the second finance provider either provides funds to the first finance provider to fund that exposure or loan (in the case of a funded sub-participation) or provides a commitment to cover any losses of the first finance provider (in the case of an unfunded sub-participation). Repayment of the second finance provider, in the case of a funded sub-participation, is normally dependent on the receipt of the corresponding amounts by the first finance provider from the debtor or obligor. This may be the case for an unfunded sub-participation. The existence of the second finance provider is normally undisclosed to the debtor or obligor. The second finance provider may, depending on the law governing the sub-participation agreement, receive a derivative interest in the exposure or loan or may simply acquire rights against the first finance provider rather than the debtor or obligor.

Subrogation It is the acquisition of the rights of a creditor by a third party who pays the original creditor.

Supplier Financing It is the arrangement where the vendor of the products allows the buyer an extended period of time after shipment to pay for the products.

Supply Chain Finance It is the portfolio of financing and risks mitigating practices, instruments, and techniques to optimize the management of the working capital and liquidity invested in the value network processes and transactions. It supports the trade and financial flows along end-to-end organization supply and distribution chains, domestically and internationally.

Supply Chain Finance Intermediation Platform It is a technology and organization platform, which brings vendors and buyers of value network financial assets together for the trading and settlement of transactions.

Supply Chain Management It is an integrating function with primary responsibility for linking major organization functions and organization processes within and across companies into a cohesive and high-performing business model.[65] It includes all of the logistics management activities, as well as manufacturing operations. It drives coordination of processes and activities with and across marketing, sales, product design, finance, and information technology.

Supply Chain Services It is a "super-category" or umbrella term used by the finance providers to describe their organization lines, organizational units, and activities. Supply chain financial services include a range of services such as purchase order management and digital invoicing, payments, and cash management and supply chain finance.

Sustainable Supply Chain Management It refers to the task for companies to extend sustainability-sound practices along with their supply chains.[66] For the purposes of sustainable development, tools such as the GRI (Global Reporting Initiative) enable a standardized method agreed on at the international level.[67]

Syndication It is the process of selling legal or economic interests in loans or other payment obligations to an investor or group of investors by the original organizer of such financing. Syndication may be built into the arrangement of the financing or take place subsequently, but normally promptly, thereafter. The investors may all be parties to a single agreement including the borrower or may be parties to a separate agreement not involving the borrower. The arranger of the financing is normally an agent for the investors.

System It is "A network of interacting components that cooperate to achieve the objectives of the system".[68] It can be the organization which includes customers, vendors, and the flow of materials and information.

Telegraphic Transfer It is a mean of remitting money where the financial institution, at the request and risk of its customer, sends a message (for instance, a cable) with the necessary details to its foreign agent who will act on the instructions. The transfer is normally made in the currency of the payee's country. The telegraph is now replaced by modern communication tools.

Temporary Grouping of Companies It designates a set of contractors, or vendors, or service providers, established to participate in the procedure for awarding a specific contract, by lodging a unique offer. If the offer is accepted, the grouping will manage the delivery of the solution.

Tenor It is the time at which a draft shows it is payable, such as, at sight, 60 days after the bill of lading date.

Three-Corner Model It is a situation where two trading parties are using the services of the same financial institution or service provider and use its services to carry out intermediation functions of various kinds

Throughput It is a metric on how quickly the service responds.

Time Draft It is the draft that demands payment at a specified future date rather than immediately upon presentation.

Timestamp By timestamping a file, for instance through the blockchain, it is possible to prove that the file existed at a certain point in time. A hash of the file is included in the block as a transaction. When somebody at a later stage wants to prove the existence of this file at the time of the block's creation, he/she simply regenerates the hash.[69]

Token It is created through smart contracts and represents an asset on the blockchain solution.[70]

Tolling It is a process by which raw materials or components are submitted to a third-party refining or manufacturing process prior to onward sale.

Total Cost Management (TCM) It is an organization philosophy of managing all organization resources amid the activities that consume those resources. Managing costs in a TCM approach means focusing on the activities and the events, the circumstances, or the conditions that cause or drive these cost-consuming activities.

Trade and Export Loans It is a general expression for loans made in the context of procurement-related financing. They are not defined as a specific procurement financial instrument, given the generality of the circumstances in which they are granted.

Trade Credit It is credit given by the vendor to the buyer. Compared to a financial institution loan, a trade credit is easier to arrange. It is often the cheapest form of credit for the buyer and the vendor since it is based primarily on mutual trust and interest.

Trade Credit Insurance It is an insurance policy and a risk management product offered by insurance companies and governmental export credit agencies to organizations wishing to protect their accounts receivable from loss due to credit. It is also called business credit insurance, export credit insurance, or credit insurance.

Trade Finance It is an umbrella term used by the finance providers to describe their organization lines, organizational units, and activities. Trade finance is used as a generic term for a range of traditional trade financial instruments and it is evolving in procurement finance. It is the financing of international or domestic trade. It can include letters of credit, guarantees, collections, bills of exchange, factoring, forfeiting, or export credit.

Transaction It is the action of executing a function or an application. An example of a transaction is the execution of a purchase order at the point of sale and the processing of authorization and clearing messages. In the case of Bitcoins, the transactions record monetary parameters. In other blockchains, it can also be the results of smart contracts.[71]

Transaction Fee It is a cost which is charged when sending and receiving money, normally, when funds are being transferred nationally or internationally.

Transaction Matching Application (TMA) In a BPO transaction, the TMA is the matching engine which compares submitted datasets with the baseline and declares a match or non-match. Swift's Trade Services Utility (TSU)[72] is an example of a TMA.

Trans-European Automated Real-Time Gross Settlement Express Transfer System (TARGET2) It is a real-time gross settlement system owned and operated by the Eurosystem.[73] TARGET2 handles mostly large-value central bank transactions across 20 euro area central banks (including the European Central Bank (ECB)), as well as 5 central banks from non-euro area countries which include Bulgaria, Croatia, Denmark, Poland, and Romania, which are made instantly and with immediate finality.

Transfer of Title It is a wide expression often used in relation to the transfer of real property as well as products and financial assets. In procurement finance, the transfers of title are achieved principally by assignment, assignment of rights, or endorsement.

Transferable Documentary Credit It is a documentary credit where the vendor allows the paying financial institution to pay all or part of the proceeds of the sale to another beneficiary.

Transferable Letter of Credit It is a type of letter of credit that names a middleman as beneficiary and allows him/her to give another party, the actual vendor, certain rights to present documents and receive payment under the letter of credit. The transfer must be done by a financial institution authorized to do so by the issuing financial institution and involves notifying the transferee (called the second beneficiary) of what documents he/she must present. The documents must be the same as those required in the letter of credit. The price of the products may be reduced. The middleman's name may be required to be listed in the transferee's invoices as the buyer, thereby allowing the middleman to substitute invoices at a higher price and receive the difference without disclosing the name of the actual end-buyer. The transferring financial institution is not obligated to pay documents presented under the transfer. Such obligation remains with the issuing financial institution.

True Sale It is an accounting and legal expression showing that a financial asset or negotiable instrument has been sold by one party to another in the sense of no longer being recorded in the balance sheet of the vendor. It is recorded on the balance sheet of the buyer. When this occurs effectively, the buyer will not be affected by any insolvency proceedings subsequently initiated against the vendor. It is not restricted or does not provide an absolute title to the asset in question. In this sense, it is different from secured or collateralized lending. The true sale is an important concept. It underlies many securitization and financial transactions. Some procurement finance instruments, such as forfeiting and factoring, aim to achieve the true sale.

Trust It is the ability for two parties to define a relationship with a formal authentication of the two parties.

Turnover It is the total value of all receivables assigned/sold to the factor by the assignors during the reporting period.

Two-Factor System It is a system by which a factor uses, by sub-assignment, a factor in another country (correspondent factor) to collect the receivables of an assignor exporting to a customer in that country with or without credit protection. The relationship between the correspondent factors is normally governed by an interfactor agreement.

Uncommitted Facility It is a credit or loan facility, which is uncommitted as to availability or time period.

Unconfirmed Letter of Credit It is a letter of credit that has not been confirmed under specific conditions. It is formally recorded as an obligation of a finance provider. The committed nature of the facility requires a more stringent credit assessment than in the case of an uncommitted facility.

Uniform Commercial Code (UCC) It is the USA statute covering the rights and obligations of the various parties involved in the purchase and sale of products.[74] The UCC includes coverage of drafts and other negotiable instruments, documents of title, transfers of funds between financial institutions, and security interests in assets as well as draft collections (in Article 4) and letters of credit (in Article 5).

Uniform Customs and Practice (UCP) It is the abbreviation for Uniform Customs and Practice for Documentary Credits.[75] The 1993 revision is referred to as UCP500 being the publication number 500 of the International Chamber of Commerce.

Uniform Customs and Practice for Documentary Credits It is the international standards of the letter of credit practice established for bankers by the International Chamber of Commerce.[76] The UCP is constantly being revised to keep up with changing practices. Although the UCP defines rights and obligations of the various parties in a letter of credit transaction, it is not a law. A letter of credit is subject to the UCP only to the extent shown in the letter of credit itself.

Uniform Rules for Collections It is the international standards of draft collection practice established for bankers by the International Chamber of Commerce.[77] The Uniform Rules are not laws.[78] They are more properly viewed as a handbook for financial institutions used to establish the common understanding of terminology and expectations.

Uniform Rules for Forfeiting (URF800) It is a set of standard rules for the primary and secondary forfeiting markets published by the ICC in collaboration with International Trade and Forfaiting Association (ITFA)[79] in effect since January 1, 2013.[80]

Unsecured It describes a situation when the lender has no security other than a legally enforceable commitment by the borrower to repay the loan.

Value It is defined by the customer and the end user. Conceptually, it is the relationship between benefits and cost/damage of a product or service. It is expressed in terms of a product/service ability to meet the required needs at a given price and at a given time. It is also possible to talk of the value perceived by the customer as all the features of the product/service that the customer deems necessary and valuable. Any activity that consumes resources (including time) and does not create value is waste (*muda* in Japanese).

Value Network It is a set of activities required to design, order, transport, manufacture, and supply (or provide in the case of a service) a given product. These activities cover the entire crossing of the product/service organization to the end customer. Objective analysis of the value network is to classify tasks into categories. The value network can be seen as the set of activities that brings value to the customer (and indirectly to the organization). It is a generalization of the supply chain.

Vendor It is a person or an organization that provides products or services for use by the process that is designed.

Vendor (Forfeiting) It is an initial vendor and any subsequent vendor of the payment claim in the secondary market.

Vendor Credit It is a financing arranged by a vendor with or without a finance provider to enable it to provide credit terms to a buyer of its products or services. Normally the buyer pays a portion of the contract value in cash and issues a promissory note or accepts a draft as evidence of its obligation to pay the balance over a period of time. The vendor thus accepts a deferred payment from the buyer. It may be able to obtain cash payment by discounting or selling the draft or promissory notes created with its financial institution.

Vendor Payments It is a synonym for payables finance. It denotes the idea that payables finance can be described as offering early payment of an invoice to a vendor.

Vendor Rating It is the process that appraises the performance of vendors/contractors qualified to perform the jobs awarded to them.

Vendor-Centric It is a description of a procurement finance transaction, where the origination takes place through a relationship with a vendor of products and services.

Vendor-Managed Inventory It is a family of business models and financial instruments in which the buyer of a product provides certain information to a vendor of that product. The vendor takes full responsibility for maintaining an agreed inventory of the material or components, normally at the buyer's consumption location (such as a store or a factory). It is analogous to the holding of consignment inventory.

Verification It is a service offered by the factor/financier to establish the validity of a debt/receivable before its due payment date.

Virtual Currency It is a type of unregulated, digital money, which is issued and normally controlled by its developers. It is used and accepted among the members of a specific virtual community.

Wallet In terms of cryptocurrencies, it is the software that stores public and private keys and interacts with blockchains. It is used for storing, sending, and receiving cryptocurrencies.[81] Tokens can be stored in some wallets as well.[82]

Warehouse Finance It is a synonym for inventory finance. This expression derives from the fact that the inventory being financed is normally located in a warehouse or in similar conditions.

Warehouse Receipt It is a document that provides proof of ownership of commodities or products that are stored in a warehouse, vault, or depository for safekeeping. Warehouse receipts may be negotiable or non-negotiable. Negotiable warehouse receipts allow transfer of ownership of that commodity without having to deliver the physical commodity or products. The status of and then nature and scope of the obligations, arising under a warehouse receipt or its equivalent, varies according to the jurisdiction.

Warranty It is generally a guarantee or promise which provides assurance by one party to another party that specific facts or conditions are true or will happen in relation to products and services or an obligation to perform.

Whole Turnover It is a provision in factoring, where all the receivables generated by an organization are assigned to the factor.

With and Without Recourse In the case of "with recourse", the finance provider relies on the vendor (of a receivable or claim) for any shortfall in the event of non-payment. In a "without recourse" facility or agreement, the finance provider relieves the vendor of any further liability for the debt and accepts the entire credit risk of non-payment itself. Even where without recourse facilities are provided in respect of the credit risk, it is likely that limited recourse to the vendor is maintained for warranties given in respect of, or disputes arising out of, the quality of products, fraud, and the correctness of the transactions.

With Banking Coordinates (ICPO) It is an ICPO which includes the organization's financial institution details in order for the vendor to conduct a soft discovery on their accounts for the vendor to satisfy himself/herself that there are sufficient funds in place to cover the cost of the purchase.

Working Capital It is the difference between an organization's current assets and current liabilities. It is the capital needed to finance the operating cycle of an organization (for instance, payment of employees, vendors, tax authorities, and so on). More precisely, it is the part of the current assets that is not financed by the resources generated by the operating activities.

Working Capital Services It is not normally treated as a procurement finance instrument but as a "super-category" or umbrella term used by finance providers to describe their organization lines, organizational units, and activities. Working capital services normally include short-term working capital related financing such as many procurement finance instruments and related transaction financial institutions services.

Yield It is the income produced by an investment. This could be expressed as a percentage. It can be paid at fixed intervals (annually, semiannually, or quarterly). There are different types of yields: current yield and yield to maturity.

Notes

1. The definitions in this glossary are synthetic and therefore necessarily not very accurate. Please refer to the text for a more proper presentation. This glossary includes only a few terms on the basis of the possible need to find a rapid clarification in the course of reading this book. The definitions used are drawn and modified by the author from a variety of sources, including definitions already used in official publications, from other sources defining terms commonly experienced in business, and expressions defined by the author of this document as a guide to understanding. Some sources for the definitions included are (All Accessed July 10, 2018):

   www.cips.org/Documents/CIPSAWhitePapers/2006/Definition_of_Procurement.pdf

   euf.eu.com/glossary-and-translator.html

   SMEs, E.X.P.O.R.T.I.N.G. (2009). *How to access Trade Finance. A guide for exporting SMEs*, International Trade Centre, Genève, CH.

supplychainfinanceforum.org/glossary/
www.iccgermany.de/fileadmin/user_upload/Content/Banktechnik_und_-praxis/Standard_Definitions_for_Techniques_of_Supply_Chain_Finance_Global_SCF_Forum_2016.pdf
businessdocbox.com/Logistics/70918884-Import-export-terminology.html
www.bankingcircle.com/payments-terminology-acronyms-glossary www.crossoverlending.com/glossary.html
www.linkedin.com/pulse/international-trade-glossary-terms-zahira-oubaiche/www.umts-forum.org/glossary.asp?id=180, 18.05.2005,
euf.eu.com/what-is-euf/objectives/glossary-on-factoring-and-commercial-finance.html
iccwbo.org/content/uploads/sites/3/2016/11/SCF-Techniques-Draft-version-03112015.pdf
cdn.iccwbo.org/content/uploads/sites/3/2017/01/ICC-Standard-Definitions-for-Techniques-of-Supply-Chain-Finance-Global-SCF-Forum-2016.pdf.

2. Madeira, A. (2018). *What Are Atomic Swaps?* www.cryptocompare.com/coins/guides/what-are-atomic-swaps/, Accessed 24 June 2018.
3. Salinger, F. R. (2006). *Factoring: the law and practice of invoice finance.* Sweet & Maxwell, London, UK.
4. Härle, P., Lüders, E., Pepanides, T., Pfetsch, S., Poppensieker, T., & Stegemann, U. (2010). Basel III and European banking: Its impact, how banks might respond, and the challenges of implementation. *EMEA Banking*, 16–17.
5. Nakamoto, S. (2008). *Bitcoin: A Peer-to-Peer Electronic Cash System.* bitcoin.org/bitcoin.pdf, Accessed 28 June 2018.
6. Sikorski, J. J., Haughton, J. & Kraft, M. (2017). Blockchain technology in the chemical industry: Machine-to-machine electricity market. *Applied Energy*, 195, 234–246.
7. Xu, X., Weber, I., Staples, M., Zhu, L., Bosch, J., Bass, L., Pautasso, C. & Rimba, P. A. (2017). Taxonomy of Blockchain-Based Systems for Architecture Design. *2017 IEEE International Conference on Software Architecture (ICSA)*, 3–7 April 2017 2017 Gothenburg. IEEE, 243–252.
8. Osterwalder, A., & Pigneur, Y. (2010). *Business model generation: a handbook for visionaries, game changers, and challengers.* John Wiley & Sons, Hoboken, NJ.
9. Sikorski, J. J., Haughton, J. & Kraft, M. (2017). Blockchain technology in the chemical industry: Machine-to-machine electricity market. *Applied Energy*, 195, 234–246
10. https://www.cls-group.com/about-us. Accessed 09 August 2018.

11. Sikorski, J. J., Haughton, J. & Kraft, M. (2017). Blockchain technology in the chemical industry: Machine-to-machine electricity market. *Applied Energy*, 195, 234–246.
12. Ravall, S. (2016). *Decentralized Applications: Harnessing Bitcoin's Blockchain Technology*, O'Reilly Media, Sebastopol, CA.
13. ec.europa.eu/info/business-economy-euro/banking-and-finance/consumer-finance-and-payments/payment-services/single-euro-payments-area-sepa_en. Accessed 29 July 2018.
14. Swan, M. 2017. Anticipating the Economic Benefits of Blockchain. *Technology Innovation Management Review*, 7, 6–13.
15. www.tradefinance.training/blog/articles/urc-522-key-concepts/. Accessed 28 June 2018.
16. International Chamber of Commerce (2006). *ICC Uniform Customs and Practice for Documentary Credits – UCP 600*. ICC Publication No. 600E, 2006 Edition.
17. www.sc.com/hk/business-banking-sme/_document/en/terms-conditions/general_trade_terms.pdf, Accessed 20 March 2018. iccwbo.org/global-issues-trends/banking-finance/global-rules/, Accessed 20 March 2017
18. eur-lex.europa.eu/legal-content/EN/ALL/?uri=celex%3A32009L0110. Accessed 09 August 2018.
19. Leon, A. (2014). *Enterprise resource planning*. McGraw-Hill Education, New York City, NY.
20. Ethereum Community. (2016). *Frequently Asked Questions* ethdocs.org/en/latest/frequently-asked-questions/frequently-asked-questions.html-where-do-the-contracts-reside. Accessed 28 June 2018.
21. www.ebaclearing.eu/services/euro1/overview/. Accessed 09 August 2018.
22. www.cen.eu/Pages/default.aspx. Accessed 08 July 2018.
23. euf.eu.com/. Accessed 08 July 2018.
24. International Chamber of Commerce (ICC) (2010). *Incoterms® 2010 English Edition*. ICC Publication No. 715E, 2010 Edition.
25. www.investopedia.com/terms/e/export-credit-agency.asp. Accessed 8 July 2018.
26. fci.nl/about-factoring/legal-basics-of-international-factoring.pdf. Accessed 28 June 2018.
27. store.iccwbo.org/icc-uniform-rules-for-forfeiting-urf-800. Accessed 09 August 2018.
28. www.iso.org/member/2176.html. Accessed 29 July 2018.
29. fci.nl/about-factoring/legal-basics-of-international-factoring.pdf. Accessed 10 August 2018.
30. The Linux Foundation. (2018). *About Hyperledger.* The Linux Foundation. www.hyperledger.org/about. Accessed 28 June 2018.

31. International Chamber of Commerce (ICC) (2010). *Incoterms® 2010 English Edition*. ICC Publication No. 715E, 2010 Edition
32. Jaffe, J. 2018. *Initial coin offerings, explained* [Online]. cnet. www.cnet.com/how-to/initial-coin-offerings-explained/ Accessed 28 June 2018.
33. International Chamber of Commerce (ICC) (2010). *Incoterms® 2010 English Edition*. ICC Publication No. 715E, 2010 Edition
34. www.factoringcompanyguide.com/factoring-organizations/factors-chain-international-international-factors-group/. Accessed 28 June 2018.
35. www.factoring.org. Accessed 10 August 2018.
36. Itfa.org. Accessed 10 August 2018.
37. www.ifc.org/, Accessed 10 August 2018.
38. Thani, N., Abdullah, M. R. M., & Hassan, M. H. (2010). *Law and practice of Islamic banking and finance*. Selangor: Sweet & Maxwell Asia, Selangor, Malaysia.
39. Nicoletti, B., (2012), *Lean and Digitize: An Integrated Approach to Process Improvement*. Gower Publishing, Farnham, UK. ISBN-10: 1409441946.
40. www.investopedia.com/terms/l/libor.asp. Accessed 10 August 2018.
41. ec.europa.eu/info/law/markets-financial-instruments-mifid-ii-directive-2014-65-eu_en. Accessed 10 August 2018.
42. Sikorski, J. J., Haughton, J. & Kraft, M. (2017). Blockchain technology in the chemical industry: Machine-to-machine electricity market. *Applied Energy*, 195, 234–246
43. www.nist.gov. Accessed 10 August 2018.
44. www.itic-insure.com/resources/publications/intermediary/article/ucp-500-and-ucp-600-an-update-2777/. Accessed 10 August 2018.
45. Morabito, V. (2017). *Business Innovation Through Blockchain*. Springer International Publishing, Basel, Switzerland.
46. Narayanan, A., Bonneau, J., Felten, E., Miller, A. & Goldfeder, S. (2016). *Bitcoin and Cryptocurrency Technologies: A Comprehensive Introduction*. Princeton University, Princeton, NJ.
47. www.businessdictionary.com/definition/norm.html. Accessed 28 June 2018.
48. www.theglobaltreasurer.com/2014/12/01/forfeiting-updating-the-guidelines-for-trade-financing/. Accessed 28 June 2018.
49. The "nonce" in a bitcoin block is a 32-bit (4-byte) field whose value is adjusted by miners so that the hash of the block will be less than or equal to the current target of the network. The rest of the fields may not be changed, as they have a defined meaning.
50. Narayanan, A., Bonneau, J., Felten, E., Miller, A. & Goldfeder, S. (2016). *Bitcoin and Cryptocurrency Technologies: A Comprehensive Introduction*. Princeton University, Princeton, NJ.
51. Swan, M. (2015). *Blockchain: Blueprint for a New Economy,* Sebastopol, California, O'Reilly Media, Inc., Sebastopol, CA.

52. Asq.com. Accessed 13 June 2018.
53. Juran, J. M. (2003). *Juran on leadership for quality.* Simon and Schuster, New York City, NY.
54. Elkington, J. (1999). Triple bottom-line reporting: Looking for balance. *Australian Cpa*, *69*, 18–21.
55. ec.europa.eu/info/business-economy-euro/banking-and-finance/consumer-finance-and-payments/payment-services/single-euro-payments-area-sepa_en. Accessed 29 July 2018.
56. Cline, P. B. (2004). The merging of risk analysis and adventure education. In *Wilderness Risk Management Conference:* Banff, Canada.
57. as9100store.com/downloads/risk-management-awareness-iaqg.ppt. Accessed 21 July 2018.
58. www.sgs.com. Accessed 11 August 2018.
59. www.ecb.europa.eu/paym/retpaym/paymint/sepa/html/index.en.html. Accessed 11 August 2018.
60. Morabito, V. (2017). *Business Innovation Through Blockchain.* Springer International Publishing, Basel, Switzerland.
61. www.swift.com. Accessed 11 February 2018.
62. www.investopedia.com/terms/s/spv.asp. Accessed 8 July 2018.
63. www.ebaclearing.eu. Accessed 11 August 2018.
64. www.ebaclearing.eu. Accessed 11 August 2018.
65. cscmp.org/CSCMP/Educate/SCM_Definitions_and_Glossary_of_Terms/CSCMP/Educate/SCM_Definitions_and_Glossary_of_Terms.aspx?hkey=60879588-f65f-4ab5-8c4b-6878815ef921. Accessed 18 June 2018.
66. Seuring, S., & Müller, M. (2008). Core issues in sustainable supply chain management–a Delphi study. *Business strategy and the environment*, *17*(8), 455–466.
67. Initiative, G. R. (2018). Sustainability report. *Disponvel em [www. globalreporting. org]. Acessado em*, *17*, 01–09.
68. Deming, W. E., & Edwards, D. W. (1982). *Quality, productivity, and competitive position* (Vol. 183). Cambridge, MA: Massachusetts Institute of Technology, Center for advanced engineering study.
69. Swan, M. 2015. *Blockchain: Blueprint for a New Economy*, O'Reilly Media, Inc., Sebastopol, CA.
70. Chen, R. Y. (2018). A traceability chain algorithm for artificial neural networks using T–S fuzzy cognitive maps in blockchain. *Future Generation Computer Systems*, *80*, 198–210.
71. La Rosa, M., Loos, P. & Pastor, O. (2016). *Business Process Management. 14th International Conference, BPM 2016,* Rio de Janeiro, Brazil, September 18–22, 2016. *Proceedings.* Springer International Publishing, Cham, Switzerland.

72. www.swift.com/node/17351. Accessed 11 August 2018.
73. www.ecb.europa.eu/paym/t2/html/index.en.html. Accessed 11 August 2018
74. www.law.cornell.edu/ucc. Accessed 11 August 2018.
75. www.tradefinanceglobal.com/glossary/ucp/. Accessed 11 August 2018.
76. http://store.iccwbo.org/icc-uniform-customs-and-practice-for-documentary-credits. Accessed 11 August 2018.
77. iccwbo.org/. Accessed 11 August 2018.
78. www.law.kuleuven.be/personal/mstorme/URC522.pdf. Accessed 11 August 2018.
79. Itfa.org. Access 11 August 2018.
80. store.iccwbo.org/icc-uniform-rules-for-forfeiting-urf-800. Accessed 11 August 2018.
81. Max, K. (2017). *Cryptocurrency Secrets.* Lulu.com. www.kobo.com/gb/en/ebook/cryptocurrency-secrets. Accessed 28 June 2018.
82. Ledger. (2018). *Check the list of cryptocurrencies and tokens supported by Ledger here.* Ledger. support.ledgerwallet.com/hc/en-us/articles/115005304449-Check-the-list-of-cryptocurrencies-and-tokens-supported-by-Ledger-here. Accessed 28 June 2018.

Bibliography

Aberdeen Group. (2007). *Technology platforms for supply chain finance*. Boston.

Aberdeen Group. (2016). *New strategies for financial supply chain optimization*. Boston.

Alex, K. (2010). *Is it finally time for m-Commerce* (Ovum White Paper). ovum.com/wp-content/uploads/2011/10/ST_IT_Q2_2010.pdf. Accessed 22 Aug 2017.

Alibaba Press. (2017). *Unlocking opportunities for SMEs*.

Anckar, B., & D'Incau, D. (2002). *Value-added services in mobile commerce: An analytical framework and empirical findings from a national customer survey*. csdl.computer.org/comp/proceedings/hicss/2002/1435/03/14350086b.pdf. Accessed 26 Aug 2017.

Angelus, A., & Porteus, E. L. (2002). Simultaneous capacity & production management of short-life-cycle, produce-to-stock products under stochastic demand. *Management Science, 48*(3), 399–413.

APEC Policy Support Unit. (2014). *Regulatory issues affecting trade and supply chain finance* (Issues paper no. 8).

Ardagna, C. A., & Zhou, J. (2011). Information security theory and practice: Security and privacy of mobile devices in wireless communication. In *5th IFIP WG 11.2 International Workshop, Computer Science/Security and Cryptology*, Heraklion, Crete, Greece.

Arnold, G. (2008). *Corporate financial management*. Harlow: Pearson.

Atanasova, C. (2012). How do firms choose between intermediary and vendor finance? *Financial Management, 41*(1), 207–228.

B. Nicoletti, *Procurement Finance*,
Palgrave Studies in Financial Services Technology,
https://doi.org/10.1007/978-3-030-02140-5

Babich, V. (2010). Independence of capacity ordering & financial subsidies to risky vendors. *Manufacturing & Service Operations Management, 12*(4), 583–607.

Babich, V., Burnetas, A. N., & Ritchken, P. H. (2007). Competition & diversification effects in supply chains with vendor default risk. *Manufacturing & Service Operations Management, 9*(2), 123–146.

Bakker, V., & Claesson, M. (2018). *Enabling continuous knowledge combining*. Master's Thesis at Chalmers University of Technology Gothenburg, Sweden.

Balasubramaniam, A., & Shanmugam, S. S. (2012). *Mobile banking: Growth, adoption and acceptance in India*. Saarbrücken: LAP Lambert Academic Publishing.

Barnes, D. (2001). *Understanding business: Processes*. London: Routledge.

Barnes, S. J. (2002). The mobile commerce value chain: Analysis and future developments. *International Journal of Information Management, 22*(2), 91–108.

Barnes, S. J., & Corbitt, B. (2003). Mobile banking: Concept and potential. *International Journal of Mobile Communications, 1*(3), 273–288.

Basi, S. (2012). *Touchscreen strategy: Planning and monetizing mobile apps & games*. Lavergne: CreateSpace Independent Publishing Platform.

Basu, P. (2012). Supply chain finance enabled early pay: Unlocking trapped value in B2B logistics. *International Journal of Logistics Systems and Management, 12*(3), 334.

Beck, T., & Demirguc-Kunt, A. (2006). Small and medium-size enterprises: Access to finance as a growth constraint. *Journal of Banking & Finance, 30*(11), 2931.

Beck, T., Demirguc-Kunt, A., & Peria, M. (2005). *Reaching out: Access to and use of banking services across countries*. Washington, DC: World Bank.

Berger, A. N., & Udell, G. F. (2006). A more complete conceptual framework for SME finance. *Journal of Banking & Finance, 30*(11), 2945–2966.

Berk, J. (2007). *Corporate finance*. Boston: Pearson.

Bishop, M. (2004). *Introduction to computer security*. Boston: Addison Wesley Professional.

Black, N. J., Lockett, A., Ennew, C., Winklhofer, H., & McKechnie, S. (2002). Modelling customer choice of distribution channels: An illustration from financial services. *International Journal of Financial Institution Marketing, 20*(4), 161–173.

Blackman, I. D., Holland, C. P., & Westcott, T. (2013). Motorola's global financial Supply Chain strategy. *Supply Chain Management: An International Journal, 18*(2), 132–147.

Blake, M. (2004). Growing mobile market in Africa. *The Electronic Library, 22*(4), 370.

BMWA. (2005). *E-Commerce und Recht, Information by the German Ministry of Economics and Labor*. www.bmwa.bund.de. Accessed 24 Aug 2013.

Boadi, R. A., Boateng, R., Hinson, R., & Opoku, R. A. (2007). Preliminary insights into m-commerce adoption in Ghana. *Information Development, 23*(4), 253–265.

Board of Governors of the Federal Reserve System. (2012). *Customers and mobile financial services.* Washington, DC: Board of Governors of the Federal Reserve System.

Borade, A. B., & Bansod, S. V. (2010). Study of vendor-managed inventory practices in Indian industries. *Journal of Manufacturing Technology Management, 21*(8), 1013–1038.

Boyd, C., & Jacob, K. (2007). *Mobile financial services and the underbanked: Opportunities and challenges for mbanking and mpayments*, Research paper from the Center for Financial Services Innovation.

Brealey, R. (2011). *Principles of corporate finance.* New York: McGraw-Hill.

Brennan, M., Maksimovic, V., & Zechner, J. (1988). Vendor financing. *Journal of Finance, 43*(5), 1127–1141.

Brunner, A., Decressin, J., Hardy, D., & Kudela, B. (2004). *Germany's three-pillar banking system – Cross-country perspectives in Europe* (Occasional paper). Washington, DC: International Monetary Fund.

Brunner, A., et al. (2017). Trade finance disrupted: A blockchain use case. *The Capco Institute Journal of Financial Transformation Journal, 4.*

Bruque, S., Cámara, J., & Fuentes Maqueira Marín, J. M. (2015). Cloud computing, Web 2.0, and operational performance: The mediating role of supply chain integration. *International Journal of Logistics Management, 26*(3), 426–458.

Bryant, C. (2014). *Supply chain finance – EBA European market guide.* Paris: European Banking Association.

Bryant, C., & Camerinelli, E. (2013). *Supply Chain finance.* Paris: EBA (Euro Banking Association).

Bryant, C., & Camerinelli, E. (2014). *Supply Chain finance: EBA European market guide.* Paris: European Banking Association.

Busch, J. (2013). *Supply chain and risk management: Finance/procurement trends intersection.* Spend Matters Network.

Buzacott, J. A., & Zhang, R. Q. (2004). Inventory management with asset-based financing. *Management Science, 50*(9), 1274–1292.

Cai, G., Chen, X., & Xiao, Z. (2014). The roles of bank & trade credit: Theoretical analysis & empirical evidence. *Production & Operations Management, 23*(4), 583–598.

Caldentey, R., & Chen, X. (2010). The role of financial services in procurement contracts. In P. Kouvelis, O. Boyabatli, L. Dong, & R. Li (Eds.), *Handbook of integrated risk management in global supply chain* (pp. 289–326). Hoboken: John Wiley & Sons, Inc.

Camerinelli, E. (2009a). Supply chain finance. *Journal of Payments Strategy & Systems, 3*(2), 114–128.

Camerinelli, E. (2009b). *Measuring the value of the supply chain: Linking financial performance and supply chain decisions.* Brookfield: Gower Publishing, Ltd.

Camerinelli, E. (2010a). *Supply chain finance: A taxonomy* (Report from Aite Group).

Camerinelli, E. (2010b). Trends in cash, liquidity and working capital management digitization: The role of technology. *Journal of Corporate Treasury Management, 3*(2), 141–148.

Camerinelli, E. (2012). *Why is supply chain finance so slow to grow?* https://www.finextra.com/blogposting/7312/why-is-supply-chain-finance-so-slow-to-grow. Accessed 18 November 2018.

Camerinelli, E. (2015). *Blockchain business scenarios.* https://www.finextra.com/blogposting/11913/blockchainbusiness-scenarios. Accessed 19 November 2018.

Camerinelli, E. (2016). Blockchain in the supply chain. *Enrico Camerinelli Google Scholar.*

Camerinelli, E., & Bryant, C. (2014). *Supply chain finance—EBA European market guide version 2.0.* Paris: European Banking Association.

Camerinelli, E., & Candtu, A. (2006). Measuring the value of the supply chain: A framework. *Supply Chain Practice, 8*(2), 40–59.

Camerinelli, E., & Schizas, E. (2014). *A study of the business case for supply chain finance.* The Association of Chartered Certified Accountants, Studie.

Campello, M., Graham, J. R., & Harvey, C. R. (2010). The real effects of financial constraints: Evidence from a financial crisis. *Journal of Financial Economics, 97*(3), 470–487.

Caniato, F., Gelsomino, L. M., Perego, A., & Ronchi, S. (2016). Does finance solve the supply chain financing problem? *Supply Chain Management, 21*(5), 534–549.

Caridi, M., Crippa, L., Perego, A., Sianesi, A., & Tumino, A. (2010). Measuring visibility to improve supply chain performance: A quantitative approach. *Benchmarking: An International Journal, 17*(4), 593–615.

Carpenter, E., & Petersen, B. C. (2002). Is the growth of small firms constrained by internal finance? *The Review of Economics & Statistics, 84*(2), 298–309.

Carter, C. R., & Easton, P. L. (2011). Sustainable supply chain management: Evolution and future directions. *International Journal of Physical Distribution & Logistics Management, 41*(1), 46–62.

Carter, C. R., Rogers, D. S., & Choi, T. Y. (2015). Toward the theory of the supply chain. *Journal of Supply Chain Management, 51*(2), 89–97.

Cavenaghi, E. (2014). Supply-chain finance: The new frontier in the world of payments. *Journal of Payments Strategy & Systems, 7*(4), 290–293.

Cerruti, C., Mena, C., Skipworth, H., & Tavoletti, E. (2016). Characterizing agile supply partnerships in the fashion industry. *International Journal of Operations & Production Management, 36*(8), 923–947.

Chaki, N., & Cortesi, A. (2012). Computer information systems – Analysis and technologies. In *10th International Conference, CISIM 2011*, Computer and Information Science, Kolkata, India.

Chang, C. T., Teng, J. T., & Goyal, S. K. (2008). Inventory lot-size models under trade credits: A review. *Asia-Pacific Journal of Operational Research, 25*(1), 89–112.

Chao, X., Chen, J., & Wang, S. (2008). Dynamic inventory management with cash flow constraints. *Naval Research Logistics, 55*(8), 758–768.

Charles, A., Lauras, M., & Van Wassenhove, L. (2010). A model to define and assess the agility of supply chains: Building on humanitarian experience. *International Journal of Physical Distribution & Logistics Management, 40*(8/9), 722–741.

Chen, X., & Hu, C. (2011). *The value of Supply Chain finance.* In M. Habib (Ed.), *Supply chain management – Applications & simulations* (pp. 111–132). Croatia: InTech, Rijeka.

Chilmon, B., & Tipi, N. (2014). Modelling an end to end supply chain system using simulation. In *LRN Annual Conference and PhD Workshop 2014, 3rd–5th September 2015*, University of Huddersfield, Huddersfield.

CIPS knowledge team. (2013). *The definition of procurement.* Melbourne.

Claassen, M. J., Van Weele, A. J., & Van Raaij, E. M. (2008). Performance outcomes and success factors of vendor managed inventory (VMI). *Supply Chain Management: An International Journal, 13*(6), 406–414.

Clark, A. J., & Scarf, H. (1960). Optimal policies for a multi-echelon inventory problem. *Management Science, 6*(4), 475–490.

Coelho, F., & Easingwood, C. (2003). Multiple channel structures in financial services: A framework. *Journal of Financial Services Marketing, 8*(1), 22–34.

Committee on the Global Financial System. (2014). *Trade finance: Developments and issues.* Basel: Banks for international settlement.

Cooper, H. M. (2009). *Research synthesis & meta-analysis: A step-by-step approach.* Los Angeles: Sage Publications, Inc.

Cornett, M. M., McNutt, J. J., Strahan, P. E., & Tehranian, H. (2011). Liquidity risk management and credit supply in the financial crisis. *Journal of Financial Economics, 101*(2), 297–312.

Cosse, M. (2011). *Case studies in Supply Chain Finance.* Cranfield: University of Cranfield.

Coulibaly, B., Sapriza, H., & Zlate, A. (2013). Financial frictions, trade credit, and the 2008–09 global financial crisis. *International Review of Economics & Finance, 26*(6), 25–38.

Cousins, P. D., & Spekman, R. (2003). Strategic supply and the management of inter- and intra-organizational relationships. *Journal of Purchasing and Supply Management, 9*(1), 19–29. Amsterdam: Elsevier.

Coyle, J. (2003). *The management of business logistics – A supply chain perspective.* Mason: South-Western/Thomson Learning.

Croxton, K. L., García-Dastugue, S. J., Lambert, D. M., & Rogers, D. S. (2001). The Supply Chain management processes. *The International Journal of Logistics Management, 12*(2), 13–36.

Darwish, M. A., & Odah, O. M. (2010). Vendor managed inventory model for single-vendor multi-retailer Supply Chains. *European Journal of Operational Research, 204*(3), 473–484.

Das, S., & Abdel-Malek, L. (2003). Modeling the flexibility of order quantities and lead-times in supply chains. *International Journal of Production Economics, 85*(2), 171–181.

Das, S. R., Duffie, D., Kapadia, N., & Saita, L. (2007). Common failings: How corporate defaults are correlated. *The Journal of Finance, 62*(1), 93–117.

De Goeij, C. (2017). Gaining insight into the effects of supply chain finance: The vendor perspective. *Vervoerlogistike Werkdagen*, 5.

Deloitte. (2016). *Blockchain. Enigma, paradox, opportunity*. London.

Deloitte University Press. (2016). *The rise of the digital supply network*. London.

Demica. (2016). *State of supply chain finance industry*. www.demica.com/library/gbi-2016-state-of-scf-april-21.pdf. Accessed 21 July 2018.

Deng, A., & Chen, Z. (2017). Managing online supply chain finance credit risk of "asymmetric information". *World Journal of Research and Review, 4*, 29–32.

DeSmet, B. (2018). *Supply chain strategy and financial metrics: The supply chain triangle of service, cost and cash*. London: Kogan Page Publishers.

Dietsch, M., & Petey, J. (2002). The credit risk is SME loans portfolios: Modeling issues, pricing, & capital requirements. *Journal of Banking & Finance, 26*(2–3), 303–322.

Dimitri, N., Piga, G., & Spagnolo, G. (2006). *Handbook of procurement*. Cambridge: Cambridge University Press.

Dong, Y., & Xu, K. (2002). A Supply Chain model of vendor managed inventory. *Transportation Research Part E: Logistics & Transportation Review, 38*(2), 75–95.

Dong, Y., Xu, K., & Dresner, M. (2007). Environmental determinants of VMI adoption: An exploratory analysis. *Transportation Research Part E: Logistics & Transportation Review, 43*(4), 355–369.

Duclos, L., Vokurka, R., & Lummus, R. (2003). A conceptual model of supply chain flexibility. *Industrial Management & Data Systems, 103*(6), 446–456.

Duygulu, E., Ozeren, E., Işıldar, P., & Appolloni, A. (2016). The sustainable strategy for small and medium sized enterprises: The relationship between mission statements and performance. *Sustainability, 8*(7), 698.

Elliot, G., & Phillips, N. (2004). *Mobile commerce and wireless computing systems*. Boston: Addison Wesley.

EU (2005). *Law and e-Commerce, internet portal of the European Union for regulatory framework of electronic commerce*. europa.eu.int/information_society/topics/ebusiness/ecommerce/8epolicy_elaw/law_ecommerce/index_en.htm. Accessed 8 Mar 2017.

Euro Banking Association (EBA), Factors Chain International (FCI), International Chamber of Commerce (ICC), International Trade and Forfaiting Association (ITFA). (2016). *Standard definition for techniques of Supply Chain Finance*.

Fairchild, A. (2005). Intelligent matching: Integrating efficiencies in the financial supply chain. *Supply Chain Management: An International Journal, 10*(4), 244–248. 112.

Farris II, M. T., & Hutchison, P. D. (2002). Cash-to-cash: The new Supply Chain management metric. *International Journal of Physical Distribution & Logistics Management, 32*(4), 288–298.

Federal Reserve Board. (2012, March). *Customers and mobile financial services.* Federal Reserve Board Publication. www.federalreserve.gov/econresdata/mobile-device-report-201203.pdf. Accessed 15 Aug 2017.

Ferrari, R. (2016). *L'era del Fintech. La rivoluzione digitale nei servizi finanziari.* Milano: FrancoAngeli.

FinExtra. (2009, October 13). *Philippines mobile phone-based microfinance financial institution set for launch.* Finextra.com: www.finextra.com/fullstory.asp?id=20598. Accessed 22 Aug 2017.

Fiorina, P. (2009). *Key trends in mobile financial services in the European Union* (Research paper by Celent Group).

Fisman, R., & Love, I. (2003). Trade credit, financial intermediary development, & industry growth. *The Journal of Finance, 58*(1), 353–374.

Fung Business Intelligence Center. (2015). *Supply Chain Finance.* Li & Fung management book series. Hong Kong.

Garcia-Appendini, E., & Montoriol-Garriga, J. (2013). Firms as liquidity providers: Evidence from the 2007–2008 financial crisis. *Journal of Financial Economics, 109*(1), 272–291.

García-Olalla, M. (2018). *Contemporary issues in banking: Regulation, governance and performance.* Berlin: Springer.

Gardner, J. (2009). *Innovation and the future proof bank: A practical guide to doing different business-as-usual.* London: John Wiley & Sons.

Garioni, G. (2004). Trade Finance: un caso pratico. *Commercio internazionale, 6*, 19–24.

Gelsomino, L. M., Mangiaracina, R., Perego, A., & Tumino, A. (2016a). Supply Chain finance: A literature review. *International Journal of Physical Distribution & Logistics Management, 46*(4), 348–366.

Gelsomino, L. M., Mangiaracina, R., Perego, A., & Tumino, A. (2016b). Supply chain finance: Modelling a dynamic discounting programme. *Journal of Advanced Management Science, 4*(4).

Giannakis, M., & Michalis, L. (2016). A multi-agent based system with big data processing for enhanced supply chain agility. *Journal of Enterprise Information Management, 29*, 706–727.

Global Business Intelligence. (2016). *State of Supply Chain finance industry: Entering a new era of maturity.* www.demica.com/library/gbi-2016-state-of-scf-april-21.pdf. Accessed 26 Dec 2017.

Gomm, M. L. (2010). Supply Chain finance: Applying finance theory to Supply Chain management to enhance finance in Supply Chains. *International Journal of Logistics Research & Applications, 13*(2), 133–142.

Goyal, M., & Netessine, S. (2011). Volume flexibility, product flexibility, or both: The role of demand correlation and product substitution. *Manufacturing & Service Operations Management, 13*(2), 180–193.

Graaf, D. M. (2016). *SCF appetite: A first analysis* (p. 2). Zwolle: Windesheim UAS.

Grosse-Ruyken, P. T., Wagner, S. M., & Jonke, R. (2011). What is the right cash conversion cycle for your Supply Chain? *International Journal of Services & Operations Management, 10*(1), 13–29.

Gupta, D., & Wang, L. (2009). A stochastic inventory model with trade credit. *Manufacturing & Service Operations Management, 11*(1), 4–18.

Haar, S. (2016). The power of collaboration. What happens when procurement, finance, and IT team up. *17*(3), 17. sapinsider.wispubs.com/Assets/Articles/2016/August/SPI-The-Power-of-Collaboration. Accessed 4 Feb 2018.

Härer, F. (2018). Decentralized business process modeling and instance tracking secured by a blockchain. In *26th European Conference on Information Systems (ECIS 2018)*, Portsmouth.

Harris, T. (2009, January). *Cloud computing – An overview* (Whitepaper). Torry Harris Business Solutions.

Hawser, A. (2017). Trade finance getting its E-legs, the innovators. *Global Finance Magazine*. London.

He, Y., Chen, Y., & Dai, Y. C. (2016). Analysis over the supply chain financing model of Jingdong. *Journal of Finance and Accounting, 17*, 20–22.

Herath, G. (2015). *McKinsey on payments, McKinsey Papers, 8*(22). London. www.demica.com/library/gbi-2016-state-of-scf-april-21.pdf. Accessed 26 Dec 2017.

Hillier, D. (2011). *Fundamentals of corporate finance*. Maidenhead: McGraw Hill.

Hofmann, E. (2005). Supply Chain finance: Some conceptual insights. In R. Lasch & C. G. Janker (Eds.), *Logistik Management. Innovative Logistikkonzepte* (pp. 203–214). Wiesbaden: Universitätsverlag.

Hofmann, E. (2010). A supply chain-oriented approach of working capital management. *Journal of Business Logistics, 31*(2), 305–330.

Hofmann, E. (2017). *Supply chain finance and blockchain technology*. Cham: Springer.

Hofmann, E., & Belin, O. (2011). *Supply chain finance solutions*. Heidelberg, Berlin: Springer-Verlag Berlin.

Hofmann, E., & Kotzab, H. (2010). A Supply Chain-oriented approach of working capital management. *Journal of Business Logistics, 31*(2), 305–330.

Hofmann, E., Wetzel, P., & Röck, D. (2018). *Blockchain can solve the pain points of trade and Supply Chain Finance, Supply Chain Finance-Lab (SCF-Lab)*. www.alexandria.unisg.ch/253971/. Accessed 7 July 2018.

Hong, L. I. N. (2017). Research on the risk management of the online supply chain finance. *DEStech Transactions on Economics, Business and Management* (eced).

Hua, S. (2013). *Supply chain perspectives and issues in China: A literature review*. Hong Kong: Fung Global Institute Limited and Fung Business Intelligence Centre.

Institute of International Finance. (2015). *Banking on the blockchain*. Washington, DC.

International Finance Corporation IFC. (2017). *Technology-enabled supply chain finance for small and medium enterprises is a major growth opportunity for banks* (p. 113).

International Trade Administration. (2012). *Trade finance guide*. Washington, DC: Office of Public Affairs, U.S Department of Commerce.

ITA'S Office of Finance. (2008). *Trade finance guide. A quick references for U.S. exporters*. Washington, DC: US Department of Commerce, International Trade Administration.

Ivashina, V., & Scharfstein, D. (2010). Bank lending during the financial crisis of 2008. *Journal of Financial Economics, 97*(3), 319–338.

Jack, E., & Raturi, A. (2003). Measuring and comparing volume flexibility in the capital products industry. *Production and Operations Management, 12*(4), 480–501.

Jansen, J. H. (2016a). *Supply chain finance*. Chelyabisnsk State University, Vestnik, Russia Federation.

Jansen, J. H. (2016b). *Is SCF ready to be applied in SMEs?* Vestnik (Chelyabinsk State University), No. 14, Vestnik, Russia Federation.

Jansen, J. H. (2016c). *Quick scan supply chain finance* (White paper). Arnhem.

Jansen, J. H. (2017). *Conceptual model for supply chain finance for SMEs At operational level. An Essay on the supply chain finance paradigm*. Chelyabisnsk State University, Vestnik, Russian Federation.

Jarvis, C. B., MacKenzie, S. B., & Podsakoff, P. M. (2003). A critical review of construct indicators and measurement model misspecification in marketing & consumer research. *Journal of Consumer Research, 30*(2), 199–218.

Jegher, J. (2010). *Small business and corporate mobile banking solutions gaining popularity*. A Blog at Celent Research Website. bankingblog.celent.com/?p=1621. Accessed 2 Oct 2017.

Jiang, J., Li, Z., & Lin, C. (2014). Financing difficulties of SMEs from its financing sources in China. *Journal of Service Science and Management, 7*(3), 196–200.

Jingming, P., Hongjiang, M., & Xiaowo, T. (2006). Study on multi-products supply chain volume flexibility decision model related to producing under demand uncertainty. In *Service Systems and Service Management, 2006 International Conference on* (Vol. 2, pp. 1409–1414).

Karjaluoto, H. (2002). Selection criteria for a mode of bill payment: Empirical investigation among Finnish financial institution customers. *International Journal of Retail and Distribution Management, 30*(6), 331–339.

Kazemargi, N., Cerruti, C., & Appolloni, A. (2016). Adopting open innovation in supply networks. *International Journal of Management and Enterprise Development, 15*(2–3), 174–190.

Khambadkone, K. (2011). Are you ready for big data? *InfoGain*. www.infogain.com/organization/perspective-big-data.jsp. Accessed 23 Aug 2017.

Klapper, L. F. (2006). The role of factoring for financing small & medium enterprises. *Journal of Banking & Finance, 30*(11), 3111–3130.

Klapper, L. F., Laeven, L., & Rajan, R. (2011). Trade credit contracts. *Review of Financial Studies, 25*(3), 838–867.

Klapper, L. F., & Randall, D. (2011). Financial crisis and supply-chain financing. In J. Chauffour & M. Malouche (Eds.), *Trade finance during the great trade collapse* (pp. 73–86). Washington, DC: The World Bank.

Knospe, H., & Schwiderski-Grosche, S. (2004). Secure mobile commerce. In C. Mitchell (Ed.), *Security for mobility* (pp. 325–346). London: Institution of Electrical Engineers.

Kondabagil, J. (2007). *Risk management in electronic banking: Concept and best practices*. Singapore: John Wiley and Sons Asia.

Kouvelis, P., Dong, L., & Turcic, D. (2017). Introduction to the special issue on supply chain finance, foundations and trends® in technology. *Information and Operations Management, 10*(3–4), 209–219. https://doi.org/10.1561/0200000058. Accessed 26 Dec 2017.

Kouvelis, P., & Zhao, W. (2011). *Supply chain finance. The handbook of integrated risk management in global supply chains* (pp. 247–288). New York: Wiley.

Kouvelis, P., & Zhao, W. (2012). Financing the newsvendor: Vendor vs bank, & the structure of optimal trade credit contracts. *Operations Research, 60*(3), 566–580.

Kristofik, P., Kok, J., de Vries, S., & van Sten-van't Hoff, J. (2012). Financial supply chain management – Challenges and obstacles. *ACRN Journal of Entrepreneurship Perspectives, 1*(2), 132–142. Melbourne: University of Melbourne.

Kumar, V., Fantazy, K., Kumar, U., & Boyle, T. (2006). Implementation and management framework for supply chain flexibility. *Journal of Enterprise Information Management, 19*(3), 303–319.

Lamoureux, J.-F., & Evans, T. A. (2011). *Supply chain finance: A new means to support the competitiveness and resilience of global value chains* (Working paper 2179944). Rochester: Social Science Research Network.

Laukkanen, T. (2006). Customer perceived value of e-financial services: A means-end approach. *International Journal of Electronic Finance, 1*(1), 5–17.

Lee, C. H. H., & Rhee, B. D. B.-D. (2011). Trade credit for Supply Chain coordination. *European Journal of Operational Research, 214*(1), 136–146.

Lemay, S., Helms, M. M., Kimball, B., & Mcmahon, D. (2017). Supply chain management: The elusive concept and definition. *International Journal of Logistics Management, 28*, 1425–1453.

Li, L., Shubik, M., & Sobel, M. J. (2013). Control of dividends, capital subscriptions, & physical inventories. *Management Science, 59*(5), 1107–1124.

Lin, H., & Lin, Q. (2018). Research on the impact of supply chain integration of startups: Service supply chain perspective. *Open Journal of Social Sciences, 6*(4), 255.

Liu, X., Zhou, L., & Wu, Y. (2015). *Supply chain finance in China: Business innovation and theory development*. Beijing: Business School, Central University of Finance and Economics.

Locker, A., & Grosse-Ruyken, P. T. (2017). *Chefsache Finanzen in Einkauf und Supply Chain – Mit Strategie-, Performance- und Risikokonzepten Millionenwerte schaffen*. Berlin: Springer Verlag.

Luo, W., & Shang, K. (2013). *Managing inventory for entrepreneurial firms with trade credit & payment defaults* (Working paper). Barcelona: IESE Business School, University of Navarra.

Luo, J., & Zhang, Q. (2012). Trade credit: A new mechanism to coordinate Supply Chain. *Operations Research Letters, 40*(5), 378–384.

Maddah, B., Jaber, M., & Abboud, N. (2004). Periodic review (s, S) inventory model with permissible delay in payments. *Journal of the Operational Research Society, 55*(2), 147–159.

Malaket, M. A. (2014). *Financing trade and international Supply Chains: Commerce across borders, finance across frontiers*. Abingdon: Ashgate Publishing.

Mangiaracina, R., Melacini, M., & Perego, A. (2012). A critical analysis of vendor managed inventory in the grocery Supply Chain. *International Journal of Integrated Supply Management, 7*(1–2), 138–166.

Martin, J., & Hofmann, E. (2017). Involving financial service providers in Supply Chain Finance practices: Company needs and service requirements. *Journal of Applied Accounting Research, 18*(1), 42–62.

Mason, S. J., Ribera, P. M., Farris, J. A., & Kirk, R. G. (2003). Integrating the warehousing and transportation functions of the Supply Chain. *Transportation Research Part E: Logistics and Transportation Review, 39*(2), 141.

Mathis, J. F., & Cavinato, J. (2010). Financing the global Supply Chain: Growing need for management action. *Thunderbird International Business Review, 52*(6), 467–474.

Meixell, M. J., & Norbis, M. (2008). A review of the transportation mode choice and carrier selection literature. *The International Journal of Logistics Management, 19*(2), 183–211.

Metternich, J., Böllhoff, J., Seifermann, S., & Beck, S. (2013). Volume and mix flexibility evaluation of lean production systems. *Procedia CIRP, 9*, 79–84.

Mills, D., Wang, K., Malone, B., Ravi, A., Marquardt, J., Chen, C., Badev, A., Brezinski, T., Fahy, L, Liao, K., Kargenian, K., Ellithorpe, M., Ng, W., & Baird, M. (2016). *Distributed ledger technology in payments, clearing, and settlement* (Finance and Economics Discussion Series 2016-095). Washington, DC: Board of Governors of the Federal Reserve System. https://doi.org/10.17016/FEDS.2016.095

More, D., & Basu, P. (2013). Challenges of Supply Chain finance: A detailed study and a hierarchical model based on the experiences of an Indian firm. *Business Process Management Journal, 19*(4), 624–647.

Naone, E. (2011, August 22). The new big data. *MIT Technology Review*, Cambridge, MA.

Natarajarathinam, M., Capar, I., & Narayanan, A. (2009). Managing Supply Chains in times of crisis: A review of literature and insights. *International Journal of Physical Distribution & Logistics Management, 39*(7), 535–573.

Nicoletti, B. (2008). Libro del Mese Alliances and co-evolution: Insights from the banking sector. Ed. Rehan ul-Haq, *Sistemi e Impresa*, no. 7, 77, Lug.–Ago.

Nicoletti, B. (2009, January 11). *Review of building a Global Bank* (Guillén, M. F. & Tschoegl, A., Ed.). www.academici.com.

Nicoletti, B. (2011). Applicare il Lean & Digitize nei servizi finanziari, *Bancamatica*, Gen.–Feb., 12–14.

Nicoletti, B. (2012). *Lean and digitize: An integrated approach to process improvement.* Farnham: Gower Publishing. ISBN-10: 1409441946.

Nicoletti, B. (2013a). *Cloud computing and financial services.* Houndsmill: Palgrave Macmillan (Also translated in Chinese).

Nicoletti, B. (2013b). CT-enabled integrated operations, APMS 2013, Philadelfia Sep. In *Advances in production management system.* Berlin: Springer.

Nicoletti, B. (2013c). *Lean procurement.* Milano: FrancoAngeli.

Nicoletti, B. (2013d). Lean six sigma and digitize procurement. *International Journal of Lean Six Sigma, 4*(2), 184–203.

Nicoletti, B. (2014a). Lean and digitize e-procurement. In *New development on e-public procurement.* Dedham: Amazon Books.

Nicoletti, B. (2014b). *Mobile banking: Evolution or revolution.* Houndsmill: Palgrave Macmillan Also translated in Chinese.

Nicoletti, B. (2016). *Digital insurance.* Houndsmill: Palgrave Macmillan. Also translated in Chinese. https://doi.org/10.1057/9781137553270_8.

Nicoletti, B. (2017a). *Agile procurement. Volume I: Adding value with lean processes.* London: Springer International Publishing. isbn:978-3-319-61082-5.

Nicoletti, B. (2017b). *Agile procurement. Volume II: Designing and implementing a digital transformation.* London: Springer International Publishing. isbn:978-3-319-61085-6.

Nicoletti, B. (2017c). *The future of fintech.* London: Springer International Publishing. isbn:978-3-319-51414-7.

Nienhuis, J. J., Cortet, M., & Lycklama, D. (2013). Real-time financing: Extending e-invoicing to real-time SME financing. *Journal of Payments Strategy & Systems, 7*(3), 232–245.

Novak, R. A., & Simco, S. W. (1991). The industrial procurement process: A Supply Chain perspective. *Journal of Business Logistics, 12*, 145–167.

Nzioka, D., & Palakurthi, P. (2011). *Impact of mobile banking on microfinance institutions: A case study of Small and Micro Enterprise Program (SMEP)*. Riga: LAP Lambert Academic Publishing.

Osservatorio Supply Chain Finance. (2015). *L'evoluzione dell'offerta di Supply Chain Finance*. Milano: Politecnico di Milano.

Palia, D., & Sopranzetti, B. J. (2004). Securitizing accounts receivable. *Review of Quantitative Finance & Accounting, 22*(1), 29–38.

Pell Mell, T. G. (2011). *NIST definition of cloud computing*. NIST Tech Beat.

Perego, A., Perotti, S., & Mangiaracina, R. (2011). ICT for logistics & freight transportation: A literature review and research agenda. *International Journal of Physical Distribution & Logistics Management, 41*(5), 457–483.

Petersen, M. A., & Rajan, R. G. (1997). Trade credit: Theory & evidence. *The Review of Financial Studies, 10*(3), 661–691.

Pezza, S. (2011). *Supply Chain Finance: Gaining control in the face of uncertainty*. Boston: Aberdeen Group.

Pfohl, H. C., & Gomm, M. (2009). Supply chain finance: Optimizing financial flows in supply chains. *Logistics research, 1*(3–4), 149–161.

Pilbeam, C., Alvarez, G., & Wilson, H. (2012). The governance of supply networks: A systematic literature review. *Supply Chain Management: An International Journal, 17*(4), 358–376.

Polak, P., Sirpal, R., & Hamdan, M. (2012). Post-crisis emerging role of the treasurer. *European Journal of Scientific Research, 86*(3), 319–339.

Price WaterhouseCoopers. (2009). *Demistify Supply Chain finance – Insight into the what, why, how, where & who*. Available at: www.pwc.com/us/en/issues/surviving-the-financial-downturn/assets/supply_chain_finance.pdf. Accessed 20 Jan 2018.

Protopappa-Sieke, M., & Seifert, R. W. (2010). Interrelating operational & financial performance measurements. *European Journal of Operational Research, 204*(3), 439–448.

Raghavan, S. N. R., & Mishra, V. K. (2011). Short-term financing in a cash-constrained Supply Chain. *International Journal of Production Economics, 134*(2), 407–412.

Randall, W. S., & Farris II, M. T. (2009). Supply Chain financing: Using cash-to-cash variables to strengthen the Supply Chain. *International Journal of Physical Distribution & Logistics Management, 39*(8), 669–689.

Rappaport, A. (1998). *Creating shareholder value*. New York: Free Press.

Report Leadership. (2007). *Guide to key performance indicators. Communicating the measures that matter*. London: PricewaterhouseCoopers.

Ronchi, S. (2014). *Supply Chain Finance: Nuove opportunità di collaborazione nella filiera*. Milano: Osservatori Digital Innovation.

Salvador, F., Rungtusanatham, M., Forza, C., & Trentin, A. (2007). Mix flexibility and volume flexibility in a build-to-order environment: Synergies and trade-offs. *International Journal of Operations & Production Management, 27*(11), 1173–1191.

Sánchez, A., & Pérez, M. (2005). Supply chain flexibility and firm performance: A conceptual model and empirical study in the automotive industry. *International Journal of Operations & Production Management, 25*(7), 681–700.

Sari, K. (2007). Exploring the benefits of vendor managed inventory. *International Journal of Physical Distribution & Logistics Management, 37*(7), 529–545.

Schmidt-Eisenlohr, T. (2013). Towards a theory of trade finance. *Journal of International Economics, 91*, 96–112. Amsterdam: Elsevier.

Schütz, P., & Tomasgard, A. (2011). The impact of flexibility on operational supply chain planning. *International Journal of Production Economics, 134*(2), 300–311.

Seifert, R. E. (2009). *Supply Chain Finance – What is it worth?* Lausanne: IMD.

Seifert, D. (2010). *Collaborative working capital management in supply networks*. Lausanne: École Polytechnique Fédérale De Lausanne.

Seifert, R. W., & Seifert, D. (2009). Supply Chain finance – What is it worth? *IMD Perspectives for Managers, 178*, 1–4.

Seifert, R. W., & Seifert, D. (2011). Financing the chain. *International Commerce Review, 10*(1), 32–44.

Seifert, D., Seifert, R. W., & Protopappa-Sieke, M. (2013). A review of trade credit literature: Opportunities for research in operations. *European Journal of Operational Research, 231*(2), 245–256.

Shaw, M. J. (Ed.). (2006). *Electronic commerce and the digital economy*. New York: M. E. Sharpe.

Sheehan, D. (2018). *Inventory and supply chain finance*. Pdf, http://scholar.google.it/scholar_url?url=works.bepress.com/duncan_sheehan/37/download/&hl=en&sa=X&d=18354609868663928656&scisig=AAGBfm08e9bgc2fpAdH4J4U4YNzyd2YPTg&nossl=1&oi=scholaralrt. Accessed 5 July 2018.

Sherehiy, B., Karwowski, W., & Layer, J. K. (2007). A review of organization agility: Concepts, frameworks, and attributes. *International Journal of Industrial Ergonomics, 37*, 445–460. Amsterdam: Elsevier.

Shi Jinzhao, & Guo Jue. (2015). Supply Chain finance development and domestic practice from the perspective of internet. *Journal of Xi'an Jiao Tong University: Social Science Edition, 35*(4), 10–16.

Shi, J., Katehakis, M., & Melamed, B. (2013). *Cash-flow based dynamic inventory management* (Working paper). Atlanta: Robinson College of Business, Georgia State University.

Shire, K. A., & Leimeister, J. M. (2012). *Technologiegestützte Dienstleistungsinnov. in der Gesundheitswirtschaft* (German edition). Wiesbaden: Springer Gabler.

Shuguang, T., & Jianbiao, R. (2010). *Bank Supply Chain finance: Small and medium-sized enterprises*. Beijing: Chinese Financial and Economic Press.
Silvestro, R., & Lustrato, P. (2014). Integrating financial and physical Supply Chains: The role of banks in enabling Supply Chain integration. *International Journal of Operations & Production Management, 34*(3), 298–324.
Singh, R., & Acharya, P. (2013). Supply chain flexibility: A frame work of research dimensions. *Global Journal of Flexible Systems Management, 14*(3), 157–166.
Slack, N. (1987). The flexibility of manufacturing systems. *International Journal of Operations & Production Management, 7*(4), 35–45.
SMEs, E.X.P.O.R.T.I.N.G. (2009). *How to access trade finance. A guide for exporting SMEs*. Geneva: International Trade Centre.
Soni, H., Shah, N. H., & Jaggi, C. K. (2010). Inventory models and trade credit: A review. *Control & Cybernetics, 39*(3), 867–882.
Sopranzetti, B. J. (1999). Selling accounts receivable & the underinvestment problem. *Quarterly Review of Economics & Finance, 39*(2), 291–301.
Soroor, J., Tarokh, M. J., & Shemshadi, A. (2009). Initiating a state of the art system for real-time supply chain coordination. *European Journal of Operational Research, 196*, 635–650.
Soufani, K. (2001). The role of factoring in financing UK SMEs: A supply side analysis. *Journal of Small Business & Enterprise Development, 8*(1), 37–46.
Soufani, K. (2002). On the determinants of factoring as a financing choice: Evidence from the UK. *Journal of Economics & Business, 54*(2), 239–252.
Stair, R. M., & Reynolds, G. (2008). *Fundamentals of Information Systems* (5th ed.). Stamford: Course Technology.
Steeman, M. (2013). Supply chain finance. In *EVO, logistics yearbook 2013*. White Paper. Zoetermeer: EVO.
Steeman, M. (2014). *The power of supply chain finance*. Windesheim Knowledge & Research Series (No. 50). Windsheim: University of Zwolle.
Steeman, M. (2015). *Supply chain finance* (White paper). London.
Steeman, M. (2016). Getting insight to the effects of supply chain finance: The vendor perspective. *Vervoerslogistieke Werkdagen*.
Stevenson, M., & Spring, M. (2007). Flexibility from a supply chain perspective: Definition and review. *International Journal of Operations & Production Management, 27*(7), 685–713.
Stewart, G. (1995). Supply chain performance benchmarking study reveals keys to Supply Chain excellence. *Logistics Information Management, 8*(2), 38–44.
Swinney, R., & Netessine, S. (2009). Long-term contracts under the threat of vendor default. *Manufacturing & Service Operations Management, 11*(1), 109–127.
Tanrisever, F., Cetinay, H., Reindorp, M. J., & Fransoo, J. C. (2012). *Value of reverse factoring in multi-stage Supply Chains* (Working paper). Eindhoven: Eindhoven University of Technology.

Tapscott, D., & Tapscott, A. (2016). *Blockchain revolution: how the technology behind bitcoin is changing money, business, and the world*. London: Penguin.

Tasca, P., Aste, T., Pelizzon, L., & Perony, N. (2016). *Banking beyond banks and money*. London: Springer International Publishing.

Tassabehji, R., & Moorhouse, A. (2008). The changing role of procurement: Developing professional effectiveness. *Journal of Purchasing and Supply Management, 14*, 55–11, 68. Amsterdam: Elsevier.

Templar, S. (2016). *Financing the end-to-end supply chain*. London: Kogan Page Publishers.

Templar, S., Cosse, M., Camerinelli, E., & Findlay, C. (2012, September). An investigation into current supply chain finance practices in business: A case study approach. In *Proceedings of the Logistics Research Network (LRN) Conference*, Cranfield.

Thompson, J. (2016). *IT + Procurement + Finance: A powerful triad*. www.digitalistmag.com/cio-knowledge/2016/07/11/it-procurement-finance-powerful-triad-04299256. Accessed 27 Dec 2017.

Tiger, A., & Simpson, P. (2003). Using discrete-event simulation to create flexibility in APAC supply chain management. *Global Journal of Flexible Systems Management, 4*(4), 15–22.

Tiwari, R., & Buse, S. (2007). *The mobile commerce prospects: A strategic analysis of opportunities in the banking sector*. Hamburg: Hamburg University Press.

Tseng, Y. H., & Lin, C. T. (2011). Enhancing organization agility by deploying agile drivers, capabilities and providers. *Information Science, 181*, 3693–3708. Amsterdam: Elsevier.

Uçaktürk, A., Uçaktürk, T., & Yavuz, H. (2015). Possibilities of usage of strategic business intelligence systems based on databases in agile manufacturing. *Procedia-Social and Behavioral Sciences, 207*, 234–241. Amsterdam: Elsevier.

Uzo, U., Shittu, O., & Meru, A. K. (2018). Introduction: Indigenous management practices in Africa. In *Indigenous management practices in Africa: A guide for educators and practitioners* (pp. 1–7). Bingley: Emerald Publishing Limited.

van der Vliet, K., Reindorp, M. J., & Fransoo, J. C. (2015). The price of reverse factoring: Financing rates vs payment delays. *European Journal of Operational Research, 242*(3), 842–853.

Van Nes, W. R. (2017). *Do not be fooled by the blocks that it got*. Rotterdam: Thesis at Erasmus University Rotterdam.

Van Weele, A. J. (2009). *Purchasing and Supply Chain management: Analysis, strategy, planning and practice*. Andover: Cengage Learning EMEA.

Varshney, U., & Vetter, R. (2002). Mobile commerce: framework, applications and networking support. *Mobile Network and Applications, 7*(3), 185–198.

van der Vliet, K., Reindorp, M. J., & Fransoo, J. C. (2013). *Maximizing the value of Supply Chain finance* (Working paper, Vol. 405). Eindhoven: Eindhoven University of Technology.

Wang, H. (2010). Study on Supply Chain Finance in E-business Circumstances. In *International Conference on e-Education, e-Business, e-Management and e-Learning*.

Witthaut, M., Deeken, H., Sprenger, P., Gadzhanov, P., & David, M. (2017). Smart objects and smart finance for supply chain management. *Logistics Journal, 2017*.

World Trade Organization. (2016). *Trade finance and SMEs. Bridging the gaps in provision*. Geneve.

Wuttke, D. A., Blome, C., Foerstl, K., & Henke, M. (2013). Managing the innovation adoption of supply chain – Empirical evidence from six European case studies. *Journal of Business Logistics, 34*(2), 148–166.

Wuttke, D. A., Blome, C., & Henke, M. (2013). Focusing the financial flow of Supply Chains: An empirical investigation of financial Supply Chain management. *International Journal of Production Economics, 145*(2), 773–789. https://doi.org/10.1111/jbl.12016.

Xu, X., Chen, X., Jia, F., Brown, S., Gong, Y., & Xu, Y. (2018). Supply chain finance: A systematic literature review and bibliometric analysis. *International Journal of Production Economics, 204*, 160–173.

Xu, X., Sun, Y., & Hua, Z. (2010). Reducing the probability of bankruptcy through supply chain coordination. *IEEE Transactions on Systems, Man, & Cybernetics, Part C: Applications & Reviews, 40*(2), 201–215.

Yan, H., & Wang, W. L. (2015). Financial supply chain innovation at the internet financial perspective. *Journal. Accounting & Finance, 3*, 78–95.

Yang, S. A., & Birge, J. R. (2010). *How inventory is (should be) financed: trade credit in Supply Chains with demand uncertainty & costs of financial distress* (Working paper). London: London Business School.

Yangyang, H., & Fang, W. (2016). Research on financing model of the Chinese SMEs in supply chain finance. *International Journal of Economics, Finance and Management Sciences, 2016, 4*(5), 235–240.

Yao, Y., & Dresner, M. (2008). The inventory value of information sharing, continuous replenishment, and vendor-managed inventory. *Transportation Research Part E: Logistics & Transportation Review, 44*(3), 361–378.

Zeballos, A. C., Seifert, R. W., & Protopappa-Sieke, M. (2013). Single product, finite horizon, periodic review inventory model with working capital requirements and short-term debt. *Computers & Operations Research, 40*(12), 2940–2949.

Zhang, Q., & Liu, H. (2014). Research on small and medium enterprises financing mode based on supply chain finance. *Journal of Chemical and Pharmaceutical Research, 6*(5), 1818–1824.

Zhao L., & Huchzermeier A. (2018). Supply Chain Finance. In *Supply chain finance. EURO advanced tutorials on operational research*. Cham: Springer.

Zhou, Q., & Lee, T. S. (2014, January 4). Financial supply chain management and supply chain finance: A concise literature. In *First International Conference on Supply Chain for Sustainability*, Hang Seng Management College.

Websites

Adwww.ingwb.com/Corporate/Finance
blog.arkieva.com/balancing-cash-cost-service-supply-chain-triangle
cdn.iccwbo.org/content/uploads/sites/3/2017/06/2017-rethinking-trade-finance.pdf
danskebank.com/en.../trade-finance/Newsletter/.../Trade-Finance-Newsletter.asp...
fci.nl/about-factoring/the-bank-payment-obligation-bpo-a-new-start-for-supply-chain-finance.pdf
Currencies – FITA.org fita.org/trade_finance.html
liquidx.com/marketplace-in-action
newsroom.nex.com/news/01022017/ebs-live-ultra-to-provide-data-at-5ms-intervals?ref=Home
steemit.com/blockchain/@lighthouse7/ubs-santander-deutsche-bank-and-bny-mellon-are-working-on-bitcoin-for-banks
tradefinanceanalytics.com/
tradefinanceanalytics.com/Magazine
www.3plstudy.com
www.abe-eba.eu
www.abfa.org.uk
www.alf.pt
www.asf-france.com
www.assifact.it
www.bernardonicoletti.com
www.bis.org
www.bofaml.com/Trade/SupplyChain
www.cfa.com
www.cfla.cz
www.ciosummits.com/B2B_Payments_Supply_Chain_Finance__E-invoicing_Market_Guide_2015.pdf
www.codecs.ro/International-Trade-Finance
www.eba.europa.eu
www.ebf-fbe.eu
www.ecb.europa.eu
www.efrag.org
www.esrb.europa.eu
www.euf.eu.com
www.export.org.uk/page/Newsletters
www.ey.com/Publication/vwLUAssets/EY-infinite-possibilities-procurement-in-2025/$FILE/EY-infinite-possibilities-procurement-in-2025
www.factoring.de

www.factoringasociacion.com
www.faktoring.pl
www.fatf-gafi.org
www.fci.nl
www.febelfin.be/fr/node/3012
www.finansogleasing.dk
www.Fireapps.com
www.fmlogistic.ru/eng-gb
www.fsb.org
www.gtreview.com/
www.hellenicfactors.gr
www.hindawi.com/journal
www.iccwbo.org
www.iccwbo.org
www.i-law.com/.../browse_newsletters.htm?...Internationalpercent20Trade percent20Finan...
www.itfa.org
www.lean-digitize.com
www.scfcommunity.org
www.singlelaw.com/international-trade-finance
www.supplychainquarterly.com
www.swedishbankers.se
www.swift.com
www.telegraph.co.uk/technology/2017/08/01/bitcoin-cash-everything-need-know-bitcoins-hard-fork
www.trade.gov/publications/ita-newsletter/
www.ueapme.com

Index[1]

[1] Note: Page numbers followed by 'n' refer to notes.

B. Nicoletti, *Procurement Finance*,
Palgrave Studies in Financial Services Technology,
https://doi.org/10.1007/978-3-030-02140-5

CPSIA information can be obtained
at www.ICGtesting.com
Printed in the USA
LVHW081125271019
635467LV00011B/742/P

9 783030 021399